BEYOND DICHOTOMIES

SUNY series

EXPLORATIONS

in

POSTCOLONIAL STUDIES

Emmanuel C. Eze, editor

BEYOND DICHOTOMIES

Histories, Identities, Cultures,
and the Challenge of Globalization

edited by

ELISABETH MUDIMBE-BOYI

STATE UNIVERSITY OF NEW YORK PRESS

Published by
STATE UNIVERSITY OF NEW YORK PRESS, ALBANY

© 2002 State University of New York

For information, address State University of New York Press,
90 State Street, Suite 700, Albany, NY 12207

Production, Laurie Searl
Marketing, Michael Campochiaro

Library of Congress Cataloging-in-Publication Data

Beyond dichotomies : histories, identities, cultures, and the challenge of globalization /
edited by Elisabeth Mudimbe-boyi.
    p. cm. — (SUNY series, explorations in postcolonial studies)
  Includes bibliographical references and index.
  ISBN 0-7914-5383-9 (alk. paper) — ISBN 0-7914-5384-7 (pbk. : alk. paper)
  1. Globalization. 2. Africa—Civilization—Philosophy. 3. Social sciences. 4. Developing
countries—Social conditions. 5. History—Philosophy. 6. Cultural policy. I.
Mudimbe-boyi, M. Elisabeth. II. Series.

D883 .B48 2002
901—dc21
                                                                          2002017724

        10   9   8   7   6   5   4   3   2   1

*To my sons Daniel and Claude,
whose vision of the world
goes beyond dichotomies.*

Contents

ACKNOWLEDGMENTS

The 1998 Stanford University conference, *Beyond Dichotomies: Histories, Identities, Cultures, and the Challenges of Globalization*, from which this book originates, was made possible by the support and assistance of many people. Although I had the primary intellectual responsibility for the conference, its organization and success would have been impossible without their presence and cooperation. I especially wish to thank my assistants before and during the conference Beverly Foulks and Kenric Tsethlikai for their efficient collaboration. Adrienne Janus, Trina Marmarelli, and Matthew Tiews extended their presence and careful attention to detail during the two days of the conference. For this book, I thank my assistants Sara Johnson and particularly Trina Marmarelli: she worked very efficiently and with great patience in dealing with computer problems, the technical preparation of the manuscript, the copyediting, and the proofreading.

I also wish to acknowledge some colleagues and friends for their interest, encouragement, and support: Bogumil Jewsiewicki of the History Department at Laval University; David Palumbo-Liu of the Department of Comparative Literature at Stanford University; Richard Roberts of the Department of History at Stanford University; and Haun Saussy of the Stanford University Department of Asian Languages and Literatures, who so diligently translated from the French version Edouard Glissant's keynote speech and accepted the difficult task of providing a consecutive translation during the speech and the discussion that followed. I am thankful as well to the following colleagues, who generously agreed to chair panels: Karl Britto of the French and Comparative Literature Departments at the University of California, Berkeley; Claire Fox of the Department of Spanish and Portuguese at Stanford University; Inderpal Grewal, chair of the Department of Women Studies at San Francisco State University; and Richard Roberts of the Department of History, director of the Center for African Studies at Stanford University. For their invaluable contributions to the conference and the lively discussions that their presentations generated, I am grateful to all of my colleagues who, spontaneously and graciously, accepted my invitation to come to Stanford—their papers constitute the chapters of this book. Some of the papers could not be included in this book, as their authors were committed elsewhere—Chris Connery of the University of California, Santa Cruz; David Palumbo-Liu; Vincent Rafael of the Department of Communication at the University of California, San Diego; Professor Emerita Sylvia Wynter of the Department of Spanish and Portuguese at Stanford University; and Joachim Warmbold of the Division of Foreign Languages at Tel Aviv University.

At Stanford, I would particularly like to thank John Etchemendy, former Associate Dean of the School of Humanities and Sciences and current Provost, for providing the seed money for the conference. My thanks also to the many departments, centers, and programs that lent financial support: the Dean of Students; the Departments of Anthropology, Asian Languages and Literatures, Comparative Literature, English, French and Italian, German Studies, History, Spanish and Portuguese; the Division of Languages, Cultures, and Literatures; the Center for Comparative Studies in Race and Ethnicity; the Center for International Studies; the Committee on African Studies; the Latin American Council; the Modern Thought and Literature Program; and the Stanford Humanities Center. A 1999–2000 sabbatical leave at the Stanford Humanities Center allowed me to advance some projects and to complete this book.

My two sons, Daniel and Claude, as well as Vida Bertrand, Jenny Chiwengo, Doris Jakubec, Françoise Lionnet, Mildred Mortimer, Mireille Rosello, Ronnie Scharfman, and Thomas Spear, have been steadfast friends. In their own ways, they all helped me complete this project, thanks to our conversations and their encouragement and support.

Finally, I thank the anonymous readers of this manuscript as well as Laurie Searl, the production editor and Jane Bunker, State University of New York Press acquisitions editor, for her interest and involvement in this project. Arif Dirlik's chapter was previously published under the same title in *The Review of Education/Pedagogy/Cultural Studies* 21:2 (1999): 95–131. We thank the *Review* for graciously granting permission to reprint the article in this book.

Preface

Not because Socrates said so, but because it is in truth my own disposition—and perchance to some excess—I look upon all men as my compatriots, and embrace a Pole as a Frenchman, making less account of the national than of the universal and common bond.

—Montaigne, *Essays*

The new electronic interdependence recreates the world in the image of a global village.

—Marshall Herbert McLuhan,
The Medium Is the Massage

Several decades ago, reflecting on the power of travel books and their capacity to create an illusion of worlds that no longer exist, swallowed or submerged by the "order and the harmony" of "the great civilization of the West," Claude Lévi-Strauss concluded with a bittersweet nostalgia that ". . . humanity has taken to monoculture, once and for all, and is preparing to produce civilization in bulk, as if it were sugar-beet. The same dish will be served to us every day" (1961, 39). Yet a few pages further, thinking of "*real* travel," he pronounces this other conclusion: "The paradox is irresoluble: the less one culture communicates with another, . . . the less likely it is, in such conditions, that the respective emissaries of these cultures will be able to seize the richness and significance of their diversity" (ibid., 45). These quotations from *Tristes Tropiques* prelude, to some extent, the dialectic tension embodied in the challenge of globalization and also anticipate the conclusion of this book with a text by Edouard Glissant.

It is indeed well established that the expansion of the market economy and of capital mobility and the circulation of goods (Wallerstein 1974, 1984), of information technology, and of people have generated

new subjectivities and sensitivities, new narratives and kinds of knowledge. At the same time, these phenomena have initiated and accelerated
the globalization process, reducing the dimensions of the planet and
leading the contemporary world to some form of a "monoculture." In
this new world system ruled by a capitalist economy, nations, communities, and individuals are searching for ways to participate in but at the
same time to not be absorbed by a world culture, even when interacting
with it and functioning within it (Wallerstein 1991). At the academic
level, these changes and anxieties have brought about epistemological
shifts and have opened new perspectives that have contributed to a
rethinking of such concepts as identity, nation and tradition, the local
and the global. A public discourse on globalization, directed at policy
makers and international businesses, approaches globalization primarily
in terms of the economy, technology, and the media (Friedman 1999;
Sassen 1988). Globalization in its relation to culture—the focus of this
book—also has become a major topic in academic discourse (Appadurai
1996; Bhabha 1994; Dissanayake and Wilson 1996; Jameson and
Miyoshi 1998). Questions and problems have been raised, and the
debate around globalization has taken various forms: criticism or reser-
vation about globalization coexists with its acceptance as an unavoidable predicament of modernity, while some embrace a "critical globalism" (Appadurai 1996; Cox 1997; Dirlik 1997; Featherstone 1990;
Featherstone, Lash, and Robertson 1995; Gilroy 1993; Hay and Marsh
2000; Nederveen Pieterse 1995; Sassen 1998). On the other hand, during its nearly two decades of strong presence and dominance, the colo-
nial/postcolonial dichotomy that introduced a new geographical configuration of the world resulting from the imperial period created its own
kind of homogenization and has thus come under scrutiny (Mukherjee
1998; Moore-Gilbert 1997; Spivak 1999).

   The conference I convened at Stanford University on May 8 and 9,
1998, *Beyond Dichotomies: Histories, Identities, Cultures, and the
Challenge of Globalization,* continues to resonate here. This book
focuses on some of the challenges mentioned above by examining concrete local practices within the context of modernity and globalization.
It examines the ways in which some societies, or individuals from those
societies, interrogate or confront the complexification of cultures; the
emergence of new modes of self-representation or self-ascription; and
the formulation or construction of new individual or collective identities
engendered by new global cultural forms in the presence of new prob-
lematics, such as displacement and relocation or transnationality and

transculturality, as well as new technologies, the expansion of the market economy, and the invasion of the media and their obtrusive presence. All of these tend to erase some lines and boundaries and reduce all to the Same. Through critical reflection, rethinking, and reconceptualization, the various contributions engage in an interrogation of the necessity, the validity or the legitimacy of dichotomized representations of contemporary societies, cultures, and collective or individual identities. In discussions and exchanges during the conference, it soon became apparent that the formula "Beyond Dichotomies," proposed since the inception of the conference project as an affirmation, had to be rephrased as an interrogation: "Beyond Dichotomies?" What appeared to be at stake could be summarized by the following questions, which simultaneously delineate the theoretical framework of this book and translate collective or individual subjects' anxieties in the face of "the end of the world as we know it" (Wallerstein 1991, 1999). Shall we go beyond dichotomies? If so, what are the conditions of possibility for such a shift? How can we account for the persistence or recurrence of the binaries colonizer/colonized, center/periphery, Empire/its Others, local/global, premodernity/modernity, all of which are still prevalent despite a widespread public discourse on globalization? Is there room for heterogeneity within the new global space? If so, how can we conceptualize the conjunctions and the disjunctions obliterated by a binarist conceptualization? How can we create, write, and preserve local historical memories? How might it be possible to transmit local knowledge, create national literatures in the language of the colonizer, and at the same time be able to translate the cultural signs of one's own people in that language? What are the markers of linguistic appropriation? How do displaced or transplanted people live and express their new identities? How can we convey the ambiguities, the ambivalence and the contradictions, as well as the continuities and the ruptures, inherent to transnational and transcultural contexts? Finally, how can one inscribe oneself in the contemporary culture "without diluting oneself," as Edouard Glissant put it in his keynote address at the conference? That is, how can we negotiate the relationship between the global and modernity in its relation to the local and the traditional? In short, how can we articulate and reconceptualize particular social and cultural identities in a time of global culture and global economy?

Léopold Sédar Senghor has been a major twentieth-century proponent of "métissage" and "civilisation de l'universel," grounded in a dialogue between cultures and a reciprocal relation of "donner et

recevoir" rather than in a hegemonic relation (1964, 1977, 1993). Senghor's forceful claims seemingly were ignored, or at least overlooked. It
is only during the last decades that a new theoretical discourse on identity has emerged, and a number of concepts have been advanced to
account for the cultural practices, phenomena, and spaces generated in
a context of cultural contacts or globalization: transculturation (Liu
1999; Morejòn 1982; Ortiz 1963), the contact zone (Pratt 1992), *métissage* (Amselle 1990; Lionnet 1989), hybridity (Ahmad 1992; Bhabha
1994; Young 1995), and *créolité* (Bernabé, Chamoiseau, and Confiant
1993 [1989]). These concepts are not necessarily referred to or explicitly discussed in this book's chapters, yet they maintain an underlying
presence. Combined with the above interrogations, they have informed
the organization of this book into its present components, centered
around several major interwoven and overlapping axes: the conceptual,
the historico-geographical, and the linguistico-cultural. The specificity
of the book, however, resides less in a general theorization generated by
these concepts than in their problematization and reconceptualization
based on particular cases of geographical, historical, and cultural location. Particular also is the diversity of the ways in which the space
between the two poles of dichotomy is configured: it emerges as shifting
rather than fixed and rigid. Some chapters do implicitly take a stand
against one of the limitations of postcolonial studies by emphasizing the
necessity of historicization and inscribing places in their particular history in order to make relevant the new configuration of power relations
within today's global world. Other chapters directly or indirectly raise
methodological questions concerning the status of ethnic studies or area
studies, calling for a collaboration between the disciplines. The remaining chapters focus on places, the inadequacy or ambivalence of ascriptions, the indeterminacy and ambivalence of translating without fully
translating, and the inadequacy of rigid dichotomies.

The chapters of this book are diverse in their topics but are linked
by their interrogations about the challenges of globalization, which
provide multiple points of convergence, as well as by the conversations
made possible between them, through the locations from which each
author speaks: disciplinary, ethnic, cultural, historical, national, or geographic origin. The topics discussed in this book center around Africa,
Asia, Europe, and the Americas, and particularly around the liminal
cultural spaces within which transplanted, transnational, transcultural,
and multilingual subjects evolve. The scholars who gathered in 1998
and the diversity of their expertise illustrate the goal of the conference:

a truly global academic dialogue that would cross the boundaries of nationalities and disciplines, the frontiers and the borders of continents and cultures, without forsaking the relevance of place and location as meaningful signifiers.

The chapters in part 1 explicitly posit and reflect on familiar power-based binaries such as insider/outsider, inclusion/exclusion, us/them, colonizer/colonized, premodern-mythical/modern-scientific, and center/periphery. With "The Perspective of the World: Globalization Then and Now," Michel-Rolph Trouillot opens the book from a historical perspective, seeking to relativize globalization as a completely new phenomenon: if it is new, its newness resides not in the process but rather in its causes and manifestations. He emphasizes a first moment of globalization, the "Atlantic moment," which occured prior to the fragmented moments of contemporary globalization: a Euro-centered pespective on the world has shadowed that "first moment of globality." At the heart of Trouillot's reflection lies thus a weighty interrogation: "For can we talk about globalization without taking seriously the various paces and temporalities involved?"—since, as he asserts further, "a world perspective on globalization requires attention to differential temporalities and the uneven spaces they create." A "silencing of the past" in the dominant discourse of today's globalization seems to perpetuate the marginalization of some groups excluded from or placed on the periphery of nineteenth-century cultural discourse, continuing throughout the twentieth century. Trouillot alludes to current concepts and designations such as hybridity, transnationality, and diasporas that have been proposed to characterize the cultural existence of such groups in today's global world. Without dismissing them, Trouillot nonetheless poses a caveat to their uncritical use, warning of their potential for homogenization.

    For some theorists, globalization constitutes one of the trends of modernity. In her chapter, "Modernity and Periphery: Toward a Global and Relational Analysis," Mary Louise Pratt, in the wake of postmodernity, reviews the work of contemporary theorists who connect postmodernity to modernity, postmodernity marking an end to the West's self-constructed position of centeredness in defining modernity. Pratt suggests instead the urgency of "creating a global and relational account of modernity" whose conditions of possibility reside at once in questioning the West's normative centrality and in taking into account societies' historical trajectories, imprinted with the colonial encounter.

In relation to the major affirmation and interrogation of this book, "Beyond Dichotomies . . . (?)," Pratt raises a central question with her statement that "the discourse on modernity encodes the periphery," and "the center encodes the periphery." How, then, not to bring the periphery into presence? Some Latin American thinkers discussed by Pratt offer "alternative formulations" of modernity. Located at the periphery, these "peripheral modernities" deconstruct the center/periphery binary and initiate the "space in between" inhabited by "peripheral intellectuals," as exemplified in cultural processes such as hybridity.

While Pratt's focal point is Latin America, Emmanuel Chukwudi Eze concentrates on Africa in his chapter "Beyond Dichotomies: Communicative Action and Cultural Hegemony." He brings back the question of modernity by interrogating the totalizing and generalizing significance of "universal," apprehended from the perspective of Europe as the center. Through a textual close reading, he takes to task Habermas' *Theory of Communicative Action*, which reveals itself as a reproduction of existing dichotomies: the West's rationality and the asserted superiority of its worldview, as opposed to Africa's "archaic" and "mythical" one; the Western, scientific mind versus the African, magical one; and the non-European's "closed" mind against the European's "open" one. Eze seems to suggest a politics of concealment or a paradox in Habermas' reference to progressive anthropologists such as Evans-Pritchard, Lévi-Strauss, and Maurice Godelier, rather than to Gobineau or Lucien Lévy-Bruhl, who are echoed in a binarist representation of Africa. Eze's chapter connects to the other ones in this book in its questioning of a totalizing, Western universal and of a lack of historicization that precludes grasping the interwoven character of Europe's and Africa's histories, particularly since the "Atlantic moment." The acknowledgment of this interwovenness is what makes going beyond dichotomies possible.

In "Mankind's Proverbial Imagination: Critical Perspectives on Human Universals As a Global Challenge," Mineke Schipper privileges a transborder perspective on humankind's proverbial imagination, which functions outside of modernity, and she introduces the gender category through a cross-cultural examination of proverbs about women. Deploring an overemphasis on difference in the academic discourse of recent decades, Schipper chooses instead to consider what might constitute humankind's cultural universals. Similarities are not necessarily created by recent globalization, she argues: rather, they belong to a set of commonalities shared by humankind. Using a comparative methodology, she locates some of these universals in an abundant corpus of proverbs collected from all over the world, beyond the borders of geography and nationality, ethnicity and race. In her discussion of theories about the "universals," Schipper suggests a nonessentialist position that acknowledges, on the one hand, the interconnection of women's roles and social structures, and, on the other hand, the socially constructed characteristics of maleness or femaleness. Urbanization and industrialization have transformed societies and mentalities, and as a consequence, attitudes and representations about women. The real and major transformation brought about by today's globalization has largely benefited educated women worldwide, reproducing a dichotomy at a different level: a class division based on Western education and the introduction and access to modernity that it provides.

A second group of chapters deals with the question of places and the construction of new identities in these places. In "Bringing History Back In: Of Diasporas, Hybridities, Places, and Histories," Arif Dirlik, as in some of his previous publications, takes a critical stance in his examination of two concepts used in the current theorization of identities: diaspora and hybridity. Dirlik seeks instead to emphasize the distinctions "between different differences." Using Chineseness as an illustration, he raises several important points, emphasizing, among other things, the multiplicity of situations within the same diasporic population or between different diasporic groups: a multiplicity based on economic status, gender, political affiliations and connections, and social position in the new land. What does a diasporic identity or hybridity mean for a Chinese American, a Chinese overseas, or other Asian Americans when we consider the realpolitik: their political, financial, or economical interests, divergences, or differences, linked to the places where they live and operate?

In "The Romance of Africa: Three Narratives by African-American Women," Eileen Julien raises the issue of belonging and the complexity of identities summarized in compound ascriptions such as "African American." If Julien calls for a more realistic vision of Africa, she does not neglect the importance of looking at the present-day place, which is America, a place where the history of African descendants has been shaped differently from that of those Africans who remained on the continent. In fact, Julien questions the significance of a diasporic identity based on race as "a unifying principle across national boundaries." She connects with Dirlik in her interrogation of a diasporic identity as constructed, and again like Dirlik, she emphasizes particular histories and places. Interestingly—or paradoxically—in Julien's chapter, instead of engendering a different consciousness and a more lucid gaze, the place (America), with its history of race and gender discrimination and exclusion, creates and perpetuates a "fictioning of Africa" and a dichotomous representation of a romanticized "there," as opposed to a "here" of oppression. The question, then, is how to negotiate a double belonging, both African and American, that is, how to inscribe oneself in the new place from which one feels excluded, and at the same time preserve lucidly the specificity of one's origins against the present larger and more global culture of modernity embedded in the Americas.

The quote, "Today British identity, which used to be so often just a synonym for Englishness, has given way before the resurgence of cultural nationalisms. . . . The arrival for the most part after the Second World War of peoples from the Caribbean, South Asia, and Africa broadened the mixture. They transformed the situation decisively not merely by the degree of cultural difference, but also because their physical differences were not invisible," clearly summarizes the major question around which Robert J. C. Young centers his chapter "Ethnicity As Otherness in British Identity Politics." In contemporary Britain, a shift in position has occurred, replacing the primacy of a globalizing Englishness with the prevalence of local cultural nationalisms and ethnicities. The interrogation of "Englishness" has another side: how to define the identities of these Others in today's Britain. It implies questions embedded in such couplings as race and biology, ethnicity and culture, bringing Young to a critical reflection on the concepts and categories that come into play in identity politics and that are considered markers of difference: race and ethnicity, center and periphery, and (self) ascription and "resistance to the center."

Akhil Gupta, in "Reincarnating Immigrant Biography: On Migration and Transmigration," raises a series of questions pertaining to autobiography, history, culture, and identity in relation to immigration; this last, as he puts it, is "reconsidered from perspectives that themselves historicize the nation-state, or position immigration within a field of global capitalist relations." Gupta approaches the question of the Self and culture through the analysis of Dhan Gopah Mukerji's autobiography *Caste and Outcast* (1923). He proposes a reading of this narrative and the immigrant's experience not only as a narrative of the Self but also as one in which individual and collective histories are conflated. On the other hand, by emphasizing Mukerji's transcontinental itinerary as a spiritual journey and quest, Gupta transposes the narrative to a symbolic level, which allows him to pair the "vagrancy of the soul" with the immigrant's geographic journey and quest for identity. Highlighting the proeminence and pervasiveness of transmigration and reincarnation in local practices and religious beliefs, as well as in Mukerji's narrative, allows Gupta to transform the latter into an embodiment of culture and a site for the "nation biography." Reincarnation and transmigration thus function as categories disruptive to life stages, literary conventions, and immigrants' life narratives, contesting the linear structure of the autoreflexive genres. At the same time, the spiritual aspects of the narrative move it beyond the reductive opposition between birth and death and beyond the dominant thematic of the immigrant's experience as embedded in the binaries of loss and gain, of a before and a now, or of "'sending' nations" and "'receiving' nations."

Among the questions raised in his analysis, Gupta recalls Mukerji's anguishing interrogation concerning the interpretation and cultural translation of Hindu culture for his anticipated audience of Western readers. The chapters in part 3 foreground the difficulty and inadequacy of translating contexts into a dualist mode, but also the frequent impossibility of escape from this dilemma, thus pointing to the ambivalence and ambiguities that characterize contexts located between the two poles of the dichotomy.

Emily Apter's chapter, "Warped Speech: The Politics of Global Translation," is grounded in the larger context of a "cultural globalization," with a focus on writings produced in the colonial languages. Her chapter's subtext includes several hotly debated questions in African postcolonial literatures: What is a national literature? How can literature in colonial languages and national identity be conciliated? Apter reflects more specifically on the cultural translation of the local into the appropriated or recreated language of the colonizer: her interrogation centers around the problematic of inscribing and safeguarding local cultural signs, including the vernacular, in these literary works produced in colonial languages, while still ensuring their production, circulation, and dissemination in today's global market economy. As she puts it, "How does a foreign, linguistically unconventional text go global?" Through an analysis of works by authors from Scotland, Anglophone Africa, and the French Caribbean, she shows how, in these texts, the interference of the vernacular functions as a trope to contest and challenge the system's dominant linguistic, political, or intellectual discourse of power, thus subverting the dualistic opposition. By the same token, her examination of the various processes of appropriation and recreation illuminates the ways in which the emergence of varieties of French or English and their transliteration relativize the homogeneity of the imperial language, in the process blurring the traditional, rigid separation between a written, normative, acceptable standardized literary language and the nonacceptability of a spoken, nonliterary, nonstandard, but innovative "popular" language. Apter demonstrates the possibility of transnational, transliterated literatures that mark the "denationalization" of imperial languages such as English or French and contest the traditional identification of a national literature or culture with a national language.

In "National Identity and Immigration: American Polity, Nativism, and the 'Alien,'" Ali Behdad alludes to the relation between the economic needs of cheap labor, unemployment, and immigration in the United States. His chapter primarily draws on the evolution of U.S. immigration laws in order to illustrate the progressive evolution of American nationalism from opening to closing borders, or at least to a policy of "border control," which delineates space and place, separating the citizens of the nation from the bodies "alien" to it. As Behdad reminds us, the immigrant nation that is the United States has been "gradually moving from a more lenient and receptive tendency to a more restrictive and regulatory one." Apparently contradictory, the coexisting notions of a nation of immigrants and one of borders control, constitute, and translate a fundamental ambivalence. They are the marks of a nation-state whose receptiveness goes back to the principles of its foundation, embedded in diversity and heterogeneity. They also constitute the signs of a nation-state and state apparatus and its restrictiveness, calling rather for homogeneity and thus the exclusion of elements from the periphery which, according to public discourse and official documents, are capable of "polluting" the body of the nation.

Although framed differently, the questions of borders, belonging, and cultural translation form the axes of Abdul JanMohamed's chapter "Richard Wright As a Specular Border Intellectual: The Politics of Identification in *Black Power*." Analyzing Wright's African travel journal, JanMohamed revives the ambivalence of hyphenated identities and echoes Mukerji's anxiety about being both "casted" and "outcasted." This chapter reveals the painful ambiguity and dilemma of Wright's status as simultaneously an insider and an outsider to both Africa and the Americas, oscillating between (self)-inclusion and (self)-exclusion: that is, he identifies with the oppressed group in which, as a black American, he feels included and includes himself, while his history as a Westerner and as an American, as well as "the specter of slavery," causes him to disidentify himself from the Africans. JanMohamed expresses this ambivalence through the notion of the "border intellectual," advanced previously in his work. Using a Lacanian grid, he argues that during his reversed Middle Passage back to Africa as a guest, Wright actually tried to negotiate between an "imaginary identification" with Africans and a "symbolic identification" that would definitively overwhelm the former. Wright's ambivalence to some extent reiterates Julien's interrogation of a construction of identity based solely on a community of race. As a corollary question, one might wonder how to rearticulate an African-American identity that would take into account the ambiguous African legacy and the ambivalent present-day reality of being a black American.

In the final chapter, "Beyond Dichotomies: Translation/Transculturation and the Colonial Difference," Walter Mignolo and Freya Schiwy argue for the necessity of going beyond a purely linguistic translation, calling rather for the promotion of a cultural translation of the native culture into the foreign language of the colony. Earlier in the book, Trouillot rightly locates the "Atlantic moment," in the sixteenth century, which marked the European expansion and established a power relation between Europe and its Others. In the context of that relation, originating from the colonial encounter between the West and Meso-America, as well as the Western methods of conceptualization through dichotomies, Mignolo and Schiwy discuss the notions of "colonial difference" and the "coloniality of power," both of which lead to a reconceptualization of translation/transculturation. The authors argue for a new theorization of translation and transculturation that will take translation beyond a merely linguistic conception, thus creating the possibility of transcending the hierarchization and dichotomization of missionary and colonial translation. From that shift emerges a new form of knowledge they call "border thinking," which introduces the subaltern Amerindian's intervention and implicates him/her and his/her world vision in the language and grammar of coloniality.

Finally, Edouard Glissant's keynote speech "The Unforeseeable Diversity of the World" comes as a poetic conclusion, grounded in the concept of the "Diverse" on which Glissant has elaborated in his major essays *Poétique de la relation*, *Introduction à une poétique du Divers*, and *Traité du Tout-monde*. His is a concluding reflection that brings to the forefront the cultural and linguistic aspects of globalization as a global diversity in which the variety of world cultures, languages, aesthetic modes, and literary creations will encounter one another. Glissant's keynote speech offers an invitation to accept the Diverse, conceived of as a liberation of human imagination and creativity going beyond the separation between literary genres, between the oral and the written, liberated from the differences of languages and cultures, and therefore finally able to blossom, to open up to new histories and new identities and to express "dans toutes les langues du monde" the diversity of these cultures and languages.

Most of the chapters in this book bring into presence the relevance of history, location, and place. Global thinking requires a historicization, a consideration of differences in historical and local contexts, times, and moments of encounter. In assembling these chapters I sought to focus on globalization in a way that would allow the articulation of continuities and ruptures rather than to emphasize oppositions and vertical relationships. Globalization raises complex questions regarding people's histories, identities, and cultures, as well as the relationship between individual and collective identity. It also confronts the West, as well as the non-West, with multiple challenges. The West, as a stable, unique center and generator of hierarchical dichotomies, has been destabilized from inside and outside. In *The Black Atlantic*, Paul Gilroy affirms the strong connection between the West and a modernity in which the non-West is undeniably involved. Emmanuel Chukwudi Eze, referring to Anthony Appiah's *In My Father's House,* revisits Gilroy's position in different terms, observing that its Others cannot escape Europe, and vice versa. In a context of globalization, the "colonial difference" of which Mignolo and Schiwy remind us still manifests its presence, reinscribed in different terms instead of reproducing a rigid dichotomization.

    With the plurality, the new mobility, and the immigration and displacement of people around the world that characterize contemporary times, many live daily in transcultural and transnational spaces. What emerges from this book is an oscillation between "Beyond Dichotomies" as an affirmation and as an interrogation. Going—or not going—beyond dichotomies remains per se an ambiguous and ambivalent process or project. On the one hand, going beyond dichotomies appears as a necessary condition of evading isolation and self-exclusion from a world becoming more and more global, of escaping the prison house of reductive representations of otherness and difference, of avoiding and disentangling oneself from what Amin Malouf calls "identités meurtrières" (Malouf 1998). On the other hand, if the "colonial difference" is still pervasive, despite its reformulation and its subversion in academic discourse, what will become of the particular and the local?

In the context of what Mignolo and Schiwy call the modern/colonial world system, going beyond dichotomies could only be inscribed in a continous act of reappropriation and recreation, a dialectic and a discursive tension between a "here" and a "there," a nomadic trajectory translated into a constant fluctuation and mediation between the transparency and opacity of Difference (Glissant, in Victor Segalen's path, will say the "Diverse"), as well as between a disconnecting deterritorialization opening up to the outer, global world and a reterritorialization reconnecting the subject to the local, as exemplified in Mukerji's *Caste and Outcast* or Wright's *Black Power*. Rethinking histories, identities, and cultures only reflects the present time and the necessity for a reconfiguration of cultures and intercultural relations in a global world. In other words, living between borders or in a state of "double consciousness" as an ordinary or a daily condition, navigating within the space of ambiguity and ambivalence, that, in itself, constitutes a challenge.

Elisabeth Mudimbe-Boyi

WORKS CITED

Ahmad, Aijaz. 1992. *In Theory: Classes, Nations, Literatures*. London: Verso.

Amselle, Jean-Loup. 1990. *Logiques métisses. Anthropologie de l'identité en Afrique et ailleurs*. Paris: Payot.

Appadurai, Arjun. 1996. *Modernity at Large: Cultural Dimensions of Globalization*. Minneapolis: University of Minnesota Press.

Appiah, Anthony. 1992. *In My Father's House: Africa and the Philosophy of Culture*. London: Methuen.

Bernabé, Jean, Patrick Chamoiseau, and Raphaël Confiant. 1993 [1989]. *Eloge de la Créolité*. Paris: Gallimard/Presses Universitaires Créoles.

Bhabha, Homi. 1994. *The Location of Culture*. London and New York: Routledge.

Cox, Kevin, ed. 1997. *Spaces of Globalization: Reasserting the Power of the Local*. New York: Guilford Press.

Dirlik, Arif. 1997. *The Postcolonial Aura: Third World Criticism in the Age of Global Capitalism*. Boulder: Westview Press.

Dissanayake, Wimal, and Rob Wilson. 1996. *Global/Local: Cultural Production and the Transnational Imaginary*. Durham: Duke University Press.

Featherstone, Mike, ed. 1990. *Global Culture: Nationalism, Globalism, and Modernity*. London: Sage.

Featherstone, Mike, Scott Lash, and Roland Robertson, eds. 1995. *Global Modernities*. London: Sage.

Friedman, Thomas. 1999. *The Lexus and the Olive Tree: Understanding Globalization*. New York: Farrar, Strauss, and Giroux.

Gilroy, Paul. 1993. *The Black Atlantic: Modernity and Double Consciousness*. London: Verso.

Glissant, Edouard. 1990. *Poétique de la relation*. Paris: Gallimard.

———. 1993. *Tout-Monde*. Paris: Gallimard.

———. 1995. *Introduction à une poétique du Divers*. Montréal: Presses de l'Université de Montréal.

———. 1997. *Traité du Tout-Monde*. Paris: Gallimard.

Hay, Colin, and David Marsh, eds. 2000. *Demystifying Globalization*. Basingstoke: Macmillan.

Jameson, Fredric, and Massao Miyoshi. 1998. *The Culture of Globalization*. Durham: Duke University Press.

Lévi-Strauss, Claude. 1961. *Tristes Tropiques*. Translated by John Russell. London: Hutchinson.

Lionnet, Françoise. 1989. *Autobiographical Voices: Race, Gender, Self-Portraiture*. Ithaca, N.Y.: Cornell University Press.

Liu, Lydia, ed. 1999. *Tokens of Exchange: The Problem of Translation in Global Circulation*. Durham: Duke University Press.

Malouf, Amin. 1998. *Les Identités meurtrières*. Paris: Grasset.

McLuhan, Marshall Herbert. 1967. *The Medium is the Massage*. New York: Bantam.

Moore-Gilbert, Bart. 1997. *Postcolonial Theory: Contexts, Practices, Politics*. London: Verso.

Morejòn, Nancy. 1982. *Naciòn y mestizaje en Nicolàs Guillèn*. La Habana: Uniòn de escritores y artistas de Cuba.

Mukherjee, Arun. 1998. *Millenial Postcolonial: My Living*. Toronto: TSAR.

Nederveen Pieterse, Jan. 1995. *The Development of Development Theory: Towards Critical Globalism*. The Hague: Institute of Social Sciences.

Ortiz, Fernando. 1963. *Contrapunto cubano*. La Habana: Consejò Naciònal de Cultura.

Pratt, Mary Louise. 1992. *Imperial Eyes: Travel Writing and Transculturation.* London and New York: Routledge.

Sassen, Saskia. 1988. *The Mobility of Labor and Capital: A Study in International Investments and Labor Flow.* Cambridge and New York: Cambridge University Press.

———. 1998. *Globalization and Its Discontent: Essays on the New Mobility of People and Money.* New York: The New Press.

Senghor, Léopold Sédar. 1964. *Liberté I. Négritude et humanisme.* Paris: Seuil.

———. 1977. *Liberté III. Négritude et civilisation de l'universel.* Paris: Seuil.

———. 1993. *Liberté V. Le Dialogue des cultures.* Paris: Seuil.

Spivak, Gayatri Chakravorty. 1999. *A Critique of Postcolonial Reason: Towards a History of the Vanishing Present.* Cambridge: Harvard University Press.

Wallerstein, Immanuel. 1974. *The Modern World System,* vol. 1. New York: Academic Press.

———. 1984. *The Politics of the World Economy.* Cambridge: Cambridge University Press.

———. 1991. *Geopolitics and Geoculture: Essays on the Changing World System.* Cambridge: Cambridge University Press, and Paris: Editions de la Maison des Sciences de l'Homme.

———. 1999. *The End of the World As We Know It: Social Science for the Twenty-First Century.* Minneapolis: University of Minnesota Press.

Young, Robert. 1995. *Colonial Desire: Hybridity in Theory, Culture, and Race.* London and New York: Routledge.

PART 1

BEYOND DICHOTOMIES

CHAPTER ONE

THE PERSPECTIVE OF THE WORLD

Globalization Then and Now

MICHEL-ROLPH TROUILLOT

"Globalization" is a fuzzy word. What hidden histories are silenced by this fuzziness? What would the many phenomena heavily packaged and heavily publicized under the word "globalization" look like from a world perspective? In particular, what would a world perspective tell us about cultural flows and processes?

INTRODUCTION: COFFEE . . . CON LECHE?

Whereas the word "globalization" has been defined at least by some economists (see Trouillot 2001), its increasing use by students of culture and society has generated little attention to—and even less agreement on—what it actually means. The further we move away from economics, the more anecdotal and impressionistic our vision of globalization seems to be. Thus anthropology and literary and cultural studies in particular have yet to spell out what, if anything, globalization means to culture. Indeed, throughout the human disciplines, the relation between culture and globalization is as evanescent as it is pervasive (but see Ohnuki-Tierney 2001; Tsing 2000; Appadurai 1996).

It is not easy to fight a spook. Yet cultural globalization is a spook insofar as it is impossible to locate *in thesis* in academic discourse and almost as difficult to find in the world outside of academia. There are reasons for this, which suggest why cultural globalization is a dream for advertisers ("United Colors of Benetton"?), and I will allude to some of them. But first I will give flesh to the thesis. The enterprise is opinioned but intellectually honest. In making explicit a number of tacit but pervasive propositions about cultural globalization, I hope to render a dominant narrative more real and more conscious of its premises but, indeed, more vulnerable.

In synthetic form, the cultural globalization thesis goes as follows: economic and technological transformations since the 1970s have led to an unprecedented flow of capital, goods, ideas, and people across state and continental borders. These flows, in turn, have contributed to the demise of institutions of power, notably the state. Our times are thus marked by the incapacity of state-built or state-sponsored boundaries (borders, citizenship, ethnicity) to regiment populations and affect cultural practices and identities. In short, the world is fast turning into a single cultural unit.

At this point, the cultural globalization thesis splits into two parts, best captured in two subliminal images. The first image is that of a blending, a coffee increasingly *con leche*, at the end of which awaits cultural homogeneity across states and continents. The second is that of a shopping mall of cultures within which individuals and groups will be able to pick their preferred components and return home, as it were, to self-construct the culture (s) of their choice—with, indeed, the capacity to return the next day if the shoe does not fit.

There is a tension between these two images, but it is exactly because the images are subliminal that this tension rarely surfaces explicitly, even in scholarly studies of globalization, let alone in the public arena. When it does, notably in the hands of advertisers, spin doctors, or media handlers, it is hyped and projected in such terms that its harmonious resolution denies the very contradictions that produced the tension in the first place. Thus golf prodigy Tiger Woods, the blend of blends, the mixture of mixtures, can successfully shop for the cultural attributes of his choice—notably the American Dream—and sell some of his wares back to us in the form of shoes that fit all. The tension between story one (the unending blending) and story two (I am what I decide to be) is happily resolved because of the boldness of the move. That is, both images revel in the alleged newness of the phenomenon, and that mutual newness is exactly what makes one support the other. Thus we buy the image—and the shoes. Again, Benetton comes to mind as a precursor, daring to juxtapose the obviously incompatible and claiming to resolve the incompatibility in a future marked by congenital innocence.

Yet claims of innocence are suspicious when it comes to globalization. Indeed, a narrative of political and economic change is fundamental to these images. These images work in part because we are convinced that the world is changing—fast, too fast—and that the motor of change is the inexorable hand of technology and trade (Gibson-Graham 1996). A critical reading of cultural globalization should therefore never lose sight of the political economy against which the narrative is deployed.

Is Globalization Unprecedented?

Back to economics, therefore, to check on that feeling of newness. Is globalization unprecedented? We may approach the answer with this quote:

> International finance has become so interdependent and so interwoven with trade and industry . . . that political and military power can in reality do nothing. . . . These little recognized facts, mainly the outcome of purely modern conditions (rapidity of communication creating a greater complexity and delicacy of the credit system) have rendered the problems of modern international politics profoundly and essentially different from the ancient. (Angell 1910)

The elements of a thesis are there: new technology—especially the speed of communication—creates an interdependence which in turn leads to a fundamentally different world. Does this suggest a radical break? Yes, except that the quote is from Norman Angell's *The Great Illusion*, published in 1910. Thus in the first decade of this century, some knowledgeable observers had already proposed that the main features we associate today with globalization fully obtained in the world of finance and politics. Were they wrong?

The figures that best measure economic globalization reveal that, in relative terms, the flow of goods and capital across state boundaries was at least as high during the period immediately preceding World War I as it is today. Ratios of export trade to GDP may have been higher in 1913 than in 1973. In the period 1913–1914, Foreign Direct Investment

(FDI) was around 11 percent, about the same level as in 1994. Capital flows relative to output were higher during the Gold Standard period than in the 1980s. To sum up a number of authors and arguments:

1. There is absolutely no evidence to suggest that the economic facts we most often associate with globalization are unprecedented;
2. There is evidence to indicate that the changes of the last twenty years are not as massive as we think they are;
3. There also is evidence that they are much more limited in geographical scope than the ideology of today suggests (Banuri and Schorr 1992; Trouillot 2001; Weiss 1997).

We should not draw from the figures highlighting the period preceding World War I that globalization first happened then—if only because two world wars should help temper such presumption. Rather, the most important lesson of the comparison between the first and last decades of this century is about the sense of newness that the awareness of global flows provoked then and now. Angell's pompousness is indeed refreshing when we know the date of his statement. Yet we need also to remember that at about the same date, Rosa Luxemburg (1968, 1972) was insisting that capitalism had always been a global process, needing from its inception new spaces to devour. Read as a process, economic globalization is inherent in capitalism and therefore as old as that system (Harvey 1995; Luxemburg 1972).

The lesson is thus one of humility, a mere suggestion that we may need eyeglasses to see things that are too near. If the economic flows we now associate with globalization are not as different or as massive as we may believe, should we not question the apparent newness of the cultural, social, and demographic flows that supposedly derive from this globalized economy?

In economics as in politics, in cultural as in social studies, the main narrative of globalization hides the very facts of power that make it both desirable and possible. All narratives impose silences (Trouillot 1995). The particularity of the narrative of globalization when it touches culture-history is a massive silencing of the past on a world scale, the systematic erasure of continuous and deeply felt encounters that have marked the last 500 years of human history. For sushi in Chicago to amaze us, we need to silence that the Franciscans were in Japan as early as the fifteenth century. For Muslim veils in France to seem out of place, we need to forget that Charles Martel stopped 'Abd-al-Raman only 300 miles south of Paris, two reigns before Charlemagne. To talk of a global culture *today*, we need to forget that Chinese chili paste comes from Mexico, French fries from Peru, and Jamaican Mountain Blue from Yemen.

TIME, SPACE, AND HISTORY

Studies of globalization have been eminently parochial in their premises, eminently limited in their handling of either time or space, and of the time-space conflation itself. It is thus both ironic and necessary to insist that studies of globalization need to develop a global perspective. How do we do it? To start with, we need a better handle on two sets of issues that I will call, for short, temporality and historicity.

Narratives of globalization say something about the history of the world, but they often assume naively as their premises the state of affairs of the *Wall Street Journal*. If globalization is about world history, scholars of globalization need to ask: which world? whose history? We cannot answer the first question, "which world," without a firm handle on temporality and the time-space relation.

You may have noticed that my title alludes to Fernand Braudel's *The Perspective of the World* (1992 [1979]). Yet Braudel was less interested in the perspective *of* the world than in a perspective *on* the world. The original French title of the third volume of *Civilisation matérielle* ... is *Le Temps du monde*, "World-time" or, more accurately, "the pace of the world." Mistranslation aside, Braudel focused on that duration whose tempo was set by the global development of capitalism.

Still, Braudel's perspective on the world is a crucial step in a search for a perspective of the world. For can we talk about globalization without taking seriously the various paces and temporalities involved? Braudel himself was careful to insist that there were temporalities other than the tempo of world capitalist development. World time does not affect the entire world in the same way. World time is not universal time. The pace of the world is uneven on the ground. Indeed, Braudel insisted, following Marx-Luxemburg and anticipating Harvey, that world-time itself necessarily created spatial hierarchies.

There are lessons here for those of us interested in the movement of global flows. Which temporalities do we privilege? Which spaces do we ignore? How do we set the criteria behind these choices? A world perspective on globalization requires attention to differential temporalities and the uneven spaces that they create.[1]

Having distinguished, as we should, the temporalities involved, we need to return to the ground where those temporalities overlap. We need to observe how these temporalities coalesce, mix, disjoint, and contradict themselves among historically situated populations. Just as world space is not everyone's space, the history of the world is not everyone's history. We need to ask whose history is being told by the most fashionable narratives of globalization, and whose history is being silenced?

If temporalities overlap in inherently uneven spaces, this overlap enables and limits sensibilities and subject positions that can arise from within these spaces. In other words, we need to move from temporality to historicity, that two-pronged field in which human beings become both actors and narrators of their own story.

The rules of the game being what they are, it is no accident that the temporalities most successfully isolated by economic history are most successfully mixed in literature. I will not dare discuss Third World literature, whatever that may be, but I will dare suggest that Caribbean literature in all languages, of which I know something, is a world where time collapses into historicity.

> Five hundred years that je cooperate, je pacify, je collaborate, that je dream American, socialize old-Europe style, that euros penetrate my ass with dollars a la leche. Here I am, plexiglass prostitute from Curacao to Amsterdam, soccer player on the French team, sweeper of all sixtine chapels in the chassé-croisé of exotic transfers. Ah, if for once I was the world, how they would laugh in Nigger's Corner! (Trouillot 1997, 31)

THE FIRST MOMENT OF GLOBALITY

The world became global five centuries ago. The rise of the West, the conquest of the Americas, New World slavery, and the Industrial Revolution can be summarized as "a first moment of globality," an *Atlantic moment*, culminating in U.S. hegemony after World War II. Europe became Europe in part through severing itself from what lay south of the Mediterranean, but also in part through a westward move that made the Atlantic the center of the first truly global empires.

I cannot deal here with the empirical details of that moment, which encompass five centuries of world history and the shrinking of huge continental masses, including Asia. Indeed, my Atlantic moment is not restricted geographically to societies bordering the Atlantic Ocean. The designation does not refer to a static space but to the locus of a momentum. Spain's conquest of the Philippines, the British conquest of India, and the United States' control of Korea all fall within that moment. I will insist, however, that it is no accident that such non-Atlantic ventures often took place when the respective power claimed partial or total control of the Atlantic Ocean.

This Atlantic moment of globality entailed at the onset massive flows of money, capital, goods, ideas, motifs, and people not only across states but across continents.

Global flows of population include, of course, the Castilian invasion of the Americas, the nearly 12 million enslaved Africans taken to the New World, and the hundreds of thousands of Asians brought to succeed the slaves on Caribbean plantations. As the North Atlantic states forcibly moved populations all over the world, their own citizens also moved from one continent to another, most often from temperate to temperate climate. Australia, Canada, New Zealand, Southern Africa, and the United States bear the marks of these demographic flows.

As peoples moved, so did goods. Massive flows of gold and silver, crops and spices, and plants and diseases, from tobacco to coconuts, from syphilis to smallpox, and from the mines of Peru to the Kews sprinkled over the British Empire and enmeshed world populations into encounters and confrontations unrestricted by physical distance. Economically these flows of goods and money sustained the life of the North Atlantic both before and after its Industrial Revolution. By the late eighteenth century, almost two-thirds of France's external trade rested on the shoulders of the Caribbean colony of Saint-Domingue-Haiti and the slaves who died there. Similarly, in the nineteenth century, the opium trade proved vital to the British economy. Crops such as sugar, coffee, tea, or cocoa concretely tied together populations separated by oceans (Trouillot 1980; Mintz 1985; Brockway 1977).

This first moment of globality also produced its self-proclaimed hybrids, from the many *convertos* who joined the Castilian venture, to the early Americans who discovered they had become Indians, to the mulattos of Cuba, Brazil, or Saint-Domingue. *Cafe con leche* is not new, certainly not in Latin America. Already in 1815 Simon Bolivar had officialized a narrative of hybridity: "We are . . . neither Indian nor European, but a species midway between the legitimate proprietors of this country and the Spanish usurpers." Assessing the cultural evolution of the Caribbean, Edouard Glissant insists that creolization requires the consciousness of mixed origins, but he also contends that the notion of hybridity is too narrow to capture the richness of the situation.

The Human Disciplines and the
Legacies of the North Atlantic

The initial reaction of the men of robes and letters of the North Atlantic to this first moment of globality was one of intellectual curiosity. The new geography of imagination that arose during the Renaissance (and made possible the conversion of Latin Christendom into Europe) implied a global projection of power. That projection, which still serves as the foundation of what we call "the West," inherently divides and segregates populations, cultures, areas, religions, and races. Yet it would be a mistake to think that it did so then the way it does now. From the sixteenth to the early nineteenth century, a number of writers expressed wonder at the globality just discovered but took it seriously enough to explore its social, moral, and cultural implications across a wide spectrum of philosophical and political positions.

From Amerigo Vespucci's letters and the debates between Las Casas and Sepulveda through the sixteenth-century proponents of a total history, the reflections of Montaigne and Montesquieu, down to Diderot-Raynald or even Adam Smith on colonization, there is indeed an "us" and a "them." But the "us" keeps changing, and the "them" is open-ended, for there is also a sense that what we say about "them" says something about "us." To that extent, the Atlantic moment of globality was handled, at least by some of the most prominent European thinkers, as a truly global—that is, open if not open-ended—phenomenon.[2]

A precision is necessary. I am not arguing that Renaissance and Early Modern European thinkers were *not* ethnocentric. On the contrary, I have suggested elsewhere that the roots of scientific racism, as it first appears in the early 1700s before gaining full speed during the nineteenth century, go back to the ontology and geographical imagination of the Renaissance (Trouillot 1995, 74–78). This does not contravene the proposition that in the scholarly world, the impact of that geography was not homogenous. It implied closure and segregation, but it also implied degrees and forms of openness. Las Casas' position at Valladolid was intellectually and *politically* defensible. It would look insane today.

When did this break occur?

In the nineteenth century, right at a moment when the North Atlantic nurtured jointly and with equal ardor nationalist rhetorics and myths of "scientific" racial supremacy, the scholarly world took what increasingly appears in retrospect as a "wrong turn" in the institutionalization of the human disciplines.

In a context marked by the increasing evocation and deployment of state power outside of academia and the reorganization of power within institutions of knowledge, the nineteenth century saw a qualitative break in both the notion and practice of "social science" as objective knowledge of the human world. Three fundamental changes sealed that break: the search for objectivity itself; the use of that "objective" knowledge as a guide for the management of social change, now perceived as inevitable; and the sense that such change would occur in a context where (political) sovereignty resided in the people (Wallerstein 1991). Objectivity and the manageability of data *and* populations fed on each other, separating the task into "disciplines," increasingly removed from the humanities and from each other (Wallerstein et al. 1996).

So stated, the project created major zones of exclusion inherent in its aims and claims. To start with, in practice and for purposes of management, the bulk of the data to be analyzed came from the five countries where that institutionalization took place: Britain, France, the Germanies, the Italies, and the United States. More important, the project left out *by definition* the populations thought to be impervious to change by nature or by practice, including most of the non-West, which became the purview of a particular discipline, anthropology (Trouillot 1991). It left out, by definition also, populations—often the same—that were not thought to be worthy of self-sovereignty. Indeed, sovereignty and the capacity for progress went hand in hand in North Atlantic social thought, if not from the days of Las Casas, certainly at least from the days of Condorcet. The project also left out the populations—again, often the same—that were thought to be (or, later on, chose to be) outside of the capitalist order as defined from the North Atlantic.

Tailing along, fighting for their own institutional space and microsites of power, the humanities tended to mimic the parcellation of the social sciences. The result is still horrific. The human disciplines rewrote their past and polished their theoretical apparatus, drawing primarily from the North Atlantic experience, as though what we now call the West encapsulated the entire richness of humankind. They did not simply neglect the experience of the non-West—and, some would add, that of quite a few fellow Westerners. Rather, they actively silenced that experience within their self-designed domains. They made it inconsequential to theory.

Within the self-designed domains, theoretical segregation paralleled the closure of human populations within the political boundaries designed by the North Atlantic or—in the lack of such—within the boundaries that most resembled home in the minds of North Atlantic observers. Tribes, nations, regions, and ethnicities became not only natural units of analysis, which is bad enough, but they became the real thing. Not only was what was here to be studied, but it was what was "out there," entities imbued with an internal life and enclosed in fixed boundaries. Anthropologist Eric R. Wolf evaluates the intellectual disaster thus:

> The habit of treating named entities such as Iroquois, Greece, Persia, or the United States as fixed entities opposed to one another by stable internal architecture and external boundaries interferes with our ability to understand their mutual encounter and confrontation. . . . We seem to have taken a wrong turn in understanding at some critical point in the past, a false choice that bedevils our thinking in the present.
>
> That critical turning point is identifiable. It occurred in the middle of the past century, when inquiry into the nature and varieties of humankind split into separate (and unequal) specialties and disciplines. This split was fateful. (Wolf 1982, 7)

CULTURE IN A BOTTLE

One consequence of that discursive narrowness is an essentialist approach to cultures, the borders of which supposedly overlap the imagined community of the nation-state or similar political boundaries within it. Anthropology, notably American cultural anthropology, played its part in this theoretical segregation, making culture not only both an object and a unit of analysis—an enterprise intellectually doubtful at best—but something "out there" that people obviously similar shared somewhat in their head when not through their practice.

To be sure, in the mind of many Boasians, the enterprise was partially intended to sever race from culture. Yet a century later it is not at all certain that cultural determinism's possible victory over biology has done much to destroy racism. At any rate, willingly or not, anthropology, and American cultural anthropology in particular, sold the general public an ahistorical, classless, essentialist notion of culture that breeds determinism. Culture became something evanescent and yet palpable, shared by a community whose borders just happened to replicate political boundaries. One nation, one state, one culture. One subnation, one subculture. Where racial boundaries were also fundamental political boundaries, as in the United States, culture and race became conflated.

If a number of North Americans now think that there is more cultural affinity between a black boy from inner-city Detroit and a Kalahari bushman than between that boy and his white Bostonian counterpart, American anthropologists have to take part of the blame.

The notion of single, isolated, and identifiable cultures thus channeled the geographical imaginary of the Renaissance through some of the worst intellectual catheters designed by the nineteenth century. Never mind that this notion of an isolated culture was never adequate to describe any population in or out of the North Atlantic. It fit nationalist ideologies of what the world should look like.

But suddenly, alas, the world does not look as it should. The problem is not that cultures are suddenly changing: they have always been changing. Nor is it new that cultures are porous. Human groups have always been open, in various degrees, to new experiences, outside influences, borrowings, and impositions. The difference now is that the fiction of isolated cultures built by the nineteenth century on the assumptions of the Renaissance no longer fits the lived experiences of the populations of the North Atlantic. I now turn to this second moment of globality.

THE SECOND MOMENT OF GLOBALITY: MASS AND VELOCITY

Since the end of World War II, a number of changes have deeply affected the globalization process. The first major change is not in the nature of global flows. As I suggested earlier, capital, goods, populations, ideas, motifs, and sensibilities have traveled across state and continental borders for a long time. They continue to do so. But they now do it at speeds and in quantities unthinkable just fifty years ago. It is not the relative importance of global flows that is unique to our times. Rather, it is the sheer volume of these flows and the speed at which these masses move. Mass and velocity are unique to our times. Unique also is the widespread awareness of global flows. That awareness grows everywhere, largely because of the increase in both size and velocity.

We can now start reading the unspoken tensions that characterize a number of cultural icons of our times, from Tiger Woods to postcolonial theorists. Capital, populations, and information move in much greater mass and at increasing speed, producing a centripetal effect of perception: we are the world; we are at its center, since everything around us moves. But that imaginary center is also the eye of a hurricane, for not only does everything move around us, but everything moves too fast and too soon.

To phrase the proposition in slightly different terms, while global flows increase in speed and velocity, most human beings continue to think and act locally. There is thus a disjuncture between the awareness of globalization and the capacity to come to terms with its consequences. While the first moment of globality produced tremendous cultural upheavals felt deeply in the colonies, in the second moment of globality globalization hits consciousness as a never-ending shock, the echoes of which seem to circle around the world.

Two contradictory reactions thus dominate the popular responses to global flows: wonderment and fragmentation.

WONDERS AND FRAGMENTATION

The most visible products of the two moments of globality do not fit the essentialist categories we inherited from the nineteenth century. They disturb the sense we had of what the world was or should have been. Thus wonder emerges as one of the reactions among the public.

We knew—we thought we knew—that a Chinese looks Chinese, speaks Chinese, and acts Chinese—until we walk into a Cuban restaurant, say, on New York's Upper West Side or in Miami's Little Havana—and discover a Chinese face with Latin flavors and Spanish accent. We think: the world has changed. But the world has not changed. We have simply moved closer to it. Chinese laborers stood next to African slaves on Cuban sugarcane plantations without much surprise on their or their masters' parts.

The example brings home a difference of our times set in three propositions: (1) wonder is premised in the incompatibility between essentialist categories and the products of global processes; (2) the nineteenth century has left us with the habit of conceptualizing humankind fundamentally in essential terms; (3) the speed of the late twentieth century makes it impossible for us not to notice the nonessentialist products of global flows. Wonder and puzzlement increase accordingly.

Academics reproduce this wonder in part by providing new labels that attempt to reconcile the world we face and the one we think we left behind. Used uncritically, these labels couch the treatment of globalization—or some of its avatars: hybrids, transnationals (corporations or peoples), diasporas—in an essentialist mode that tries to recover the assurance of nineteenth-century pronouncements. Their fluidity once stated, we treat our new hybrids as entities—as givens rather than as moments to be unpacked.

The political danger is obvious. One of the least banal effects of the Tiger Woods, Hybrid qua Star phenomenon is a thicker mask on the formation of racial identity and the workings of racism in the United States. There is a mess out there, and the temptation to order the mess by inventing new labels, by naming the results rather than deciphering the process, is great. From nominalization to essentialism, the bridge is rather short.

Wonder does not exhaust our dominant responses to the second moment of globality. A second reaction is a feeling of fragmentation.

Since the end of World War II, a number of political and intellectual leaders have promised us, intermittently and with varying degrees of certitude, an end to racial and ethnic conflicts, both within and across political borders. Yet during that same period, such conflicts have erupted repeatedly in various parts of the globe, pushing millions of individuals to unexpected levels of verbal and physical violence. That violence does not exempt Western democracies such as the United States, Germany, or France. Further, even when mass violence is absent, race and ethnicity creep into personal relations, often with surprising twists of perversity. From the vote of the United Nations Charter in 1945 to today's headlines from Bosnia or Los Angeles, these last fifty years can be read as an ongoing tension between the promise of a future where religion, language, and phenotype would become increasingly immaterial and the reality of a present where differences, presumed irrelevant, would become suddenly pristine. The twenty-first century is likely to be marked by the speed and brutality of similar conflicts.[3]

Academics also have reproduced this tension both within and across disciplinary lines. Whereas some disciplines can be said to have emphasized the processes of integration rather than the facts of fragmentation, all have had to take both into account, albeit to different degrees. Overlapping the disciplines are, again, the labels that tie this new world together: globalization, global culture, and diasporas.

One danger in these labels is the extent to which they replace the old universalisms of nineteenth-century thought—or of development studies—with a new universalism that is equally blind to its parochial roots. The experience of globality is always that of historically situated individuals with specific resources and limits.

I am not convinced that we gain more understanding of globalization by suggesting that the world is now moving to a "global culture," or that cultures are now engaged in flows of exchange that propel them as equal partners in a global market of patterns and ideas. McDonald's in Beijing is not the same as sushi in Evanston. Or at least we should not assume so until we do the research that would confirm this assumption. The challenge is to face the reality that cultural landscapes are open, that their openness has always been an occasion for exchanges and flows, and that these exchanges have always been modulated by power. In better words, how do we study the cultural practices of human populations and take power into account?

THE HISTORICIZATION OF THE WEST

We cannot start with a clean deck. The history of the last 500 years has marked us all in ways that we cannot deny. Indeed, if there is proof of what I call the Atlantic moment of globality, the proof is that few of us can think about the last 500 years as though they were not inevitable, as if North Atlantic hegemony was not in the very premises of human activity. Thus the first task is to ask how and why that hegemony became not only so pervasive but also so convincing, and the ideal tool for that task is the parochialization of the North Atlantic. The historicization of the West—its practices, concepts, assumptions, claims, and genealogies—is a central theoretical challenge of our times.

That has been said by many, including notable subaltern and postcolonial theorists. My own insistence is that this historicization, properly conceived, requires a global perspective. It cannot be reduced to an empirical focus on the successive geographical areas or populations (Greece, Rome, Latin Christendom, or the North Atlantic) that the West now claims in its genealogies. To limit the investigation to the physical West would be to accept naively the West's own genealogies and forget that the current challenge comes to the human sciences, in part, from changes in the globalization process.

Theoretical ethnocentrism is not intellectually equipped to face that situation, nor are the marginal responses, such as Afrocentrism, that this ethnocentrism provokes. Nor can ethnic studies, legitimate in their own terms, fill that void, unless we are willing to argue that North American minorities can serve as historical proxies for the vast chunks of humankind abandoned by the Latin and Teutonic canons. Chicano studies, as legitimate as they are, cannot replace Latin American studies. Black studies, as legitimate as they are, cannot replace African or Caribbean studies. In short, we need to cross political and linguistic boundaries to place whichever population we study, and the very places we come from, in a global perspective.

The difficulty in achieving such a global perspective may be the Achilles heel of postcoloniality, the main reason it has not delivered on the promises of a new theory and politics. To put it differently, postcolonial theory has broken a silence less than it has generated a new position within an ongoing conversation. The postcolonial intellectual *her*self entered the conversation only inasmuch as her positioning vis-à-vis that center demanded a generous attention that denies the facts of power that made this positioning necessary in the first place. As such, she may have changed the themes but not the terms of a conversation that preceded her entry and will likely continue after her departure.

The capacity to read one's own position and generate from that reading multiple, shifting, and questioning new locations seems to me the singular lesson from the most progressive academic trends of the last few years. The deployment of that capacity—in what I insist should be a global perspective—may be the key difference in evaluating the effectiveness of recent strategies of discourse and practice in and out of academia. If so, the difficulties that self-described postcolonials have in developing a critical reading of their own conditions of possibility may be a testimony to the limits of the enterprise.[4] As others have suggested (Ahmad 1992, 1995; Harvey 1989, 350–52), the need remains for a more critical reading of the context of intellectual production in and around academia.

CROSSING BOUNDARIES

Within academia itself we need to cross disciplinary boundaries much more often than we do now. Today, no single discipline has the capacity to conceptualize the experience of the people dismissed by the nineteenth century. Anthropologist Eric R. Wolf (1982) again says it best: "It is only when we integrate our different kinds of knowledge that the people without history emerge as actors in their own right. When we parcel them out among several disciplines, we render them invisible."

While parochialism, including that of the disciplines, leads to obvious dead ends and centrisms of all kinds—including the renewed search for universalist paradigms, such as rational choice theory—these now convince mostly the believers. The human sciences are going through what historian Jacques Revel (1995) calls a time of "epistemological anarchy," in part because of the greater empirical base available for theory. Yet if we make use of that empirical base, this very anarchy is an opportunity for new conversations that take into account the entire historical experience of the world, with the various sensibilities and viewpoints that this experience implies.

Endnotes

This chapter was written in 1998, when versions of it were presented at Stanford University, the University of Chicago, the University of Virginia at Morgantown, Duke University, and at the workshop on Theory and Politics after Postcoloniality (Institute for Global Studies, Johns Hopkins University). Since then I have substantially refined my thoughts on these issues in later articles noted in the bibliography below. I have also added later references to the text for the benefit of the reader. My thanks to Michael Dorsey, Jeffrey Mantz, Nabiha Megateli, and Clare Sammells, whose research tips inform this text, and to Vivek Dhareshwar, for the ongoing conversation that provoked some of these lines.

1. Yet when we turn to most of the literature on globalization from the *Wall Street Journal* to the liberal-minded literature of anthropology, and literary and cultural studies, we discover a peculiar handling of the space-time relation: a silencing of the past, an obsession with what Annales historians called derisively "la conjoncture," a patchwork of current headlines projected as the duration of the future over a world unfettered by mountains and other sinuosities. The world started this morning when sushi first reached Peoria, and guess what—it is a flat world.

2. Trails of this wonderment can still be found in studies of the Americas, notably creolization studies focusing on Brazil or the Caribbean (Trouillot m.s.).

3. In February 1998, Zapatista Indians seized control of the Web page of Mexico's Ministry of Finance. What could be more global than a Web page? Yet what is more grounded in locality and historicity than the claim of the Zapatistas?

4. Yet some of these are rather obvious: England's difficulties in sustaining the Commonwealth as an economic and intellectual umbrella; the uncontested dominance of English as the Latin of the late twentieth century; the ideological and personnel relay points between the United Kingdom and the United States—from Thatcher–Reagan to Clinton–Blair—however weak the structural parallels; and the conditions of academic production in the United States, including the politics of racism, all seem parts of a landscape begging for critical description.

WORKS CITED

Ahmad, Aijaz. 1992. *In Theory: Classes, Nations, Literatures.* London: Verso.

———. 1995. "Postcolonialism: What's in a Name?" Pp. 11–32 in *Late Imperial Culture*, ed. Roman de la Campa, E. Ann Kaplan, and Michael Sprinker. London: Verso.

Angell, Norman. 1910. *The Great Illusion.* New York and London: G. Putnam's Sons.

Banuri, Tariq, and Juliet R. Schorr, eds. 1992. *Financial Openness and National Autonomy: Opportunities and Constraints.* Oxford and New York: Oxford University Press.

Braudel, Fernand. 1992 [1979]. *The Perspective of the World.* Translated by Siân Reynolds. Berkeley: University of California Press. *Le temps du monde.* Paris: Colin, 1979.

Gibson-Graham, J. K. 1996. *The End of Capitalism (As We Knew It): A Feminist Critique of Political Economy.* Oxford and Cambridge: Blackwell.

Harvey, David. 1989. *The Condition of Postmodernity: An Enquiry into the Origins of Cultural Change.* Oxford and Cambridge: Blackwell.

———. 1995. "Globalization in Question." *Rethinking Marxism* 8:4 (winter 1995): 1–17.

Luxemburg, Rosa. 1968. *What is Economics?* Translated by T. Edwards. Colombo, Ceylon: Sydney Wanasinghe.

———. 1972. *The Accumulation of Capital: An Anti-Critique.* New York and London: Monthly Review Press.

Mintz, Sidney Wilfred. 1985. *Sweetness and Power: The Place of Sugar in Modern History.* New York: Viking.

Ohnuki-Tierney, Emiko. 2001. "Historicization of the Culture Concept." *History and Anthropology* 12:3:231–54.

Revel, Jacques, and Lynn Hunt, eds. 1995. *Histories: French Constructions of the Past.* Translated by Arthur Goldhammer. New York: New Press.

Trouillot, Lyonel. 1997. *Les Dits du fou de l'île: nouvelles.* Port-au-Prince: Editions de l'île.

Trouillot, Michel-Rolph. 1991. "Anthropology and the Savage Slot: The Poetics and Politics of Otherness." Pp. 17–44 in *Recapturing Anthropology: Working in the Present*, ed. Richard G. Fox. Santa Fe: School of American Research Press.

———. 1995. *Silencing the Past: Power and the Production of History.* Boston: Beacon Press.

————. 1998. "Culture on the Edges: Creolization in the Plantation Context." Special Issue, "Who/What is Creole?," ed. A. James Arnold. *Plantation Society in the Americas* 5:1:8–28.

————. 2001. "The Anthropology of the State in the Age of Globalization: Close Encounters of a Deceptive Kind." *Current Anthropology* 42:1:125–38.

Tsing, Anna Lowenhaupt. 2000. "The Global Situation." *Cultural Anthropology* 15:3:327–60.

Wallerstein, Immanuel. 1991. *Unthinking Social Science: The Limits of Nineteenth-Century Paradigms*. Cambridge, UK: Polity Press.

Wallerstein, Immanuel, et al. 1996. *Open the Social Sciences: A Report of the Gulbenkian Commission on the Restructuring of the Social Sciences*. Stanford, Calif.: Stanford University Press.

Weiss, Linda. 1997. "Globalization and the Myth of the Powerless State." *New Left Review* 225:3–27.

Wolf, Eric R. 1982. *Europe and the People without History*. Berkeley: University of California Press.

CHAPTER TWO

MODERNITY AND PERIPHERY

Toward a Global and Relational Analysis

MARY LOUISE PRATT

When the term *postmodern* began circulating the planet in the 1980s, two reactions prevailed among Latin American colleagues, both of them ironic. One was "Dammit, we haven't even got modernity yet, and they've called it off!" The other was "Fragmentation? decenteredness? co-existence of incommensurate realities?—if that's it, we've *always* been postmodern. *They* are catching up to *us*." This is by way of saying, as Graciela Montaldo so clearly puts it, "In general, postmodernism serves in Latin America primarily as a way of thinking about the scope of our modernity" (1997, 628). This, she argues, has been the case in Europe and in the United States as well. She is right. Despite the apparently infinite capacity of the term *postmodern* to displace other analytical categories, the 1980s and 1990s have seen a rich and an interesting rethinking of modernity by scholars in many parts of the world. What is emerging is an account of modernity that is more complex, and above all more intelligible, than before. In particular, in keeping with the decolonization of knowledge that began in the 1960s and accelerated in the 1970s and 1980s, modernity is currently being analyzed from a much more global perspective than before. One thinks, in Latin America, of

Beatriz Sarlo's pioneering *Una modernidad periférica* (1988), analyzing Buenos Aires in the 1920s, the essays of Roberto Schwarz on modernity in Brazil (1992), or the wide-ranging Consejo Latinoamericano de Ciencias Sociales (CLACSO) volume *La modernidad en la encrucijada post moderna* ([Modernity at the postmodern juncture], 1988a), edited by Fernando Calderón. In Britain, Paul Gilroy's *The Black Atlantic* (1993) approaches modernity in terms of the African diaspora. One thinks, in the United States, of the recent debate on modernity in *Thesis Eleven* (see Arnason 1994; Grumley 1994; Smith 1994; Touraine 1994), Arjun Appadurai's *Modernity at Large* (1996), or ethnographic investigations such as Anna Tsing's *In the Realm of the Diamond Queen: Marginality in an Out-of-the-Way Place* (1993). Indeed, the argument is made that the process of decolonizing knowledge is the source of the "post" in postmodernity, not because it put an end to modernity but because it put an end to the center's self-interested and deluded understanding of modernity, provoking, among other things, a crisis in intellectual authority that academies are still struggling to confront and contain. The texts I have just cited, and many others, bear out this claim.

Jürgen Habermas has invited us to think about modernity as an "incomplete project." I would like to suggest that what also remains incomplete is our (and his) understanding of modernity. As I will suggest in these pages, intellectuals now confront a collective challenge that is also an imperative and a possibility: that of creating a *global and relational* account of modernity. This is both a conceptual and an empirical project. Until such an account exists, the term *postmodern* has no referent and remains a gesture of premature closure on modernity, foreclosing the decolonization of knowledge and the decentering of the center. A global account of modernity will provide necessary historical and conceptual grounding for inquiries about globalization in the present and for reflection on the institutions of knowledge in which such inquiries take place.

In what follows, I propose to review briefly (1) the ways in which modernity has customarily talked about itself at the metropolitan center; (2) the ways in which the center encodes the periphery in accounts of modernity; (3) the ways in which modernity is characterized from the perspective of the periphery. The goal is to suggest some of the outlines for a global and relational account of modernity, and also to suggest that the opacity and incoherence of accounts of modernity constructed at the center derive in significant degree from their elision of the periphery and of center-periphery relations, that is, from a dramatic failure to recognize the diffusionist character of modernity as one of its most central features. The argument goes on to ask, on the one hand, the source of this failure and, on the other hand, how one might construct an account that brought this diffusionism, from the sending and receiving ends, into focus. To deploy the terms *center* and *periphery* is of course to revive a vocabulary now seen as anachronistic, supposedly replaced by an unaligned concept of globalization. I wish to suggest, however, that it is arbitrary and unnecessary to regard the concept of globalization as replacing a center-periphery perspective. Indeed, to do so reauthorizes the center to function unmarked as a center. Perhaps this concern lies behind the recent emergence of the dyad "North" and "South"—capitalized—in place of the vocabularies of center-periphery and first, second, and third worlds.

MODERNITY AT THE CENTER

How does modernity talk about itself at the center, that is, in Northern Europe and North America? Six characteristics of metropolitan discourses on modernity are of interest here.

1. They display an impulse to establish an *array of features* considered constitutive or symptomatic of modernity. Equally important, the distinction between constitutive and symptomatic features is not usually drawn, so the latter can be freely identified as the former, or vice versa. The array includes, for example:

- democracy, the nation-state, class formation
- industrialization and industrial divisions of labor
- the high/low culture distinction in the cultural sphere
- urbanization, mass culture, mass society, mass education
- expansion of markets and wild capitalist growth
- the hegemonization of instrumental rationality, the bureaucratization of society
- the rise of science as a truth-seeking discourse
- the privileging of reason as the path to true knowledge
- the rise of the individual and the idea of his freedom
- the idea of progress, progressive time
- change as an inherently positive value[1]

The specific items on the list are less important than the fact that accounts of modernity tend to assume that there should be such a set of features, and that it should be finite and noncontradictory; at the same time, the features cited seem potentially infinite and readily contradict each other.

2. Accounts of modernity display widely varying *narratives of origin*. There is an argument that starts modernity in 1436 with Gutenberg. Another locates the starting point in the late 1400s with Portuguese expansion, or specifically in 1492. Another (Touraine) cites the "long sixteenth century"—1450–1640. Others, most recently Stephen Toulmin (1990), mark 1637, the year of Descartes' *Discourse on Method*. For others, Leibniz is the key figure. Another common argument places the starting point at the mid-eighteenth century with the rise of science and of Man. Another places it at the end of the eighteenth century with the French Revolution, though not the Haitian and Andean ones that occurred at the same time. Some philosophers mark 1800, with the publication of Hegel's *Phenomenology of Spirit*. The first decades of the nineteenth century provide yet another starting point, marked by industrialization, urbanization, and the rise of the nation-state. Other accounts place the starting line at the beginning of the twentieth century, with the rise of mass communications, mass society, and modernist aesthetic projects. This is a common position in regions colonized by the first wave of European expansion, including Latin America. Even more common in the Third World is the marking of 1945 as the starting point—the point at which center-periphery relations were redefined by the paradigm of development versus underdevelopment, and the point at which, according to Immanuel Wallerstein (1979), it began to be impossible to think of Europe as the center of the world. The last president of El Salvador observed recently that now that the guerrilla movement is dead, modernity is at last ready to begin in Central America, while José Joaquin Brunner and others make a similar claim for postdictatorship Chile. Matei Calinescu, from whose monumental *Five Faces of Modernity* (1987 [1977]) we might hopefully expect some guidance, if anything vexes things more. He reveals that the Latin term *modernus* in its modern sense dates from the sixth century A.D. (not a date that figures in anyone's account), and that in English, "modernity" was first used in 1622 (confirming one account), while in French, "modernité" turns up only two centuries later, in 1849 (confirming another account).

What kind of a thing can modernity be if it has so many beginnings? What is at stake in both needing to identify a beginning and constructing a multiplicity of beginnings that can be invoked, depending on the argument that one wants to make? Why has this state of explanatory excess not been more troubling?

3. Modernity's narratives of origin define it with respect to a range of *others*—feudalism, absolutism, the primitive (i.e., tribal or subsistence societies), the traditional (i.e., peasant and rural societies), the irrational (animals, non-Westerners, and women), and the underdeveloped or backward (the colonial/neocolonial world).[2] What remains constant is that in every account there *has* to be an other. The multifaceted borders with these others have been policed and reproduced by the modern academic disciplines institutionalized at the center in the second half of the nineteenth century. Anthropology has produced and enforced the category of the primitive, economics those of backwardness and underdevelopment. Political science has administered the distinctions between state and non-state, simple and complex societies, philosophy the distinction between the rational and the irrational, and literary studies and art history between high and low culture. History has administered the concept of progressive time, determining who occupies it and who does not. Sometimes the points of reference are explicit. Sander Gilman has traced the way images of Africans defined the borders of Western aesthetics in the work of Hegel, Schopenhauer, and Nietzsche (1982, and discussed in Gilroy 1993, 8). In social theory, the unexplained referent "tribal societies" turns up freely when the boundaries of the modern need to be marked in the sand. In a recent (1998) lecture series, *What Is Modernity?*, Agnes Heller elaborated a vivid, wide-ranging description which, often inexplicably, required continuous reference to a contrasting entity called "premodern societies." Over the course of the lectures, this concept acquired the following characteristics:

- stable social orders;
- fixed and absolute norms of goodness, truth, and beauty ("The art of Egypt and Mesoamerica remained unchanged for thousands of years");
- a pyramidal social structure with a man at the top;
- the life of the subject is completely determined at birth by its place in the pyramid; there is neither mobility nor the desire for mobility;
- subjects do not question their place in the order or desire change;

- the ancient is sacred;
- the dominant worldview is supplied by religion and founded on absolutes;
- what the subject perceives as its needs are given at birth and correspond to its place in the order; needs are assigned qualitatively;
- domestic violence exists in normalized forms;
- sex is obligatory on the woman's part;
- passions and emotions are expressed more freely; and
- happiness exists not as a subjective state but as an objective condition determined by concrete criteria.

It is easy to reconstruct for each item on this list which feature of modernity was being established in contrast, but the project of defining modernity does not require this list to have coherence, boundedness, or verifiability. Its epistemological status is somewhat mysterious. As a list of general attributes of societies outside of European modernity, it is empirically false and arbitrary. Attempts to question the empirical basis for the claims, however, were vigorously rejected as trivial.

What, in modernity's accounts of itself, is the rationale for requiring a fixed other and creating a range of them to choose from, depending, again, on the argument that one wants to make? Why has this infinity of content been a feature of, rather than a problem for, the discourse on modernity?

4. Scholars are by now accustomed to questioning the universalizing, totalizing aspects of modernity's accounts of itself, but somewhat less has been said about the *centralizing* aspects of such accounts. The effort to identify essential features, a unified other, and a narrative of origin is an effort to centralize the object of study. At the same time, since a multiplicity of features, others, and narratives of origins is generated, the object of study can be centralized and recentralized in many ways and combinations, depending on the argument that one wants to make. By the same token, every centralizing gesture is provisional. The apparent disjointedness and inconsistency of modernity's descriptions of itself are a by-product of this centralizing tendency, this centrism. If the impulse to centralize were not present, the proliferation of centralizing schemata would be unnecessary.

At an empirical level, the centrism of the metropolitan discourse on modernity depends upon a form of interpretive power that involves what might be called the *monopolistic use of categories*. I use this phrase to refer to an interpretive logic, whereby if A is a symptom of B, then every instance of A *may be read as* an instance of B. Thus if rationality is a criterial feature of modernity, then wherever the interpreter encounters it he or she, if he or she chooses, may identify it as indicating the presence of modernity. By the same token, all instances of irrationality can be read, if the interpreter chooses, as signifying the non- or premodern. This structure of possibilities grants the interpreter a huge capacity for absorbing or creating otherness. I focus here on the phrase "if the interpreter chooses" in order to stress that this is a form of interpretive power, on whose workings it is essential to reflect. Who, we may inquire, has access to the power to do such choosing and to assign such readings, and the places of power where they are done? How is access constructed and enforced? What happens when an unauthorized party— a testimonial subject, for example—contests or lays claim to this power, proposing an alternative account? Investigating the possibility of "alternative modernities," Paul Gilroy notes "the ease and speed with which European particularisms are still being translated into absolute universal standards for human achievement, norms, and aspirations" (1993, 7–8). (He could be talking about anything from the philosophy of agency to IMF [International Monetary Fund] structural readjustment programs.) This monopolistic interpretive power is an important dimension of the centrism that characterizes modernity's account of itself.

5. I have been commenting so far on the way metropolitan modernity represents itself to itself, the way it brings itself into being, the way it lines up a geographical and an epochal idea of modernity with a range of entirely real historical processes and events. The point here is not at all to deny the reality of those processes and events but to examine how they have been understood. The idea of modernity, I suggest, was one of the chief tropes through which Europe constructed itself as a center, as *the* center, and the rest of the planet as a—its—periphery. This identity-creating aspect is what Homi Bhabha alludes to when he says the story of modernity is "about the historical construction of a specific position of historical enunciation and address" (1991, 201). Note that this characterization is outer directed, involving address: in its relational dimensions, modernity is a *diffusionist* project, assigned to interpellate others from a center. One of its prime tasks was to make particular kinds of sense of, and give particular kinds of direction to, Europe's interactions with the rest of the world. I have found it quite helpful to think about modernity as an *identity discourse*, as Europe's (or the white world's)

identity discourse as it assumed global dominance. The need for narratives of origins, distinctive features, and reified Others, and the policing of boundaries combined with the slippery capacity to create and erase otherness as needed are the signposts of identity discourses. Hence, the centrism of modernity is in part ethnocentrism, though it does not readily identify itself in this manner. The monopolistic use of categories I mentioned earlier is an ethnocentric practice. Though euro-, ethno-, and androcentrism are not normally found on that list of features by which modernity characterizes itself, they come into view when modernity's others gain the interpretive power to question the monopolistic use of categories. This is the import of Gilroy's call for an "ethnohistorical reading of western modernity" (1993, 8), or of Enrique Dussel's charge that modernity is constituted by a "eurocentric fallacy." It is, he says, "a European phenomenon . . . constituted in a dialectical relation with a non-European alterity that is its ultimate content" (1995, 65).

6. Dussel's formulation points to an axis of tension with little visibility or importance in the center, but which is extremely significant everywhere else: the *contradiction* between modernity's need for fixed otherness, on the one hand, and its diffusionist, subject-producing program, on the other hand. Frederick Buell speaks of the incompatibility of the metropolitan attempt to both produce subjects on the periphery and to maintain their alterity (1994, 335), between the imperative, on the one hand, to fix others in order to define itself and, on the other hand, to modernize others through processes of assimilation. This internal contradiction intersects with another: a concept of individual liberty that depends on the subordination or self-subordination of others. In classic liberal theory, liberty consists in the possibilities the individual has to develop his (*sic*) capacities and to follow his desires and interests (Held et al. 1983). This (masculinized) concept of the individual presupposes a division of labor in which reproduction and social continuity are carried out by others. Liberty thus conceived depends a priori on the existence of population sectors that are by definition unfree, charged with the reproductive, custodial, and tutelary relations. These conflicting dynamics explain much about the ways the discourse on modernity encodes the periphery, to which I now turn.

FROM CENTER TO PERIPHERY

How does the center encode the periphery from within modernity? Postcolonial criticism has reflected richly on this question. Two key terms have surfaced: *outside* and *behind* (but not, it appears, "below.") "Primitive" and "tribal" mark the outside of modernity; "backward" and "underdeveloped" mark that which is behind. "Feudal" and "traditional" mark things as simultaneously outside and behind. Again, note the centralizing, monopolistic use of these categories: given the interpretive power, the interpreter can read anything that fails to correspond to preconception as an instance of either outsideness or behindness, rather, say, than as an instance of alternative, emergent, diasporic, or counterforms of modernity. Nor can the schema recognize phenomena that participate simultaneously in modernity and some other historical trajectory, as with postconquest indigenous social formations in the Americas, for example. This is a conceptual limit of vast consequence.

It is important to observe that in the semantics of this spatial discourse, the normative positions of "insideness" and "in-frontness" are defined only by the center. In other words, the presence or absence of modernity can be determined only from that one site. There is no room, say, for the very plausible ideas that those "in front" are pushed—or held up—by those "behind," or that those "in front" are trapped looking ahead and therefore cannot see what is going on "behind." In other words, the agency of the periphery in the creation of modernity remains systematically invisible at the center, as do the processes of diffusion from center to periphery. Obscured by those binaries of inside/outside and in front/behind is the fascinating and variegated global phenomenon of what Beatriz Sarlo (1988) has called "peripheral modernity" and the relatively unexamined history of the *constitutive* relations between metropolitan modernity, on the one hand, and colonialism, neocolonialism, and slavery, on the other hand. These latter phenomena no longer appear to scholars as "outside" or "behind" the modern, but the nature of their "insideness" has yet to be well researched and theorized. That is probably the central empirical and conceptual task at hand in producing a global and relational account of modernity. So the experimental ethnographer Anna Tsing, writing about "marginality in an out-of-the-way place," laments "the poverty of an urban imagination which has systematically denied the possibilities of difference *within* the modern world, and thus looked to relatively isolated people to represent its only adversary, its dying Other" (1993, x). The "romance of the primitive," she goes on to say, "is a discourse of hope for many Europeans and North Americans—as well as urban people everywhere"—but it must be given up.

Tsing calls for "a different set of conceptual tools," the most important of which are the concepts of marginality and gender. As Sarlo also observes, to be marginal or peripheral is precisely not to be disconnected from a center but to be intimately connected in particular, highly meaningful ways that are local, not in the sense that one sees only part of the picture but in the sense that one sees the whole picture from a particular epistemological location that is not a center. For similar reasons, gender is Tsing's other deconstructive category. Precisely because women are systematically trivialized and ignored by modernity, women's knowledges have developed—globally—with a degree of autonomy and distance from both the assimilationist and the othering mechanisms of modernity. The product of forms of agency and meaning making invisible to modernity, women's knowledges systematically offer alternative conceptualizations of the global relations and states of affairs that the centrist lenses of modernity misidentify. In the terms being proposed here, Tsing's concepts of marginalization and gender are points of entry to a global, relational account of modernity.

MODERNITY ON THE PERIPHERY

Beyond the center, which is to say across most of the planet, the roster of features, narratives of origins, and relations of self and otherness that I have been discussing routinely fail to describe the world. Within the terms of modernity, these divergences all have the same explanation: backwardness, the time lag. The periphery is simply behind and will in time catch up, so that at a particular point in the future, all will be fully and equally modern. That positivist account is what made it possible to posit modernity's universals as universals—they will indeed correspond universally when everyone has caught up. As soon as the time lag is revealed as a lie, however, the teleology of catching up breaks down, and center-periphery relations come into view as a structure of inequality that is *constitutive* of the center. Though scholars today take this structure of inequality as a given, the teleology of catching up (alias "progress" or "modernization") lost its monopoly only quite recently— in the 1970s, when import substitution policies broke down and produced the debt crisis. This breakdown has been key in making peripheral modernities available for reflection. It is the context for the rich body of discussion upon which this chapter draws. At the same time, the paradigm of modernization—conveniently treated as synonymous with modernity—continues to exert enormous power in the world. Indeed, it was revived in the 1980s and 1990s as a founding myth of the new neoliberalism, whose false narratives of diffusion obscure the torrential flow of profit from the Third World to the First.

Among intellectuals outside of the center, the epistemology of backwardness and the teleology of progress have been meaningful, indeed, compelling, interpretive frameworks. At one time they underwrote discourses of optimism and powerful senses of futurity. In the neoliberal era they also generate diagnostics of irremediable lack. "Truncated, partial, incomplete, fragmented"—these are the terms used to describe Latin American modernity in two recent Latin American collections (Calderón 1988a; *David y Goliath* 1987). While many thinkers accept this incompleteness as a fact, others question the interpretive monopoly that enables the center to project reductive and negative self-definitions upon its others. "Among us," says José Joaquín Brunner, "cultural unease does not come from the exhaustion of modernity, but from exasperation with it" (1987, 39). In his landmark essay, "Brazilian Culture: Nationalism by Elimination" (1986; in Schwarz 1992), Brazilian critic Roberto Schwarz speaks eloquently of the painful existential conditions that the diffusionist structure of modernity creates for intellectuals, requiring them to respond to trends and vocabularies arriving one after another from abroad, produced in reference to alien sociocultural contexts and epistemological dilemmas. On the receiving end, these become "ideias fora do lugar" (ideas out of place). Ideas, of course, can be adapted—it is no accident the theory of transculturation originated in Latin America (Ortiz 1978 [1947]; Rama 1982)—but, argues Schwarz, a deeper problem remains. The exports come in such rapid sequence that there is never time to domesticate each one or follow it through before the next one arrives. This pacing is not an accident but a dynamic of power. Schwarz speaks eloquently of the psychic, human, and social cost of this condition of imposed receptivity, which deprives the society of the chance to create forms of self-understanding of its own making, grounded in its own reality and history. He foregrounds the self-alienation that results when accepting a diagnosis of backwardness and incompleteness is the price of admission to a club in which membership is not optional. On the periphery, according to Schwarz and others, the price of living by the ideological compass of modernity has been to live one's own reality in terms of lack, fragmentation, partiality, imitativeness, and unfulfillment—while plenitude and wholeness are seen as existing at the center (one of modernity's most powerful planetary fictions).

While Schwarz denounces what Spivak calls the "epistemological violence" of the center's diffusionism, others embrace the epistemological privilege of the periphery, its power to reveal the center as it cannot reveal itself. This is the case with Schwarz's compatriot Silviano Santiago (1996), for whom the peripheral intellectual occupies "o entre-lugar" (the space between), a site from which she or he can reflect back to the center images of itself that the center could never generate but from which it stands to learn. The periphery's work includes the ironizing task of enlightening the center. Though his diagnosis is very different from Schwarz's, Santiago does not seem to deny the painful existential conditions that Schwarz emphasizes. He simply notes that there is a payoff, not for the nation (Schwarz's domain of concern) but for a humanistic field shared by center and periphery. Santiago's argument has a historical dimension. He argues that the self-critical, self-interrogating current of modernity is the result of the ongoing intervention of voices from the periphery. The latter thus have played a clearly discernible historical role in the development of modernity at the center. René Antonio Mayorgal (1988, 139) makes this point as well, asserting the periphery as a source of insight for the center, because the "insufficiencies" of modernity are displayed there. This also makes the periphery a source of solutions that cannot be generated at the center.

As attested by the texts to which I have been referring, in the 1980s, non-European thinkers as well as experimental ethnographers have increasingly laid claim to the periphery's power to describe and define itself, offering empirical and conceptual alternatives to the centrist imagery of backwardness and lack. A rich and suggestive literature has resulted, whose Latin American component I am drawing on here. Rejecting the center's account, which treats diffusion as a kind of natural by-product of modernity, this literature postulates a variety of relations between central and peripheral modernities, forming a counterdiscourse to the centrism of metropolitan accounts. Three kinds of relations seem to be emphasized: contradiction, complementarity, and differentiation.

Contradiction

The power structure of center-periphery is in open contradiction with the emancipatory, democratizing project of modernity, as intellectuals in the Americas have been pointing out for 500 years. In the very export of its ideas, in other words, modernity is in contradiction with itself, though this is systematically invisible at the center. Thus Homi Bhabha asks: "What is modernity in those colonial conditions where its imposition is itself the denial of historical freedom, civic autonomy, and the ethical choice of self-fashioning?" (1991, 198). For Bhabha, the history of the periphery generates an alternative narrative of emancipation: freedom and agency are not given by modernity but rather have to be fought for within it. Modernity comes into view, then, not as an agent that grants freedom but as an agent that sets in motion certain conflicts and that is itself constituted by those conflicts.

Complementarity

The center generates narratives of diffusion. These are essential to its self-concept as a center. Their content, however, from the standpoint of the center, is unproblematic and inconsequential. Far from being a constitutive feature of modernity or an aspect of a global division of labor, diffusion appears as a spontaneous and an inessential side effect of developments at the center. The specifics of what gets diffused, when, and to whom make no difference to how modernity sees itself. On the periphery, however, diffusion translates into processes of reception and transculturation; the content and character of processes of diffusion, far from being unproblematic or inconsequential, constitute reality. At the center, for example, the dual phenomena of European out-migration and African slavery scarcely appear as events in narratives of modernity. Europe's displaced peasantries simply disappear from its history the moment they board ship, while Africans do not come into view at all. But in the Americas, both groups are crucial historical actors without whom the history of modernity in the Americas cannot be told. The "backward" peasantries displaced by modernization in Europe were invited to the Americas as a modernizing force to overcome "backward" indigenous and mestizo peoples, so such immigration has been recognized as involving a process of "becoming white" (Ignatiev and Garvey 1996). (From the Americas, one can wonder what European modernity would have looked like if those displaced peasantries had had nowhere to go. Would Italy and Ireland have had agrarian revolutions as well as Mexico and Russia?) Gilroy, Schwarz, Mintz, and others call for slavery to be located firmly within the modern. Gilroy demands that we "look more deeply into the relationship of racial terror and subordination to the inner character of modernity" (1993, 70–71). Gilroy's *The Black Atlantic* makes one of the most comprehensive attempts to set terms for a transatlantic account of modernity, particularly with respect to culture. Gilroy insists on the idea of countercultures within modernity and of cultural formations that are simultaneously inside and outside of its borders, simultaneously immanent and transcendent.

When uncontested, the center's diffusionist accounts of culture assume a transparent and an inconsequential process of assimilation on the reception end. Nothing at the center calls for a questioning of this assumption. From an epistemological standpoint on the reception end, however, the idea of "assimilation" lacks explanatory power. Again, it is no accident that the theory of transculturation developed in Latin America (Calderón 1988a; Rama 1982), or that vocabularies of hybridity, *mestizaje*, and *créolité* have become the bases for powerful cultural paradigms and identity discourses in the Americas.

Differentiation

Challenging the center's self-endowed interpretive monopoly involves asserting difference against false claims of sameness. For instance, it has been common to assume that "progress" on the periphery has the same referential meaning as "progress" at the center. The center's normative interests are served by this equation, but on the periphery it becomes apparent that "progress" in such senses as "bettering the human condition" or "moving toward greater plenitude" is not at all the same as "progress" in the sense of "catching up" or "reproducing what has already happened elsewhere." The latter teleology, as many critics point out, imposes a permanent identity crisis.

Beyond the center, the concepts of modernity and modernization tend to differentiate sharply. The relation of homology or identity they hold at the center cracks apart. In Latin America, for instance, modernization is overwhelmingly seen as displacing modernity. Reflection on this question has been rich and diverse. Gino Germani (1969) believes that modernization works as much against modernity as for it. Aníbal Quijano (1988) argues that after World War II, modernization eclipsed all other aspects of modernity, obscuring the fact that while Latin America has been a passive recipient of modernization, it has since 1492 been an active producer of modernity. Quijano blames British capitalism for bringing modernization without modernity to Latin America. Alain Touraine (1988) rejects not only the equation of modernity and modernization but any fixed relation between the two. What is at stake, he argues, is the way any particular social formation combines modernity with some particular form of modernization. Norbert Lechner (1990) posits an irreducible tension between the two. He defines modernization as the unfolding of instrumental rationality, and modernity as the unfolding of normative rationality leading toward autonomy and self-determination. In the Latin American context, the former is destructive of the latter. In Peru, Rodrigo Montoya (1992) makes a similar argument, defining modernity as self-determination and autonomy and modernization as capitalist development and the Western civilizing project. On the periphery, he argues, it is impossible to achieve modernity through modernization. This is the basis for Montoya's counterproposal of a distinct modernity based on Andean indigenous values. This tension between modernity and modernization seems to have resolved itself in favor of the latter. In the work of a number of recent theorists, including Brunner (1994), García Canclini (1989), Appadurai (1996), and Buell (1994), the two terms seem to be used interchangeably, usually reducing modernity to modernization. Perhaps this reduction registers the impact of postmodern (and post-cold war) paradigms that insist that modernist emancipatory projects are dead, and that citizenship is now anchored in consumption.

CONDITIONS OF PERIPHERAL MODERNITY

I suggested that a global and relational account of modernity is an empirical and a conceptual project. In such an account, peripheral modernities will be described in relations of contradiction, complementarity, and differentiation, with respect to those of the center. Two existential and epistemological conditions will, I believe, also play a key role in accounts of the character and trajectories of modernity outside of Europe. Both are relational: (1) the condition of *imposed receptivity* and (2) the *copresence of modernity's "selves" and "others."* These final pages will attempt to elaborate on these two observations.

By "imposed receptivity," I refer to the circumstances lamented by Schwarz above, of being on the receiving end of an asymmetrical relation of diffusion. García Márquez's *Macondo* often is read as an attempt to capture the dynamic whereby things descend on the periphery unpredictably. The peripheral social formation has power to determine *how* but not *whether* they are received. By "copresence of self and other," I refer to historical situations in which the European-identified subjects of modernity—sometimes colonial elites—face the task of founding a social and spatial order shared with modernity's others—indigenous inhabitants or imported slaves, for example. These two dynamics turn up repeatedly when scholars trace the historical and cultural dynamics of modernity in the Americas. A few examples illustrate the point.

After independence from Spain, the map of modernity that Latin American thinkers produced for themselves envisioned enlightened elites governing unenlightened masses. What "held things back," it was understood, were the latter (Rama 1984). Recent analyses, however, have argued the opposite. Among elites, that is, the diffusion of modernity's programs often had the effect of reinforcing existing social structures and *preventing* "progress." In particular, in the heterogeneous societies of the Americas, modernity's need for reified Others had the effect of widening dissociations between the elites (seen as governed by modernity) and masses (seen as governed by tradition, tribalism, or barbarism). The core terminologies of modernity located indigenous and mestizo masses outside of the very history the enlightened elites saw themselves assigned to make. Peruvian sociologist José Guillermo Nugent makes this argument with respect to Peru in an essay wonderfully titled *El laberinto de la choledad* (1992). In the nineteenth century, Nugent argues, Peru's indigenous majority was rapidly "expulsados del tiempo" (expelled from time) and ceased to be seen as players in the production of the Peruvian nation, or of history.[3] As Nugent puts it, "los señores se hicieron más señores y los indios más indios" (the lords became more lordly and the Indians became more Indian) (1992, 71). The categories of modernity legitimated, and indeed imposed, what in modernity's own terms was a social regression. There was no space in the modernist imaginary of the center for the heterogeneous social formations that were the norm wherever European expansionism had left its mark. In Argentina, where indigenous peoples were a minority by the time of independence, the result was not simply an expulsion from time but the well-known campaigns of genocide set in motion by Domingo Faustino Sarmiento, possibly the most cosmopolitan, modern president in the hemisphere at the time. Eradicating the indigenous population and importing displaced European peasants were complementary rather than contradictory strategies.

In Peru, Nugent argues, the elites created what he calls a "contramodernidad" (countermodernity) in which aspects of modernization were used to bolster a colonial social order that the center would have seen as archaic. This resulted, says Nugent, from a "selective reception" of modernity, which landed elites saw as essentially foreign to themselves. In the terms being proposed here, such a selective reception was inevitable given the condition of imposed receptivity on the periphery. The option of simply rejecting modernity outright did not exist, but why would Peru's elites experience modernity as "essentially foreign"? Often this is seen as evidence of their backwardness. This may be true, but a logically prior explanation suggests itself as well, namely, the copresence of the self and other. In Peru, the existence of an indigenous majority and three centuries of colonial cohabitation were more than sufficient to make ideologies of modernity foreign. Centrist modernity did not allow for the type of social formation that the elites on the periphery were charged with modernizing.

Roberto Schwarz elaborates a related argument with respect to Brazil. "When Brazil became an independent state," he says, "a permanent collaboration was established between the forms of life characteristic of colonial oppression and the innovations of bourgeois progress" (1992, 14). The fact that Brazil remained a slave-holding society, for example, determined the idea of freedom that developed there. To be free was to be unenslaved. Schwarz argues that in Brazil, the society of "free" individuals developed not around a Rousseauian idea of personal agency and autonomy but around the idea of patronage or *favor*, a form of bondage radically distinct from slavery. In this system, "free" persons, in order to survive, had to make themselves dependent on the favor of individuals of wealth and power. The resulting patronage system was at odds with modern individualism and liberalism, but it was sustained—and even imposed—by the modern categories of freedom and individuality projected from the center. The result, argues Schwarz, is a form of peripheral modernity peculiar to Brazil. "Favor" came to shape Brazil's modern institutions, its bureaucracies, and its system of justice, all of which, "though ruled by favor, affirmed the forms and theories of the modern bourgeois state" (ibid., 24). Schwarz underscores the "extraordinary dissonance that results when modern culture is used to this purpose" (ibid.).

Again, centrist formulas interpret the *favor* system as backwardness, as the absence of modernity. Failing to absorb modern democratic ideals, it is argued, the elites acted out of cynical self-interest, but Schwarz insists on asking: how could it be otherwise? The fact was, liberal ideas could be neither rejected nor implemented in Brazil (or Peru or the United States) in the nineteenth century. Imposed receptivity makes it impossible to reject the modern and assume an independent trajectory; the copresence of modernity's others makes it impossible to reproduce the metropolitan script. Under no circumstances does Schwarz accept the diagnosis of backwardness (or "behindness") to account for the situation. "Modern" centers and "backward" peripheries belong to the same order of things and are products of the same historical conditions, he points out. Slavery existed in Brazil till 1888 not as an archaic hangover of premodernity but as a modern structure fully integrated into the historical process of the time. The conditions upholding slavery in Brazil were the same *modern* conditions producing the mode of production at the center.

This is the global, relational dimension that modernity's accounts of itself systematically obscure. From the point of view of the center, the *process* of diffusion/reception of modernity abroad has been regarded at best as a spontaneous and collateral effect that can reveal nothing important about modernity itself. It does not appear as an aspect of an international division of labor or a web of global relations for whose content Europe might be in part accountable. On the reception end, however, the diffusionist momentum of modernity becomes a powerful determinant of reality in all of its dimensions; its empirical particularities are very consequential. This is a truism, but it is one to which metropolitan theorizing on modernity remains remarkably immune—Berman, Toulmin, Heller, and their interlocutors take no notice of it, for instance, and even today little in their intellectual spheres appears to compel them to do so.

One cannot resist inserting here a parallel anecdote from the history of modernity on another periphery, northern Africa. Paul Rabinow, in a fascinating study of French colonial cities, argues that "it was in Morocco that France's first comprehensive experience in urban planning took place" (1989, 277). The French urban planners he studies despised France, because it was so bound by tradition that it could not be truly modernized. At the turn of the twentieth century, in their view, the colonial frontier was the place where modernity could truly develop—not least because there everything could be done by fiat. Negotiation with tradition was not required. Working by fiat, the French colonial authorities designed new, ultramodern cities in which the copresence of the other was a given. One of the priorities was to make possible and aesthetically rewarding the permanent cohabitation of French and Muslim populations in segregated, adjacent, and aesthetically appealing spaces. In this account, the colonial frontier is the vanguard of modernity, not the site of backwardness. Morocco was an opportunity to use urban form to create a modern social formation, an opportunity sustained by the violence of colonial power.[4]

Rabinow's point is to revindicate the early-twentieth-century French planners by noting that they worked out of a deep respect for cultural differences that would later be replaced by homogenizing, technocratic attitudes. One cannot help observing, however, that in Lyautey's designs the copresence of the other is taken into account through segregation, a practice that enforces and reinforces the categories of otherness which, I have argued, are key to modernity as an identity discourse. Do such formations on the periphery represent a "dissonant" deployment of modernity, to use Schwarz's term? Are they instances of "contramodernidad," to use Nugent's term, or the "pseudomodernidad" lamented by Octavio Paz (Brunner 1988, 96)? Or are they alternative realizations of modern plenitude, as Gilroy might say? To the extent that they leave the normativity of the center unquestioned, none of these formulations is fully satisfactory.

Periphery and Plenitude

Can peripheral or alternative modernities result in peripheral or alternative plenitudes? In Latin America, the first decades of the twentieth century often are seen as the moment at which modernity consolidated itself. Political participation democratized, and urban middle classes emerged, along with consumer markets, industrialization, technological transformation of daily life, and modern oppositional movements—unions, feminism, Marxism, and anarchism. Cities grew and acquired influence over landed gentry. In the arts, radio, photography, cinema and avant-garde movements flourished. What happens if this consolidation is examined through the lenses that I have been proposing here? Examples from the domain of literature and aesthetics suggest a few dimensions of the question.

In the arts, metropolitan modernity is profoundly linked to urbanization and urban aesthetics, from Baudelaire's flaneur in Paris in the 1860s to Walter Benjamin's study of Baudelaire's flaneur in the 1930s. The aesthetic projects of the European avant-gardes originated in the city. The city *is* the vanguard of modern civilization, its cutting edge, its most dramatic creation. In its absence, modernity also is absent. The rural becomes synonymous with backwardness. From the point of view of this urban norm, how would one view an Argentine novel such as *Don Segundo Sombra* (1926) by Ricardo Güiraldes? It is a nostalgic *bildungsroman* about the Argentine *pampa* that narrates the relationship between a young gentleman and an old gaucho or cowboy. Within metropolitan norms, it is scarcely believable that such a folkloric pastoral appeared in the year between, say, the two experimental masterpieces of

Virginia Woolf: *Mrs Dalloway* (1925) and *To the Lighthouse* (1927). Güiraldes' novel seems a clear case of anachronism or backwardness.

But the fact is that in the Americas, north as well as south, modernity produces a flourishing of experiments in nonurban aesthetics, of artistic projects anchored not in the city but in the countryside, the jungle, the mountains, in border regions, and in the heterogeneous social order.[5] The avant-garde movement in Brazil, for example, was launched in 1921 by an outrageous document called the "Anthropophagist Manifesto" ("anthropophagist" means cannibal), by poet and cultural activist Oswald de Andrade. The aesthetic program it proposes, with seriousness and irony, embraces the (decidedly nonmodern) figure of the cannibal as the basis for a modern Brazilian identity. Anthropophagist aesthetics resignified the relation of imposed receptivity: what comes to us from abroad, it said, we will neither imitate nor obey; rather we will devour it, defecate what is not of use to us, and absorb the rest into our own flesh. For critic Silviano Santiago, the co-existence of castration and liberation in anthropophagist thought both evokes a "situation of real 'cultural dependency'" and posits "the possibility of an original Third World culture which necessarily participated in the European ethnocentric tradition at the same time as it questioned it" (1996, 177). The other central figure of Brazilian modernism, Mario de Andrade, was a very cosmopolitan poet, novelist, ethnographer, musicologist, photographer, pedagogue, and autodidact. He wrote the canonical novel of Brazilian modernism, *Macunaíma* (1928), a comic prose fantasy whose hero is a Tupi Indian who travels throughout the territory of Brazil causing trouble. At the same time, de Andrade also wrote one of the great urban poems of all time, the *Paulicea Desvairada*, in 1922, the same year that James Joyce published *Ulysses*. Both country and city were privileged terrains for the new modern artist of the Americas.

The same would be said of a perhaps better-known contemporary, Guatemalan novelist Miguel Angel Asturias, winner of the Nobel Prize for Literature in 1967. Asturias wrote a famous urban novel about dictatorship (*El Señor Presidente*, 1948) and the equally famous rural novel *Hombres de maiz* (1949). The latter is an extraordinary experimental text in which the author tries to construct a Guatemalan national imaginary by recuperating and resignifying Maya mythology. In fact, Asturias exemplifies the anthropophagic aesthetic canonized by the Brazilians. His contact with Maya mythology did not and could not have taken place in a modernizing Guatemala. It happened at the Sorbonne, where he was sent to study. Alongside Asturias, such Mexican writers as Nelly Campobello, Agustín Yañez, and Juan Rulfo were experimenters in rural aesthetics, as were José Lins do Rego, Graciliano Ramos, Jorge Amado, and Raquel de Queiroz in Brazil. Campobello and Queiroz are part of a rich wave of women's writing that included Gabriela Mistral and Marta Brunet (Chile) and Teresa de la Parra (Venezuela). Mistral, who received the Nobel Prize for Literature in 1945, wrote a vast text titled *Poema de Chile* (Poem of Chile, 1967), in which the poet traverses the territory of her nation in the company of an indigenous child. The city is nowhere in sight. For Latin American women writers, the city often represents immobilization and unfreedom. In Europe, it is difficult to encounter anything resembling this kind of nonurban women's writing; in North America, however, one does.

Yet another set of experiments takes place in what could be called "frontier aesthetics," in which such writers as Horacio Quiroga, Eustacio Rivera, Romulo Gallegos allegorize the borders of modernity and the relationship between modernity and modernization. Fernando Coronil and Julie Skurski (1993), in a fascinating study of Gallegos' novel *Doña Bárbara* (Venezuela, 1929), argue that the text exemplifies a "return to the rural," which was an attempt to resolve ambivalent relations to the high modernism of the center. The Venezuelan countryside—the periphery of the periphery—became the site of an elite's effort to resolve the double consciousness of its dependent condition. Read against European psychological fiction of the time, this allegorization tends to appear anachronistic. Read against the contradictions of peripheral society, the anachronism disappears (Lechner 1990). One also finds attempts, distorted by ignorance and racism, at what might be called "ethnographic aesthetics," from folklore collections to works of social realism and indigenism.

Such projects in rural, frontier, and ethnographic aesthetics reflect important dimensions of modernity in the Americas, which do not yet seem to appear in accounts of that modernity. We see their legacy in the famous boom of the Latin American novel in the 1950s and 1960s. It is not often observed that the novels of the boom are heavily nonurban: from Carpentier's *Los pasos perdidos* (Cuba, 1953) through Arguedas' *Los rios profundos* (Peru, 1958), Fuentes' *La muerte de Artemio Cruz* (Mexico, 1962), Vargas Llosa's *La casa verde* (Peru, 1966), and Darcy Ribeiro's *Maíra* (1976). Marginality is of course the foundational myth of García Márquez's compelling fictional worlds. When in his masterpiece *Grande Sertão: Veredas* (1956; English title *The Devil to Pay in the Backlands*), the Brazilian João Guimarães Rosa wanted to imitate James Joyce, he substituted the city of Dublin with the vast interior plains (the *sertão*) of Brazil.

One cannot help but be intrigued by the dynamism of these projects. In the terms under discussion here, they often involve reversals of imposed receptivity, that is, a reclaiming of the center by the periphery. Equally striking is the degree to which they are anchored in the copresence of selves and others. These were creative engagements with reality and history beyond the center, in terms not entirely laid down by the center. To return to the relational categories introduced above, they are peripheral modernisms standing in relations of contradiction, complementarity, and differentiation with those of the center. Their emancipatory power, as critics often have noted, lies chiefly in refusing the self-alienated position of imposed receptivity, as Schwarz would have it, or using that position as a site of creative authenticity, as Silvano Santiago would have it.

RISING THROUGH THE POPULAR

The "magic" of Latin American magic realism, as Jean Franco often has pointed out, derives from another feature alien to the metropolis: an engagement by writers with the popular. In metropolitan accounts of modernity, popular and vernacular cultures have no place. If anything, they are perceived as forms of alterity ("tradition," for example). But as a number of researchers have shown, one of the most conspicuous characteristics of Latin American modernities is the interaction between currents imported or imposed from the center and the deep, heterogeneous cultural formations developed among the racially, ethnically, and regionally diverse popular classes. Research on this subject (one thinks of Jesus-Martin Barbero, Nestor García Canclini, Jean Franco, Angel Rama, William Rowe and Vivian Schelling, and others) suggests an imperative of understanding how cultural diffusion has worked within modernity. Emphatically rejecting the centrist idea of a diffusion that displaces that which preexisted it, these scholars argue that even that which is imposed must enter *through* that which is already there.

This point is argued at length in an influential book by William Rowe and Vivian Schelling, *Memory and Modernity* (1991). "In Latin America," they argue, "modernity rises through the popular" (3). The centrist assumption of a diffusion entering and replacing what is there is aggressively rejected. Like America's theorists of heterogeneity, hybridity, and *créolité*, Rowe and Schelling are theorizing the reception end of a diffusion that at the center is seen as unproblematic and inconsequential. Even that which is imposed, they argue, must enter through what is already there, through everything that is already there—which means that modernity enters through the very things that at the center are defined as its others: religion, the traditional, the tribal, the non-Western, the unlettered, and the unenlightened. How could it be otherwise? (How could it have been otherwise in Europe as well?) In example after example, Rowe and Schelling look at how popular mythology, local drama, and ritual encode the history of modernity, how popular religion, with its feasts, saints, ritual calendar, art forms, and cosmologies, engages and is engaged by modernity. They observe how vernacular culture generates its own cast of character types—the malandro, the cholo, the chola—codifying forms of subaltern agency within modernity. They discuss sports, crafts, forms of urbanization, social movements, and the impact of oral traditions on electronic media. The obvious conclusion, upheld by contemporary Latin American *cronistas* across the hemisphere, is that in its dynamic, mobile engagement with modernity, popular culture cannot be contained by the modernist geography of outsideness or behindness, nor by Raymond Williams' concepts of the emergent and residual, nor, one suspects, by García Canclini's powerful image of subjects "entering and leaving modernity," or Eduardo Galeano's idea of an American "modernidad barroca" distinct from Europe's "modernidad ilustrada." At the same time, in terms of social and economic empowerment and access to citizenship and institutions, the promises of modernity have neither risen up nor trickled down. If postmodernity is indeed the moment of reflection on "the scope of our modernity," the task has barely begun.

NOTES

This chapter was published in a different version in German: "Modernität und Peripherie. Zur analyse globaler Verhaltnisse," *Exzentrische Räume: Festschrift für Carlos Rincón*, edited by Nana Badenberg, Florian Nelle, and Ellen Spielmann. Stuttgart: Heinz, 2000, 33–50.

1. For a valuable summary of theories of modernity on which I draw here, see Larraín Ibañez (1996).

2. There is one other who rarely shows up in modernity's accounts of itself, namely, the enslaved person, the person as property of another. As will be discussed below, this other assumes great importance on the periphery.

3. This erasure from history contrasts with the Andean eighteenth century, when elaborate, power-sharing arrangements prevailed between criollo elites and indigenous nobility, and when the indigenous masses participated in a relentless series of revolts, culminating in the pan-Andean Tupac Amaru-Tupac Katari rebellion of 1781–1782. The indigenous elites were disempowered in the wake of this revolt.

4. Lyautey was not the only one to imagine Africa as the site of a modern urban dream in the early twentieth century. In the 1920s, Chilean Vicente Huidobro wrote a novel in which Europe is destroyed and the survivors go to Africa to found a truly modern urban society, called Chaplandia. I am grateful to Guillermo Giucci for introducing me to this text.

5. Sandra Benedet has made a similar observation for political movements. Anarchism, an urban phenomenon in Europe (and in Argentina), had powerful rural variants in Latin America, such as that of the Flores Magón brothers in Mexico.

WORKS CITED

Appadurai, Arjun. 1996. *Modernity at Large*. Minneapolis: University of Minnesota Press.

Arguedas, José María. 1958. *Los ríos profundos*. Buenos Aires: Losada.

Arnason, Johann. 1994. "Touraine's Critique of Modernity: Metacritical Reflection." *Thesis Eleven* 38 (1994): 36–45.

Asturias, Miguel Angel. 1948. *El Señor Presidente*. Buenos Aires: Losada.

———. 1949. *Hombres de maiz*. Buenos Aires: Losada.

Barbero, Jesus Martin. 1991. *De los medios a las mediaciones*. México: G. Gil.

Berman, Marshall. 1982. *All That Is Solid Melts into Air*. New York: Simon and Schuster.

Bhabha, Homi. 1991. "Race, Time, and the Revision of Modernity." *Oxford Literary Review* 13:1 (1991): 193–219.

Brunner, José Joaquín. 1987. "Notas sobre modernidad y lo postmoderno en la cultura latinoamerica." *David y Goliath* 17:52 (September): 30–39.

———. 1988. "Existe o no la modernidad en América Latina?" Pp. 95–100 in *Imágenes desconocidas: La modernidad en la encrucijada post moderna*, ed. Fernando Calderón. Buenos Aires: Consejo Latinoamericano de Ciencias Sociales.

———. 1994. *Bienvenidos a la modernidad*. Santiago: Planeta.

Buell, Frederick. 1994. *National Culture and the New Global System*. Berkeley: University of California Press.

Calderón, Fernando, ed. 1988a. *Imágenes desconocidas: La modernidad en la encrucijada post moderna*. Buenos Aires: Consejo Latinoamericano de Ciencias Sociales.

———. 1988b. "Identidad y tempos mixtos o como pensar la modernidad sin dejar de ser boliviano." Pp. 25–29 in *Imágenes desconocidas: La modernidad en la encrucijada post moderna*, ed. Fernando Calderón. Buenos Aires: Consejo Latinoamericano de Ciencias Sociales.

Calinescu, Matei. 1987 [1977]. *Five Faces of Modernity*. Durham: Duke University Press.

Carpentier, Alejo. 1953. *Los pasos perdidos*. Mexico City: Edición y Distribución Iberoamericana de Publicaciones.

Coronil, Fernando, and Julie Skurski. 1993. "Country and City in Postcolonial Landscapes: Double Discourse and the Geopolitics of Truth in Latin America." Pp. 231–59 in *Views Beyond the Border Country: Raymond Williams and Cultural Politics*, ed. Dennis L. Dworkin and Leslie G. Roman. New York: Routledge.

David y Goliath. 1987. Vol. 17, no. 52. Special issue on modernity and postmodernity. Buenos Aires. 1–81.

de Andrade, Mario. 1992. *Paulicea desvairada*. São Paulo: Cara Mayença.

———. 1928. *Macunaíma, o heroi sem neuhum caracter*. São Paulo: Oficinas graficas de E. Cupolo.

Dussel, Enrique. 1995. "Eurocentrism and Modernity: Introduction to the Frankfurt Lectures." Pp. 65–76 in *The Postmodernism Debate in Latin America*, ed. John Beverley, Jose Oviedo, and Michael Aronna. Durham: Duke University Press.

Echeverría, Bolívar. 1991. "Modernidad y capitaismo (quince tesis)." Pp. 73–122 in *Debates sobre modernidad y postmodernidad*, comp. J. Echeverría. Bogotá: Nariz del Diablo.

Echeverría, Julio de, comp. 1991. *Debates sobre modernidad y postmodernidad*. Bogotá: Nariz del Diablo.

Franco, Jean. 1999. *Critical Passions*. Durham: Duke University Press.

Fuentes, Carlos. 1962. *La muerte de Artemio Cruz*. Mexico City: Fondo de Cultura Económica.

Gallegos, Romulo. 1929. *Doña Bárbara*. Barcelona: Araluce.

García Canclini, Nestor. 1989. *Culturas híbridas: estrategias para entrar y salir de la modernidas*. México: Grijalbo.

———. 1995. *Consumidores y ciudadanos: conflictos molticulturales de la globalización*. México: Grijalbo.

Germani, Gino. 1969. *Sociologia de la modernización*. Buenos Aires: Paidós.

Gilman, Sander. 1982. *On Blackness without Blacks*. Boston: G. K. Hall.

Gilroy, Paul. 1993. *The Black Atlantic: Modernity and Double Consciousness*. Cambridge: Harvard University Press.

Grumley, John. 1994. "Watching the Pendulum Swing—Agnes Heller's Modernity." *Thesis Eleven* 37 (1994): 127–40.

Guimarães Rosa, João. 1956. *Grande sertão: veredas*. Rio de Janeiro: J. Olympio.

Güiraldes, Ricardo. 1926. *Don Segundo Sombra*. Buenos Aires: Proa.

Held, David et al., eds. 1983. *States and Societies*. Oxford: Martin Robertson and the Open University.

Ignatiev, Noel, and John Garvey, eds. 1996. *Race Traitor*. New York: Routledge.

Joyce, James. 1922. *Ulysses*. Paris: Shakespeare & Co.

Lander, Edgardo. 1991. *Modernidad y universalismo*. Caracas: Nueva Sociedad.

Larraín Ibañez, Jorge. 1996. *Modernidad, razón e identidad en América Latina*. Santiago: Editorial Andrés Bello.

Lechner, Norbert. 1990. "¿Son compatibles la modernidad y la modernización?: El desafío de la democracia latinoamericana." Documento de trabajo, no. 440. Santiago: Facultad Latinoamericana de Ciencias Sociales.

Mayorgal, René Antonio. 1988. "Las paradojas e insufiencias de la modernidad y el proceso de la democracia en América latina." Pp. 139–44 in *Imágenes desconocidas: La modernidad en la encrucijada post moderna*, ed. Fernando Calderón. Buenos Aires: Consejo Latinoamericano de Ciencias Sociales.

Mintz, Sidney. 1985. *Sweetness and Power: The Place of Sugar in Modern History*. New York: Viking.

Mistral, Gabriela. 1967. *Poema de Chile*. Santiago de Chile: Pomaire.

Montaldo, Graciela. 1997. "Strategies at the End of the Century: A Review Essay." *Organization* 4:4 (November): 628–34.

Montoya, Rodrigo. 1992. *Al borde del naufragio: democracia, violencia y problema etnico en el Peru*. Madrid: Talasa.

Nugent, José Guillermo. 1992. *El laberinto de la choledad*. Lima: Fundación E. Ebert.

Ortiz, Fernando. 1978 [1947]. *Contrapunteo cubano: Dialéctica del tabaco y del azúcar*. Caracas: Biblioteca Ayacucho.

Quijano, Aníbal. 1988. "Modernidad, identidad y utopía en América Latina." Pp. 17–24 in *Imágenes desconocidas: La modernidad en la encrucijada post moderna*, ed. Fernando Calderón. Buenos Aires: Consejo Latinoamericano de Ciencias Sociales.

Rabinow, Paul. 1989. *French Modern*. Cambridge: Massachusetts Institute of Technology Press.

Rama, Angel. 1982. *Transculturación narrativa en América Latina*. Mexico: Siglo XXI.

———. 1984. *La ciudad letrada*. Hanover: Ediciones del Norte.

Ribeiro, Darcy. 1976. *Maíra*. Rio de Janeiro: Civilização Brasiliera.

Rowe, William, and Vivian Schelling. 1991. *Memory and Modernity*. London: Verso.

Santiago, Silviano. 1996. "The Course of Literary Modernity in Brazil." *Journal of Latin American Cultural Studies* 5:2:175–82.

Sarlo, Beatriz. 1988. *Una modernidad periférica. Buenos Aires 1920 y 1930*. Buenos Aires: Nueva Vision.

Schmidt, Wolfgang. 1991. "En los limites de la modernidad." Pp. 57–72 in *Debates sobre modernidad y postmodernidad*, comp. J. Echeverría. Bogota: Nariz del Diablo.

Schwarz, Roberto. 1992. *Misplaced Ideas*. Edited by John Gledson. London: Verso.

Smith, Bernard. 1994. "Modernism and Post-Modernism: Neo-Colonial Viewpoint Concerning the Sources of Modernism and Post-Modernism in the Visual Arts." *Thesis Eleven* 38:104–17.

Toulmin, Stephen. 1990. *Cosmopolis*. New York: Free Press.

Touraine, Alain. 1988. "Actores sociales y modernidad." Pp. 175–78 in *Imágenes desconocidas: La modernidad en la encrucijada post moderna*, ed. Fernando Calderón. Buenos Aires: Consejo Latinoamericano de Ciencias Sociales.

———. 1992. *Critique de la modernité*. Paris: Fayard.

———. 1994. "Mutations of Latin America." *Thesis Eleven* 38:61–71.

Tsing, Anna. 1993. *In the Realm of the Diamond Queen: Marginality in an Out-of-the-Way Place*. Princeton: Princeton University Press.

Vargas Llosa, Maria. 1966. *La casa verde*. Barcelona: Seix Barral.

Wallerstein, Emmanuel. 1979. *The Capitalist World Economy*. Cambridge: Cambridge University Press.

Woolf, Virginia. 1925. *Mrs Dalloway*. New York: Harcourt Brace.

———. 1927. *To the Lighthouse*. New York: Harcourt Brace.

CHAPTER THREE

BEYOND DICHOTOMIES

Communicative Action and Cultural Hegemony

EMMANUEL CHUKWUDI EZE

> If the other is not a shadow or a mannequin, he belongs to
> a definite and concrete social-historical community. Con-
> crete means particular. . . . But then, the appeal to the
> other's point of view floats uneasily between vacuousness
> and tautology. It is vacuous if the addressee is supposedly to
> be found in each and every particular community. It is tau-
> tologous if it is an appeal to our community: for then it is
> an appeal to go on judging as beautiful what has already
> been so judged.
>
> —Cornelius Castoriadis,
> *Philosophy, Politics, and Autonomy*

INTRODUCTION

In the first quarter of Jürgen Habermas' *The Theory of Communicative Action, Volume One: Reason and the Rationalization of Society*,
Africa serves as the paradigmatic "mythical" world against which the
author establishes, through contrasts, the achievements of the modern

49

Occidental "rational" worldview.[1] In addition, the modern societies analyzed by Habermas—through conceptions such as "internal colonization," "the uncoupling of system and lifeworld," "the welfare state," and so on—in the second volume of the same work (*Lifeworld and System: A Critique of Functionalist Reason*) are European capitalist societies and nation-state formations whose economic and political growth presupposed, from the seventeenth century onward, imperial dominions, transatlantic slavery and subsequent colonization, and accompanying ideologies of white-racial supremacy.[2] Africa is therefore *negatively* present in Habermas' thought.[3]

When Talcott Parsons wrote, in *The System of Modern Societies*, that what is thought of as modern society took shape in the seventeenth century in the northwest corner of the European system of societies, in Great Britain, Holland and France, he added that subsequent development of modern societies included three processes of revolutionary structural change: the industrial revolution, the democratic revolution, and the educational revolutions. Parsons left unsaid and out of view in this influential work, however, the complex historical relationships between the northwest corner of the European system of societies and the southeast rest of the world. The sources, the logics, and the effects of the "revolutionary structural change" that occurred in Europe during and after the seventeenth century cannot be fully accounted for if one focuses only on the endogenous and neglects exogenous forces such as Europe's economic, political, cultural, and military encounters with non-European worlds such as China, India, Africa, and America. These are events that shaped and continue to shape the world we live in today. Attempts to thematize these traumatic and enduring forms of exogenous relationships between Europe and non-European nations ("the North" and "the South") have been variously theoretically organized under "imperialism," "colonialism," and more recently "postcolonialism." These, however, are analytic categories for which one would search in vain in Habermas' theories of modernity, and this, too, is what renders paradoxical the uses of Africa in *The Theory of Communicative Action*. How could one speak of Africa as a way of understanding Europe without reference to the imperial and colonial encounters? An answer that illuminates this paradox, a paradox whose conditions of possibility I wish to examine, can be succinctly stated: Habermas' idea of Africa is ahistorical. As such, it is conceptually hardly enlightening and essentially politically regressive.

HABERMAS AND AFRICA

The ahistoricity of Habermas' idea of Africa is an issue, because it occludes not only a progressive understanding of the actually existing Africa but also the nature of Europe's own history. In *In My Father's House: Africa in the Philosophy of Culture*, Kwame Anthony Appiah warns that "to forget Europe is to suppress the conflicts that have shaped [African] identities" (1992, 155, 72). A similar caution, addressed also to Africans, exists throughout the essays of James Baldwin. In *Nobody Knows My Name: More Notes of a Native Son*, he writes: "Africans are . . . whether they like it or not related to Europe, stained by European visions and standards [in] their relations to themselves, and to each other, and to their past" (1961, 198).[4] Implicit in these warnings, however, is their obverse: for Europe or the modern West to think itself without Africa is to suppress the conflicts that shaped and continue to shape modern and postmodern European history and identities. Otherwise stated, Europeans and European-descended peoples are, whether they like it or not, related to Africa, stained by Africa, in their relations to themselves, to each other, and to their history. The truth and the consequences of these observations are lost when either Africa or Europe is theorized as Habermas has done: abstractly, ahistorically, and mythologically.

Were it not for the crucial roles, substantive and strategic, that "Africa" plays in *The Theory of Communicative Action*, one would probably not bother to read the texts as I do. One could argue, for example, though explicit, that Habermas' intention about Africa in the book was, in his words, merely an "excursus into the outer court of the theory of argumentation . . . [to] supplement . . . provisional specification of the concept of rationality" (Habermas 1984, 43). But this concept of modern rationality, to which Africa plays the function of an "outer" court—the role of spatial (geographical) and temporal (historical) limits, the limits of reason—is the central building block not just of a theory of argumentation in the narrow sense but also ultimately of Habermas' understanding of communicative praxis in general. In this way, Africa, already assumed not only to be outer but more crucially opposite, was brought in from the possible ends of civilization and pressed into a systematic service—the service of the interior court of the Empire. Why was this appeal to Africa necessary? Habermas explains:

> Even when we are judging the rationality of individual persons, it is not sufficient to resort to this or that expression. The question is,

rather, whether A or B or a group of individuals behaves rationally *in general*; whether one may systematically expect that they have good reasons for their expressions and that these expressions are correct or successful in the cognitive dimension, reliable or insightful in the moral-practical dimension, discerning or illuminating in the evaluative dimension; . . . that they exhibit understanding in the hermeneutic dimension; or indeed whether they are "reasonable" in all these dimensions. When there appears a systematic effect in these respects, across various domains of interaction and over long periods (perhaps even over the space of a lifetime), we also speak of the rationality of a *conduct of life*. And in the sociocultural conditions for such a conduct of life there is reflected perhaps the rationality of a lifeworld shared not only by individuals but by collectives as well. (ibid.)

It is in the attempt to show that the modern Western "collective" life is not only rational but superiorly so that one steps out of court to bring in Africa, a continent whose inhabitants and worldview are suspected of being "irrational,"[5] the antithesis of the rational West. Through this antithesis, Habermas hopes, one would see that (1) the modern West is indeed not just "rational" but rational in the way Habermas says it is, and (2) the modern Western rational worldview is superior to all others known to humans. Yet more strategically, it is further explained:

I shall take up the cultural interpretive systems or worldviews that reflect the background knowledge of social groups and guarantee an interconnection among the multiplicity of their action orientations. Thus I shall first inquire into the conditions that structures of action-orienting worldviews must satisfy if a rational conduct of life is to be possible for those who share such a worldview. This way of proceeding offers two advantages; on the one hand, it forces us to turn from conceptual to empirical analysis and to seek out the rationality structures embodied in worldviews; and, on the other hand, it keeps us from supposing *without further ado* that the rationality structures specific to the modern understanding of the world are generally valid and forces us instead to consider them in an historical perspective. (1984, 43–44, emphasis added)

"Without further ado"? How does one theoretically guarantee that the modern Western worldview is "rational"? How does one show that it is generally—or universally—"valid"? What does "validity" in this situation mean, and how can one presume this meaning without further ado—when the very concepts of "rational" and "validity" are drawn from one of the traditions under interrogation? Was the journey to the "outer court" a shortcut to the rapid execution of a series of claims? In other words, to "ground" an idea of Occidental reason and prove its universal validity and superiority, all we have to do is take a look at it?[6]

To render more convincing this difference and superiority of the Western worldview, however, Habermas appears to have been forced to take great pains to construct, in a series of appropriations from a specific school of anthropology, an Africa that looks as antithetical to "the West" as one could possibly imagine. The most significant example of this can easily be shown: notice the admission that his approach "forces us to turn from conceptual to empirical analysis" and to adopt "an historical perspective." There is something radical about these gestures, but the radicality is not located where one might think, for the adoption of the empirical attitude yielded nothing more than a "presentist" conception of Africa,[7] and the supposedly "historical" perspective meant a comparison between a West deemed historical and an Africa deemed ahistorical. The exercises become aimed at contrasting a "dynamic" "modern" "culture" and a "static" "traditional" one, the "rational" West and a "mythical" Africa. The shine and the glow of Europe's history, progress, and modernity are therefore framed against the darkness of Africa.

> In determining the significance of this claim [to the universality and superiority of "our" Occidental rationality], it would be well to draw a comparison with the *mythical* understanding of the world. In *archaic* societies myths fulfill the unifying function of worldviews in an exemplary way—they permeate life-practice. At the same time, within the cultural traditions accessible to us, they present the *sharpest contrast* to the understanding of the world dominant in modern societies. *Mythical worldviews are far from making possible rational orientations of action* in our sense. With respect to the conditions for a rational conduct of life in this sense, *they present an antithesis* to the modern understanding of the world. Thus the heretofore unthematized presuppositions of modern thought should become visible in the mirror of mythical thinking. (1984, 44, emphasis added)

The presuppositions that one makes for modernity, presumptions heretofore "unthematized," were rendered clear through the uses and, let it be said, abuses of Africa as Limit and Other. One must wonder, to what extent is the other worldview wholly "archaic" and "mythical," a "sharp contrast," "antithesis," and "outside" the court, precisely because the inner court of the Empire wishes for a strong opponent, an outer court against which to work out its clearly robust claims about itself? Is this a way to fashion Europe's image and identity by proposing, as a precondition, a deserving enemy?

HABERMAS' "AFRICA"

Why and in what ways for Habermas must Africa function as a "mirror" of the modern West? Is "archaic" and "mythic" Africa a mirror for the West in the sense that Sander Gilman explained the peculiarly German phenomenon of "Blackness without blacks" (1982), or is it of a more ancient origin, as in Günter Grass' description of the presence of the Romanies and Sinti in contemporary Europe?[8] What could Habermas mean by the "mythical," in light of Adorno's and Horkheimer's understanding of mythology in their "two theses: myth is already enlightenment; and enlightenment reverts to mythology" (1992, xvi)?[9] In light of these well-known studies of the West in general and of Germany in particular, what should one make of an eagerness to prove that Africa is the truly "mythical"?

It is no surprise that when Habermas engages in a detailed discussion of the debates about the nature of the Zande "mythical worldview," he relies on the later rather than the early models in the anthropological literature. Instead of Lévy-Bruhl and Gobineau, for example, Habermas guides the reader to Africa through Evans-Pritchard and Lévi-Strauss, supplemented by the Marxist work of Maurice Godelier.

> The earlier discussion of Lévy-Bruhl's theses on the mentality of "nature peoples" showed that we cannot postulate a "prelogical" stage of knowing and acting for the "savage mind." The well-known investigations of Evans-Pritchard concerning the belief in witchcraft among African Azande confirmed the view that the differences between mythical and modern thought do not lie at the level of logical operations. The degree of rationality of worldviews evidently does not vary with the stage of cognitive development of the individuals who orient their action within them. Our point of departure has to be that adult members of primitive tribal societies can acquire basically the same formal operations as the members of

modern societies, even though the higher-level competences appear less frequently and more selectively in them; that is, they are applied in more restricted spheres of life. (1984, 44–45)

Lévy-Bruhl, in *La Mentalité primitive* [*Primitive Mentality*, 1923] and *Les fonctions mentales dans les sociétés inférieures* [*How Natives Think*, 1926] had argued that Africans are incapable of logical thought: instead, they "know" things through mystical and magical emotions. Lévy-Bruhl did revise this opinion in a diary published posthumously,[10] but it was Evans-Pritchard's work that succeeded in overturning the original anthropological image of these African people as devoid of reason and logic. Hence, Habermas' position: if Evans-Pritchard's assessment of the African mind should be correct ("the degree of rationality of worldviews evidently does not vary with the stage of cognitive development of the individuals who orient their action within them"), then the "primitive" rationality is only inferior, and "our" point of departure has to be that "the higher-level competences appear less frequently and more selectively" among the African people. But compare these qualified claims, made in deference to Evans-Pritchard, to Habermas' original and more radical postulate: "Mythical worldviews are *far from making possible rational orientations of action*"; or, "With *respect to the conditions for a rational conduct of life* in this sense, *they present an antithesis* to the modern understanding of the world." If these original arguments are correct, and if the Zande worldview is mythical as interpreted at this time, then the claim derived more directly from Evans-Pritchard should appear inexplicable.

But there is a more easily intelligible perspective of these unstable claims. First, the differences and divergence between the goals of Habermas' "rationality debates" uses of Africa and Evans-Pritchard's empirical research projects are quite obvious. The divergent programs make room for different and varying interpretations that ultimately produce competing versions of Africa. Second, there are deeper historical bases—economic, political, and cultural—that account for the shifting views of Africa held by dominant European thinkers at various times, sometimes by the same thinker.

In the earliest modern encounters between European and African kingdoms, in the fifteenth century, for example, recorded accounts reveal a remarkable relationship of equals: the exchange of diplomatic counsels was routine, as were glowing accounts of thriving and vibrant nations of Bini, Dahomey, Ashanti, and so on, whose organizational powers and influence were constantly favorably compared to the Roman Papacy.[11] However, as the plantations in the Americas developed and Afro-European trade demands shifted from raw material to human labor, there also was a shift in the European anthropological, literary, artistic, and philosophical characterizations of "the African" or "the Negro."[12] Africans became identified as a subhuman race, and speculations about the "savage" nature of "the African mind" became widespread and intertextually entrenched within the *univers du discours* of the French, Scottish, and German Enlightenment thinkers.[13] Finally, when slave trade and plantation slavery declined (due to a combination of shifts in economic interests as well as in moral and political attitudes) and the relationship between Africa and Europe transformed itself into various projects of active occupation of Africa and *in situ* administration of its populations (officially marked by the 1884 Berlin Conference), the theory of Africans shifted to accommodate this new reality. Henceforth, Africans are not prerational but only endowed with inferior forms of reason. This new theory fit adequately the need to train local bureaucrats and clerks and the need to exploit the positions of African kings and chiefs through a system of colonial administration known variously as "indirect rule" and, in the case of the French, "association." In fact, where Africans had no monarchs, "warrant chiefs" were created to facilitate bureaucratic and colonial administration; yet the chief's responsibility must conform to his "mental" capacity: "selectively" and in "restricted spheres." Since, theoretically, only the European District Officer or colonial administrator had the "higher level competences," the colonial subjection of the African monarchs and warrant chiefs is thereby logically consistent and receives its practical completion.[14]

That Habermas' practice and language must be located in this historical frame is self-evident. He writes:

> I shall begin with (A) a rough characterization of the mythical understanding of the world. For the sake of simplicity I shall confine myself to the results of Lévi-Strauss' structuralist investigations, above all to those stressed by M. Godelier. (B) Against this background the basic concepts constitutive of the modern understanding of the world, and thus intuitively familiar to us, begin to stand out. In this way we can, from a cultural-anthropological distance, link up again with the concept of rationality introduced above. (1984, 45)

A "cultural-anthropological distance" is asserted, yet "Africa" stands here as something that is posited as "other" in order merely to be reappropriated as the familiar. The language throughout is that of "we," "our," and "us" versus "they," "their," and "them," yet the attempt is, bluntly and throughout, to legitimate "the basic concepts constitutive of the Occidental modern understanding of the world" (ibid.).

A PARADOX

While holding onto an original proposition that a worldview comprises the "background knowledge" that guarantees an interconnection among the multifarious rational activities of a group (1984, 43), Habermas presented a "rough characterization" of the African worldview, thematized some presuppositions about modern European rationality by contrasting it to the African "mythical" mind, and highlighted, against the background of the African mythic worldview, the claim that the modern European understanding of the world is universal. This schematization finally allows Habermas to assert that there are further bases for the Comtean claims about a world-historical evolutionary process of rationalization.[15] Noting that what most characterizes the mythic worldview is the "strongly totalizing power of the 'savage mind'" (1984, 45), he draws the conclusion that the Zande "savage mind" is incapable of differentiating reality into subject and object, concrete and abstract, and culture and nature. The world-historical evolutionary process, however, moves in the opposite direction: rationalization.

> What *we* find most astonishing [about the "savage mind"] is the peculiar leveling of the different domains of reality: nature and culture are projected onto the same plane. From this reciprocal assimilation of nature to culture and conversely culture to nature there results, on the one hand, a nature that is outfitted with anthropomorphic features, drawn into the communicative network of social subjects, and in this sense humanized, and on the other hand, a culture that is to a certain extent naturalized and reified and absorbed into the objective nexus of operations of anonymous powers. (Habermas 1984, 47)

Furthermore, "What irritates us members of a modern lifeworld is that in a mythically interpreted world we cannot, or cannot with sufficient precision, make certain differentiations that are fundamental to our understanding of the world" (ibid., 48). The modern European mind, declared not only unmythical but also universal, faced with an African mind presumed universally mythical, experiences not just astonishment but also irritation. Why? Because unlike the differentiation of social spheres that, from Hegel to Weber, has been recognized as the defining characteristics of European capitalist modernity, the unmodern African mind presents the world in "a seamless totality," a "confusion," or "a giant maze of mirrors in which the opposing images of man and world are infinitely reflected in each other" (Habermas 1984, 46). Habermas gives, as an example of this "confusion," the African conceptualization of nature under the category of spirit ("animism") rather than causality ("science") (Ingram 1987, 23–24). While Africa is animistic, socially totalistic, and alien, Europe is scientific, socially differentiated, and familiar.

Conceptually frozen in this binary is however an internally insufficient account of the "modern" and the "mythical," including their coexistence. Little wonder that the philosopher feels astonished and irritated: Africa is "confusing" and "irritating" because it is not Europe. This is, surely, a modern mythical account of Africa.

One could not be surprised that Habermas essentially agrees with ethnologist Evans-Pritchard that the difference between modern and mythic thinking is not that of logical and illogical aptitudes; rather, the "savage" world understanding is different from that of the modern because of the way the mythic mind confuses nature with culture and culture with nature. "This associative nature of mythic understanding is diametrically opposed to the analytic sundering of objective, subjective, and social domains of reference fundamental to modern rationality" (Ingram 1987, 23). Because the mythic mind is not sufficiently analytical, it also is not critical, and therefore the mythic worldview is "closed."[16]

However, in *The Theory of Communicative Action*, one feels cheated out of even a minimally adequate philosophical and historical familiarity with Africa. Absent is any account of Africa's centuries-old and complex relationships to the capitalist societies of modern Europe. This situation results from the fact that Habermas appears to be more interested in the ideological (or, as he prefers, "normative") work of "discover[ing] through the quite contrasting structures of the 'savage mind' important presuppositions of the modern understanding of the world" (Habermas 1984, 53) than in providing knowledge of an actually existing Africa, Europe, and their interwoven histories. It is this "normative" interest, I believe, that accounts for the relentless effort (and irritation at having) to prove that the Zande worldview, held here as the best representative example of non-European mentality, is "closed," while the European one is "open" (ibid., 61–66).

Closedness for Habermas signifies a lack of capacity for critical reflectivity, unlike openness, which allows for a critical sense and in turn makes possible the progressive acquisition of (scientific and moral) knowledge (ibid., 52). It, however, goes without saying that from the point of view of the ability to understand modern Europe or modern capitalist culture in general, the danger—and thus the regressive element in Habermas' typologies of the "modern" and the "mythical"—is to suppose that the mythical is located elsewhere, and always already so. How much of the modern is not only scientific and differentiated but also mythical and totalistic?[17] And how much of the "mythical" worldview and its totalities are irrevocably ruptures, from within and without?

When he situates himself in the debate between Peter Winch and Robin Horton regarding the epistemological legitimacy of Evans-Pritchard's anthropological work, in particular, the classic *Witchcraft, Oracles, and Magic among the Azande* (1937), and with an eye to proving not only the openness but also the objectivity and universal validity of the scientific and modern, Habermas (1984) argues:

> Evans-Pritchard's study of witchcraft, oracles, and magic in the African tribe of the Azande is one of the best examples showing that one can exhibit a high degree of hermeneutic charity toward obscure expressions without drawing the relativistic consequences that Lukes sees connected with this manner of proceeding. I would like to open the second round with an argument from Evans-Pritchard, who clarifies the belief in witches, and thereby also the reasons for the corresponding magical practices, in such a way that his readers can recognize the coherence of the Zande worldview. At the same time, as an anthropologist he holds fast to the standards of scientific rationality when it is a question of objectively assessing the view and techniques of this tribe (55–56). [Furthermore] the charge of a category mistake raised against the European anthropologist can be understood in a strong and in a weak sense. If it says merely that the scientist should not impute to the natives his own interest in resolving inconsistencies, the question naturally arises, whether this lack of a theoretical interest may not be traced back to the fact that the Zande worldview imposes less exacting standards of rationality and is in this sense less rational than the modern understanding of the world (61). [And finally] th[e] dimension of

"closed" *versus* "open" seems to provide a *context-independent standard for the rationality of worldviews.* Of course the point of reference is again modern science. (62)

Should we need to point out, however, that the "context-*in*dependent" status of modern science is not, so to speak, a closed case? In any event, the presumption here is that Africa is the place where one can locate an inferior form of rationality that, as is claimed, pretends to be universal. Unlike the scientific universality of Western reason, however, Africa's is a universal presence of "myth" and an equally universal absence of "science."

Fairly, to the extent that the terms of the binary constructions allow, Habermas entertains the thought that just because he thinks the mythic worldview is closed and the modern scientific worldview is open does not necessarily prove the truth of his *presuppositions* about the modern worldview ("Of course, this does not *yet* prove that the supposed rationality expressed in our understanding of the world is more than a reflection of the particular features of [our] culture" [1984, 53]). He also raises what he considers "the fundamental question," namely, the potential circularity of a desire to validate one's very own system of validation: "whether and in what respect the standards of rationality by which the investigator was himself at least intuitively guided might claim universal validity" (ibid.). Finally, one is invited to seriously consider an issue at the core of Peter Winch's critique of Evans-Pritchard in particular and certain traditions of Western anthropology in general:

[W]e come upon a perspective from which Winch's misgivings concerning the hypostatization of scientific rationality can be rendered intelligible and at the same time freed from precipitate conclusions. Scientific rationality belongs to a complex of cognitive-instrumental rationality that can certainly claim validity beyond the context of particular cultures. Nevertheless, after Winch's arguments have been examined and defused, something of his pathos survives, to which we have not given its due: "My aim is not to engage in moralizing, but to suggest that the concept of 'learning from' which is involved in the study of other cultures is closely linked with the concept of *wisdom*." Can't we who belong to modern societies learn something from understanding alternative, particularly premodern forms of life? Shouldn't we, beyond all romanticizing of superseded stages of development, beyond exotic stimulation from the contents of alien cultures, recall the losses required by our own path to the modern world? (Habermas 1984, 65)

Well intended as this pathos-eliciting openness may sound, the argument surrounding and constraining it highlights what is precisely a problem: why and in what ways must—if this is what it is—"alternative" forms of life in "outside" cultures be invariably defined as "pre-"modern? Could this form of life be anything other than that which must always be already haunted, bounded, and contained by Europe's historical particularity expressed in a specific modernity? In addition, how would one understand the talk about "superseded stages of development"? In what (metaphorical) sense has Europe "superseded" the "stage" of Africa's existence? Are there modern features of Africa? Has Europe today exhausted its Africa-like "pre-" or, better yet, un-modern features? Do answers to these questions exist "normatively," and without recourse to actual histories of both Africa and Europe and their relationships? Should we, for example, understand that the West has suffered "losses"—and therefore must now content itself in "recall"—of the mythical qualities in its worldview—even with regard to religion, gender, race, or any number of aspects of modernity's relationships to itself and to others?

In the long run, with all of the nods and dues paid to opposing arguments, the thrust of Habermas' position remains to "defuse" and "free" Winch's arguments in ways that allow one to go on "judging as beautiful what has already been so judged."

> The course of our argument can perhaps be summarized as follows: Winch's arguments are too weak to uphold the thesis that inherent to every linguistically articulated worldview and to every cultural form of life there is an incommensurable concept of rationality; but his strategy of argumentation is strong enough to set off the justified claim to universality on behalf of the rationality that gained expression in the modern understanding of the world. (Habermas 1984, 66)

Even if one admitted that there could be conceptual problems attached to a defense of an "incommensurable concept of rationality,"[18] there is a question that remains: namely, if we subtract from the concessions made to the strength of Winch's arguments the modern "fix[ation] on knowing and mastering external nature"—a fixation that Habermas acknowledges is shared by Zande and other cultures as well—then what is special about the "normative" defense of a singular universality of a supposedly unique rationality of the West? Stated otherwise, if "Scientific rationality belongs to a complex of cognitive-instrumental rationality that can certainly claim validity beyond the context of particular cultures," the easy task is to show that all cultures have some "complex of cognitive-instrumental rationality" (Habermas 1984, 66); the hard task is to prove that the specifically European modern expression of this rationality also is an attribute that *any* culture or society must have in order to be "developed," "civilized," or adequately "rational." Habermas seems to be arguing that it is not enough to be rational; one also has to be Occidentalized.

So What?

Habermas' recognition that the "self-interpretation" of Europe's modernity since Descartes may be "uncritically . . . fixed" on "knowing and mastering external nature," that is, on knowledge/power, is an interesting acknowledgment, for it allows one to reopen the question of whether the "universality" acquired by this modernity must always predominantly express itself as will to power, not only over nature but also over other humans commodified as natural resources. In addition to the fact that "scientific rationality . . . can certainly claim validity beyond the context of particular culture," in what ways have the uncritical practices of modern science distorted Europe's self-understanding and contributed to the incapacity to "understand" non-European peoples as also humans and equals? As one can discern from Habermas' work, the "force" of a scientific argument often is made palpable and rendered effective by underlying and presupposed attitudes or interior dispositions, by a *will* to knowledge. The dichotomies—modern/premodern, Europe/Africa—reveal this will which, much like the mythical mind, works in an orchestrated binary consumed in a longing for the "normative" or the "universal." What is lacking is adequate attention to histories of specific peoples and the contradictions that such histories reveal about precipitous claims to normativity and universality.

Notes

A longer version of this chapter, under the title "Out of Africa," appeared in *Telos* 111 (spring 1998): 139–61.

1. See Habermas 1984, 8–74.

2. Hannah Arendt clearly demonstrates these historical connections in *The Origins of Totalitarianism* (1951).

3. The suggestion that (the idea of) Africa functions for Habermas as a "negative" principle is quite different from the sort of lack or "deficiency" that Nancy Fraser has found between Habermas' work and, for example, gender issues. Writing about the difficulty of establishing a dialogue between Habermas's work and key theoretical-political concerns proper to issues of gender in general, Fraser notes:

This would be a fairly straightforward enterprise were it not for one thing: apart from a brief discussion of feminism as a "new social movement" . . . Habermas says virtually nothing about gender in *The Theory of Communicative Action.* Now, according to my view of critical theory, this is a serious deficiency, but it need not stand in the way of the sort of inquiry I am proposing. It simply necessitates that one read the work in question from the standpoint of an absence, that one extrapolate from things Habermas does say to things he does not, that one reconstruct how various matters of concern to feminists would appear from his perspective had those matters been thematized. (Fraser 1989, 114)

The use of the Azande as the figure of Africa in *The Theory of Communicative Action* is quite explicit and thematic.

4. An interesting feature of these observations is Appiah's and Baldwin's choice of words, respectively, "contamination" and "stain." The "pure" European race (or African race as the case may be) "contaminated" and "stained" by the "other" race?

5. "[T]he Azande themselves experience unavoidable absurdities . . . as soon as they enter upon a stubborn consistency check such as the anthropologist undertakes. But a demand of this kind is *brought* to bear upon them; . . . and when an anthropologist confronts them with it, they generally evade it. But isn't this refusal, this higher tolerance for contradiction, a sign of a more irrational conduct of life? Must we not call action orientations that can be stabilized only at the cost of suppressing contradictions irrational?" (Habermas 1984, 60).

6. According to Habermas, "In attempting to elucidate the concept of rationality through appeal to the use of the expression 'rational,' we had to rely on a *preunderstanding* anchored in modern orientations. Hitherto we have naively presupposed that, in this modern understanding of the world, structures of consciousness are expressed that belong to a rationalized lifeworld and make possible in principle a rational conduct of life. We are implicitly connecting a claim to *universality* with our *Occidental understanding of the world*" (Habermas 1984, 44).

7. I use "presentism" here in the same sense that Habermas had applied it to some of Foucault's historiography, an analysis that "remains hermeneutically stuck at its starting point"; in other words, a historical study that takes place reductively and surreptitiously through the concerns of the present. See Habermas 1990, 276–78.

8. "The Romanies and Sinti are the lowest of the low . . . Why? Because they are different. Because they steal, are restless, roam, have the Evil Eye and that stunning beauty that makes us ugly to ourselves. Because their mere existence puts our values into question. Because they are all very well in operas and operettas, but in reality—it sounds awful, reminds you of awfulness" (Grass 1992, 107).

9. Compare Habermas' ahistoric "Africa" to Adorno's and Horkheimer's awareness in the *Dialectic of Enlightenment* of the complex relationships between "conflicts in the Third World," "the Nazi terror," and "the transition to the world of administered life" (1992, ix).

10. See Lucien Lévy-Bruhl (1857–1939) 1949. In a chapter entitled "Discussion des faits 'Afrique Occidentale Française' au point de vue logique" Lévy-Bruhl wrote: "Maliki semble d'abord incapable de saisir qu'il affirme deux choses incompatibles et qu'il est contradictoire de les dire vraies toutes les deux. Si sa fille a été kidnappée, elle n'est pas morte dans sa case; s'il est exact qu'elle est morte dans sa case, elle n'a pas été kidnappée. Si son corps a été mis en terre, elle n'a pas été cuite et mangée, il ne se peut pas que son père ait enterré son cadavre intact. Maliki est-il incapable de comprendre cet *entweder-oder*?" In a question that anticipates Habermas' conclusions at the end of his arguments with Winch, Lévy-Bruhl continued: "Il faudrait alors expliquer ce qui cause chez lui cette incapacité; et se demander, comme je le faisais, si les exigences logiques de son esprit ne sont pas moindres que les nôtres." However: "Un examen plus attentitif de la conduite et des paroles de Maliki . . . montre que la question est mal posée ou pour mieux dire n'a pas à être posée. Maliki n'est pas incapable de voir qu'entre deux affirmations incompatibles, il faut choisir, et que dans ce cas d'*entweder-oder*, une des affirmations exclut l'autre. Car il y a incompabilité *pour nous* mais non pas *pour lui*. Il est vrai que sa fille est morte dans sa case; il l'a vue expirer et se refroidir. Mais cela n'exclut pas qu'elle a été victime d'un rapt spirituel; son âme, son principe vital lui ont été enlevés par les sorcières, et c'est précisément cela qui l'a fait mourir. Il est vrai qu'il a lui-même enseveli sa fille, et il montre sa tombe, d'ou l'on retire le corps. Mais cela n'exclut pas que les sorcières l'ont mangée, à leur façon, qui est invisible: anthropophagie spirituelle. Nous n'avons donc pas de raison de supposer chez Maliki, en cette circonstance, quelque chose de spécifiquement différent au point de vue logique de ce qui se passe chez nous. Il suffit de savoir que les croyances et les expériences mystiques communes à son groupe rendent raison de ses paroles et de ses actes. Une fois données leurs idées de la maladie, de l'anormal de la mort, de la puissance et des maléfices des sorcières, le reste s'ensuit. Maliki est conséquent avec lui-même, et trouve que c'est le blanc qui est incapable de comprendre."

In yet another section, more emphatically entitled "Abandon définitif du caractère prélogique," Lévy-Bruhl, providing further details about why on this issue he decided to put "beaucoup d'eau dans [s]on vin," concludes: "Un examen plus serré m'a donc conduit à une interprétation meilleure des faits recueillis dans les documents de l'Afrique Occidentale Française. Je me suis plus préoccupé de vérifier l'idée préconçue d'une différence au point de vue logique entre l'attitude mentale des indigènes, en certaines circonstances, et la nôtre. En ce qui concerne le caractère 'prélogique' de la mentalité primitive j'avais déjà mis beaucoup d'eau dans mon vin depuis vingt-cinq ans; les résultats auxquels je viens de parvenir touchant ces faits rendent cette évolution définitive, en me faisant abandonner une hypothèse mal fondée" (57–58, 60). One should notice that despite his "examen plus serré" and "examen plus attentif" of the Maliki, Lévy-Bruhl's conclusions about the African mind bring us no further than Winch's popular position: the European anthropologist in judging the African worldview irrational commits a *category mistake*. As such, both Lévy-Bruhl's revised position and Winch's contemporary formulations remain wounded by Habermas' critique—a critique whose seeds were already discernable in Lévy-Bruhl: "Must we not call action orientations that can be stabilized only at the cost of suppressing contradiction irrational?" (or: "se demander," in regard to Maliki "si les exigences logiques de son esprit ne sont pas moindres que les nôtres"). Of course, Lévy-Bruhl in his revision also inserted a caveat that should be important even in regard to both his and Winch's claims of "categorical" difference for the African mind: "pour autant que nous pouvons admettre que nous avons ses propres paroles, puisqu'il faut les prendre telles que l'interprète nous les donne" (ibid., 57–58).

11. See, for example, Basil Davidson 1966, 1969.

12. See, for example, Martin 1993; Honor 1982; Gates 1978.

13. See, for example, Eze 1997a, 1997b; Gates 1986; Mills 1998; West 1993; Faull 1994; Kramnik 1995.

14. For an extended discussion of the various stages in the European philosophical theories about the "African mind" and its correlation to pressures from economic, political and, on occasion, moral considerations, see, for example, Lloyd 1996.

15. It is instructive to keep in mind Lévy-Bruhl's key theses in his *The Philosophy of Auguste Comte* (1903) as a way of making sense of the similarities between the regressive views about the "savage" held by Lévy-Bruhl and Habermas.

16. The concepts of "open" and "closed" societies have a longer history as a dichotomy established by Karl Popper. Popper meant the concepts to reflect the more general distinctions that he makes between "dogmatic" and "critical" attitudes. According to Popper, "an uncontrolled wish to impose regularities, a manifest pleasure in rites and in repetition as such, are characteristic of primitives and children; and increasing experience and maturity sometimes create an attitude of caution and criticism rather than of dogmatism" (Popper 1968, 49). Robin Horton, through discussions in many of his works, popularized Popper's "open" and "closed" concepts for descriptions of the difference between African

and European worldviews. According to Horton, "traditional" Africa is a "closed" society, because its forms of thought are not "modern," that is, critical or scientific (see, for example, Horton 1986). Habermas endorses a more sophisticated version of the "open/closed" dichotomy in relation to his conception of what it means to be "rational," through appropriations of Piaget and critique of the debate between Horton and Winch (see Habermas 1984, 61–142).

17. When, for example, Habermas writes that "the Azande themselves experience unavoidable absurdities . . . as soon as they enter upon a stubborn consistency check such as the anthropologist undertakes. But a demand of this kind is *brought* to bear upon them; . . . and when an anthropologist confronts them with it, they generally evade it. But isn't this refusal, this higher tolerance for contradiction, a sign of a more irrational conduct of life? Must we not call action orientations that can be stabilized only at the cost of suppressing contradictions irrational?" (1984, 60). One is tempted to ask: why did the anthropologist need to travel all the way to Africa to discover this form of behavior? And what is so peculiarly non-European about it?

18. See, for example, Donald Davidson's "On the Very Idea of a Conceptual Scheme," as well as other essays collected in *Inquiries into Truth and Interpretation* (1984).

Works Cited

Adorno, Theodor W., and Max Horkheimer. 1992. *The Dialectic of Enlightenment*. Translated by John Cumming. New York: Continuum.

Appiah, Kwame Anthony. 1992. *In My Father's House: Africa in the Philosophy of Culture*. New York: Oxford University Press.

Arendt, Hannah. 1951. *The Origins of Totalitarianism*. New York: Harcourt, Brace.

Baldwin, James. 1961. *Nobody Knows My Name: More Notes of a Native Son*. New York: Dial Press.

Castoriadis, Cornelius. 1991. *Philosophy, Politics, and Autonomy*. Edited by David A. Curtis. New York: Oxford University Press.

Davidson, Basil. 1966. *Africa: History of a Continent*. New York: Macmillan.

———. 1969. *The African Genius: An Introduction to African Cultural and Social History*. Boston: Little, Brown, and Company.

Davidson, Donald. 1984. *Inquiries into Truth and Interpretation*. Oxford: Clarendon.

Evans-Pritchard, E. E. 1937. *Witchcraft, Oracles, and Magic among the Azande*. Oxford: Clarendon.

Eze, Emmanuel Chukwudi. 1997a. *Race and the Enlightenment*. Oxford: Blackwell.

———. 1997b. *Postcolonial African Philosophy: A Critical Reader*. Oxford: Blackwell.

Faull, Katherine. 1994. *Anthropology and the German Enlightenment: Perspectives on Humanity*. London: Bucknell and Associated University Presses.

Fraser, Nancy. 1989. *Unruly Practices: Power, Discourse, and Gender in Contemporary Social Theory*. Minneapolis: University of Minnesota Press.

Gates, Henry Louis. 1978. "The History and Theory of Afro-American Literary Criticism, 1773–1831: The Arts, Aesthetic Theory, and the Nature of the African." Ph.D. diss., Cambridge University.

———. 1986. *Race, Writing, and Difference*. Chicago: University of Chicago Press.

Gilman, Sander. 1982. *On Blackness without Black: Essays on the Image of the Black in Germany*. Boston: G. K. Hall and Company.

Grass, Günter. 1992. "Losses." Translated by Michael Hoffman. *Granta* 42 (winter): 98–108.

Habermas, Jürgen. 1984. *The Theory of Communicative Action, Volume One: Reason and the Rationalization of Society*. Translated by Thomas McCarthy. Boston: Beacon Press.

———. 1990. *The Philosophical Discourse of Modernity*. Translated by Frederick G. Lawrence. Boston: Massachusetts Institute of Technology Press.

Honor, Hugh. 1982. *The Representation of the Black in Western Art*. Cambridge: Harvard University Press.

Horton, Robin. 1986. "Tradition and Modernity Revisited." Pp. 210–60 in *Rationality and Relativism*, ed. Martin Hollis and Steven Lukes. Cambridge: Massachusetts Institute of Technology Press.

Ingram, David. 1987. *Habermas and the Dialectic of Reason*. New Haven: Yale University Press.

Kramnik, Isaac, ed. 1995. *The Portable Enlightenment Reader*. New York: Penguin Books.

Lévy-Bruhl, Lucien. 1903. *The Philosophy of Auguste Comte*. New York: G. P. Putnam's Sons; S. Sonnenschein and Company.

———. 1923. *Primitive Mentality*. Translated by Lilian A. Clare. *La mentalité primitive*. New York: Allen & Unwin.

———. 1926. *How Natives Think*. Translated by Lilian A. Clare. *Les fonctions mentales dans les sociétés inférieures*. New York: Allen & Unwin.

————. 1949. *Les Carnets de Lucien Lévy-Bruhl*. Paris: Presses Universitaires de France.

Lloyd, David. 1996. "Race under Representation." Pp. 249–72 in *Culture/Contexture*, ed. E.Valentine Daniel and Jeffrey M. Peck. Berkeley: University of California Press.

Martin, Peter. 1993. *Schwarze Teufel, edle Mohren: Afrikaner in Bewußtsein und Geschichte der Deutschen*. Hamburg: Junius.

Mills, Charles. 1998. *The Racial Contract*. Ithaca, N.Y.: Cornell University Press.

Parsons, Talcott. 1971. *The System of Modern Societies*. Englewood Cliffs, N.J.: Prentice Hall.

Popper, Karl. 1968. *Conjectures and Refutations*. New York: Harper.

West, Cornel. 1993. *Keeping Faith: Philosophy and Race in America*. New York: Routledge.

CHAPTER FOUR

Mankind's Proverbial Imagination

*Critical Perspectives on Human Universals
As a Global Challenge*

MINEKE SCHIPPER

Over the last decades the academic debate has been dominated by an emphasis on difference: difference between "us" and "them," and difference in race, class, ethnicity, culture, nation, continent, and so on. In this debate solutions have been sought for existing dichotomies in "mixture" concepts, such as creolization or hybridity. Such "solutions" have been mainly invented by scholars in the West as a result of the multinational Otherness industry that has been developed there.

Beside our own views of ourselves and others, others' views of themselves and us exist—it is as simple as that. However, people's demand for alternative perspectives is not generally acute, and curiosity about the answers of others tends not to be particularly intense in the camp of most "selves."

The most crucial dichotomy academia has to go beyond is the enormous information and facilities gap between the rich and poor areas of our world. Globally speaking, there is a huge imbalance in available scholars and available data, in library access, in communication and information technology, and in the quantitative representation of existing cultural, regional, and gender diversities.

GLOBALIZATION

Today, all continents are incorporating the same basic economic ingredients as well as some common cultural features (due to the mass media and electronic culture). Tomlinson (1996, 22–23) defines cultural globalization as "the particular effects which the general social processes of time-space compression and distanciation have on that realm of practices and experience in which people socially construct meaning."

The concept of "globalization" seems to suggest an active process of conquest and unification of the global space, but who is globalizing and who is globalized, and to what effect? Will the ongoing global unification process destroy our diversities and therewith *en passant* the dichotomies referred to in our conference theme ("Beyond Dichotomies: Histories, Identities, Cultures, and the Challenge of Globalization")? Some of us wonder and worry about whether uniformization is threatening all "deviant" identities; culture is the way in which members of society create meaning, but existing meanings also create people and determine the behavior of men and women as members of their society through ongoing flows of interactions. Globalization interacts with local realities, negatively and positively.

As humans, we have in common the fact that we are all earthlings, and we are products of genetic, cultural, and societal forces that in some ways seem to provoke similar reactions among humans all over the globe.

My starting point in this chapter is that a number of human similarities, and possibly some universals, are not at all due to contemporary globalization effects. In spite of all of our dichotomies, there also are similarities, since all peoples belong to humankind. What we have in common first of all has to do with very early common basic human drives, such as food, shelter, safety, and procreation. Such primary drives and needs determine behavior and are determined by innate representations. At the level of social structures, institutions, and culture, these primary drives are articulated in order to secure continuity (and to cope with change, if need be) in specific geographical, historical, and sociocultural contexts. Still, the primary drives and needs and the anatomy and physiology of the human body underlie human social, cultural, and linguistic universals, as Brown (1991, 39) argues in an interesting book, *Human Universals*.

HUMAN UNIVERSALS

It is not at all self-evident that invariants in human affairs exist. Anthropologists, for instance, have been mostly suspicious and hostile to the search for universals (particularly in the United States). In anthropology as a discipline, there has been a gradual shift away from generalizations, due to the success of cultural relativism. If cultures are considered completely autonomous, cultural universals are rather unlikely (Brown 1991, 63). Anthropologists prefer to distinguish sharply between biology and anthropology: their doctrine is that animals are supposed to be controlled by their biology, and humans are supposed to be determined by culture.

In his book *The Language Instinct* (1995), Steven Pinker doubts this Standard Social Science Model (SSSM), which for a long time has been the dominant basis for research on humankind within the academic world. This model also has dictated the dominant ideology of our time: this is the position that a decent member of society should hold, and, indeed, history has taught us that biological determinism leads to slavery, colonialism, racism, sexism, and so on. Pinker, however, states that we need not regress into this mindless dichotomy of heredity versus environment. Both play a role: a child brought up in Japan will speak Japanese; the same child brought up in the United States will end up speaking English, while the child's pet in the same environment does not start speaking at all. Language, he says, needs "intricate mental software," as do other accomplishments of mental life. He attributes to the human mind a universal design (ibid., 409): a language refers to the process of different speakers in the same community who do acquire highly similar mental grammars. Culture, in a similar way, is the process by which particular kinds of learning "contagiously spread from person to person in a community, and minds become coordinated into shared patterns" (ibid., 406, 411). But what about cross-cultural similarities?

Those who dwell on differences will certainly find differences between peoples (as well as between individuals), while those who dwell on similarities will find similarities. Perhaps some elements of Pinker's "universal design of the human mind" are at the basis of cultural

similarities. Human universals have been found in individuals and societies, in cultures and languages. All peoples breathe, have language, and
are sexually active. Anatomical and physiological features have been
mostly neglected in anthropological studies although, as we said earlier,
they do underlie social and cultural structures and institutions in society.
Culture is transmitted horizontally and vertically between individuals
and collectivities, and to a great extent, it is much less created by individuals than it is imposed upon them (Brown 1991, 40).

We can try to classify certain human phenomena, even where the
contents may differ, for example, cooking, courtship, etiquette, funeral
rites, fire making, incest taboos, property rights, numerals, and so on. In
a number of cases, though, there also are universals of content, with universal details, such as general similarities all over the world in the emotions that people express during bereavement, for instance, shortening
and easing bereavement by final funeral rites (Levinson and Malone
1980, 297).

However, universality can never be proved 100 percent, because
the arguments will always rest on limited evidence, as Murdock (1975)
has already observed. People classify the world about them in a variety
of words, but there are some basic universal conceptions in the semantic components beneath the cultural varieties in vocabulary, as Goldschmidt (quoted in Brown 1991, 76) argues: "Underlying the diversity
of human institutions is a universal set of problems or functions that
must be solved or discharged in all societies, [and] these functions provide a common framework for the analysis of all societies." As far as the
research on the relations between men and women in society is concerned, most comparative studies conclude that "men exercise more
power, have more status, and enjoy more freedom" (Levinson and Malone 1980, 267).

Some scholars have distinguished universals "of essence" and "of
accident." According to Brown (1991) "essence" here refers to universals "that could not be eliminated except by unnatural interventions"
(e.g., by genetic engineering), "examples of essences being biological features of the species." In his opinion, "much of the debate concerning
male and female differences turns around the issue of whether certain of
the universal differences are essential or accidental." Since our world is
not static, universals may change or disappear, and new universals come
into being. Among the latter, Brown mentions the dog as a domestic animal and the use of metal tools: they have gradually become universals in
human culture. And, he adds, "such items as plastic containers, phosp

horus matches, and machine-factured clothing do not (alas for the romance of anthropology) seem far behind" (ibid., 50). Old universals do not necessarily have eternal life, and numerous new universals, not only material ones, but also ideas, representations, and artistic devices, will spread around the globe in the years ahead, affecting people's earlier perspectives on humanity and the universe.

THE GREAT CHAIN OF BEING

In their book *More Than Cool Reason: A Field Guide to Poetic Metaphor* (1989), Lakoff and Turner present what they call "the great chain of being" as a cultural model that places various kinds of beings on a vertical scale with "higher" and "lower" beings and properties, that is, a scale of forms of being—from human to animal, to plant and inanimate object. These are associated with a scale of the properties characterizing these forms: reason, instinctual behavior, biological function, and physical attributes. The authors consider this chain of being an unconscious model, "indispensable to our understanding of ourselves, our world, and our language." This hierarchical chain of being, they argue, "is largely unconscious and so fundamental to our thinking that we barely notice it" (ibid., 167). The highest properties of beings define their level in the Great Chain, in which human beings are thought to belong to a higher order of beings than all other kinds. Thus, for example, instinct is a generic-level parameter of animals, while mental, moral, and aesthetic qualities are generic-level parameters of human beings: "What defines a level are the attributes and behaviors distinguishing it from the next below level" (168). The attributes and behavior that define a given level are beyond those possessed by forms of being at lower levels. In this context, "beyond" means more, more complex, more powerful. Higher-level beings possess something that lower forms lack: there is a hierarchy here, from humans (higher-order attributes and behavior) down to animals (instinctual), down to plants (biological), to objects (structural) and to natural physical things (natural attributes and natural physical behavior) (cf. ibid., 168ff.).

The fixed hierarchy of this Chain of Being is combined with fixed ideas that humans tend to have about the "Nature of Things." We all have, as Lakoff and Turner put it, "a commonsense theory about forms of being—that they have essences, and that these essences lead to the way they behave or function . . . essential physical attributes result in essential physical behavior" (ibid., 169). Some of these attributes are immutable, while others are not. Our commonsense theory about the nature of things seems largely unconscious; it makes us accept as "natural" our perspective on the relationship between what things or beings are like and how they behave. Hierarchies in "the Great Chain" associated with the "Nature of Things" condition our perspective on what is considered "essential" and "accidental" (ibid.). Such commonsense perceptions may deeply influence our views on gender, for example.

The combination of the "Nature of Things" with the "Great Chain," Lakoff and Turner argue, forms a complex commonsense theory of how things work in the world. In another book, *Women, Fire, and Dangerous Things: What Categories Reveal about the Mind* (1990), Lakoff elaborates on this human commonsense theory, analyzing several concepts, such as anger, lust, and rape, and the metaphors associated with them. His conclusion is that "basic-level metaphors allow us to comprehend and draw inferences, . . . using our knowledge of familiar, well-structured domains" (ibid., 406).

The model of the Great Chain concerns not merely attributes and behavior but also dominance, because according to the "logic" of the model, higher forms of being "naturally" dominate lower forms of being by virtue of their higher natures, thus it is self-evident that humans dominate animals (Lakoff and Turner 1989, 208).

The question then is: is this "Chain," as such, a universal, or is it a limited cultural model? The authors conclude that "the basic form of the Great Chain . . . is what is unconsciously taken for granted in a wide variety of cultures" (ibid., 209). As far as the Western world is concerned, they analyze the details of the internal hierarchies constructed at the different levels of the Chain, with their far-reaching consequences: "The Great Chain is a description not only of existing hierarchies but also of what the hierarchies in the world *should be*" (ibid., 210). One may wonder how far these norms have been influencing local cultures in other parts of the world since colonial times.

Why should the influence of this extended Chain be so enormous? Lakoff and Turner speculatively answer this question as follows:

> Perhaps because in our early cognitive development we inevitably form the model of the basic Great Chain as we interact with the world, it seems that the Great Chain is widespread and has strong natural appeal. This is frightening. It implies that those social, political, and ecological evils induced by the Great Chain will not

disappear quickly or of their own accord. The Great Chain is itself a political issue. As a chain of dominance it can become a chain of subjugation. It extends over centuries to men and women today. (ibid., 213)

The basic Great Chain was elaborated into a Cultural Model of Macrocosm and Microcosm: "Each level of the chain was expanded to reflect the structure of the chain as a whole. At each level, there were higher and lower forms of being, with the higher forms dominating the lower." The examples they give are drawn from the animal kingdom, in which lions, grizzly bears, and birds of prey dominate lower forms, such as deer and snakes. At the human level they also find an internal hierarchy constructed as follows: "the king above the nobility, the nobility above the peasants, men above women, adults above children, and masters over slaves" (ibid., 209). Where does the queen fit in, one may be tempted to ask. This may seem a rather simple example, but the construction of internal hierarchies as such tends to be a human universal.

The Chain is referred to verbally in daily language as well as in artistic texts, by metaphors, for example. In his *Poetics*, Aristotle already said that using metaphors is a sign of genius, since they translate the author's intuitive perception of what is similar into what is dissimilar. Because of their artistic mastery, proverbs are highly popular and have a strong impact in oral cultures. The metaphors used *in* the proverbs double the proverbs' impact *as* metaphors, at the very moment that they themselves turn into new metaphors in the actual quotation situation.

Lakoff and Turner convincingly demonstrate how proverbs are closely linked to the Chain of Being, how respectfully they reflect and confirm its hierarchies by metaphorical mechanisms, through their continuous message that the order of dominance ought not to be subverted (1989, 210).

Normally a proverb is mapped onto a quotation situation; when proverbs are collected and referred to without their context of origin, the explicit discourse situation to indicate the target domain is lacking. However, we still know a lot about the target domain from our background thinking, or "commonsense theory," in Lakoff's and Turner's (1989, 175) terms, since proverbs are connected to basic human concerns and automatically linked to the Great Chain of Being. Proverbs are rooted in a social and cultural context, and their messages are to be understood against the background of the assumptions, norms, and values that inspired them (ibid., 187). Metaphors reveal such background thinking in a wide variety

of poetic proverbs and sayings. My aim is to compare them cross-cultur-
ally, bearing in mind the question of whether or not woman's representation in proverbs confirms the discussed basic hierarchical Great Chain
mechanisms and reflects "what is unconsciously taken for granted in a
wide variety of cultures," as stated by Lakoff and Turner.

PROVERBS ON WOMEN

Over the years I have collected thousands of proverbs on women from
many cultures all over the world, proverbs in which I have found striking
similarities in representations of women, mostly from a male perspective.

I have been working on the project "Proverbs on Women Worldwide" for more than ten years now. It has been adopted for patronage by
the United Nations Educational, Scientific, and Cultural Organization's
(UNESCO) International Fund for the Promotion of Culture. In the
Netherlands, I have published four collections of proverbs on women
from Europe, Africa, Asia, and Jewish culture respectively (Schipper 1993,
1994, 1995, 1996); in addition, a volume on the Caribbean and Latin
America is forthcoming. The collections all follow the same classification
order: *I. Phases of Life:* girl, woman, wife, co-wife, mother, daughter,
mother-in-law, widow, grandmother, and old woman; and *II. Elements of
Life:* beauty, love, sex, pregnancy, work, arguing and violence, unfaithful-
ness, unreliability, witchcraft, and power. All of these categories were frequently represented in proverbs from oral as well as written sources.

Proverbs are defined as short, pithy sayings, ingeniously embo-
dying an admitted truth or a common belief. Definitions generally
emphasize four characteristics of the proverb: (1) its concise, fixed artistic form; (2) its evaluative and conservative function in society; (3) its
authoritive validity; and (4) its anonymous origin.

In an oral culture, the experts on traditions are—mainly or exclusively—chiefs and elders. Referring to their ancestral legacy, they are
supposed to be or claim to be specialists on tradition, its preeminent
representatives. Quoting is an art, and the skillful display of one's knowledge by quoting proverbs is a source of prestige in oral societies. The
proverb is associated with the authority of old wisdom. By referring to
the wisdom's unquestionable validity, the speaker deserves respect and
authority himself or herself. Thus traditional values and existing power
relations are confirmed: "The one who quotes proverbs, gets what he
wants," in the words of the Shona (Zimbabwe).

A user of proverbs appeals to collective norms and values in the community: "Both collective acceptance and traditionality are the consequences of socialization of certain forms of expression which originally must have been individual. Collective acceptance here . . . seems to be an active factor: something that has achieved social acceptance is not only generally used but also generally accepted as correct" (Mukarovsky 1983 [1971], 99). This social acceptance results from the above-discussed hierarchies and differences in the "Great Chain."

The German, Wander (1987, v), calls language "the heart of a people" and proverbs "the veins carrying blood to all parts of the body," thus underlining their importance. In the preface to his Gikuyu collection, the Kenyan, Barra (1984 [1939], iii), calls proverbs "the essence of eloquence, . . . the true wisdom written by God in the hearts of people and a precious heritage which should not be lost in the present times of change." The proverbs as such are taken for granted by Wander and Barra, as well as by most other sources. Whether their acceptance is as general as suggested above is rarely questioned. One is morally and socially forced to agree with their eternal truth and unshakable wisdom, since the rulers' values are the ruling values in all societies.

In spite of cultural differences, some striking similarities seem to occur in proverbs from different cultures and continents—in form as well as in content.

FORMAL CHARACTERISTICS

First I will present some frequent constructions that proverbs seem to have in common, in spite of different cultural origins. Examples have been selected from my collection of proverbs on women.

1. *A is (like) B:* "A house full of daughters is like a cellar full of sour beer" (Netherlands/Germany); "A widow is like a boat without a helm" (Brazil/China); "Woman is like the earth; everybody sits down on her" (Luba, Zaïre); "The earth is like a woman [who is] mother" (Mapuche, Chili); "A wife is like a protecting wall for her husband" (Jewish).

2. *A is not (like) B:* "Woman is not a corncob to be valued by stripping off its leaves" (Baule, Ivory Coast); "A bad wife is not a good mother" (Spain); "Your wife is not a prayer shawl you replace when you don't like her anymore" (Jewish).

3. *No A without B:* "No young woman without a mirror, no old one without advice" (Spain); "No woman without big sister" (Rwanda); "No bride without a veil, no woman without jealousy" (Sephardic); "No woman without charms, no poet without rum" (Brazil).

4. *Better A than B:* "A stupid wife is better than a ruinous house" (Bassari, Togo); "It is better to live with a dragon than with a bad woman" (England); "Better to live on the corner of the roof than with a quarrelsome wife in the same house" (Jewish); "Better to starve than eat cats' dinner; better to freeze than wear old woman's clothes" (Chinese).

5. *If A, then B:* "If an old woman dances, she invites death on/to?? her yard" (Germany); "If you dance with your rival, don't close your eyelid" (Burundi); "If the father doesn't act like a father, still the daughter has to behave like a daughter" (China); "If a woman does not want to dance, she says her skirt is too short" (Jamaica); "If the son marries, he divorces his mother" (Jewish); "If you are impatient to have a child, you marry a pregnant woman" (Fulfulde, Senegal).

Artistic devices such as rhythm, rhyme, assonance, alliteration, parallelism, metaphor, contrast, wordplay, and so forth strongly contribute to the proverbs' success, but I cannot go into this important point here. Due to its attractive form, a well-known proverb, quoted in a new situation, adequately renews people's attention to its old message as well as to its new connotations.

SIMILARITIES IN CONTENT

As far as the content is concerned, proverbs should, first, be studied "live." Only then can questions such as the following be answered: Who are the addressers, and who are the addressees (e.g., man or woman, old or young)? What position do they have in society? Which proverbs are used most frequently, and what is their effect?

A proverb acquires its concrete meaning only at the moment it is used: "In the absence of the situation, there is no proverb" (Brookman-Amissah 1972, 264). Yet it is indeed true that new shades of meaning may develop in new situations. For example, a poor man complaining about his misery might quote the following saying: "Whether the widow has her period or not does not make any difference" (Baule, Ivory

Coast). In his society it means, literally, that a widow has no right to have sexual intercourse, and neither does a woman who has her period. In this man's particular situation, it means that whether it is a festive day or an ordinary day makes no difference to the poor, since their situation is always grimy and monotonous. The example makes clear that an originally simple straightforward saying with a literal meaning may become metaphorical and thus applicable to numerous other situations.

Nevertheless, the proverb also continues to make clear that in the Baule culture the widow's freedom is curtailed. Not only here but in many cultures widows are treated less respectfully than women whose husbands are alive, or they are brought under suspicion: "A widow is like a boat without a helm" (China). "Never marry a widow, unless her husband was hanged," the English say; and the French warn: "A wife who has buried a husband, doesn't mind burying another one."

For our purpose, sayings literally referring to women as well as metaphorical ones have been collected, since the two categories tell us about women in the societies concerned. In spite of varying contexts and connotations, a relatively constant core of meaning is being transmitted (see Cox 1989, 332). Bearing in mind our earlier discussion on human universals and the Great Chain of Being, I now draw a few comparative lines on the basis of some strikingly constant cores of meaning among the proverbs in my collection.

The only category of women favorably portrayed in proverbs is the mother—unique, loving, reliable, and hard working, therefore, "A wife should be like one's mother," as the Swahili in East Africa say, or "A good wife is like a mother" (Costa Rica). In childbirth, boys often are preferred to girls: "To bear a daughter is to bear a problem" (Tigrinya, Eritrea); "To bear a daughter, to bear a disaster" (China); "A whole night of labor pains, and then only a daughter" (Spain).

Except for the mothers, women in proverbs are portrayed as more unfaithful than virtuous, and men are warned time and again not to fall for their charms and evil intentions. Women and daughters have to be watched closely all of the time: "Glass and girls easily break" (Korea); "A bag full of flies can be guarded more easily than a girl" (Netherlands/Germany); "A woman is like the unpeeled bark of a tree: whoever draws near may peel it off" (Shona, Zimbabwe); "With a white horse and a beautiful wife, you are always in trouble" (Denmark/Italy).

The silent and submissive type is highly recommended: "Virtuous is the girl who suffers and dies without a sound" (Bengali, India); "Silence is a woman's most beautiful ornament" (England/Greece/Italy);

"A wise woman has a great deal to say and remains silent" (Asia, general, except in Muslim cultures).

Another point often stressed is that women ought to be (kept) inferior to men in general and to their husbands in particular: "A woman who knows Latin will never find a husband nor come to a good end" (France/Italy/Spain/Argentina). The Sena (Malawi/Mozambique) express this as follows: "Never marry a woman with bigger feet than your own." Those big feet are meant metaphorically, although a number of proverbs explicitly express the wish that women physically be smaller too: "The misfortune remains within limits, the man said, he married a small wife" (Friesland/Netherlands); "Women and sardines, the bigger they are, the greater the damage" (Portugal). If she still turns out to be bigger, then the Ngbaka (Central African Republic) find a solution in the following proverb: "A little string binds a big parcel," meaning that a small husband can very well marry a huge woman, because he stays in power (the smallest of the strong is more powerful than the biggest of the weak). The overall message seems to be that women should not have too much potential: the younger, smaller, and less educated or competent than their partners, the more acceptable they become.

I came across many more proverbs about women than about men. In *The Penguin Dictionary of Proverbs* (Fergusson 1986 [1983]) and in *Proverbs and Sayings of Ireland* (Gaffney and Cashman 1992 [1974]), for example, a reference to the category "male" in the index is lacking, while the section "female" is well provided. Maybe the proverb has become a "male genre," in the sense that men used it more (in public), and in doing so they shaped the genre to their best interest. This could explain the striking fact that proverbs about women are rather negative and often have been demonstrably formulated from the male perspective.

As far as European proverbs are concerned, the German, Daniels (1985, 18), states the following: "While proverbs judging men from a female perspective are rare, proverbs about the theme 'woman' are innumerable, among which the ones underlining the negative qualities and rigidly fixed role patterns form a striking majority" (my translation). This conclusion also is reached by the Ghanaian, Amba Oduyoye (1979), on the basis of material from West Africa.

One could object that proverbs may contradict and thereby neutralize each other. Take the question of the advantages and disadvantages of polygamy as an example: the proverb, "One wife means one eye" (Luba, Zaïre) is contradicted in, "If you marry two, you will die all the younger," coming from the same culture. Collections do indeed contain proverbs and counter-proverbs. Quantitatively, however, positive proverbs concerning women are rare birds among flocks of negative ones (see Oduyoye 1979 and Daniels 1985, among others). On the basis of his European collection, Cox (1989, 334), too, agrees on the "generally sexist features . . . in the existing, male-made collections of proverbs."

STEREOTYPES

Existing stereotypical opinions about women are reflected in proverbs. Stereotypes are beliefs expressed in words, aiming at individuals or groups. They take the form of generalized, biased statements, which simplistically and wrongly withhold or attribute certain qualities or types of behavior from or to a group of people. Stereotypes are the result of a selection of certain traits and observations that deny others, so that the "typical" traits are selected and whoever hears a proverb automatically follows it, without thinking independently about such a statement. Based on comparable clichés and rhetorical processes, the same socio-psychological mechanism is highly successful in commercials today. In order to see through such statements, certain questions from narratology are helpful, such as: (1) Who is speaking? (2) Whose views are presented? (3) Who is subject, and who is object? (4) Whose interests are promoted? (5) What impact do such quotations have? (Bal 1985; Schipper 1985). Such questions had never before been applied to proverbs as a genre.

In a number of proverbs the gender of the speaker can easily be guessed. Would a woman ever say the following: "Women and steaks, the more you beat them, the better they'll be" (Germany)? Or: "A woman is like a goat, you tether her where the thistles grow" (Rwanda)? Or: "Never trust a woman, even after she has given you seven sons" (Brazil/Japan)? The view that she has to be ruled with an iron fist makes clear who is being presented as the subject and who as the object, and it also makes clear which group does not profit from the effect of such statements. Many proverbs dictate women's roles and behavior and in doing so give a vision of what their society expects from them. In that vision, the woman has to be subservient and silent, has to work hard and preferably produce male offspring, and she is presented as being so unreliable that she is associated with destruction, devilry, and witchcraft. Of course, one has to take into account that proverbs also contain elements of playfulness and should not be taken literally and out of context. Still, the number of negative messages about women is rather astonishing.

The attractive form and rhetorical tools often are combined with forceful expressions such as: "As our ancestors used to say . . ." or "As the old wisdom has taught us. . . ." With proverbs, the aspect of authority has the function of legitimizing certain role patterns and possibly of forbidding behavior questioning these patterns. In this respect they seem to confirm Lakoff's and Turner's observations on the Great Chain and its internal hierarchies.

Proverbs on women reveal mostly male perspectives on social norms and roles. Globally, much less is as yet known about female critical perspectives on female and male roles and behavior, and this knowledge is hardly transmitted in proverbs. The proverb is a public genre, and in most cultures women are invited to speak much less than men and therefore are much less used to addressing society publicly. The highly praised silence of women in many cultures underscores this point.

The male-female information imbalance has indeed severely suffered from the fact that for many decades a majority of male anthropologists have carried out the research for studying history and society; their knowledge was mostly based on the worldview of male informants (Ardener 1975), and they either were not very interested in or had no easy access to women's perspectives on society. Ever since the rise of women's studies, the invisibility of women in anthropological studies often has been noted. In most small-scale societies, men and women live in different worlds, with women mostly interacting with other women and children, and men mostly interacting with other men. As Levinson and Malone observed, the issue of male versus female worldview needs to be addressed much more systematically by those interested in comparing the role and status of men and women (1980, 271n).

GLOBAL COMPARISONS

It is not possible to find out from where a particular proverb originally came. Researchers who have studied proverbs from a single country or language area have found the same proverb or its variant in various regions; those who have looked at a whole continent or searched for a worldwide collection have come to the conclusion that proverbs from different places can show similarities: "What we think of as real

Dutch, because it is so common to us, the Germans have too, but also the Danish and the Norwegians, and also the French and the Italians" (Ter Laan 1988, 7).

Champion (1938, xxiv) takes this much further. According to him, proverbs are the same all over the world, even though the local presentation of the same idea may vary. He gives a number of striking examples from many areas, among others, the following proverb: "I madam and you miss, but who does the housekeeping?" (Spain). His variants include: "I a queen and you a queen, but who makes the butter?" (Punjabi); "You a lady, I a lady, but who milks the cow?" (Serbia); "I the boss and you the boss, but who shines the shoes?" (Germany). The hierarchical message referring to the "Nature of Things" is obvious, although not discussed in the context.

According to Champion, it is impossible that such proverbs have spread only by borrowing. Still, they are exactly the same, he says, although the metaphors are different. He gives an explanation for this: "Love, hunger and fear are the basic facts that control humanity . . . facts that are not influenced by surrounding or culture. Not even the civilization of many centuries can destroy those primary instincts of humanity" (ibid.). The study of proverbs, in his eyes, has given a convincing proof of this lasting equality (*sic*) of people "everywhere, regardless of language or culture." Champion's argument is simple and not very subtle: proverbs do have universal traits, just like the people quoting them. Obviously, it is a question of innate instincts.

If we believe Champion, the widespread views on women in proverbs also would be part of those ineradicable primary instincts. I do not think so. Behavior, feelings, and expectations are certainly based on biological instincts, but as human beings we do have choices; we can reflect on our behavior, and we can influence it socially and culturally. Champion, who published his rich collection in 1938, does not go into this matter. Gender-related questions were not addressed at that time.

Over the past decades, the social sciences have addressed the concept of gender intensively and concluded that what is considered typically male or female is mostly a social and therefore an alterable construction. To a large extent, the biological has been detached from the social, whereby the idea is that one is more made than born to be a man or a woman. Nonetheless, both sexes continue to be subjected to their historical and cultural context and thus continue to be forced into certain roles, often unconsciously—the very roles prescribed in the proverbs.

All over the world, the limited physical differences between men and women have had far-reaching consequences that have nothing to do with those differences. The biological and the anthropological have to be looked at in combination to find out where the unchangeable biological essences have been misused to create biased social and cultural norms.

To what extent are the proverbial messages confirmed by today's realities? According to an Institute for Policy Studies press release (March 1993), only 3.5 percent of the ministers in the world are women, and they hold less than 10 percent of the seats in parliaments. On the basis of the current tendency and the slowness of earlier developments, the International Labor Organization (ILO) has calculated that it will take another 475 to 500 years before there will be more or less as many women in power positions as men and both sexes will be equally represented in public life. That does not sound optimistic, but there is no question of an unalterable fate.

A lot has changed already, especially in industrialized societies. That the stereotypes in the proverbs I have quoted may seem outdated is telling in this respect. However, these changes have especially benefited women from privileged groups, those who have always had more education and possibilities to develop intellectually than the great majority of underprivileged women. Sociological research has demonstrated that particularly in less-educated social groups, traditional ideas about what is male and what is female are extremely strong. That does not mean, though, that such ideas are no longer present in the internalized subconscious legacy of socially privileged groups too.

It is, of course, always advantageous to maneuver and keep groups other than one's own in a subordinate position. Those who have always had others do unpleasant and hard work for them want to keep things that way: "One makes the bed, and the other lies down in it" (Germany). It is a question of power, and the generous offer to share equally the annoying tasks at home is not obvious from the comfort of a dominant position.

The proverb's authority effect serves to advise against role changes, as in the Ashanti proverb: "If a woman makes the giant drum, it is kept in the men's room." Amba Oduyoye (1979, 7) gives the following commentary on this proverb from her own culture in Ghana: "Why would anyone make the effort to take such an initiative when the honor still goes to somebody else? If a woman tries to be as big as a man, it will only bring her unhappiness. . . . Such proverbs are a warning aimed at girls who display behavior which society has labeled 'male.'"

On the other hand, men are warned constantly not to do women's work: it brings chaos and misery, and it is degrading. Women are reminded that housekeeping is their business: "However beautiful a woman [is], she always ends up in the kitchen" (Indonesia); "A bad home sends you for water and firewood" (Rwanda) means that the man would became his wife's slave if he would have to do such humiliating (women's) work in her place. In Europe, a man would say that the woman is wearing the trousers, a frequently heard complaint: "Where the woman is wearing the trousers and the man the apron, things are going badly" (Italy). Badly for whom?

The proverbs present "how things ought to be" from a certain point of view, a dominant view that has contributed to the construction of people's gendered identities. We have been programmed in our behavior as men and women mostly without being aware of it. This is where we have come from, as men and women. Worldwide, our "essences" have brought about similarities in gender hierarchies.

All of those warnings for men and compelling prescriptions and rules for women reveal fear and insecurity. If women were as subservient as they should be according to those rules, fear and insecurity would be just as unnecessary as the numerous discriminating proverbs to which they give rise.

Once More: Universals

Cross-cultural research reveals links between peoples' observations of physical facts (such as bodily differences between males and females) and their reflections on these facts. In a number of cultures, perhaps in most, the result has been the justification of instituted gender hierarchies, norms and roles, on the basis of, in our case, simple physical differences. Commonsense theories on the "Nature of Things" and the "Great Chain of Being" have been based on such reflections, and the resulting gender representations in proverbs support them.

In order to define where we want to go globally, first we have to be aware of those legacies of our human sociocultural past. Proverbs can help to raise our consciousness on the matter.

According to Robertson (1992, 78), the global human condition refers to "both the world in its contemporary concreteness and to humanity as a species," and globality refers "to the circumstance of extensive awareness of the world as a whole including the species aspect of the latter."

One aspect of the global human condition is a worldwide growing awareness of our gender legacy. To date, numerous international meetings and demonstrations have been held, of which the United Nations Women's Conferences were certainly the most widely publicized and spectacularly globalizing. Many of the inequalities referred to at these conferences can be traced back to internalized oral traditions in patriarchal cultures, although concomitant sexual hierarchies were not only maintained through colonization but also further enhanced by the latter. Such mental remnants of the past, in which physical, psychological, cultural, and ideological elements have been amalgamated into representations of men and women, still dominate our human sociocultures, in which, according to Ulf Hannerz (1992, 9), three interactive dimensions can be distinguished: (1) ideas, beliefs, modes of thought, feelings, and experiences; (2) publicly meaningful forms through which ideas, beliefs, and emotions are externalized and made visible on the social scene; and (3) the lines and channels along which the meaningful external forms are socially distributed in a given society. These three points suggest more social and cultural unity than diversity in human communities. However, the publicly dominant ideas, beliefs, and experiences are questioned more than ever before by groups that have been marginalized in the past.

As Lakoff and Turner rightly argue, new perspectives can be applied to the Great Chain, "challenging old ways of understanding the world" (1989, 203). The local and the global are intertwined and mutually challenging each other all over the world. One example is women's groups in South Africa that have recently been discussing my collection of proverbs on women from all over Africa. It came out in Johannesburg after it had been published earlier in London, Chicago, and Nairobi. Having discussed the proverbs' messages in their women's groups, they then started manipulating these messages from oral traditions, changing the content by replacing the word "man" with "woman" wherever it appeared in the proverb, and vice versa. It provoked not only lots of laughter but also serious discussions on gender hierarchies in contemporary Africa. Such discussions are due to newly available data in our age of globalization, an age in which local collective images are confronted with new information, new perspectives, and new forms of awareness.

A universal is an emic universal if "it is a part of the conceptual system of all peoples"—and as such integrated in their worldview (Brown 1991, 49). My research is based on emic perspectives: the proverbs represent views from within the cultures concerned. In the proverbs a number of similar qualifications are attributed to women across cultures and continents but, as we have seen, they are mostly presented from a male perspective, and there is not much material available in this oral genre presenting man from a female perspective. The material is certainly too limited to jump to easy conclusions concerning the universality of the mentioned similarities in male representation of women. Data on female representation of men need to be collected and studied systematically, from women's songs, stories, and sayings. And what will happen to the proverbs if they are turned upside down, as the women in the South African women's groups did? Well, the Shona in Zimbabwe used to say: "Those who quote proverbs, get what they want."

The proverbial gender imagination is clearly challenged from many sides. New proverbs may be created, and new genres will be born. Change will bring them along, although change can be hard to achieve. Violations of the boundaries of deeply held systems of norms and classification are often taboo, as Mary Douglass observed in the 1960s. This may explain the violent opposition to changing traditions. In many contexts, globalization provokes not only new debates but also a hardening of local perspectives on gender differences.

On the other hand, there is among women as well as among men a worldwide, growing awareness of the irrationality on which most existing gender dichotomies have been based, an awareness that has become confident and irreversible, as the innumerable local and global ongoing actions make clear. For those who are optimistic, it seems no longer excluded that gender equality will prominently figure on the list of new human universals in the next century.

WORKS CITED

Ardener, Shirley, ed. 1975. *Perceiving Women*. London: Malaby Press.

Bal, Mieke. 1985. *De theorie van vertellen en verhalen: inleiding in de narratologie*. Muiderberg: D. Coutinho.

Barra, G. 1984 [1939]. *One Thousand Kikuyu Proverbs*. Nairobi: Kenya Literature Bureau.

Brookman-Amissah, Joseph. 1972. "Some Observations on the Proverbs of the Akah-Speaking Peoples of Ghana." *Afrika und Übersee* 50:4:262–67.

Brown, Donald E. 1991. *Human Universals*. New York: McGraw-Hill.

Champion, Selwyn Gurney. 1938. *Racial Proverbs: A Selection of the World's Proverbs Arranged Linguistically*. London: G. Routledge and Sons.

Cox, Heinrich Leonhard. 1989. *Spreekwoordenboek in vier talen. Nederlands/Frans/Duits/Engels*. Utrecht: Van Dale Lexicografie.

Daniels, K. 1985. "Geschlechtsspezifische Stereotypen im Sprichwort: Ein interdisziplinärer Problemaufriss." *Literatur in Wissenschaft und Unterricht* 16: 18–25.

Fergusson, Rosalind. 1986 [1983]. *The Penguin Dictionary of Proverbs*. New York: Penguin.

Gaffney, Sean, and Seamus Cashman. 1992 [1974]. *Proverbs and Sayings of Ireland*. Dublin: Wolfhound.

Hannerz, Ulf. 1992. *Cultural Complexity: Studies in the Social Organization of Meaning*. New York: Columbia University Press.

Lakoff, George. 1990. *Women, Fire, and Dangerous Things. What Categories Reveal about the Mind*. Chicago and London: University of Chicago Press.

Lakoff, George, and Marc Turner. 1989. *More Than Cool Reason: A Field Guide to Poetic Metaphor*. Chicago and London: University of Chicago Press.

Levinson, David, and Martin J. Malone. 1980. *Toward Explaining Human Culture*. New Haven, Conn.: Human Relations Area Files.

Mukarovsky, Jan. 1983. "Selected Passages." Pp. 96–104 in *Communicating with Quotes: The Igbo Case*, by Joyce Penfield. Westport, Conn.: Greenwood Press.

Murdock, George Pieter. 1975. *Outline of World Cultures*. New Haven, Conn.: Human Relations Area Files.

Oduyoye, Amba. 1979. "The Asante Woman: Socialization through Proverbs." *African Notes* 8:1:5–11.

Penfield, Joyce. 1983. *Communicating with Quotes. The Igbo Case*. Westport, Conn.: Greenwood Press.

Pinker, Steven. 1995. *The Language Instinct*. London: Penguin.

Robertson, Roland. 1992. *Globalization: Social Theory and Global Culture*. London: Sage.

Schipper, Mineke. 1985. "'Who Am I?': Fact and Fiction in African First-Person Narrative." *Research in African Literatures* 16:1 (spring): 53–79.

———. 1993. *Een goede vrouw is zonder hoofd. Europese spreekwoorden en zegswijzen over vrouwen*. Amsterdam: Ambo.

———. 1994. *Een vrouw is als de aarde. Afrikaanse spreekwoorden en zegswijzen over vrouwen*. Amsterdam: Ambo.

————. 1995. *Een wenkbrauw als een wilgenblad. Aziatische spreekwoorden en zegswijzen over vrouwen.* Amsterdam: Ambo.

————. 1996. *De rib uit zijn lijf. Joodse spreekwoorden en zegswijzen over vrouwen.* Amsterdam: Ambo.

Ter Laan, Kornelis. 1988. *Nederlandse Spreuken, Spreekwoorden en zegswijzen.* Amsterdam: Elsevier.

Tomlinson, J. 1996. "Cultural Globalization: Placing and Displacing the West." *The European Journal of Development Research* 8:2 (December): 22–35.

Wander, Karl F. W. 1987. *Deutsches Sprichwörterlexikon: 1867–1880.* 5 vols. Leipzig: Brockhaus.

PART 2

CONTESTED PLACES, CONTESTED (SELF) ASCRIPTIONS

CHAPTER FIVE

Bringing History Back In

Of Diasporas, Hybridities, Places, and Histories

ARIF DIRLIK

At a conference in Singapore in December 1997, a U.S. anthropologist gave a presentation on the Chinese diaspora or, as she preferred it, Chinese transnationality. When she was finished, a well-known Singapore sociologist stood up to object to her conceptualization, declaiming that he was a Singaporean, not a diasporic or transnational, adding for good measure that American scholars were always imposing identities of that kind on other people. He was joined by a distinguished historian of Chinese Overseas, who added that rather than imposing diasporic identity on all Chinese Overseas, it would be much more productive to think of it in terms of recent migrants, not yet settled in their places of arrival, and classes who were in a position to exploit or benefit from transnationality. For either scholar, the issue was not one of Singapore nationalism or an "essentialized" Singapore identity (Singapore prides itself in many ways on being a multicultural society) but a place-based identity against a transnational or diasporic one.[1]

Discussions of diasporas or diasporic identities in much of contemporary cultural criticism focus on the problematic of national identity or the necessity of accommodating migrant cultures. The concept of diaspora or diasporic identity serves well when it comes to deconstructing claims to national cultural homogeneity. It also is important in expanding the horizon of cultural difference and challenging cultural hegemony at a time when the accommodation of cultural difference may be more urgent than ever in the face of the proliferating transnational motions of people. It may be because of the urgency of these issues that relatively less attention has been paid to problems presented by notions of diaspora and diasporic identity, especially the quite serious possibility that they may reproduce the very homogenizations and dichotomies that they are intended to overcome. I will address some of these problems in this chapter, with some attention to the question of hybridity, which has acquired considerable prominence with the emergence of a diasporic consciousness. As my goal is to stimulate questions on various aspects of diasporas, I present my thoughts as a series of reflections, without too much effort to achieve a tight coherence of argument. If diasporas are my point of departure, I rest my reflections on places and place consciousness, which I offer as a counterpoint to globalism and diasporas. While on occasion I may refer to other groups, my concern here is mainly with Chinese populations in motion, and it is those populations that I draw on for purposes of illustration.

The reconceptualization of Chinese Overseas in terms of diaspora or transnationality responds to a real situation: the reconfiguration of migrant societies and their political and cultural orientations. But diaspora and transnationality as concepts also are discursive or, perhaps more appropriately, imaginary; not only do they have normative implications, but they also articulate—in a very Foucauldian sense—relations of power within populations so depicted, as well as in their relationship to societies of origin and arrival.[2] Diaspora discourse has an undeniable appeal in the critical possibilities it offers against assumptions of national cultural homogeneity, which historically has resulted in the denial of full cultural (and political) citizenship to those who resisted assimilation into the dominant conceptualizations of national culture, were refused entry into it, or whose cultural complexity could not be contained easily within a single conception of national culture. Taking their cue from Paul Gilroy's concept of "double consciousness" with reference to the African diaspora, Ong and Nonini write of Chinese in diaspora that "they face many directions at once—toward China, other Asian countries, and the West—with multiple perspectives on modernities, perspectives often gained at great cost through their passage via itineraries marked by sojourning, absence, nostalgia, and at times exile and loss" (1997b, 12).[3]

This critical appeal, however, also disguises the possibility that diasporic notions of culture, if employed without due regard to the social and political complexities of so-called diasporic populations, may issue in reifications of their own, opening the way to new forms of cultural domination, manipulation, and commodification. To quote Ong and Nonini once again, "There is nothing intrinsically liberating about diasporic cultures" (1997a, 325). In pursuit of their interests, diasporic Chinese elites have collaborated with despotic political regimes, pursued exploitative practices of their own, and utilized the notion of "Chineseness" as a cover for their own class interests. The danger of reification is implicit in a contemporary culturalism that easily loses sight of the distinction between recognizing the autonomy of culture as a realm of analysis and the rendering of culture into a self-sufficient explanation for all aspects of life, therefore rendering culture once again into an offground phenomenon available to exploitation for a multiplicity of purposes. Moreover, since much of the discussion of culture and cultural identity is mediated by the new discipline of "cultural studies," there has been a tendency to carry questions and findings concerning one group of people to all groups similarly placed, in effect erasing considerable differences in the experiences of different populations through the universalization of the language of cultural studies. In either case, the erasure is one of the social relations that configure difference within and between groups and, with them, of historicity.

Ambiguities in the discourses on diasporas and related discourses of hybridity warrant some caution concerning projects of overcoming "binarisms." While there is little question about the desirability of such projects where they seek to overcome debilitating (and worse) divisions between ethnicities, genders, and so on, it also is important to note that they also may serve as ideological covers for proliferating divisions in the contemporary world, especially the new forms of class divisions that accompany the unprecedented concentrations of wealth within nations and globally. It is important, in any case, not to take such projects at face value but to distinguish progressive efforts to overcome divisions from their manipulation in the service of new forms of power.

The problems presented by diaspora discourse may be illustrated through the recent case of John Huang, the Chinese American fund-raiser for the Democratic National Committee. When Huang was charged with corruption on the grounds that he raised funds from foreign sources, the Democratic National Committee proceeded immediately to canvass all contributors with Chinese names to ascertain whether or not they were foreigners, turning a run-of-the-mill case of political corruption into a racial issue. The Committee's action reactivated the long-standing assumption that anyone with a Chinese name might in all probability be foreign, reaffirming implicitly that a Chinese name was the marker of racial foreignness. What followed may not have been entirely novel but seemed quite logical nevertheless in terms of contemporary diasporic "networks" (perhaps more appropriately in this case, "webs"). Huang's connections to the Riady family in Indonesia, which surfaced quickly, not only underlined the probable foreignness of Chinese contributors but also suggested further connections between Chinese Americans and other Chinese Overseas that seemed to be confirmed by revelations that several other Chinese American fund-raisers or contributors had ties to Chinese in South and Southeast Asia. As these overseas Chinese had business connections in the People's Republic of China, before long a petty corruption case was to turn into a case of possible conspiracy that extended from Beijing through Chinese Overseas to Chinese Americans.[4]

This linking of Chinese Americans to diasporic Chinese and the government in Beijing has provoked charges of racism among Asian Americans and their many sympathizers. Racism is there, to be sure. But is this racism simply an extension of the historical racism against Asian Americans, or does it represent something new? If so, is it possible that at least some Asian Americans have been complicit in producing a new kind of racist discourse? The question is fraught with difficulties—chief among them shifting responsibility to the victim— but it must be raised nevertheless. My goal in raising the question is not to erase racism but to underline the unprecedented depth to which race and ethnicity have become principles of politics, not just in the United States but globally. If the Democratic National Committee used Chinese names as markers of racial foreignness, is it possible that the government in China, or some Chinese transnational looking for recruits, might do the same? Immigration and Naturalization Service (INS) agents at the United States–Mexico border, upon finding out the Turkish origins of my name, have stopped me for a special search. On account of the same name, I have been approached by Turkish "grassroots" organizations mobilizing against condemnations of Turkey for its activities against the Kurds or its refusal to acknowledge the Armenian massacres. The name does bring a burden, but the burden is the ethnicization and racialization of politics, which is open to all for exploitation.

The new consciousness of diaspora and diasporic identity, cutting across national boundaries, is at least one significant factor in this racialization of politics in its current phase. The linking of John Huang, Chinese Overseas, and the Beijing government, I would like to suggest here, has been facilitated by the new discourse on the Chinese diaspora which, in reifying Chineseness, has created fertile grounds for nourishing a new racism. The idea of diaspora is responsible in the first place for abolishing the difference between Chinese Americans and Chinese elsewhere (including in China). In response to a legacy of discrimination against Chinese Americans, which made them hesitant even to acknowledge their ties to China and other Chinese, some Chinese Americans and their sympathizers have been all too anxious to reaffirm such ties, in turn suppressing the cultural differences arising from the different historical trajectories of different Chinese populations scattered around the world. The anti-assimilationist mood (expressed most fervently in liberal "multiculturalism") itself has contributed in no small measure to such cultural reification by a metonymic reduction of the culture of the Other to "representative" ethnographic elements or texts divorced from all social and historical context that may then serve purposes of self-representation by the diasporic population or self-congratulatory consumption in the carnivals of the society at large. While in much of contemporary diaspora discourse the preferred term for representing difference is *culture*, the question of culture, to quote Gilroy, is "almost biologized by its proximity to 'race'" (1996, 263). *Because* of the fact that the very phenomenon of diaspora has produced a multiplicity of Chinese cultures, the affirmation of "Chineseness" may be sustained only by recourse to a common origin or descent that persists in spite of widely different historical trajectories, which results in the elevation of ethnicity and race over all of the other factors—often divisive—that have gone into the shaping of Chinese populations and their cultures. Diasporic identity in its reification does not overcome the racial prejudices of earlier assumptions of national cultural homogeneity but in many ways follows a similar logic, now at the level not of nations but of off-ground "transnations." The "children of the Yellow Emperor" may be all the more a racial category for having abandoned their ties to the political category of the nation.

Let me clarify here. In taking a critical stance toward the notion of diaspora, I am not suggesting that Chinese Americans should therefore renounce ties to China or other Chinese Overseas. The question is how these ties are conceived and articulated and whether or not they erase significant historical differences among the Chinese populations in different locations around the globe. I will illustrate again by reference to the John Huang case. An important part was played in publicizing the case by Professor Ling-ch'i Wang of the University of California, Berkeley, who alerted and informed many of us by gathering and electronically disseminating information on the case. Over the past year, Professor Wang's communications have ranged widely from the John Huang case to the election of Chinese officials around the country, from defense of the People's Republic of China against various allegations to reportage on anti-Chinese activity in Southeast Asia. Now a discursive field that covers all of these elements appears at first sight to differ little from what I have been calling diaspora discourse, motivated as it is by bringing together information on Chinese, regardless of place. What disrupts this field, however, is its unwavering focus on concrete problems of its immediate environment. Professor Wang was quick from the beginning to distance Asian Americans from "foreign money," drawing a national boundary between Chinese here and Chinese donors of campaign funds from Southeast Asia (Wang 1997, 7). The communications throughout have stressed issues of class and community, distinguishing community interests of Chinese Americans from the activities of transnationally oriented diasporic Chinese with economic and political interests of their own, and this electronic discourse has remained focused throughout on the issue of campaign finance reform in the United States, as campaign corruption rather than the color of money has been defined as the basic problem. In other words, the discourse, while ranging transnationally, has been quite grounded in its immediate environment. This, I think, is what distinguishes it from the diaspora discourse the way I understand that term here.

I will return to this issue of "groundedness" below. First, I will take a brief look at two products of this diasporic discourse in the realm of culture that are on the surface quite antithetical but may also reinforce one another in surprising ways: the reification of Chineseness by erasure of the boundaries among different Chinese populations, and the contrary move to break down such reification through the notion of hybridity.

In its failure to specify its own location vis-à-vis the hegemonic, self-serving, and often financially lucrative reification of "Chineseness" in the political economy of transnationalism, critical diaspora discourse itself has fallen prey to the manipulation and commodification made possible by cultural reification, and it contributes to the foregrounding of ethnicity and race in contemporary political and cultural thinking. There has been a tendency in recent scholarship, the publication industry, the arts, and literature, for instance, to abolish the difference between Asians and Asian Americans. In scholarship, contrary to an earlier refusal of Asian studies specialists to have anything to do with Asian American studies, there have been calls recently to integrate Asian American studies into Asian studies, which partly reflects the increased prominence of trans-Pacific population flows but also suggests the increasingly lucrative promise of reorienting Asian American studies in that direction. Publishers' catalogues, especially those devoted to "multiculturalism" and ethnic relations, freely blend Asian with Asian American themes, and it is not rare to see these days a catalogue in which *The Woman Warrior* is placed right next to *The Dream of the Red Chamber*. A film series on "Asian American Film" at the University of North Carolina mysteriously includes many more films from Asia than from Asian America, either due to the imaginary China of its China specialist organizer or to increase the appeal of the series, which may not matter much as the ideological effect is the same.

Moreover, and more fundamentally, within the context of flourishing Pacific economies (at least until very recently), some Asian Americans—most notably Chinese Americans—have been assigned the role of "bridges" to Asia, a role they have assumed readily for its lucrative promises. The metaphor of "bridge" as a depiction of Asian Americans is not quite novel. In a recent dissertation that analyzes with sensitivity Asian Americans' relationship to the Chicago School of Sociology, Henry Yu argues that in their association with the Chicago sociologists, second-generation Asian Americans internalized an image of themselves as "bridges" between American society and societies of origin in Asia, advantageously placed to serve as cultural interpreters (1995, 162–89). The advantage, however, came at a heavy price. The condition for successful service as "bridges" between cultures was marginality; it was their status as "marginal men" who existed between two societies without belonging fully to either that enabled the status of cultural interpreter. As one such "marginal man," Kazuo Kawai, wrote: "My decision to be an interpreter has improved my relations with both races. I am happy because I don't try to be a poor imitation of an American. I am happy because I don't vainly try to be a poor imitation of a genuine Japanese. I am simply what I am. I don't try to imitate either, so I am never disappointed when I find myself excluded from either side" (quoted in Yu 1995, 184).

Kawai, of course, was not qualified to be a cultural "interpreter" in any serious sense of the term. He was American by birth and culture, and his claims to access to Japanese culture were forced on him by alienation from American society, which excluded him, necessitating an imaginary affinity with his parents' society of origin. The notion that someone who did not belong to either society was for that very reason qualified to serve as cultural interpreter between the two glossed over fundamental problems of cultural orientation—which seems to have escaped both Kawai and his Chicago School of Sociology mentors. Be that as it may, what is important here is that the metaphor of "bridge" between two societies was ultimately a product of alienation from a society that refused to recognize him as anything but a foreigner.

While the latter may not be the case in any obvious way at the present time, the metaphor of the bridge nevertheless continues to invoke the foreignness of Asian Americans. Much more so than in the case of those like Kawai, a diasporic identification may be a matter of choice rather than necessity. Contemporary "bridges," moreover, are most prominently economic brokers rather than cultural interpreters. Nevertheless, there is a racialization at work when diasporic populations, regardless of their widely different cultural trajectories internally, are expected to bridge the gap between places of arrival and places of origin by presumed cultural legacies that are more imagined than real. Thus Ronnie C. Chan, chairman of the Hang Lung Development Group, a Hong Kong real estate company, in an article entitled "Entrepreneur Applauds U.S. Money Move," published in the *Hawaii Tribune-Herald* (June 18, 1998), urges Chinese Americans in Hawaii to become "bi-cultural" so as to serve as bridges between Chinese and U.S. business, telling them that, "We all need our cultural roots, but put them away for a while and become truly bi-cultural" (1, 10). Roots in this case take precedence over history, so Chan urges Chinese Americans not to learn to be Chinese again but to learn to be American!

The economic emergence of Chinese populations across the Pacific may be the single most important factor in the cultural rehomogenization of Chineseness. The most significant by-product of this economic emergence may be the recent Confucian revival, which attributes the economic success of Chinese (in some versions, also of Japanese and Koreans), without regard to time or place, to the persistence of "Confucian values," which were viewed earlier as obstacles to capitalism but have been rendered now into the source of everything from economic development to the production of "model minorities." As I have discussed this problem extensively elsewhere, I will simply note here that this so-called Confucian revival reproduces within a context of transnationality the most egregious prejudices of Orientalism (Dirlik 1995). It also is a transnational product itself, for its emergence in the late 1970s and early 1980s involved, at least by intertextual collusion, experts on Chinese philosophy, U.S. futurologists, and authoritarian regimes in East and Southeast Asia. According to its more enthusiastic proponents, Confucian values of thrift, diligence, educational achievement, family loyalty, discipline, harmony, and obedience to authority—a list that reads like a dream list of the ideal worker or employee—have been responsible for the unquestioning commitment of Chinese (and East Asian) populations to capitalist development. In the more socially based versions of the argument, Confucian values owe their persistence to the central importance throughout Chinese societies of kinship and pseudo-kinship ties, themselves products of the social diffusion of Confucian values: the networks of *guanxi* that distinguish the socially oriented capitalism of the Chinese from individualistic and conflict-ridden "Western" capitalism. As with the Confucian argument, there is little sense of time and place in these social arguments, as though social relations and networks were not subject to change and fluctuation. The net result is a portrayal of Chinese where, networked through *guanxi* and driven by Confucianism, Chinese around the world are rendered into a "tribe," in the words of Pacific visionary Joel Kotkin, committed to a relentless search for wealth. These same networks, needless to say, make Chinese into ideal "bridges" with Asia.

Some of this argumentation, where it is promoted by Chinese scholars or leaders, no doubt draws upon a newfound sense of economic power and presence to reassert a Chinese identity, against the century-old cultural hegemony of Eurocentrism, which utilizes earlier Orientalist representations to turn them against claims of Euro-American superiority. Nevertheless, they have been attached most prominently to questions of economic success, with a consequent commodification not only of the so-called Confucian values but of Chinese as well. To quote from a recent piece by Kotkin, "With their cultural, linguistic, and family ties to China, Chinese-American entrepreneurs like [Henry Y.] Hwang are proving to be America's secret weapon in recapturing a predominant economic role in the world's most populous nation" (1996, 25). Never mind the problematic question of "cultural and linguistic ties to China" on the part of many Chinese Americans; it may not be very far from Kotkin's portrayal of Chinese Americans as

American economic moles in China to William Safire's depiction of John Huang as a Chinese political mole in Washington, D.C.

The attitudes that lie at the root of these recent tendencies are not less productive of racism for being produced by or sympathetic to Chinese and other Asian populations. They also are quite unstable, in that the sympathy itself may be subject to significant fluctuation, on occasion even turning into its opposite. This has happened to some extent with the recent so-called economic meltdown in Asia, with which "Asian values," among them Confucianism, once again lost their luster. It turns out now that "Asian values" have been responsible for creating a corrupt "crony capitalism" that inevitably led to economic breakdown.

Chinese populations are no less divided by class, gender, ethnic, and place differences than other populations. Not the least among those differences are differences of place and history. Reification of diaspora erases, or at least blurs, such differences. As Arjun Appadurai has written of "ethnoscapes,"

> the central paradox of ethnic politics in today's world is that primordia (whether of language or skin color or neighborhood or kinship) have become globalized. That is, sentiments whose greatest force is their ability to ignite intimacy into a political sentiment and turn locality into a staging ground for identity, have become spread over vast and irregular spaces as groups move, yet stay linked to one another through sophisticated media capabilities. This is not to deny that such primordia are often the product of invented traditions or retrospective affiliations, but to emphasize that because of the disjunctive and unstable interaction of commerce, media, national policies and consumer fantasies, ethnicity, once a genie contained in the bottle of some sort of locality (however large), has now become a global force. (1990, 15)

While the globalization of ethnicity is no doubt bound up with abstract forces that contribute to global restructurations, it is important nevertheless to draw attention to agencies engaged actively in inventing traditions and producing retrospective affiliations. If differences of history and place are erased by the shifting of attention to a general category of diaspora (which I take to be equivalent to Appadurai's "ethnoscapes"), it is necessary to raise the question of whom such erasure serves. There is no reason to suppose that the government in Beijing (or, for that matter, Taiwan) is any more reluctant than the government in Washington, D.C., or U.S. transnational corporations to use diasporic Chinese for its own purposes. On the other hand, both from a political and an economic perspective, some diasporic Chinese obviously are of greater use than others, and in turn they benefit from the erasure of differences among Chinese, which enables them to speak for all Chinese.[5] Reconceptualization of Chinese populations in terms of diasporas, in other words, serves economic and political class interests (it is not accidental that Chinese American John Huang was connected to the Riady family, which made him useful in a number of ways).

The concept of hybridity is intended to destabilize cultural identities of all kinds and, at least on the surface, it provides a clear alternative to the reification of identity described above. Popularized through the works of influential theorists such as Stuart Hall, Paul Gilroy, Homi Bhabha, and Edward Soja, among others, hybridity is an important keyword of contemporary cultural studies. Judging by the pervasiveness of the term in discussions of identity, hybridity also has come to define the self-identification of intellectuals around the world, in effect becoming a social force of sorts. In the field of Asian American studies, Lisa Lowe (1991), through an influential article, has been a prominent proponent. Hybridity, too, has a lineage in its application to Asian Americans, which may not be very surprising given its kinship with marginality. While some Asian Americans may have found a resource for hope in their marginality or hybridity, others viewed it as a desirable condition to be overcome. Rose Hum Lee, another product of the Chicago School of Sociology, observed in a discussion of the "marginal man" that "when the 'cultural gaps' are closed . . . the cultural hybrid no longer poses a problem to himself and others. This is brought about by the processes of acculturation and assimilation" (quoted in Yu 1995, 229).[6]

The contemporary idea of hybridity is in a basic way quite the opposite of what Rose Hum Lee had in mind. Hybridity (along with associated terms such as "in-betweenness" and "thirdspace") is intended to challenge the homogenization and essentialization of cultural identity—most importantly in the present context, ethnic, national and racial identity (it also has been influential in discussions of gender and class identity, especially the former). Its goal is to undermine the assumption that boundaries may be drawn around nationality, ethnicity, and race on the grounds of cultural homogeneity. What marks it as diasporic is that the argument is directed not only against the society of arrival, where the dominant culture demands assimilation of the migrant for full political and cultural citizenship, but also against the society of origin, which likewise denies political and cultural citizenship to the migrant on the grounds that emigration is inevitably accompanied by distancing and degeneration from the culture of origin. Thus placed at the margins of two societies, the migrant is denied cultural identity and autonomy. Hybridity in contemporary culture is in a fundamental sense a rebellion of those who are culturally dispossessed, or feel culturally dispossessed, who not only assert hybridity as an autonomous source of identity but go further to challenge the cultural claims of the centers of power.

There is, no doubt, much that is radical in the challenge, and it is not difficult to see why the notion of hybridity should be appealing at a time of proliferation of the culturally dispossessed. Hybridity is appealing for a different, more intellectual reason. Its breakdown not just of political and cultural entities but also of the categories of social and cultural analysis releases the imagination to conceive the world in new ways. This has been most persuasively argued recently by Edward Soja (1996), who locates "thirdspace" not just between societies, but between society and imagination, where the imaginary may claim as much reality as the real of conventional social science.

Why, then, should hybridity also be a deeply problematic concept, especially in its social and political implications, and how could it reinforce the reification of identity when its intention is exactly the opposite? It is problematic, I think, because in its vagueness it is available for appropriation for diverse causes, including highly reactionary and exploitative ones. It reinforces the reification of identity, not only because the metaphor of hybridity invokes the possibility of uncontaminated identities but also because such identities are essential to the discourse on hybridity as its dialogical Other. The discourse of hybridity is a response to racial, ethnic, and national divisions but is sustained in turn by foregrounding race, ethnicity, and nation in problems of culture and politics.

Apparently transparent, hybridity is in actuality quite an elusive concept that does not illuminate but rather renders invisible the situations to which it is applied—not by concealing them but by blurring distinctions among widely different situations. Pnina Werbner (1997a) has observed as a "paradox" of the fascination with hybridity that it "is celebrated as powerfully interruptive and yet theorized as commonplace and pervasive" (1). If hybridity is indeed pervasive, it is in and of itself meaningless—if everything is hybrid, then there is no need for a special category of hybrid—and can derive meaning only from the concrete historical and structural locations that produce it. While some theorists of hybridity, such as Paul Gilroy, Stuart Hall, and Gayatri Spivak, have been attentive to distinguishing hybridities historically and structurally, others, such as Homi Bhabha and Edward Soja, have rendered hybridity (and its associated concepts of "thirdspace" and "in-betweenness") into abstractions with no identifiable locations. It is my impression that in recent years the use of the concept has unfolded in the latter direction, as hybridity has been universalized in its application, to be rendered into a "universal standardization," as Feroza Jussawalla (1997) puts it—gaining in abstraction, but progressively deprived of meaning (20–21).[7] The "off-grounding" of hybridity no doubt derives additional force from the postmodern, especially the postcolonial, suspicion of history and structures; the demand to historicize hybridity appears, from this perspective, to imprison the concept within the very categorical prejudices that it is intended to overcome.

This may indeed be the case. After all, theorists such as Bhabha and Soja do not intend hybridity or thirdspace in a physical, descriptive sense but rather to disrupt the hegemony of social and historical categories and to overcome binary modes of thinking. On the other hand, there is an elision in almost all discussion of hybridity between hybridity as a strategically disruptive idea, operating at the level of epistemology, and hybridity as an articulation of an actual human condition. It is this elision that may account for the elusiveness and opaqueness of the term. Thus Katharyne Mitchell is quite correct, I think, to inquire of Bhabha's boundary crossings, "what are the actual physical spaces in which these boundaries are crossed and erased?" or to point out with regard to Soja's liberating claims for "thirdspace" that "this space is able to accomplish all these marvelous things, precisely because it does not exist" (1997, 537; 534n.) As I noted above, hybridity no longer appears as an intellectual or a psychological stratagem but seems to be pervasive in certain quarters, mostly among intellectuals, as a self-definition, which makes it into a social and an ideological force. What is not clear is whether the hybrid is "everyman" (what Werbner observes to be the commonplaceness of hybridity) or "nowhereman" (the stranger, as Bauman [1997] puts it, who disrupts the existing order of things). The confounding of the two has led to a situation where the promotion of hybridity, out of political correctness or universal standardization, has taken the form of an intellectual and ethical imperative that will brook no alternative, as when Iain Chambers states that, "We are drawn beyond ideas of nation, nationalism and national cultures, into a post-colonial set of realities, and a mode of critical thinking that is forced to rewrite the very grammar and language of modern thought in directing attention beyond the patriarchal boundaries of Eurocentric concerns and its presumptive 'universalism'" (Chambers 1994, 77, quoted in Friedman 1997, 77). Hybridity is no longer disruptive or just descriptive, but prescriptive; if you are not hybrid, you are a Eurocentric patriarch!

Hybridity, abstracted from its social-historical moorings for critical purposes but then returned to society as an abstraction, most importantly blurs, in the name of difference, significant distinctions between different differences. Hybridity reduces all complexity to a "statement of mixture" (Friedman 1997, 87), as though the specific character of what is being mixed (from class to gender to ethnicity and race) did not matter—partly stemming from its originary assumptions that all "binarisms" are equally undesirable, regardless of context. It also reads into all mixtures a state of hybridity, disregarding the possibility that mixtures and hybridization may produce new identities. As Jussawalla puts it, "despite mixing and merging, like a martini in a cocktail shaker, the [South Asian] writers do not become hybrids or 'mongrels,' and we do not need a median point along the 'scale' or 'cline' of authenticity to alienation indicating 'hybridity'" (1997, 26). Indeed, hybridity in its abstraction serves not to illuminate but to disguise social inequality and exploitation, by reducing to a state of hybridity all who may be considered "marginal," covering up the fact that there is a great deal of difference between different marginalities: between, say, a well-placed social elite hybridized and marginalized ethnically and members of the same ethnicity further incapacitated by their class and gender locations. We have had a good illustration of this only recently, in the flare-up of anti-Chinese violence in Indonesia, which the ordinary Chinese have to deal with as best they can, while the wealthy Chinese plan refuge in Western Australia in the same spaces occupied by Indonesian generals![8] Given such inequality, the claims to undifferentiated marginality and hybridity on the part of the elite confound the culturally dispossessed with the culturally privileged, who travel with ease across cultural spaces. The result is the appropriation by the elite of the margins, making hybridity available as a tool in intra-elite competition but further erasing the concerns of the truly marginal. As Friedman puts it,

> hybrids and hybridisation theorists are products of a group that self-identifies and/or identifies the world in such terms, not as a result of ethnographic understanding, but as an act of self-defini-

tion—indeed, of self-essentializing—which becomes definition for others via the forces of socialisation inherent in the structures of power that such groups occupy: intellectuals close to the media; the media intelligentsia itself; in a certain sense, all those who can afford a cosmopolitan identity. (1997, 81)

The "unmooring" (in Mitchell's term) of hybridity from concrete social-historical referents also invites by the back door the very cultural essentializations that it has been intended to overcome, which is the second problem with hybridity. While it may be possible to speak of the hybridization of hybridity, as I will suggest below, most writing on hybridity ignores this possibility, perhaps because the acknowledgment of hybridity as a perennial condition would weaken considerably or even render irrelevant the claims made for hybridity, which is the paradox posed by Werbner. As a result, the discourse of hybridity is sustained by a tacit premise, reinforced by its claims to offer a radical alternative, of the purity of hybridity's constituent moments. "Hybridity," Friedman states, "is founded on the metaphor of purity" (ibid., 82–83). Referring specifically to Bhabha's use of hybridity, Nira Yuval-Davis writes that "it may interpolate essentialism through the back door—that the old 'multiculturalist' essentialist and homogenising constructions of collectivities are attributed to the homogeneous collectivities from which the 'hybrids' have emerged, thus replacing the mythical image of a society as a 'melting-pot' with the mythical image of society as a 'mixed salad'" (1997, 202). Hybridity taken out of history also dehistoricizes the identities that constitute hybridity which, if it does not necessarily rest on an assumption of purity, nevertheless leaves unquestioned what these identities might be.

The biological associations of the term contribute further to this underlining of an assumption if not of purity then at least of clearly identifiable entities that go into the making of hybridity; to offer an analogy that I have utilized elsewhere, the hybrid nectarine is constituted out of a peach and an apple, both of which have clear identities, whatever their levels of purity (and it may be instructive to reflect that the hybrid nectarine also has a clear identity!). In fact, the biological notion of hybridity, on the basis of clearly definable identities, even renders hybridity quantifiable, which is quite visible in the human realm in the prolific racial categories employed in nineteenth-century Latin America, still alive in the United States in the "blood quantum" used to define the authenticity of Amerindians.[9] While such quantification would be difficult to transfer to the realm of culture, it does point to serious questions that are elided in discussions of hybridity, chief among them degrees of hybridity: are all hybrids equally hybrid? There are other questions as well. Robert Young (1995) has documented the historical centrality of biological assumptions in the conceptualization of hybridity, which persist in contemporary usages of hybridity, if only as traces and inescapable reminders of the biological associations of the term, as with the author who remarked to Jussawalla that "hybridity smacks of biological blending of plants" (Jussawalla 1997, 34). While it is not my intention in the slightest to ascribe a racial intention to those who speak of cultural hybridity, it is nevertheless unavoidable that the use of a biological term as a metaphor for culture and society is pregnant with the possibility of confounding cultural, social, and political with racial entities—especially where the term is divorced from its historical and structural referents. Such is the case, I suggested above, with the reified concept of diaspora, where discussions of culture slip easily into identification by descent.

While hybridity could easily refer to "in-betweens" other than national, ethnic, or racial "in-betweens," such as the "in-betweens" of class and gender, it is remarkable that most discussions of hybridity revolve around the former categories. The mutual articulation of categories of gender, class, and race has been present all along as a basic concern in recent discussions of hybridity;[10] it is amazing nevertheless that questions of race and ethnicity—often conflated—overshadow all others. This may or may not be a consequence of the logic of hybridity as biological concept. I am inclined to think, however, that the discourse on hybridity, while it may refuse to engage the limitations of its historical and social context, is itself subject to the forces of that context. Within a social and historical context where identity claims are very much alive and proliferating, the condition of hybridity itself is quite unstable. The benign reading of hybridity perceives in such instability the possibility of opening up to the world. That may well be the case, but it is staked too much on a libertarian faith in the autonomy of the hybrid self, which can negotiate its identity at will in a marketplace of equals, as it were. There is another possibility as well: oscillation between the identities out of which hybridity is constructed and fragmentation into one or another of those identities in response to the pressures of everyday life. How else to explain the simultaneous breakdown and proliferation of identities in the contemporary world? There are also the personal stakes involved. It is worth pondering Jussawalla's observation, which may be familiar from the everyday circumstances of cultural encounters even within academia, "that true hybridity cannot be achieved because those who would most speak for hybridity most want to retain their essentialisms—the natives, the insiders of cultural studies, those who feel they best represent the post-modern condition and can speak for it" (1997, 35). Hybridity may be like interdisciplinarity in academia, which everyone lauds but no one really wants, not unless it can be shaped according to their disciplinary orientations. It often is difficult to avoid the impression that, more often than not, the motivation underlying the promotion of hybridity is to center the marginal and render visible cultural identities that have been rendered invisible by coercive or hegemonic suppression. The quite apparent predicament here is how to achieve this quite significant and worthwhile goal without slippage into the reification of the marginalized, as in the case of the diasporic identity I discussed above: to achieve genuine dialogue rather than merely assert one "essentialism" against another—especially under circumstances of unequal power.

With so much uncertainty over the content of the concept, it is not surprising that the political implications of hybridity in action should be equally indeterminate, or that hybridity should lend itself to a variety of politics, ranging from the radical to the reactionary. Hybridity in and of itself is not a marker of any kind of politics but a deconstructive strategy that may be utilized for different political ends. To a bell hooks, Stuart Hall, Homi Bhabha, or Edward Soja, hybridity may be a significant means to create new kinds of radical political alliances by opening up and articulating to one another categories of race, class, and gender. To a John Huang, or to the Hong Kong investors in Vancouver of whom Mitchell writes, hybridity is a means to creating alliances ("bridges") between different states or national and diasporic capital, the consequence if not the intention of which is to erase those radical alliances. As Mitchell writes,

> The overuse of abstract metaphors, particularly within frameworks which foreground psychoanalytic approaches, often leads to thorny problems of fetishization. As concepts such as hybridity become disarticulated from the historically shaped political and economic relations in which identities and narratives of nation unfold, they take on a life and trajectory of their own making. Second and third readings, borrowings, interventions, elaborations—all can contribute to conceptualizations that are not only removed from the social relations of everyday life, but which also, because of this very abstraction, become ripe for appropriation. The disingenuous move of the

"third space" is to occupy a position "beyond" space and time, and beyond the situated practices of place and the lived experience of history. The space thus satisfyingly transcends the kind of essential-izing locations that characterize a certain branch of work in histor-ical materialism and feminism. But without context, this "in-between" space risks becoming a mobile reactionary space, rather than a traveling site of resistance. (1997, 534)

Abstraction is one problem, as in its very divorce from its own social and historical locations, hybridity conceals and contains the dif-ferential relationship to power of different hybrids, making the concept available for appropriation by those whose goals are not to promote alternatives to the present but rather to gain entry into existing spaces of power, further consolidating its domination. What Peter McLaren and Henry Giroux write about postmodern and postcolonial preoccupation with language also applies, I think, to hybridity as discursive liberation:

As essential as these theoretical forays have been, they often abuse their own insights by focusing on identity at the expense of power. Language in these texts becomes a discursive marker for registering and affirming difference but in doing so often fails to address how they are related within broader networks of domination and exploitation. In part, this may be due to the ahistorical quality of this work. Lacking a historical context, they fail to engage the polit-ical projects that characterized older versions of critical pedagogy and end up failing to locate their own politics and its value for larger social, political, and pedagogical struggles. (1997, 17)

To engage those political projects, it is necessary, I think, to over-come the anxiety that seems to legitimize an unquestioning commitment to hybridity—anxiety over what Werbner describes as "the bogey word of the human sciences": essentialism (1997b, 226). Essentialism is surely one of the most inflated words of contemporary cultural studies. It seems as though any admission of identity, including the identity that may be necessary to any articulate form of collective political action, is open to charges of essentialism, so that it often is unclear whether the objection is to essentialism per se or to the politics, in which case essen-tialism serves as a straw target to discredit the politics.[11] In its extremist logic, such suspicion of "essentialism" may be resolved only at the level of a libertarian individualism, if even that, since the run-of-the-mill lib-ertarianism also "essentializes" the subject. Notions of hybridity informed by such extremism rule out any kind of serious radical politics, which requires at least some assumption of commonality, what Gayatri Spivak has described by compromise as "strategic essentialism." As bell hooks has written,

> One exciting dimension to cultural studies is the critique of essentialist notions of difference. Yet this critique should not become a means to dismiss differences or an excuse for ignoring the authority of experience. It is often evoked in a manner which suggests that all the ways black people think of ourselves as "different" from whites are really essentialist, and therefore without concrete grounding. This way of thinking threatens the very foundations that make resistance to domination possible.[12]

While an anti-essentialist hybridity at its extreme undercuts the possibility of "resistance to domination," no less important is its failure to come to terms with the world as it is, so as to confront its very real challenges. As a commitment to hybridity takes hold of intellectuals, the world at large currently is experiencing a proliferation of identity claims, often in the most obscurantist, essentialist guise. It will not do to dismiss this historical phenomenon as an aberration, as some kind of deviation from normalcy as stipulated by the principles of hybridity, which not only reifies hybridity contrary to its claims to open-endedness but also shows how much the contemporary discourse of intellectuals may be in need of a reality check. What needs urgent confrontation is whether or not hybridity and essentialism generate one another.

I will conclude this discussion of hybridity by returning to the paradox posed by Werbner: if hybridity is indeed a condition of everyday life, what is radical about it? One possible answer has been suggested by Robert Young in his invocation of Bakhtin's idea of hybridity in the novel (1995, 20–22). According to Young, Bakhtin's idea of hybridity was itself hybrid. Bakhtin referred to two kinds of hybridity: unconscious "organic hybridity" and "intentional hybridity." As Bakhtin put it:

> Unintentional, unconscious hybridization is one of the most important modes in the historical life and evolution of all languages. We may even say that language and languages change historically primarily by hybridization, by means of a mixing of various "languages" co-existing within the boundaries of a single dialect, a single national language, a single branch, a single group of different branches, in the historical as well as paleontological past of languages. (Bakhtin 1981, 358–59, quoted in Young 1995, 21)

On the other hand,

> The image of a language conceived as an intentional hybrid is first of all a *conscious* hybrid (as distinct from a historical, organic, obscure language hybrid); an intentional hybrid is precisely the perception of one language by another language, its illumination by another linguistic consciousness. . . . What is more, an intentional and conscious hybrid is not a mixture of two *impersonal* language consciousnesses (the correlates of two languages) but rather a mixture of two *individualized* language consciousnesses (the correlates of two specific utterances, not merely two languages) and two individual language-intentions as well. . . . In other words, the novelistic hybrid is not only double-voiced and double-accented . . . but is also double-languaged; for in it there are not only . . . two individual consciousnesses, two voices, two accents, as there are two socio-linguistic consciousnesses, two epochs, that, true, are not here unconsciously mixed (as in organic hybrid) but that come together and fight it out on the territory of the utterance. (Bakhtin 1981, 359–60)

Bakhtin, Young observes, "is more concerned with a hybridity that has been politicized and made contestatory" rather than hybridity that "remains mute and opaque," for the former is by far the more radical in its consequences (1995, 21). Young continues, "Bakhtin's doubled form of hybridity therefore offers a particularly significant model for cultural interaction: an organic hybridity, which will tend towards fusion, in conflict with intentional hybridity, which enables a contestatory activity, a politicized setting of cultural differences against each other dialogically" (ibid., 22).

If I may revise the vocabulary slightly, it seems to me that "organic hybridity" refers to what we might otherwise call historicity: that language or, in our case, cultural identity, in its historical progress is subject to transformation in the course of daily encounters with different consciousnesses, so that it becomes impossible to speak of a pure, self-enclosed consciousness traveling through time and space untouched by its many encounters. The transformations are moreover unarticulated, but concrete and specific. Intentional hybridity, on the other hand, is self-conscious and contestatory; it brings out into the open the encounters that remain unarticulated in organic hybridity and confronts them as structural contradictions. It is radical, because this very revelation of everyday encounters as contradictions may bring to the surface the relations of inequality and hegemony in everyday life, demanding some kind of resolution.

While this opposition may help explain why hybridity may be both pervasive and radical, it raises other questions. If hybridity is a condition of history, why does it remain silent most of the time while finding a voice at other times? The question is easier posed than answered, but it seems to me that the articulation as structural opposition of what is lived ordinarily as a condition of life suggests at the least that some sense of empowerment is necessary to even risk the articulation. This may be as much the case with the assertion of cultural hybridity as with class, gender, and ethnic structurations of everyday life.

The thornier and more immediate question is whether or not, having found expression in the recognition of structural contradictions, it is possible to resolve those contradictions to return cultural identity to its historicity. The question is crucial, I think. In his reading of Bakhtin, Young tends to overemphasize the conflictual nature of intentional hybridity. While endless contestation and conflict may have a place in the novel or in academia (which I also doubt), it is hardly a desirable condition of everyday life, which requires some coherence and unity.

Intentional hybridity is important to Bakhtin in challenging the hegemony of a single voice, but equally important, I think, is Bakhtin's stress on the illumination of one consciousness by another, which unites the contestants in their very contest, in a "unity of opposites"—reminiscent readily of the dialectical notion of "contradiction," which in many ways is preferable over the term *hybridity* itself, because it allows for the same open-endedness as hybridity while remaining attentive to questions of historicity and concreteness. While intentional hybridity interpreted as conflict may be radical for revealing the inequalities and hegemonies imbedded in everyday life, it also fragments—not just collectivities, but "the dialogical self" itself.

I borrow the latter term from Hubert Hermans and Harry Kempen, who apply Bakhtin's ideas to the study of individual psychology. The authors caution against the confounding of the "multiplicity of characters" implicit in the idea of the dialogical self with the pathological state of "multiple personality." The difference lies in the ability of the "multiplicity of characters" to engage in a dialogue rather than to speak sequentially, one at a time, unaware of the existence of other characters, as in the case of "multiple personality" (1993, 89). The goal of the dialogue is to synthesize the self, "to create a field in which the different characters form a community" (ibid., 93). This mental community, moreover, resonates with the social context of the individual:

> The inside and the outside world function as highly open Systems that have intense transactional relationships. The self, as a highly contextual phenomenon, is bound to cultural and institutional constraints. Dominance relations are not only present in the outside world but, by the intensive transactions between the two, organize also the inside world . . . the possible array of imaginal positions becomes not only organized but also restricted by the process of institutionalization . . . some positions are strongly developed, whereas others are suppressed or even disassociated. (ibid., 78)

The synthesizing activity takes place in a definite social context, which has a strong presence in the nature of the synthesis achieved. The inquiry into the hybrid or the dialogical self returns us to the social context of the self without reducing it to the former but underlining nevertheless the crucial importance of concrete circumstances in the shaping of subjectivity. One implication is that even intentional hybridity as a form of subjectivity is subject to organization: a return to the historicity of organic hybridity.

Returning from the self to the collectivity, we may well inquire where this synthesis, this re-historicization of hybridity, may be achieved most effectively without abandoning the self-consciousness necessary to the nonhegemonic cultural identity, and how. Other questions follow inevitably: most crucial among them, the kind of histories that could accommodate the new consciousness, and the kind of social transformation and political projects that might produce such histories.

Diasporas do not provide an answer. While the diasporic imaginary is obviously capable of disrupting a world conceived in terms of nations as homogeneous entities or even transgressing against the borders of nation-states, diasporas themselves may serve as sources of new identities in only the most off-ground, reified sense. Diasporic consciousness has no history; indeed, its claims may be sustained only in negation of history and historicity. This consciousness, whether in its homogenizing or hybrid form, may serve the purpose of cultural projects of various kinds; it is much more difficult to imagine what progressive political projects it might produce—unless it is qualified with a consciousness of place.

Criticism of diasporic consciousness need not imply an urge to return to the nation with its colonial, homogenizing, and assimilationist ideology. While recent critiques of the nation have introduced new insights, they often fail to address the question of who stands to benefit

the most from the erasure of national boundaries. Whatever its colonizing tendencies may be, the nation is still capable, properly controlled
from below, to offer protection to those within its boundaries.[13] It is not
very surprising, therefore, that those Chinese Americans devoted to
social issues and community building should be suspicious of the claims
of diasporas or the questioning of national boundaries. In this case, too,
place consciousness is a fundamental issue, for it leads to a different conception of the nation: bottom up rather than top down.[14]

To raise the question of places is to raise the issue of difference on
a whole range of fronts, including those of class, gender, and ethnicity.
It also is to raise the question of history in identity. Identity is no less an
identity for being historical (is there any other kind?). Contrary to a
hegemonic cultural reification or a whimpering preoccupation with the
location of "home," both of which seem to have acquired popularity as
alternative expressions of diasporic consciousness, what is important is
to enable people to feel at home where they live.[15] This does not require
that people abandon their legacies, only that they recognize the historicity of their cultural identities and that those identities are subject to
change in the course of historical encounters. In the words of the Indian
writer, Farrukh Dhondy, "what makes people is not their genes, is not
their nostalgia, it's their interactions of daily existence" (quoted in Jussawalla 1997, 32).

The historicity of identity is by no means transparent, since history
itself makes sense in terms of its social locations. One of the prominent
phenomena of our times is the fragmentation of history into a number
of seemingly irreconcilable spaces, most importantly ethnic spaces. The
proliferation of histories without any apparent connections to one
another, or that consciously repudiate such connections, has led to the
substitution for history of heritage, as David Lowenthal (1995) puts it,
or more pessimistically, a condition of "schizophrenic nominalism," in
Fredric Jameson's (1991) words, that has deprived history of all temporal and spatial meaning.[16]

Such negative evaluations stem at least partially from the breakdown
of a Eurocentric temporality that provided coherence, but only at the cost
of repressing histories other than its own. The breakdown of history may
be viewed, from a less pessimistic perspective, as the assault on a hegemonic history of the previously repressed, who have now returned to visibility to demand a presence for themselves. The challenge is how to create new unities out of this fragmentation, which may be a precondition for
achieving a more democratic unity to transcend an earlier illusion of unity

that could be sustained only through a hegemonic history. A further and crucial question is where to locate this new history or histories. The effort, no doubt, has to proceed at more than one location, but one location that is indispensable, I think, is places.

Diasporas are dispersals from some remembered homeland, from some concrete place, which after the fact is conceived in terms of the nation (at least over the last century), although concrete places of origin retain their visibility even in their incorporation into the language of the nation or of diaspora. The dispersed also land in concrete places in the host society, which also is captured in national terms, even if the very fact of diaspora, if nothing else, disturbs efforts to define nation and national culture. Ling-ch'i Wang tells us that one Chinese metaphor for the diasporic condition is "growing roots where landed" (*luodi shenggen*) (1991, 199–200). While a prejudice for the nation makes it possible to speak of "national soil" and demands assimilation to some "national culture," rootedness as a metaphor points inevitably to concrete places that belie easy assumptions of the homogeneity of national soil or culture. Kathleen Neils Conzen writes of German immigrants to the United States that

> as change occurred, it could proceed without the kinds of qualitative shifts implied by the familiar notions of acculturation and assimilation. Culture was more strongly localized—naturalized in the literal botanical sense of the term—than it was ethnicized, and the structures of everyday life, rather than being assimilated to those of some broader element within American society, responded to the transforming pressures of modern life on a parallel trajectory of their own. (1990, 9)

The statement points to both the concrete place-basedness and the historicity of diasporic identity. James Clifford uses the metaphor of "routes" to capture the spatio-temporality of cultural identity; I will describe it simply as "historical trajectory through places."[17] Encounters in places traversed involve both forgetting and new acquisitions. The past is not erased, therefore, but rewritten. Similarly, the new acquisitions do not imply disappearance into the new environment but rather the proliferation of future possibilities.

What attention to place suggests is the historicity of identity. The "assimilation theory" to which Conzen objects presupposed dehistoricized and placeless notions of culture; assimilation implied motion from one to the other.[18] One could not be both Chinese and American but had to move from being Chinese (whatever that might mean) to being American (whatever that might mean); hence, failure to become "fully American" could produce such notions as "dual personality," which precluded being American—suggesting that such an identity represented the degeneration of the components out of which it was formed. The very formulation of the problem precluded what from our vantage point would seem to be an obvious answer: that it is possible to be Chinese without being like other Chinese, and it is possible to be American without being like other Americans. In either case, the history traversed makes a crucial difference in the formation of new identities that unite and divide in new ways.

Ironically, contemporary critiques of assimilation theory, to the extent that they ignore place and history, end up with similar assumptions. Multiculturalism may evaluate hybridity differently than an earlier monoculturalism permitted, but it nevertheless retains similar culturalist assumptions (some notion of Chineseness conjoined to some notion of Americanness to produce a hybrid product). Since culturalism still runs against the evidence of difference, it is potentially productive of the reification of ethnicity and, ultimately, race. If diasporic reification erases the many historical legacies of the past, hybridity disallows the future. Without a clear account of how different "hybridities" may be productive of new cultures, hybridity in the abstract points merely to an existence between cultures frozen in time.

On the other hand, place consciousness is quite visible in Asian American literary texts. The inhabitants of these texts move through ethnic spaces out of choice or necessity, but the ethnic spaces themselves are located in places with a variety of cohabitants. The classic example may be Carlos Bulosan's *America Is in the Heart*, which literally traces the author's motions from place to place, starting in Philippine places, and then up and down the United States' West Coast. Place consciousness is most readily evident in contemporary Asian American literature in the literature of Hawaii—of writers such as Milton Murayama, Gary Pak, and Wing Tek Lum, whose forays into the histories of different ethnic groups share in common a language that marks them as irreducibly Hawaiian. Another example, especially interesting because of the deep contrast between the author's literary output and his more formal discussions, is Frank Chin. Chin's literary works are quite attentive to places and to the historicity of Chinese American identities. On the other hand, when the author turns to formal discussions of identity, his representation of Chinese identity matches the most egregious reifications of an earlier Orientalism. This itself may be revealing of a gap between depictions of concrete, every-day life and an imagined ethnicity constructed very much in the course of daily life but lifted out of it to be represented as an identity that tran-scends history. The contrast raises interesting questions concerning the ways in which transnationalization and diasporic consciousness may affect a place-based understanding of ethnicity.

The insistence on places against diasporic reification has consequences that are not only analytical in an abstract sense. It draws attention, in the first place, to another, place-based kind of politics. One of the dan-gerous consequences of undue attention to diasporas is to distance the so-called diasporic populations from their immediate environments, to render them into foreigners in the context of everyday life. Given the pervasiveness of conflicts in American society that pitch different dias-poric populations against one another rather than retreat behind reified identities that further promote mutual suspicion and racial division, it is necessary to engage others in political projects to create political alliances where differences may be "bridged" and common social and cultural bonds formed to enable different populations to learn to live with one another.[19] A Chinese living in Los Angeles has more of a stake in identifying with his or her African or Hispanic American neighbors than with some distant cousin in Hong Kong (without implying that the two kinds of relationships need to be understood in zero-sum terms). Following the logic of the argument above, I suggest that place-based politics offers the most effective means to achieving such ends. Place-based politics does not presuppose communities that shut out the world but refocuses attention on building society from the bottom up.

Radical (perhaps unrealistically radical)[20] as a place-based politics may seem, it is unlikely to fulfill its radical promise unless it also chal-lenges the hegemony of the global imaginary that utopianizes transna-tionalism. My use of places is somewhat different than in discussions of the "local" in some postcolonial literature, which tends to view places in isolation from the larger structures that inform them and the cate-gorical allegiances (such as class or gender) that enter into their consti-tution. The reassertion of place that I am suggesting could hardly be accomplished, therefore, without challenging those larger structures and working over such categorical allegiances. Without reference to struc-tures, the notion of historicity itself readily disintegrates into a jumble of empirical phenomena with no meaning outside themselves. To speak of places at the present time is to set them against the new global or transnational imaginaries, with their fetishism of a dehistoricized developmentalism and placeless spaces.

Liberal multiculturalism seeks to make room for different cultures, but with a hegemonic containment of difference within the structures of capitalism assumed to offer a common destiny for all, which perpetuates fundamental hegemonies under the new requirements of broadened cultural tolerance. Culturalism without history may serve to divide (as it does); it also may serve to consolidate hegemony. It may not be too surprising that we witness exactly such a hegemonic unity at the level of transnationalized ruling classes, whose claims to cultural difference are negotiated with the assumption of common interests, while the same culturalism often is manifested in deadly conflicts among the population at large. The return to history from culture is important precisely because it may serve as a reminder of how people at the level of places are not just divided by different cultural legacies but also united by common histories and interests without which those differences themselves may be incomprehensible. What needs to be resolved at this level are different memories; not just histories remembered differently but also histories remembered jointly.

History is important for a reason other than the possibilities it offers for the resolution of past and present differences. Released from a hegemonic containment within contemporary structures of power, the recognition of different pasts inevitably invites the possibility of envisioning the future differently. The historicization of cultures—the recognition of different historical trajectories—may play a crucial role in opening up a dialogue over different futures. Political projects that account for the different historical possibilities offered by their constituents may fulfill their radical promise if they may, on the basis of those possibilities, imagine alternative futures as well.

The other consequence also is political, but within the context of academic politics, for there is a pedagogic dimension to realizing such political goals. It is rather unfortunate that recent ideological formations, backed by the power of foundations, have encouraged the capturing of ethnicities in "diasporic" American or cultural studies. In studies of Asian Americans in particular, the most favored choices these days would seem to be to recognize Asian American studies as a field of its own, to break it down into various national components (Chinese, Japanese, Filipino, etc.), or to absorb it into American or Asian studies. Each choice is informed by political premises and goals. Asian American studies as a field is under attack from the inside for its homogenizing implications, as well as its domination by some groups over others. Breaking it down, however, does not offer any readily acceptable solution, as it merely replaces continental homogeneity with national homogeneities; why should there be Chinese American rather than, say, Fuzhounese American studies? And why stop at Fuzhou?

On the other hand, absorbing Asian American studies into either Asian or American studies would seem to achieve little more than bringing it as a field under the hegemony of the study of societies of origin or arrival. On the surface, American studies would seem to be an appropriate home for Asian American studies, as Asian American history is grounded in U.S. history, which continues to be the concrete location for Asian American experience. On the other hand, it is also clear that Asian American history extends beyond the boundaries of U.S. history, and by virtue of that has special requirements—chief among them language—that are not likely to be accommodated with ease within the context of American studies as currently organized. These needs have prompted some scholars to advocate some kind of a merger between Asian and Asian American studies. After all, Asian studies would benefit from a greater awareness of Asian American populations, which might complicate their notions of Asia with beneficial results. On the other hand, closer integration with Asian studies would bring into Asian American studies a closer grasp of societies of origin, as well as a disciplinary training in languages, which may be necessary for more sophisticated scholarship, as indicated by the growing number of Asian American scholars who have extended the boundaries of Asian American studies. I am thinking here of scholars such as Yuji Ichioka, Him Mark Lai, Marlon Hom, Sau-ling Wong, and Scott Wong, to name a few, who have produced works that have enriched the field by using non-English language sources.

Dialogue between the different fields is not only desirable, therefore, but necessary. Mergers are a different matter. The reasoning underlying these proposed mergers is full of pitfalls, especially when viewed from the perspective of politics. Absorption of Asian American into American studies prima facie would perpetuate the hegemonies that do not disappear but are in fact consolidated under the guise of multiculturalism. The case with Asian studies is even more problematic, as the justification for it is fundamentally diasporic, with all of the implications of that term that I have discussed above. One of the most important characteristics of Asian American studies, as of all the ethnic studies projects that were born of the political ferment of the 1960s, was its insistence on ties to community projects. This was a reason Asian studies scholars long disassociated themselves from Asian American scholarship, for such explicit ties to political projects made the field suspect in terms of scholarship (which, of course, did not apply to scholars of Asia with ties to other kinds of political projects, respectable because of their ties to power). The new interest of scholars of Asia in Asian American studies may be attributed to something so mundane as the lucrative promise of a field suddenly in demand due to the explosion in the numbers of students of Asian origins. I suspect, however, that what makes the association tolerable is the respectability that Asian American studies has acquired as it is transnationalized or diasporized, achieving respectability at the cost of alienation from its radical political projects. It may be noteworthy here that a panel at the recent annual meeting of the Association for Asian Studies ("Crossing Boundaries: Bridging Asian American Studies and Asian Studies") "bridges" the gap not by addressing Asian American issues but by including in the panel Evelyn Hu-De Hart, the only participant recognizable as a serious scholar of Asian America (to be distinguished from being Asian American). Judging by the titles of the papers listed, the panel reveals little recognition of the integrity and coherence of Asian American studies as a field with its own problems and paradigms, not to mention the intellectual and political implications of those paradigms.[21] The claim to "bridging" the two fields, as with most occasions informed by that particular term, rests on the assumption of some vague diasporic unity across the Pacific. The danger (and the quite real possibility) here is the disappearance into some vague diasporic field of problems specific to Asian America.

If education has anything to do with politics, and it does have everything to do with it, the wiser course to follow in overcoming ethnic divisions would be to reinforce programs in ethnic studies, which initially had as one of its fundamental goals the bridging of ethnic divisions and the pursuit of common projects (based in communities) to that end. Ethnic studies, since its inception, has been viewed with suspicion by the political and educational establishments and suffered from internal divisions as well. Whether or not these legacies can be overcome is a big question, embedded as they are in the structures of U.S. society and academic institutions. The irony is that while ethnic studies might help ideologically in overcoming ethnic divisions, it is not likely to receive much support unless interethnic political cooperation has sufficient force to render it credible in the first place. The ideology of globalization, of which diasporic ideology is one constituent, further threatens to under-mine its promise (and existence). Here, too, place-based politics may have something to offer in countering the ideologies of the age.

NOTES

1. While the issue of place against transnationality is quite central, as I will suggest below, in this case the criticism was not entirely fair. The anthropologist in question, Nina Glick-Schiller, is among the earliest critics of transnational cultural homogenization and its manipulation by business and political interests (see, e.g., Schiller, Basch, and Szanton-Blanc 1992). The colleagues in Singapore were Chua Beng-huat and Wang Gung-wu. A colleague in Hong Kong, Siu-woo Cheung, responded in similar fashion, this time to a talk by Greg Lee on Chinese hybridity. Cheung informs me that he feels "silenced" by a concept such as hybridity, which erases his differences from other Chinese, not just elsewhere but in Hong Kong.

2. This double aspect of the concept is investigated in several of the essays, especially the editors' introduction and epilogue, in Ong and Nonini 1997c.

3. For Gilroy, see Gilroy 1993.

4. There is a great deal of material on the John Huang case, although no studies as yet. For a blatant example of the unscrupulous linking of John Huang to the Riadys and the People's Republic of China, see William Safire, "Listening to Hearings," *New York Times*, July 13, 1997.

5. For an important discussion, see Kwong 1997, especially chapter 5, "Manufacturing Ethnicity."

6. For another study that also stresses the debilitating consequences of hybridity, see Smith 1970.

7. Lawrence Grossberg notes that there has been an increasing tendency in cultural studies to identify the field with problems of identity, which may well have something to do with the abstraction and universalization of hybridity. See Grossberg 1997, 87.

8. For a discussion of class differences, see Leo Suryadinata, "Anti-Chinese Riots in Indonesia: Perennial Problem but Major Disaster Unlikely," *Straits Times* (Singapore), February 25, 1998. For the Indonesian Chinese elite's plans, see "Elite Making Contingency Plans to Flee to Australia," *South China Morning Post*, February 28, 1998. It might be worth remembering that this is the same elite of which some members were implicated in the John Huang case.

9. See Young 1995, 176, for a tabulation of degrees of "mongrelity" in Peru. See also Maingot 1992, 229, for similar categorizations in Santo Domingo. For the blood quantum, see Guerrero 1995.

10. Theorists of abstract hybridity such as Bhabha and Soja nevertheless refer to the quite grounded work of bell hooks, who seeks such articulation from a black feminist perspective. See the essays in bell hooks 1990.

11. I have in mind here the essentialism that Lisa Lowe discovers in the early Asian American movement of the late 1960s and the 1970s. There is little in the texts of that movement to suggest that Asian American radicals assumed any kind of ethnic or social (class and gender) homogeneity for the groups encompassed under the term. If there was erasure of gender differences to begin with, that was challenged very quickly. On the other hand, the movement did have political goals that have become less desirable to new generations of Asian Americans (see Lowe 1991).

12. bell hooks, "Culture to Culture: Ethnography and Cultural Studies As Critical Intervention," in hooks 1990, 123–33, 130. See also Hall 1996 for the importance of history and place in identity. Hall distinguishes a "hegemonizing" form of ethnicity from a hybrid one, which is subject to change but does not therefore deny the importance of ethnic identity: "difference, therefore, persists—in and alongside continuity" (114). For a similar reaffirmation, this time contrasting ethnicity to race, see Werbner 1997b.

13. For a defense of the nation from what may seem to be a surprising source, see Sub-Commandant Marcos, "Why We Are Fighting: The Fourth World War Has Begun," *Le Monde diplomatique* (August–September 1997).

14. For a parallel argument, see Partha Chatterjee, "Beyond the Nation? Or Within?," *Economic and Political Weekly* (January 4–11, 1997): 30–34.

15. I am referring here to the title of a conference held in early November 1997 at New York University, "Where Is Home?" (previously the title of an exhibition on the Chinese in the United States). The preoccupation has its roots in a particularly narcissistic and manipulative offshoot of cultural studies. The "yearning" for home need not be a consequence of such narcissism. Jussawalla defends her case for "home" in response to the oppressive refusal of the society of arrival to recognize genuine political and cultural citizenship to the ethnically, racially, and culturally different, even after generations of residence in the new "home," which indeed has been the experience of many. On the other hand, I find implausible her alternative that "the answer is to assimilate and yet to keep our distinctness, our senses of nationality" (1997, 36).

16. Jameson's pessimism is related to a yearning for an earlier class politics of socialism. He describes the contemporary fragmentation of history with the same vocabulary that he uses to describe the new social movements:

as having emerged from the "rubbles" of an earlier, unified and coherent history and politics. This yearning does not allow him to see the progressive potential of the new "rubble."

17. See the collection of his essays in *Routes: Travel and Translation in the Late Twentieth Century* (1997). I may note here an aspect of the contemporary dissatisfaction with history for supposedly ignoring questions of space out of a preoccupation with questions of time. While this may be a legitimate criticism for certain kinds of histories, such criticism itself seems to be more concerned with nineteenth-century historicism and conceptions of history than with the actual practice of historians. To this historian at any rate, the concept of historicity as a concrete concept is inseparable from location in time *and* space—within a *social* context (to complete Soja's "trialectics"!).

18. Henry Yu argues that the Chicago sociologists dehistoricized the experiences of their "oriental" subjects by rendering into static universal categories what were stages in their life histories. See the discussion in Yu 1995, 185–88.

19. The divisive effects of diasporic discourse as I approach it here are similar to the divisive effects of the idea of a "model minority."

20. The difficulties are obvious, but then we do not seem to have too many choices. For a sensitive discussion of the difficulties involved in what she calls "transversal politics" (a term coined by Italian feminists), see Yuval-Davis 1997. I have discussed the problems and possibilities at greater length in my "Place-Based Imagination: Globalism and the Politics of Place" (1999).

21. A concomitant roundtable discussion subtitled "Where Do Asia and Asian America Meet?" may have been more promising with the participation of Gail Nomura and Scott Wong.

WORKS CITED

Appadurai, Arjun. 1990. "Disjuncture and Difference in the Global Economy." *Public Culture* 2:2 (spring): 1–24.

Bakhtin, M. M. 1981. *The Dialogic Imagination.* Edited by Michael Holquist. Translated by Caryl Emerson. Austin: University of Texas Press.

Bauman, Zygmunt. 1997. "The Making and Unmaking of Strangers." Pp. 46–57 in *Debating Cultural Hybridity*, ed. Pnina Werbner and Tariq Modood. London and Atlantic Highlands, N.J.: Zed Books.

Chambers, Iain. 1994. *Migrancy, Culture, Identity.* London: Routledge.

Clifford, James. 1997. *Routes: Travel and Translation in the Late Twentieth Century.* Cambridge: Harvard University Press.

Conzen, Kathleen Neils. 1990. "Making Their Own America: Assimilation Theory and the German Peasant Pioneer." German Historical Institute, Washington, D.C. Annual Lecture Series No. 3. New York: Berg.

Dirlik, Arif. 1995. "Global Capitalism and the Reinvention of Confucianism." *boundary 2* 22:3 (November): 229–73.

———. 1999. "Place-Based Globalism and the Politics of Place." *Review* 22:2:151–89.

Friedman, Jonathan. 1997. "Global Crises, the Struggle for Cultural Identity, and Intellectual Porkbarrelling: Cosmopolitans versus Locals, Ethnics, and Nationals in an Era of Global De-Hegemonization." Pp. 70–89 in *Debating Cultural Hybridity*, ed. Pnina Werbner and Tariq Modood. London and Atlantic Highlands, N.J.: Zed Books.

Gilroy, Paul. 1993. *The Black Atlantic: Modernity and Double Consciousness*. Cambridge: Harvard University Press.

———. 1996. "'The Whisper Wakes, the Shudder Plays': Race, Nation and Ethnic Absolutism." Pp. 248–74 in *Contemporary Postcolonial Theory*, ed. Padmini Mongia. London: Arnold Publishing.

Grossberg, Lawrence. 1997. "Identity and Cultural Studies—Is That All There IS?" Pp. 87–107 in *Questions of Cultural Identity*, ed. Stuart Hall and Paul du Gay. London: Sage.

Guerrero, Mariana Jaimes. 1995. "The 'Patriarchal Nationalism' of Transnational Colonialism: As Imperialist Strands of Genocide/Ethnocide/Ecocide." Paper presented at the conference "Asian Pacific Identities." Duke University, March 1995.

Hall, Stuart. 1996. "Cultural Identity and Diaspora." Pp. 110–21 in *Contemporary Postcolonial Theory*, ed. Padmini Mongia. London: Arnold Publishing.

Hermans, Hubert J. M., and Harry J. G. Kempen. 1993. *The Dialogical Self: Meaning As Movement*. San Diego: Academic Press.

hooks, bell. 1990. *Yearning: Race, Gender, and Cultural Politics*. Boston: South End Press.

Jameson, Fredric. 1991. *Postmodernism, or, the Cultural Logic of Late Capitalism*. Durham: Duke University Press.

Jussawalla, Feroza. 1997. "South Asian Diaspora Writers in Britain: 'Home' versus 'Hybridity.'" Pp. 17–37 in *Ideas of Home: Literature of Asian Migration*, ed. Geoffrey Kaine. East Lansing: Michigan State University Press.

Kotkin, Joel. 1996. "The New Yankee Traders." *Inc.* (March).

Kwong, Peter. 1997. *Forbidden Workers: Illegal Chinese Immigrants and American Labor*. New York: The New Press.

Lowe, Lisa. 1991. "Heterogeneity, Hybridity, Multiplicity: Marking Asian American Differences." *Diaspora* 1:1 (spring): 24–44.

Lowenthal, David. 1995. *Possessed by the Past: The Heritage Crusade and the Spoils of History.* New York: Free Press.

Maingot, Anthony P. 1992. "Race, Color, and Class in the Caribbean." Pp. 220–47 in *Americas: New Interpretive Essays,* ed. Alfred Stepan. New York: Oxford University Press.

McLaren, Peter, and Henry A. Giroux. 1997. "Writing from the Margins: Geographies of Identity, Pedagogy, and Power." Pp. 16–41 in *Revolutionary Multiculturalism: Pedagogies of Dissent for the New Millenium,* ed. Peter McLaren. Boulder: Westview Press.

Mitchell, Katharyne. 1997. "Different Diasporas and the Hype of Hybridity." *Environment and Planning D: Society and Space* 15: 533–53.

Mongia, Padmini, ed. 1996. *Contemporary Postcolonial Theory: A Reader.* London: Arnold Publishing.

Ong, Aihwa, and Donald Nonini. 1997a. "Toward a Cultural Politics of Diaspora and Transnationalism." Pp. 323–32 in *Ungrounded Empires,* ed. Aihwa Ong and Donald Nonini. New York: Routledge.

———. 1997b. "Chinese Transnationalism As an Alternative Modernity." Pp. 3–33 in *Ungrounded Empires,* ed. Aihwa Ong and Donald Nonini. New York: Routledge.

———, eds. 1997c. *Ungrounded Empires: The Cultural Politics of Modern Chinese Nationalism.* New York: Routledge.

Schiller, Nina, Linda Basch, and Christina Szanton-Blanc. 1992. "Transnationalism: A New Analytic Framework for Understanding Migration." *Annals of the New York Academy of Sciences* 645: 1–24.

Smith, William Carlson. 1970 [1937]. *Americans in Process: A Study of Our Citizens of Oriental Ancestry.* New York: Arno Press.

Soja, Edward W. 1996. *Thirdspace: Journeys to Los Angeles and Other Real-and-Imagined Places.* Cambridge, Mass.: Blackwell.

Wang, Ling-ch'i. 1991. "Roots and Changing Identity of the Chinese in the United States." In *Daedalus* (spring): 181–206.

———. 1997. "Foreign Money Is No Friend of Ours." *AsianWeek* (November 8).

Werbner, Pnina. 1997a. "Introduction: The Dialectics of Cultural Hybridity." Pp. 1–26 in *Debating Cultural Hybridity,* ed. Pnina Werbner and Tariq Modood. London and Atlantic Highlands, N.J.: Zed Books.

———. 1997b. "Essentializing Essentialism, Essentializing Silence: Ambivalence and Multiplicity in the Constructions of Racism and Ethnicity." Pp. 226–54 in *Debating Cultural Hybridity*, ed. Pnina Werbner and Tariq Modood. London and Atlantic Highlands, N.J.: Zed Books.

Werbner, Pnina, and Tariq Modood, eds. 1997. *Debating Cultural Hybridity: Multi-Cultural Identities and the Politics of Anti-Racism*. London and Atlantic Highlands, N.J.: Zed Books.

Young, Robert J. C. 1995. *Colonial Desire: Hybridity in Theory, Culture, and Race*. London and New York: Routledge.

Yu, Henry. 1995. "Thinking about Orientals: Modernity, Social Science, and Asians in Twentieth-Century America." Ph.D. diss., Princeton University.

Yuval-Davis, Nira. 1997. "Ethnicity, Gender Relations, and Multiculturalism." Pp. 193–208 in *Debating Cultural Hybridity*, ed. Pnina Werbner and Tariq Modood. London and Atlantic Highlands, N.J.: Zed Books.

CHAPTER SIX

The Romance of Africa

Three Narratives by African-American Women

EILEEN JULIEN

Yes! Three hundred years later the African Prince rose up out
of the seas and swept the maiden back across the middle passage over which her ancestors had come.

—Asagai, from Hansberry,
A Raisin in the Sun

"What is Africa to Me?" Unquestionably older than the poem in which
Countee Cullen wrote it down, it is a question that may well have arisen,
first, in the New World. Phyllis Wheatley clearly thought about it, as did
the innumerable enslaved Africans and their children whose voices filled
cotton and sugarcane fields, homes, and churches with the powerful
chords of chants and spirituals.

To what extent can African Americans[1] in the United States today
get beyond what Wole Soyinka has called the "fictioning of Africa,"[2] the
often constricting lenses of our own particular historical circumstances
in our mythologizing and representation of that array of peoples and
cultures known as Africa?

A long-standing object of denigration in the hegemonic, colonizing discourse of Europe and America, meant both to justify the West's imperial projects to itself and to deprive enslaved Africans and their descendants of historical and cultural heritage, rendering them malleable as well to enslaving ideologies, can Africa be more than a figure in the collective imaginary of black Americans, cut to the rhythm of our needs and ideological battles for respect as well as civic rights? If "Africa" serves to fuel our indignation or claims for dignity, can the continent be recognized as a space with its own agendas and its own dirty linen? Can we engage those agendas in ways that are instructive and productive for Africans as well as ourselves?

In her survey "What Is Africa to African American Women Writers?" Trudier Harris examines a range of works, including drama, poetry, and fiction, as of 1959, the year Lorraine Hansberry's *A Raisin in the Sun* was first performed. Harris notes that in this play Beneatha Younger "romanticizes Africa, and Mama Lena Younger has adopted the prevailing missionary Christian attitude toward it," while Asagai, the African in the play, suffers through the misguided desires of the one and sympathies of the other (1997, 29). In both this play and *Les Blancs*, her posthumously performed play that explores the means and process of revolutionary change in a fictive African country, one can see that Hansberry strives—regardless of her success in absolute terms—to imagine Africa with its own specificity, distinct from the realities and needs of African Americans in North America. The portrayal of Asagai, the representative of the continent itself, slipping through the cracks of the daughter's and mother's alternative imaginings, is emblematic of more recent texts, however.

Thus in Nikki Giovanni's "Ego Tripping," Harris finds that Africa becomes whatever the poet needs "to augment her identity and her conceptualization of self." In Toni Morrison and Paule Marshall, in Audre Lorde and Gloria Naylor, "Africa represents possibility, the mind space of escape, the imaginative power of creating myths that can counteract the negative effects of American racism by transcending them" (Harris 1997, 27). In Alice Walker's *The Color Purple*, "except for its sexism," Africa is "everything that Celie does not have in her life . . . the site [of] model communities, model behavior, and model harmony with nature" (ibid., 29). In other texts, such as Marita Golden's *A Woman's Place*, Marshall's *The Chosen Place: The Timeless People*, or Morrison's *Beloved*, "Africa becomes the *haunting*, the longing for better times and days gone by, for that—in many cases—which is irretrievably lost" (ibid., 28).[3]

These texts have done important cultural work, instilling in black women readers in particular a sense of dignity and possibility. Yet for all of the exhilaration they offer and horizons they open for African Americans, we must recognize that they are about *here*, not *there*. Harris goes on to say: "With the poetic license of imagination, most of these writers have reduced a continent into the smallness of its collectivity, its common denominators. . . . While writers such as Marita Golden make specific references to Kenya, Nigeria, or Zimbabwe, most writers simply refer to *Africa*" (ibid., 31).

Harris concludes that in this monolithic construction, "Africa in contemporary African American women's writing is a poor stepsister. . . . There is seldom a genuine desire to *know* Africa." Because of their historical tie to the continent, black Americans assume that they can "use its connotative resources however they wish in their own bids for individual and communal freedom and identity." For Harris, they create distorted images "without ever setting foot on the continent— and all for the sake of reclaiming identity or asserting political stances" (ibid.).

Writing is, of course, symbolic activity. It is inherently the liberty to take liberties, to invent. We should neither berate writers for writing nor minimize historic and ongoing struggles to promote freedom and identity. I would say, then, that these writers' images are not so much distorted as simply unrelated to African realities. In a real sense, they are not about Africa at all.[4]

There have been and continue to be impediments to an informed understanding of Africa on the part of African Americans. It bears repeating that black American experiences of oppression and racialization differ from those of Africans, as do our political status, wealth, and access to global resources.[5] Limited access to the continent over the last three centuries and the misteaching of American and African history also play no small part in African-American ignorance of or indifference to African realities. Indeed, as long as Africa cannot be recognized in mainstream America as the vital tributary of New World culture that it has been,[6] as long as African Americans are lesser citizens and race and gender provide handy explanations for deviance, then the representation of Africa, past and present, will be a site of struggle, and an informed understanding of the continent and productive dialogue with it will be foreclosed.

In a fog of ideology and contradictions, Africa has always been and remains more symbol than reality, as Trudier Harris' survey demonstrates, and we confront the limits of African-American symbolism every time Africans speak (or write) to us of *their* reality.[7]

What happens when African Americans leave the perches of our specific ecology and *encounter* Africa or Africans today? One of the more intense and revealing spaces of encounter is the terrain of romantic love.[8] This, I believe, is a new type of engagement with the continent in the tradition of African-American female letters. I focus here on *Sarah's Psalm*, a first novel published by Florence Ladd in 1996, Marita Golden's autobiographical account of her marriage to a Nigerian, *Migrations of the Heart*, published in 1983, and Maya Angelou's memoir of her relationship with a South African activist, *The Heart of a Woman* (1981), one volume of a multi-volume chronicle of her life. These are the only narratives of which I am aware by African-American women in which the love plot, featuring an African-American woman and an African man, is central.

The emphasis of each text is, of course, distinct. The title of Ladd's novel refers to the heroine's revision of a psalm that becomes a mantra throughout her story: "I will cast mine eyes upon the ocean from whence cometh my help. My help cometh from Senegal, which is heaven and earth." The novel seems to me especially inspired by reflections on a particular place and its possibilities, as well as by traditions of the novel.[9] Angelou's memoir, on the other hand, is a near documentary of a particularly rich historical period, 1957 through the early 1960s. Angelou, herself a performer and an activist, moved from California to New York, then to Egypt and Ghana, and she frequented any number of well-known artists and personalities. Golden's narrative is true autobiography: it is the means of the author's coming to terms with herself, of her self-fashioning and emergence as a self-possessed woman. While all three love stories might be read as nostalgic to a certain extent, Ladd does not associate Africa nominally with the past but casts it rather as her heroine's true spiritual home.

All three texts are first-person accounts—*Sarah's Psalm* and *Migrations of the Heart* containing snippets from letters and diaries—and all, in varying degrees, are travel journal and romance. These narratives differ significantly however from formulaic mass-market romances. They do not, for example, maintain the couple and reader in a state of "permanent foreplay," promising a happily ever after with marriage on the horizon.[10] Nor do they take place in a nameless setting, marked only by signs of upper-class lifestyles to which innumerable working women readers may aspire. Rather, they go on to explore the important next phase—marriage and home on the continent, where the stress of political and social life inhabits the couple, where the vision they had of themselves and each other during courtship is tested, resulting inevitably in readjustment or failure. Nor can they be read as lowest-common-denominator "universal" fantasies. They are rather about specific women—unmistakably black, middle-class women, fashioned by and within history. In fact, all three narratives devote considerable space to historical events, notably the civil rights movement and Pan-Africanism, and they are imbued with social purpose, if not didactic agendas. Susan Willis signals three themes that are "ways into" African-American women's writing: community, journey, and sensuality (1985, 212). These narratives also can be understood in these terms.

If the woof of these texts is romance, their warp is the travel journal. I am struck by the banality of this combination of genres and what I assume to be its rarity in the history of African-American women writers. African-American women are not typically the *narrating subjects* of travel literature and passionate love stories. This is not surprising, given restricted access to travel for most African-American women and late-nineteenth-century, early-twentieth-century anxiety about black female sexuality.

In European literary traditions, love plots are commonly yoked to travel stories and are especially tied to nineteenth-century exoticism and Orientalism, as discursive complements of imperialism. In American traditions, they also arise in the era of abolition. Peter Hulme (1986) and Mary Louise Pratt (1992) have written persuasively that in such narratives, transracial love plots come to replace bonds of slavery and force. In Hulme's words, they enact "the ideal of cultural harmony through romance" (1986, 141). Pratt notes similarly that sentimental fiction of this era often "casts the political as erotic" (1992, 101). While *Sarah's Psalm* and the other narratives I examine here could not be characterized either as transracial love stories or as stories in which romantic love replaces servitude or force, as in the narratives of those particular eras, I believe that these narratives do, as transnational narratives of the diaspora, enact the political and the ideal of (black) cultural harmony.

I come to these narratives as an African-American woman and a scholar of African rather than African-American literature. The gap between what I know of that vast array of peoples and nations of the African continent and popular representations of it in the U.S. press, films, and music has intrigued and often troubled me. This chapter is meant to contribute to raising a debate about the distance between here and there, about the pressing needs and experiences that inform our mythologies. Thus I have reservations about reading these stories, situated in part in different nations (Senegal, Egypt and Ghana, and Nigeria), as a corpus unified by the setting or theme of Africa, for the continent, as any number of commentators and scholars have demonstrated, is far from uniform. But despite their specificity, these settings are in the minds of the narrators synecdoches for the continent as a whole, just as for many African Americans, nuances of place with respect to Africa are not significant. In addition to these and other novels, popular songs and films suggest the wide currency of this assumption.

I shall read these narratives of romance as commentaries on processes of racialization and gendering, as well as on the politics of diaspora relations.[11] I shall not give a comprehensive analysis of each but will sketch out a few of the ways in which these narratives nudge us away from Harris' critique, that is, from Africa as pure signifier of black American desire. The dream of an African Prince, as Asagai puts it in *A Raisin in the Sun*, may be a significant and distinctive sign of the narrators' gender identity as African-American women.[12] That dream, conditioned by the history of American slavery and its consequences, can be read as an attempt to traverse history in reverse, to escape the anguish of the middle passage, and thus to regain a lost place in the sun. These romances mark an improvement in our grasp of racial and gender dynamics and politics. Not because black women and their desire are the subject and such an emphasis is progressive—as it once may have been. Rather, as I have stated above, these narratives incorporate a dimension not present in other writings. The African-American heroine of romance who sets foot on the continent is more vulnerable than her counterpart who stays home. Africa *resists* easy apprehension. In the trenches of lived experience, projections made from afar are queried and often undone. The novel is especially suggestive, because it can introduce a *deus ex machina* or other solutions for intractable problems and move on to explorations of womanhood and sisterhood. Its focus on differential power suggests the limits of race as a unifying principle across national boundaries and presents a challenge to discourses of cultural nationalism with their unacknowledged, masculinist biases.[13]

What becomes clear in all three narratives is that African men exercise a singularly powerful attraction over the African-American heroines that is manifest at the moment of encounter and in the subsequent moment of lovemaking. In these sequences, the contours of the heroines' desire are revealed.

Sarah, the heroine of *Sarah's Psalm*, is writing as a woman in the 1990s but situates the beginnings of her story at a historical moment of tremendous activism and hope in the black world, the era of the early 1960s, as Senegal and other African nations are in the first years of independence and as the civil rights and black power movements in the United States are reaching their stride. A young graduate student in comparative literature at Harvard University, Sarah is solidly middle class, and that status enables her education, her refined tastes, and her access to opportunity, travel, and ordinary American comforts—all of which may be the author's way of "normalizing" black life. Sarah becomes an enthusiast of the work and characters of Ibrahim Mangane, a brilliant Senegalese writer and filmmaker on whom she will write her dissertation. The United States is in the throes of civil rights demonstrations and racist violence, and Sarah perceives Africa in contrast (and regardless of the innumerable problems of the post-independence period) as a place of dignified people, of respect for the human person, and of courtesy.

Sarah's husband dismisses her interests, which are for him escapist in the context of the national civil rights struggle. On the surface, Sarah rejects the masculinist logic implicit in her husband's devaluations of her interest in literature (rather than social protest) and in Africa (as opposed to the national civil rights movement, which many have argued was the occasion for an unabashed drive for male power). Nonetheless, she remains fascinated with African presidents and prime ministers, whom she sees on television and admires for their "crisp analyses in richly accented English, their attire and proud carriage. . . . With confidence, they spoke of commanding their continent's destiny" (Ladd 1996, 14).

Maya Angelou narrates her encounter in similar terms. A young single mother in the late 1950s, Maya has just moved with her son Guy from Southern California to New York, where opportunities for her career as a writer and performer will be better. Once there, Maya takes a job with the Southern Christian Leadership Conference and finds her social niche with Abbey Lincoln, Max Roach, John Killens, Paule Marshall, and other intellectuals and performers. When she is eventually engaged to a young black American jail bondsman, she meets Vusumzi Make, a South African who has come to the States to seek support from the United Nations against apartheid and who is welcomed by the community of black artists residing in Manhattan. Make's accent, she writes, is "delicious"; he wears "a beautifully cut pin-stripe suit." He is a compelling, charismatic spokesman, "brilliant," evincing "Old World formality" (Angelou 1981, 107–21). Of another diplomat, an additional specimen of "African man," she writes that he was "blue-black and spectacular. His unquestionable dignity gave lie to the concept that black people . . . had been naked subhumans living in trees three centuries before, when the whites raided them on the African continent. That elegance could not have been learned in three hundred years" (ibid., 112).

Marita Golden narrates comparable experiences. She opens her autobiography with her girlhood in Washington, D.C., in the 1960s, her tremendous love for her parents, their difficult relationship with each other, their successive deaths, and her own loss and emptiness. Lonely and a voracious reader, she nonetheless is an active participant in civil rights activities in D.C. Marita goes off to study journalism at Columbia University, during which time she goes from one unsatisfying relationship to the next. She meets Femi, a Nigerian student in architecture at Cornell. Once married and settled in Lagos, she reflects on her own and other women's attraction to Nigerian men:

> Lagos is an aggressively masculine city, and its men exude a dogmatic confidence. . . . The intensity of their kinship was startling. Belligerently patriarchal, the men assumed their worth and waited indifferently for the women to prove theirs. . . . Yet it was this masculinity that made the men so undeniably attractive. Their self-consciousness translated into a roughhewn charm. Watching their deft, often obvious interplay, I understood why Femi gained my loyalty and why, if what I was told was true, so many black women followed these men back home. Nigeria was their country to destroy or save. That knowledge made them stride and preen in self-appreciation. This assurance became for an Afro-American woman a gaily wrapped gift to be opened anew every day. (Golden 1983, 90)

One would search in vain in the annals of African women's writing for such a passage or an attitude. By and large, in African texts with which I am familiar, a man's handsome and attractive demeanor might be the visible sign of personal strength and character, while what seems to pertain in these romances, however, is the power of these men as seen by the narrators. All of them have public, if not political, roles. They are leaders of their countries and continent. Just as Pan-Africanists of this hemisphere and decolonizing nationalist poets and novelists of Africa such as Léopold Sédar Senghor of Senegal, Okot p'Bitek of Uganda, and Ngugi wa Thiong'o of Kenya, to name a few, have conflated Africa with

"Woman," the African-American female imaginary in these heterosex-
ual love relationships figures the continent as "Man."[14] The particular
attractiveness of this self-confident masculinity has as its condition of
possibility, I believe, several centuries of American racism and the
mythology of an emasculated black masculinity. Thus Sarah's response,
like Maya's and Marita's, reveals the allure of male power, even to a
nascent black American feminist consciousness.

The attractiveness of the preening African man would seem to be
the promise of higher status for the black American woman, the attain-
ment of a true womanhood as the woman of a true man. One of the
important signs of that new status is that the heroine comes alive sensu-
ally and erotically. Marita's narrative is the exception in this regard.
Lovemaking, in her case, is not presented as exhilarating but rather, in
keeping with her emotional timidity, *comforting*: "I became his with an
ease that only confounded me later, when there was no turning back. He
did not evoke in me an immediate rush of passion but elicited instead a
sense of safety" (Golden 1983, 54). Emotional security is the fundamental condition of her self-realization.

In the novel, heightened passion seems to be a product both of the
African lover and of the "more civil place" that is Senegal. Thus when
Sarah, over the protestations of her husband and family, finally arrives in
Senegal to begin her research, the narrative takes on a lyrical voice that
revels in the colors of the Sandaga Market and the perfume of its fruits. It
is significant, it seems to me, that in the novel the space of encounter and
discovery is *outside* of the United States, in a context where normal relations of power are suspended for Sarah, or where they are, at the very
least, different from those that have come to define black American life. In
Senegal, even though Sarah enjoys the comforts of middle-class life, she
experiences neither the social burdens of American middle-class ignorance
and narcissism nor those of racism. Her journey toward a powerful
African man, toward Africa, is her flight from class as well as from race.

It is precisely beyond the strictures of American life that her sensuality can blossom. One has only to compare the perfunctory lovemaking with Lincoln—as a young, promising bourgeois couple, they
"make love in haste and detachment, then fitfully fall asleep" (Ladd
1996, 11)—to the erotic scenes of her lovemaking with Ibrahim (ibid.,
93, 169). This, at this early moment of the text, is an unmistakable sign
of her having found her true self.

When Maya, who is engaged to a young and "boring" black
American jail bondsman, breaks up with her fiancé and agrees to marry

Make, she too undergoes a metamorphosis, at once political and sensual. Make exclaims, "'This is the joining of Africa and Africa-America!
Two great peoples back together again'" (Angelou 1981, 120). It is
Make himself who conflates the African-American female with the
dream of Pan-Africanism, but curiously Maya takes over his vision and
articulates her role (as she believes he sees it) in her very own voice: "Vus
saw me as the flesh of his youthful dream. I would bring to him the vitality of jazz and the endurance of a people who had survived three hundred and fifty years of slavery. . . . With my courage added to his own,
he would succeed in bringing the ignominious white rule in South Africa
to an end" (ibid., 123). There is obviously a complex dynamic of mirroring operating in these mutual attractions. She concludes with the
older narrator's observation, "Infatuation made me believe in my ability
to create myself into my lover's desire" (ibid., 123). This is a heady mixture: sensuality and sexual desire are clearly embedded in and partake of
political contexts and strivings.

Thrilled with Make's stories of "Warrior queens, in necklaces of
blue and white beads [leading] armies against marauding Europeans, . . .
nubile girls [dancing] in celebrations of the victories of Shaka, the Zulu
king," Maya, "all [her] senses . . . tantalized," is led off to make love.
Angelou, the older and wiser narrator, comments on the youthful Maya:
"I looked into the mirror and saw *exactly what I wanted to see*, and
more importantly *what I wanted him to see*: a young African virgin,
made beautiful for her chief" (ibid., 128, emphasis added). The youthful Maya conflates sensuality and female power and political prowess.
Clearly, the narrator's desire springs from a new vision of herself as
African, as noble, as powerful. One might ask: whose vision, in fact,
dominates here?[15]

The narratives of Angelou and Golden were published over fifteen
years ago. Furthermore, the stories they tell are situated in an intensely
passionate political climate for black American men and women. By the
end of their stories, both narrators have grown in self-awareness, and
their narratives deconstruct their youthful vision. But what remains is
the unveiling of a distinctive racialized gender identity that carries the
problematic traces of American history.

Moreover, the seductiveness for the African-American woman of
African manhood, in its most "belligerent" manifestations is, it seems to
me, one nail in the coffin of an assumed natural sisterhood between
African and African-American women.[16] Just as our experiences of
oppression—colonialism on the one side and slavery on the other—are

different, so too is our identity, the combination of gender, racialization, and degrees of power. As we shall see, *Sarah's Psalm* will become explicit on this point.

The plenitude that these princely Africans promise at first blush meets serious challenges once the couples go about the messy business of daily living. Each love story falls upon the shoals of patriarchy, manifest either in the couple's very relationship or structurally, within each African context. The marriages come to dissolution, leading to the African-American heroine's survival and self-fulfillment outside of the marriage.

Maya, for example, is infantilized by her husband, who monitors her interior decorating as well as her housekeeping:

> It seemed to me that I washed, scrubbed, mopped, dusted, and waxed thoroughly every other day. Vus was particular. He checked on my progress. Sometimes he would pull the sofa away from the wall to see if possibly I had missed a layer of dust. If he found his suspicions confirmed, his response could wither me. He would drop his eyes and shake his head, his face saddened with disappointment. I wiped down the walls, because dirty fingerprints could spoil his day. (Angelou 1981, 141)

Maya accepts this psychological tyranny as part of the role (or what she thinks is the role) of the woman of an African man. She has been an independent woman up until this point, in every sense—emotionally mature, financially self-sufficient, working as a performer and political activist. Under the new regime, she is given an allowance; she does not know the source of her partner's money and the family income, and she does not know if the household bills are being paid (and, indeed, some of them are not). Vus is, of course, a lavish spender. He also begins to seek out other lovers.

At a later point in their marriage, during their time in Cairo, their problems are exacerbated. When the couple's financial situation becomes precarious, Maya takes a job as associate editor of the *Arab Observer*. Vus, feeling demeaned as a man at not having been consulted, grows angry and enraged. Maya has mismanaged the episode, she admits, but:

> With the awareness of my unfortunate mismanagement came the shocking knowledge that I was no longer in love.
> The man standing over me venting his fury, employing his colorful vocabulary was no longer my love. The last wisps of mystery

had disappeared. There had been physical attraction so strong that at his approach, moisture collected at every place where my body touched itself. Now he was in hand's reach, and tantalization was gone. He was just a fat man, standing over me, scolding. (Angelou 1981, 227)

Here the narrator deconstructs the spell with which her story begins. Gone are the bodily responses, moisture and tantalization, that characterized their early lovemaking, because what remains of the mysterious, that is, the *imagined* prince is his shell, the only-too-human and imperfect flesh of a simple man. Maya, who loves but is no longer "in love with" her husband, heads confidently for West Africa, where Guy will attend the University of Ghana and where a job awaits her in Liberia.

In Marita's case, the marriage collapses under the weight of social and family expectations and, above all, because of Femi's temperament and a context in which his masculinity—measured by his having a son, by the type of job he holds, and by his financial independence, wealth, and contributions to his family—is threatened. These are Femi's manly worries, but Chinua Achebe's *Things Fall Apart* (1959) should have left none of us doubting the imbrication of gender and national identities, whether the latter is writ small or large. Femi begins to withdraw, to wallow in self-pity, and grows disdainful and uncommunicative with his wife. Not only is he a poor communicator, but Marita's gender status as wife effectively takes her words away:

> Without Femi's brothers, Tope and Jide, and without his mother I wondered how I would ever reach him. They were barriers and conduits between us. . . . I—who wrote to save and manage my life, who sculpted from words explanations and truths, who confidently lectured to classrooms of students, who was awed by the potency and charm of words—was mute, as verbally incompetent as my child in the face of my husband's resistance. . . . He was as dense as a rainforest, its trees twisted and tangled into an enticing threat, silent and fearsome. He was a country I had lived in, it seemed, all my life. He was a territory in which I found myself lost. (Golden 1983, 200)

Marita's disillusionment is of another type than Maya's, and it is far more fierce. Maya jousts verbally with her husband, but Marita is silenced and invisible, required to pass through translators, as though her gender and status as wife consign her to another country and to a language that has no meaning.

After the birth of their son and Marita's coming into her own, she realizes that she can no longer live with her husband. Desperate to survive and to keep her child, she plots an escape with the help of a lover. She lands in New York and will go through a long period of anger and self-examination before emerging as a whole woman.

Unlike Maya and Marita, Sarah lives a fabled life—in the mode of high romance—as the wife of a prosperous, charismatic, international figure. Ibrahim is the closest thing to a (black) prince that the late twentieth century is able to offer, and Sarah becomes a princess. In the initial phase of the story, Ibrahim is Sarah's mentor in some sense, an older man, more sophisticated, worldly, and broad-minded than Sarah's youthful husband. A benign patriarch, he is more appreciative of Sarah, but she begins to founder nonetheless. Apart from the responsibilities of mothering their son Isaac and Ibrahim's son Ousmane, Sarah loses her professional identity as a researcher and as an intellectual in bolstering Ibrahim. His success renders her invisible, but it is, above all, the neglect and silencing of Sarah and other women intellectuals during an international black arts festival, most notably their exclusion from public debate, that crystallize her sense of oppression. This bitter moment is a deeply ironic reversal. Sarah suffers the same plight as did the African women who were rendered invisible by the male presidents and prime ministers on American television whom she admired as a young woman.

At one point in her marriage, when she discovers the tremendous strength and moral resources of village women, Ibrahim rebuffs her suggestion that he do a film on them: he would rather foment action than affirm and inspire.[17] Sarah's focus is shifting, her awareness growing. These conflicts produce tensions that are never resolved. Finally, in a melodramatic twist, Ibrahim's progressive views—especially those on women—win him the Nobel Prize as well as the enmity of Muslim fundamentalists, including Ousmane. Ibrahim is promptly assassinated, along with his son who, full of regret, tries to save his father. Sarah, with the help of Isaac, a newfound spiritual sister, Aisha, and other friends, slowly recovers and goes on to lay the groundwork for an intellectual and activist institute for women of the diaspora. Ladd grants her heroine (and her readers) the plenitude of romance and then, through Ibrahim's death, opens a space beyond it, in which Sarah comes to independence and self-fulfillment. The novel suggests that men are not enough, or in a feminist version of the Wolof proverb, "the remedy for woman is woman."[18]

It should be noted that the failure of romance and the strain of marriage delineated in these narratives do not amount to diatribes against African men or gloomy portraits of a continent. Maya and Sarah stay on. Marita deeply wishes she could do so; her pain is partly the pain of losing a place she has come to love. Their stories suggest, rather, complexity—possibilities and limits, strengths and weaknesses, and successes and failures in varied doses. These narratives of mixed blessings and pains are, then, narratives of maturity, of success in coming to see individuals and societies in multiple dimensions rather than through one-dimensional lenses.

As I indicated above, Susan Willis has written that journey, sensuality, and community are "ways into" African-American women's writing. We have examined elements of journey and sensuality in all three narratives and have begun in fact to look at elements of community, which is another way of thinking about identity. We shall now look more closely, for these narratives can also be read as attempts to expand the concept of community from the narrowly national to the diasporic and the difficulties in doing so. It is precisely this aspect of the narrative that seems to me to expand our understanding of "Africa" and diaspora.

Marita, for example, notes explicitly the limits of racial unity by focusing on questions of gender and national identity. She describes at several moments Nigerian women's competence and savvy, and she signals also their submission, the performance of the feminine gender role: "Bisi ran her home and business with demonlike efficiency. Yet Jide inherited total control over her life when he entered the house at ten minutes after five. The voice that barked—ordering the children to begin their homework, Iyabo to fry plantains—became a whimper" (Golden 1983, 107). She also observes that patriarchal privilege makes Nigeria more hospitable to African-American men than to African-American women: "No matter what their status (single or married) or occupation, no matter how long they had been in the country, much of their idealism remained intact. They spoke to me of power, of being unable to attain it in America but finding it in Nigeria. . . . But foreign wives were forced to bend to the collective will of clan, family and custom" (ibid., 192). At another moment in her story, she signals the significant difference between herself and her Nigerian friends and acquaintances: "Looking at me they saw skyscrapers, spaceships and Technicolor movies. I looked at them and saw a chance to reclaim a past that spat me out onto the shores of another world. We stumbled through these illusions to find one another" (ibid., 107).

Yet Marita's narrative is ambivalent on this point, for she refuses to relinquish the illusion of racial unity. One of the striking moments of that presumed unity is an exchange about interracial relationships between Marita and Ikpoi, an Igbo colleague at the University of Lagos:

> "Did you marry your wife because no black women would have you?" I asked, proud of my straightforwardness.
>
> "I married her because I love her." We walked in silence for a few moments, our appetites for revelation perked. "In the States, would you have shunned me because of Ann?" he asked.
>
> "I'd have found it unsettling. Hard to accept. I'd have felt betrayed. You are black, after all, and belong to me."
>
> He stopped in mid stride, seemingly offended by my claim. Shaking his head, he laughed. "That's preposterous."
>
> "No, Ikpoi, it's the truth." (ibid., 144)

Marita holds onto the presumption that a shared black skin gives her rights over Ikpoi, thereby repeating the stance of cultural nationalism that sees only through the lenses of race that are the sine qua non of black American experience. One comes away from this narrative with the sense that the heroine has disclosed the contradictions of patriarchal privilege but struggles still with the mythology of racial essence.

Maya concludes *The Heart of a Woman* with a series of subtle reflections on the possibilities, limits, and contradictions of her hyphenated identity that could serve as a model for postmodernist perspectives. When African friends in Cairo gather to try to resolve Vus' and Maya's differences, Maya insists in her narration, as during the event, on the *American* dimension of her "African-American" identity: "African women hardly ever used profanity in mixed company, but I wasn't strictly an African, and, after all, they had gathered to hear me speak and I was a black American. Mentioning slavery in present African company was a ploy. Their forefathers had been spared, or had negotiated for the sale of my ancestors. I knew it and they knew it. It gave me a little edge" (Angelou 1981, 252). Although it has nothing to do with allegiance to the United States, Maya uses her difference *as an American* both to justify nonconformist behavior and to weaken the authority of her African friends.

Shortly after, as she works in her newspaper office during the Cuban missile crisis in 1962, she observes: "Actions by people thousands of miles away, men who didn't know I was alive and whose

sympathy I would never expect, influenced my peace, and rendered
me odious. Kennedy was an American, and so was I. I didn't have the
language to explain that being a black American was qualitatively different from being An American" (ibid., 255). With Arab co-workers
and readers alike, she would like to stress her *difference from* the
average (read: white, male) American, thereby distancing herself from
policies and people with whom she profoundly disagrees and which
have also victimized her. And yet for the outside, she remains American, sharing American power, and therefore she becomes the perceived enemy, the butt of Arab resentment.

Finally, en route from Cairo to Ghana, as the plane traverses the
Sahara, she mourns her ancestors; she announces her identification as
African American:

> I could look down from my window seat and see trees, and bushes,
> rivers and dense forest. It all began here. The jumble of poverty-
> stricken children sleeping in rat-infested tenements or abandoned
> cars. The terrifying moan of my grandmother, "Bread of Heaven,
> Bread of Heaven, feed me till I want no more." The drugged days
> and alcoholic nights of men for whom hope had not been born. The
> loneliness of women who would never know appreciation or a
> mite's share of honor. (ibid., 257)

What is striking about this identification, given the earlier one in which
Maya saw herself as the young African maiden, is the quality of those
with whom she identifies: poor children, lonely women, drugged men,
terrified grandmothers. This is a political solidarity rather than a
romantic one.

By narrative's end, she too is prepared to "act out" another part to
get what she wants. When her son unknowingly attacks the scholarship
of the vice chancellor of the University of Ghana on his entrance exam,
Maya is, as she puts it, "prepared to shuffle and scratch" in order to get
her son into the University of Ghana. "My people had written the book
on dealing with white men" (ibid., 271). Surprised that she will not have
to do so, she observes humorously: "Sooner or later, I was going to have
to admit that I didn't understand black men or black boys and certainly
not all white men" (ibid., 271). Here she is particularly conscious of her
gender identity, its limits, and the limits of racial categories as well.
These many moments in the narrative suggest the narrator's ever-grow-
ing awareness of identity as textured and multilayered. Different aspects
of that identity can be called upon and put into play, depending on con-

text. Such play on identities is not a postmodernist invention. It is certainly as old as marriage and slavery themselves.

With respect to diaspora politics and identity, the most interesting aspect of *Sarah's Psalm* is Sarah's encounter with African women, rural women especially. While Sarah lives a comfortable life, away from American stratification, she nonetheless comes to discover her own privilege vis-à-vis other women. "Africa" is not thus simply a site in which the heroine comes to self-realization: it is its own site of struggle. Sarah begins to make those connections during her marriage, when she decides to take off on her own and visit a village sustained by women. These women are neither "divine complements" to their men,[19] nor mere "bearers of culture."[20] They are rather bearers of burdens: they work! Sarah lives, works with, and learns from them, "women who had demonstrated their competence in life-sustaining skills, women whose actions were articulate, although not a syllable of their language could I understand. Through them I had realized that an organized collective of women could be a self-reliant community" (Ladd 1996, 222). Sarah neither has a romantic view of African women as queens, even as she witnesses their agency, nor does she victimize women, even as she admits their handicaps.

Sarah also comes to understand that the gender and race she shares with these women—all of the people are women, and all of the women are black—are less significant than the fact that she is wealthy and relatively powerful, whereas they are not: "I wondered whether I would have found life in the bush exhilarating if it were my only life, if I were not returning to the comfort of our well-staffed compound" (ibid.). It is this experience that allows her to see that her leisure is "linked . . . to their work," that what she "had found beautiful, restorative, and stimulating in the lore, language, and quality of life in my quarter of Dakar, was derived, in part, from the toil of village women" (ibid., 223), that "the labor of village women was part of the infrastructure that supported the entire continent."

Sarah will act on her experience and bring this new knowledge to fruition by building political solidarity with women across class and national boundaries around women's felt needs—this, the text suggests, is firmer ground than identity politics. One might argue that the autobiographical framework and first-person voice undercut these revelations and resolutions—the rural women do not speak, they do not participate in Sarah's decision—just as the novel's delight in consumption through its fascination with wine labels, savory foods, and elegant dress may undermine its critique of class. But even a thematic valorization of Sarah's newfound awareness cannot be underestimated, for it is an important precondition for black women's solidarity within and across our nations, especially for those of us standing on this side of the ocean. The understanding of wealth and power differentials and of the lesser importance of gender and racial identities is crucial: a natural sisterhood cannot be assumed.

Sarah's Psalm, The Heart of a Woman, and *Migrations of the Heart* offer complex inquiries into the meaning of Africa as they interrogate and reinvent the identities of women of African descent. They leave off with celebration and turn to questions of power between women and men, between Africa and the Americas. They make clear that none of us can save the other. Our relationships are, above all, subject to our ever-changing needs and continuous negotiations.

Of one thing I am certain, then: until women and men of African descent listen to the plurality and heterogeneity of contemporary African voices, until we encounter Africa as an autonomous if nonetheless kindred space, as a space that therefore "resists" us and perhaps challenges our most cherished myths, and until we found our solidarity on more than race and the past, we will persist in insular and self-absorbed "fictions," perhaps no less damaging than those of imperial and colonial apologists. Ladd, Golden, and Angelou have the merit, in my view, of having shown us the way.

Notes

Versions of this chapter were presented at the University of Yaounde, Cameroon, in January 1999 and at the annual meeting of the African Literature Association in Fez, Morocco, in March 1999. I extend special thanks to Susan Andrade, Biodun Jeyifo, Janis Mayes, Carol Polsgrove, and Sandra Zagarell, who helped me think through the issues presented here and offered invaluable suggestions. I also am grateful to the West African Research Center, Dakar, Senegal, and Indiana University's Institute for Advanced Study at Bloomington, which facilitated the writing of this chapter.

1. While the term *African American* designates all Africans and their descendants who reside in North, Central, or South America, regardless of the date or means of their coming, this chapter focuses primarily on U.S. nationals who are the descendants of enslaved Africans. I shall also use the term *black* American which, unlike African American, acknowledges a history of racialization that has enduring effects.

2. This was the title of a lecture given by Soyinka at Indiana University, September 10, 1997.

3. For an instructive comparison of Morrison's and Walker's symbolic uses of Africa, also see Kadiatu Kanneh's chapter on African-American appropriations of Africa (1998, 109–35).

4. Paul Gilroy also indicates the comparably local focus (what he sees as the myopia) of the African-American critical establishment, exemplified in its reception of Richard Wright's novel *The Outsider*, written in Paris (1993, 155–56).

5. This argument has been made time and again. See Wright 1956 and, in more recent versions, Kwame Anthony Appiah's discussion of Pan-Africanism in *In My Father's House* (1992), or Kadiatu Kanneh's *African Identities* (1998), chapter 3.

6. See, for example, Hall 1992; Cartwright 1997.

7. I am reminded of Kenny, a young black man who was profoundly troubled by the texts that I had chosen for an introductory African literature course, because they did not portray the continent in the glorious light he had imagined, and he found them embarrassing before his white classmates.

Thus, for example, the writings of African women, focused on the Africa that is their home, are characterized by specificity, nuance, and scrutiny. While Ghanaian novelist, playwright, poet, and short story writer Ama Ata Aidoo emphasizes the value of foremotherly wisdom associated with village cultures, as do several African-American writers, she examines also the freedoms and limits that characterize women's lives in village communities, as well as the varied impacts of colonial and postcolonial patriarchy. Novelist Mariama Bâ, writing about her native Senegal, on the other hand, emphatically defends the proposition that urban, middle-class women, at least, have greater resources for self-realization as a result of colonialism. Buchi Emecheta, the Nigerian novelist who lives in exile in London, also acknowledges a customary set of rights and freedoms as well as obligations for Igbo women away from colonial centers but finds little that is redeeming in any setting, under any form of governance, as does Calixthe Beyala of Cameroon, now residing in Paris. Tsitsi Dangarembga, the Zimbabwean novelist, playwright, and filmmaker, now living in Germany, also offers a sober evaluation of women's possibilities in a traditional rural economy or within institutions and systems introduced by colonialism. These are just a few of Africa's prominent writers, but there are no texts by African women of which I am aware that portray the continent as an uncomplicated space of self-fashioning, escape, or longing.

8. Several travel diaries or memoirs have been published in recent years as well. The most (in) famous may be Keith Richburg's *Out of America* (1997). A journalist who spent the period 1991–1994 covering the wars in Rwanda and Somalia, Richburg exposes what is for him the horror of Africa and his relief: "Thank God my ancestor got out. . . . Thank God that I am an American" (ibid., xiv).

For Africans and for those who study and work on Africa, there is unfortunately no news in the fact that the continent has had its share of brutal dictators, repressive militaries, violent upheavals, poverty, and corruption. What is lost here, of course, is a comparable history of brutal dictators, repressive armies, violent upheavals, poverty, and massive corruption that is Europe's fate in history—because that history has no usable meaning in contemporary America.

What Richburg's story reveals, ironically and pathetically, it seems to me, is how deeply wounded he has been by the processes of racialization in the very United States to which he clings as home and salvation. This becomes clear when one tries to imagine a single white American for whom contemporary carnage in Europe leads to a disavowal of his "European racial heritage."

9. Florence Ladd, author of the only fiction among these narratives and a first-time published writer, describes the novel's heroine and hero as composites of many friends and acquaintances. Ladd's own career clearly provided opportunities for thought and experience that inform her novel. After many years as an educator, she served as associate executive director of Oxfam America, making site visits throughout Africa, and she concluded her career in 1998 after a ten-year stint as director of Radcliffe College's Bunting Institute, a center for the promotion of women scholars, artists, and activists from around the world.

10. See Ann Snitow's (1986) and Rosalind Coward's (1986) studies of mass-market romances.

11. Ann du Cille notes that, "Until recently, love and marriage were all but dismissed as female or, at least, feminized themes little worthy of study when juxtaposed to the masculinized racial and freedom discourse assumed to characterize the African-American novel" (1993, 3). Recent scholarship by du Cille and Claudia Tate (1992) has rehabilitated the romance in African-American literary traditions. Tate focuses on post–Reconstruction, woman-authored novels, from the period 1877–1915.

12. What importance, one might ask, is assigned to marriage with Italian or Irish men, for example, in comparable narratives by Italian American or Irish American women?

13. I am referring to the writings of figures such as Martin Delany, W.E.B. DuBois, Richard Wright, Amiri Baraka and, more recently, Molefi Asante. The essay of social analysis and critique has been their favored literary medium.

14. Susan Andrade has offered a particularly useful reading of Maryse Condé's novel in which she argues that, "As the phallus that (temporarily) fills in the absence of history, Ibrahima Sory [Veronica's Sahelian lover] thus represents a gendered inversion of the symbol of Mother Africa or the feminized landscape commonly used by Antillean male writers" (1993, 218).

15. Angelou provides the most explicit remarks on the particular attractiveness of the African-American female for the African man in the 1960s. Make

admits that he has come to the States "'with the intention of finding a strong, beautiful black American woman, who would be a helpmate, who understood the struggle, and who was not afraid of a fight'" (1981, 117). Once he has met Maya, he is impressed with the "manliness" of her son and her sensuality. There are obviously large numbers of strong, beautiful, black African women to go around. So it is their American difference—perhaps their education and "modernity"—that makes these African-American women appealing to African men. This, too, of course, would be a double-edged bargain. See also Harold R. Isaacs' (1961) article on black Americans in Ghana in the 1960s.

16. In *Black Women, Writing, and Identity* (1994), Carole Boyce Davies offers a strong critique of the dominance of African-American (U.S.) models in black feminist criticism, revealing the strain on the category "black women." Such a broad category, encompassing British, African, Latin American, and North American black women, may well be untenable.

17. There is a parallel to African-American letters. Claudia Tate points out that "the representation of freedom found in masculine black protest critiques or an unconsciously male rendition of black cultural nationalism" has led the critical establishment and readers to disparage "domestic stories as narratives of confinement, as narratives of status quo" (1992, 80).

18. It is particularly instructive to contrast this novel's ending to that of Maryse Condé's *Heremakhonon* (1982 [1976]). Veronica, the Guadeloupian heroine of *Heremakhonon*, goes to Africa in pursuit of a prince also or, as she dubs him, a "nigger with ancestors." But Veronica's desire for a Sahelian lover renders her incapable of engaging with the Africans among whom she lives and of exercising all moral judgment regarding her lover's murderous activities on behalf of his nation's dictator. Condé ends her story at the height of a violent political crisis with Veronica's abrupt departure for France, thus suggesting an impasse and the difficulty, if not the impossibility, for a woman of African descent to know Africa through the phallus. Veronica cultivates no friendships with women and must leave West Africa, suggesting, as the inverse of *Sarah's Psalm*, that women are central to women's health.

19. Amiri Baraka's black power movement's pronouncements on "healthy African identities," on the need to embrace "a value system that knows of no separation but only of the divine complement the black woman is for her man" (quoted in hooks 1981, 95) provide evidence of the way Africa was and still is invoked as a justification for male dominance. While this stance was seen as politically oppositional by Baraka and others in the 1960s, hooks offers compelling evidence to the contrary.

20. In *Contemporary African Literature and the Politics of Gender*, Florence Stratton dubs this construction of women in the writings of African men "pots of culture" (1994).

Works Cited

Achebe, Chinua. 1959. *Things Fall Apart*. New York: McDowell, Oblensky.

Andrade, Susan Z. 1993. "The Nigger of the Narcissist: History, Sexuality and Intertextuality in Maryse Condé's *Heremakhonon*." *Callaloo* 16:1: 213–26.

Angelou, Maya. 1981. *The Heart of a Woman*. New York: Random House.

Appiah, Kwame Anthony. 1992. *In My Father's House: Africa in the Philosophy of Culture*. New York: Oxford University Press.

Cartwright, Keith. 1997. "Reading Africa into American Literature." Ph.D. Diss., Indiana University.

Condé, Maryse. 1982 [1976]. *Heremakhonon*. Translated by Richard Philcox. Washington, D.C.: Three Continents Press.

Coward, Rosalind. 1986. Reprint, *Feminist Literary Theory: A Reader*. Edited by Mary Eagleton. Oxford: Basil Blackwell, 145–48. Excerpt from *Female Desire: Women's Sexuality Today*. London: Grafton Books.

Davies, Carole Boyce. 1994. *Black Women, Writing, and Identity: Migrations of the Subject*. London: Routledge.

Du Cille, Ann. 1993. *The Coupling Convention: Sex, Text, and Tradition in Black Women's Fiction*. New York: Oxford University Press.

Gilroy, Paul. 1993. *The Black Atlantic: Modernity and Double Consciousness*. Cambridge: Harvard University Press.

Golden, Marita. 1983. *Migrations of the Heart*. New York: Ballantine.

Hall, Gwendolyn Midlo. 1992. *Africans in Colonial Louisiana*. Baton Rouge: Louisiana University Press.

Harris, Trudier. 1997. "What Is Africa to African-American Women Writers?" Pp. 25–32 in *Contemporary Literature in the African Diaspora*, ed. Olga Barrios and Bernard W. Bell. Leon, Spain: Universidad de Salamanca.

hooks, bell. 1981. *Ain't I a Woman*. Boston: South End Press.

Hulme, Peter. 1986. *Colonial Encounters: Europe and the Native Caribbean, 1492–1791*. New York: Methuen.

Isaacs, Harold R. 1961. "A Reporter at Large: Back to Africa." *The New Yorker*, May 13, p. 105.

Kanneh, Kadiatu. 1998. *African Identities*. London: Routledge.

Ladd, Florence. 1996. *Sarah's Psalm*. New York: Scribner.

Pratt, Mary Louise. 1992. *Imperial Eyes: Travel Writing and Transculturation*. London: Routledge.

Richburg, Keith. 1997. *Out of America: A Black Man Confronts Africa*. New York: Basic Books.

Snitow, Ann. 1986. Reprint, *Feminist Literary Theory: A Reader*. Edited by Mary Eagleton. Oxford: Basil Blackwell, 134–40. Excerpt from "Mass Market Romance: Pornography for Women Is Different." *Radical History Review* 20 (1979): 141–61.

Soyinka, Wole. 1997. "The Fictioning of Africa." Patton Lecture. Indiana University, September 10, 1997.

Stratton, Florence. 1994. *Contemporary African Literature and the Politics of Gender*. London: Routledge.

Tate, Claudia. 1992. *Domestic Allegories of Political Desire*. New York: Oxford University Press.

Willis, Susan. 1985. "Black Women Writers: Taking a Critical Perspective." Pp. 211–37 in *Making a Difference: Feminist Literary Criticism*, ed. Gayle Greene and Coppelia Kahn. London: Methuen.

Wright, Richard. 1956. "Tradition and Industrialization." *Présence Africaine* 8, 9, 10: 347–60.

CHAPTER SEVEN

ETHNICITY AS OTHERNESS
IN BRITISH IDENTITY POLITICS

ROBERT J. C. YOUNG

The famous inability of an insomniac sun to ever manage to set on the British Empire—until, that is, the stroke of midnight, on August 15, 1947—suggests that British imperialism constituted the first historical experience of globalization. The local became the global before it became the local again. This systolic imperial rhythm scattered local Anglo-Saxons over the globe, settling in North America, South Africa, and Australasia before the flow turned and a reverse colonization from the margins of the Empire to the metropolitan center made the global local, or rather, in Harish Trivedi's felicitous reformulation, the glocal lobal. As an Indian–Pakistani joke puts it, "Oh, no," they said to the British as they were leaving in 1947, "you won't get rid of us that easily!"[1] Or, in Salman Rushdie's (1988) more vengeful version in *The Satanic Verses*: "He would show them—yes!—his *power*. These powerless English!—Did they not think their history would return to haunt them? 'The native is an oppressed person whose permanent dream is to become the persecutor' (Fanon)" (353).

The Empire strikes back: "We are here because you were there." This combative and simultaneously defensive piece of immigrant graffiti testifies to the dramatic transformation that has occurred in Britain since the Second World War. The British withdrew fairly rapidly from the countries that made up their empire after 1947, but no one in Britain anticipated that postcolonial Britain itself would be transformed in the next fifty years into a culture that has incorporated diversity in such a radical, new, creative form. This reorientation has meant that English identity no longer comprises the singular scenario of a garlic-free world of pinstripe suits and clipped, high-pitched, staccato voices. Of course, it had never been just like that anyway, but one of the more curious achievements of imperial culture was to impress upon the world the properties of Englishness that encapsulated the identity only of its elite, ruling class. In the nineteenth century, the class war was won at the level of representation as well as political power. Today, however, the world has begun to perceive that the British as a whole come in a range of models, not only in class terms but also as a result of the increasing emphasis on the national and ethnic diversities contained within the not very United Kingdom of Great Britain and Northern Ireland. As a result, in recent years, English identity as such has been left in something of a vacuum. Everyone has been so busy deconstructing Englishness and English nationalism, according to its identity of the past, that they have only recently begun to notice that it has been suffering something of an identity crisis—no one these days is quite sure what properties constitute Englishness—aside, that is, from the continuing class snobbery of the abject remnants of the prewar middle and upper classes. This is a crisis not only for the English but also for anyone else in Britain, such as the Scots—or abroad, in places such as Australia—who defines their identity against them. There is, as it were, no same for the other. One indication of this situation is that no one admits to being just English any more. Whereas in the old days many people used to cover up any non-English ancestry, today everyone has suddenly rediscovered their forgotten Irish grandmothers, their Anglo-Indian grandfather, or their Scottish roots. What used to be the most valuable attribute, to be English, has lost its value in cultural terms, whereas what used to have a negative value, being Irish, has gained positive value. This is true also of that curious category "English Literature," which is in the process of breaking up into its regional traditions and identities. Today, British identity, which used to be so often just a synonym for Englishness, has given way before the resurgence of cultural nationalisms—particularly among the Scots and Welsh, who look to the success of Irish cultural nationalism for their political model. The arrival, for the most part after the Second World War, of peoples from the Caribbean, South Asia, and Africa broadened the mixture. They transformed the situation decisively, not merely by the degree of cultural difference but also because their physical differences were not invisible.

Since the 1950s, British society, formerly divided up according to class interests, found itself challenged by new forms of minority politics. Of course, Britain had always had a form—a rather different form—of minority politics, in the sense that it had always been (and probably still is) ruled by a minority. The new forms of minority politics were different: they involved minorities who were not politically disenfranchised but rather disadvantaged solely because of their being part of a minority. Such politics, whether of ethnic minorities or the women's movement, involved conceptual as well as political strategies. They were similar in that they both had to deal with disadvantage resulting from physical markers of difference. Both groups had to contend with the prescription of biology as destiny and to counter the prejudiced assumption of social and cultural inferiority as an effect of biological difference. As a result, a parallel conceptual distinction was forged that disputed the cultural values that followed from the properties of biological difference: for women, between the female (biology) and the feminine (culture); for ethnic minorities, between race (biology) and ethnicity (culture). With a little help from Althusser and Lacan, this was accompanied by an attack on essentialism, that is, any form of identification between the two now distinct categories, biology and culture, whose interrelation was more or less denied, most famously in that awesome dictum that we must *never* confuse the phallus with the penis.

The separation of culture from biology allowed the active construction of positive identities in the place of the negative ones that had formerly been ascribed to the minority by the majority. In both cases, the problem remained of what to do about the biological. Some feminists, such as Judith Butler, have moved to a view in which gender attributes are regarded not as expressive but as performative, with nothing essential or biological determining them (Butler 1990). Ethnicity was trickier. The initial form of the word, ethnic, originally simply constituted the adjectival form of the noun, race. It was only after Auschwitz that race was officially deconstructed at the UNESCO conference on race in 1950, where it was recommended that "the use of the term race be dropped, and the term 'ethnic group' be adopted instead" (UNESCO 1969, 497). The notion of an "ethnic minority" was invented in 1945, with "ethnicity" following in 1953, in order to provide a way of describing what the

Oxford English Dictionary, in a significant hedge, calls "a group of people differentiated from the rest of the community by racial origins or cultural background, and usually claiming or enjoying official recognition of their group identity."

The category of race, insofar as it was connected to any biological basis, is today disavowed in favor of a cultural-political grouping. The notion of ethnicity allows the denial of any biological determinism, and the claim from some that one can simply choose one's ethnicity on the analogy of being able to choose one's sexuality, or one can perform one's ethnicity on the analogy of being able to turn gender into performance. But what does one do then with the physical properties of difference? One cannot turn forms of ethnicity associated with the property of skin color into something entirely performative—although one can construct any performance one likes from the signifier. The signifier may be floating, but one cannot choose to deny one's ownership of it altogether if the majority, or even a minority of the majority, enforces its significance. This situation is nicely exposed in a passage in Samuel Selvon's *The Lonely Londoners* (1985 [1956], 88–89):

> And Galahad would take his hand from under the blanket, as he lay there studying how the night before he was in the lavatory and two white fellars come in and say how these black bastards have [made] the lavatory dirty, and they didn't know that he was there, and when he come out they say hello mate have a cigarette. And Galahad watch the colour of his hand, and talk to it, saying, "Colour, is you that causing all this, you know. Why the hell you can't be blue, or red or green, if you can't be white? You know is you that cause a lot of misery in the world. Is not me, you know, is you! I ain't do anything to infuriate the people and them, is you! Look at you, you so black and innocent, and this time so you causing misery all over the world!"
>
> So Galahad talking to the colour Black, as if is a person, telling it that is not *he* who causing botheration in the place, but Black, who is a worthless thing for making trouble all about. . . .
>
> Galahad get so interested in this theory about Black that he went and tell Moses. "Is not we that the people don't like," he tell Moses, "is the colour Black.". . .
>
> Moses tell Galahad, "Take it easy, that is a sharp theory, why you don't write about it."

Ethnicity may be a cultural construction, so that one can contest and then construct one's own identity. But one cannot refuse the materiality of the signifier, the "racial epidermal schema" of one's skin color, if it has been given a social significance by others for one (Fanon 1986 [1952], 112). In a racialized confrontation, one is owned by the color of one's skin. The social meaning of its properties has already been written. As Fanon put it four years before Selvon in "The Fact of Blackness," in *Black Skin, White Masks*: "I am given no chance. I am overdetermined from without. I am the slave not of the "idea" that others have of me but of my own appearance" (1986 [1952], 116). Like Galahad upon his arrival in Britain, Fanon finds that the social meaning of the property of blackness has already been written. He is "overdetermined from without." The trick, therefore, is to rewrite it.

Writing race. Race has always been written. It has always been the signifier of otherness, the written mark of the body, whether of skin color or of hair and eyes. That is why race slips so easily into a form of paranoia—because it essentially involves overinterpretation—interpreting something of little or no significance as being significant, or rather overwhelmingly significant. Paranoia is the result of interpreting meaningless signs as meaningful. Race was predominantly written in the nineteenth century in the form of a biological and cultural typology; its reinstitution as ethnicity involves wresting the power of the already written to a power of writing, of choosing the signifiers and controlling their meaning. This is the real difference between the concept of ethnicity and that of race, and it suggests why ethnicity still hovers uneasily on any complete denial of the biological. It accounts for the some of the differences in the models of cultural identity between, say, Scots and British African-Caribbeans. That is because the former do not have the disadvantage—or advantage—of possessing the signifier that produces that flash of recognition—of a meaning that is already written—from the English other. They have to assert it, to lay claim to it, through the invocation of cultural properties, of language, history, and place. The difference for anyone who is white in a white-dominated society is that one can turn the signifier on and off, one can decide whether to be same or to come out as the other—it is as easy as putting on one's kilt or taking it off. This flexibility is clear from the variable force with which Scottish nationalism and the different forms of its ethnic identifications have been asserted at different historical moments. Galahad, in *The Lonely Londoners* (Selvon 1985 [1956]), had no such choice of identification with his black skin, nor does anyone today with any skin that looks a shade away from white.

Race, therefore, continues uneasily to shadow ethnicity. The attempt to separate the biological from the cultural always creates an unsustainable dichotomy—even the scientific accounts of race were never just biological. In the face of this, the distinction between race and ethnicity could be usefully reformulated by starting out with the fact that both share a set of common properties, cultural and biological. Whereas the thesis of race as the biological, ethnicity as the cultural, claims a complete separation between the two, if one thinks of race and ethnicity as possessing common forms of property, the dynamics between them can become clearer. Race, in its traditional historical usage, gives the greatest cultural value to the property of the body, whose intrinsic properties then prompt the devaluation of all of the other properties that a race may possess, regarded as comparatively peripheral, a by-product of a particular physical and mental capacity, that is, a shared history, geographical space, language, religion, culture, cultural aesthetic, cuisine, and so on (no individual one of which is, of course, essential). Ethnicity, on the other hand, sees ethnic identity in terms of a shared set of properties, of which history, language, religion, culture, and so on are the determining and therefore the most valuable, while the properties of the communal body—skin color, physiognomy— though in many respects still essential, are comparatively peripheral and of no determining significant status. The race, therefore, shares exactly the same properties with the ethnic group, but the cultural value of the different elements that define it differs radically.

There is a major conceptual difference, however, in ethnicity's claim, apart from the relation to the biological, and that is a political one. Race, as it was developed in the nineteenth century by racial theorists such as Gobineau, in the *Essay on the Inequality of Races* (1853–1855), constituted a taxonomy of an absolute physical and cultural difference that would never change, resulting in a claim of a permanent hierarchy between the races. Race, in other words, meant that the races were not only different but also unequal—and that difference meant inequality on a permanent basis. Today, however, otherness is, in a sense, no longer an absolute otherness, for its otherness is bound up with the condition of also being part of the same. Today, with the transformation of the markers of difference into the category of ethnicity, the equation has been decisively rewritten: with ethnicity, one is allowed to be different, but it goes along with a recognition that at a fundamental level, both in terms of intellectual and cultural capacity and in terms of political rights, one is essentially the same. This is why, incidentally, it makes no sense to reject universals for a postmodern particularity in the name of difference—because in demanding general political rights, anyone is assuming universals.[2]

Ethnicity, therefore, like identity and race, involves both sameness and difference, a hybrid formation that could be said to be at the heart of postcolonialism as such. If ethnicity, however, is still constructed as otherness by a dominant social group, that otherness is today generally predicated on an equal assumption of sameness. The other is not, as it was formerly for race, an absolute other but a form of difference. Ethnicity operates within the boundaries of the social and is thus not completely other, whereas race is cast out, beyond the pale. This is very different from African-American politics in the United States, where race has been reclaimed, giving it some biological value, blackness, but changing its associated cultural value, a movement that was formally instituted by African Americans in the United States with the founding of the National Association for the Advancement of Colored People (NAACP) in 1909 (Kellogg 1967). African-American commentators such as bell hooks, Henry Louis Gates Jr., or Cornel West insist that, to cite the title of West's book, *Race Matters* (1993). Gates and West (1997) have recently published a book in which they pronounce on *The Future of the Race*.[3] In the United States, the term *race* has a history of being used as a synonym for what is now called "African American" or "black," as, for example, in the "Victor Race Records" that were devoted to recordings of blues singers. In contemporary U.S. "critical race theory," race and "the race" have been turned around and retrieved as positive terms, allowing a continuing acknowledgment of the realities of the body, while giving black culture an ever-more powerful, positive, and coherent value. This is simply because ethnicity as a concept denies the foundations of what makes African Americans African Americans; it erases the history—and the history of the rewriting of that history—of their construction as a race, as well as the heroic countercultural constructions of the past, such as Booker T. Washington's "New Negro."[4] The concept of ethnicity denies the obvious racial experience that African Americans have to live every day, as well as the basis for their own cultural communities. The perpetuation of African-American identity as that of a "race" reflects the fact that socially as well as economically, the United States is a society that remains deeply divided along racial lines. As a result, "race" is, in a sense, owned by African Americans, with the term *people of color* operating as its related supplement to describe other groups such as Chicanos and Chicanas. The term *eth-nicity* tends to be used exclusively rather for white people, for Euro-peans—Italians, Jews, and so on. Here ethnicity and race continue the division and distinction in nineteenth-century racial theory between proximate and distant races. Britain has no comparable history of reconstructing "race"—black activism in London before the Second World War was concerned with the politics of the African and Caribbean independence movements; since the war, it has been directed toward the politics of anti-racism and the discrediting of any concept of race.

In the United States, race is a given. It has its own long, agonistic, domes-tic history that cannot simply be denied. In the British model, identifiable with the positions of Stuart Hall (1988, 1990, 1991a, 1991b), Paul Gilroy (1993), Kobena Mercer (1994), and Kwame Anthony Appiah (1992), race is rejected as absolutist, biological, essentialist, or intrinsic. In its place, ethnicity, no longer an "otherness" proper, is affirmed as a form of differential identity, and this constitutes the basis of an identity politics that can be adapted for any minority. If ethnicity is a marker of difference, then that means that it is not fixed or essential. You can add properties or take them away. What the ethnic minority itself can do is to attempt to reverse or shift the significance of the dominant culture's neg-ative interpretation of the signifier in what Voloshinov called the struggle for the sign. If race was a category through which groups of individuals were othered, ethnicity is a means through which that group can control and construct its forms of otherness, investing itself with a dynamic form of cultural agency. The minority can resist the dominant by becoming the agent of its own signification and cultural representation, and this is what has been done with such success by ethnic minorities in Britain in the past decades. This began with the anti-racist movement and the politicization of the term *black* to describe all ethnic minorities who were subject to oppression. In recent years, that political solidarity among ethnic minori-ties, still observable in names such as the "Southall Black Sisters," who are in fact Asian, has broken down, with different groups seeking to establish individual, specific cultural identities. However, other forms of solidarity have developed in different ways through the politics of repre-sentation. The claim to self-representation, resistance through self-repre-sentation, has been articulated and achieved above all in the area of the popular culture, particularly music, of British youth culture. Indeed black British, or more accurately perhaps black Atlantic, culture has become so much the dominant music scene today that both Asian and white teenagers have started to emulate black street style and dress, a phenomenon that has come to be known as "whiggery." This development undoes any multiculturalist assumption that each ethnic group will always pursue its own individual identity, its own form of self-expression, its own future. Rather, what we have here are common forms of identification across different ethnic groups that are more concerned with participating in contemporary youth subcultures and marking themselves with their forms of difference than perpetuating discrete ethnic identities. This process forms the main subject of Hanif Kureishi's novel *The Buddha of Suburbia* (1990). Such forms of identification do not stop at music: they also can be found in the popularity, among younger sections of different ethnic groups, of Louis Farrakhan's "Nation of Islam."

Ten years ago, Stuart Hall remarked on this dynamic feature of contemporary black British culture. What he noticed was that those at the periphery of society seemed to be simultaneously at its center, those who had no economic or political property to hold the cultural property of greatest value:

> I've been puzzled by the fact that young black people in London today are marginalized, fragmented, unenfranchized, disadvantaged and dispersed. And yet, they look as if they own the territory. Somehow, they . . . in spite of everything, are centered, in place: without much material support, it's true, but nevertheless, they occupy a new kind of space at the centre. And I've wondered again and again: what is it about that long discovery-rediscovery of identity among blacks in this migrant situation, which allows them to lay a kind of claim to certain parts of the earth which aren't theirs, with quite that certainty? I do feel a sense of—dare I say—envy surrounding them. Envy is a very funny thing for the British to feel at this moment in time—to want to be black! Yet I feel some of you surreptitiously moving toward that marginal identity. (1987, 44)

"This moment was registered as a 'break,'" recalls Kobena Mercer (1994, 19): the moment when marginal identity and diaspora aesthetics became, in contemporary British culture, almost the typical, most widely felt, or most desired form of identification.

Identification with the migrant as the center of British culture also operates in a different way in the cultural and academic sphere. The Booker Prize (the British equivalent of the Pulitzer) has transformed the identity of contemporary British fiction by broadening the metropolitan mainstream to include many international writers in English, from Salman Rushdie to Ben Okri to Arundhati Roy. These writers are balanced by those representing Britain's older ethnicities, such as Roddy Doyle. In the 1960s, it was the working-class culture that seized the void left at the center of a post-imperial English identity, defining the "swinging London" of the Wilson era. Oddly, perhaps, and against all expectations, in the course of the era of Mrs. Thatcher, British ethnic minorities have come to dominate the cultural self-representation of contemporary Britain—or rather, England. Arguably, multicultural identity is more relevant to England than to Britain as a whole, in the sense that it is more England than Wales or Scotland that tends to be represented as multicultural in this way (Ireland's multiculturalism, of course, is of an entirely different order, usually designated in negative terms as sectarianism). Significantly, the brilliant black poet, Jackie Kay, who was brought up in Scotland, has now moved south of the border. Multicultural England now represents itself as "British," as opposed to Scottish, Welsh, or Irish, while "English" is used more specifically within England as a synonym for "white," not only by those on the right but also within ethnic minority communities. This transformation of the culture of England into a more heterogeneous British identity often has gone unnoticed by those whose own cultural identity has been defined against the union—it was striking, for example, that despite a lifetime of analysis of "The Break-up of Britain," Tom Nairn could recently describe the parents of murdered black teenager Stephen Lawrence as "*English.*"[5] The cure for "anti-Englishness" that, according to Nairn, Scotland badly needs, and which can only be found "by her own efforts," could begin with the recognition of the present-day realities of life in England today.

At a cultural level, this translated reality is best represented in Rushdie's hybridized postcolonial London, but think also of the work of so many other writers—Kazuo Ishiguro, Timothy Mo, Sunetra Gupta, Joan Riley, Caryl Phillips, Merle Collins, and Diran Adebayo, to name just a few—along with films that seem to define, yet transgress, contemporary British hybridized culture, such as *My Beautiful Laundrette*, *Sammy and Rosie Get Laid*, *Bhaji on the Beach*, or Isaac Julien's *Looking for Langston*. The work of such writers, filmmakers, and musicians is increasingly supported by those in the media, the arts councils, and the academy, which now see as their duty articulating the voices of the silenced, marginalized minorities of the present and the past. The same forces provide institutional funding from Channel 4 television and the British Film Institute for black cinema and institutionalize such forms of cultural production in academic degree courses, in conferences in and outside of the United Kingdom, hosted by the British Council, a British government agency. All of these things suggest that Britain's ethnic minorities have captured the cultural center ground, so much so that they have created what has become the dominant form of self-representation of British culture today. Ethnicity has been so successful in moving in on contemporary English culture that, as Stuart Hall observed, the margin has become the center.

Or has it? Despite Hall's claim, that is not how it often feels on the street. How can we account for this disparity? Music provides the obvious answer: the music of youth cultures, as Dick Hebdige (1979) has shown, is always subcultural or countercultural. It is not the center itself but an act of resistance to the center. What Hall has done is to mistake the first as the second. Cultural authority appears to have shifted to the margins and left the center disempowered. But as black American culture makes clear, the cultural properties of what is cool and fashionable are not necessarily possessed by the center of power and economic well-being—a fact vividly brought out when it was reported that Cheryl Mills, President Clinton's black woman lawyer, was only the third African American ever to speak on the floor of the American Senate. If the center lacks the fashionable, it can always be bought, appropriated. Ethnicity gets commodified. Its culture gets celebrated. It is the government that provides, through its various liberal institutional intermediaries, much of the funding for black culture in Britain today.

The problem with any claim that minority artists and writers have become the center is that the status, and in many cases the implicit aesthetic, of ethnic minority artists, writers, and academics is in some sense still guaranteed and authenticated by the continuing marginalization and social deprivation of Britain's ethnic minorities. The latter are no longer culturally marginalized, but economic disadvantage, particularly for African Caribbeans, is as great as ever. The emphasis on positive identities and on the politics of self-representation means that the signifier has started to float again. Just as with the old colonial stereotypes, there has been a slippage between the representation and the real, between the image and the realities of poverty and social deprivation. Moreover, as the *Satanic Verses* affair indicated, the problem with the representations of minorities by minority writers is that their cultural values often are implicitly directed at the white majority and constructed in terms which that majority will find sympathetic. In fact, it is the government that provides, through its various intermediaries, much of the funding for black cultural production in Britain today. Crudely, minority artists who endorse the dominant liberal view are celebrated. Those who do not, or whose work does not address the majority, or who do not work in the appropriate media remain unheard and unregarded. The case of *The Satanic Verses* brought out these issues very clearly. Here the British government found itself in the ultra-liberal position of defending one of its former critics, because Rushdie's assertion of his right to liberal values (artistic freedom above morality) accorded with the government's position against that of so-called Islamic fundamentalism. What the outcry showed is that Rushdie, like many ethnic minority artists, could not cash in his claim to speak for the minority whom he had been presumed to represent. For once the subaltern spoke and was heard. The minority refused to be treated as Rushdie's own cultural property, to allow its own cultural representation to be transformed and translated into the paradigms of Western liberal ideology, just as it refused to accept his recontextualization of the *Qu'ran* in a hybridized "composite" of translations, mediated, as Rushdie put it, "with a few touches of my own" (1988, 549).

Rushdie could be said to offer a paradigm for a certain version of postcolonial studies, which likes to imagine that its politics of difference subverts the dominant (Western) culture, but there is little reason to assume that postcolonial values toward cultural difference are in themselves subversive for Western cultures. Consider a recent questionnaire in a British newspaper:

Do you have a global mind-set?

- When you interact with others, do you assign them equal status regardless of national origin?
- Do you regard your values to be a hybrid of values acquired from multiple cultures, as opposed to just one culture?
- Do you consider yourself as open to ideas from other countries and cultures as you are to ideas from your own country and culture of origin?

If one can answer in the affirmative to all of these questions, then the paper assures that one has "a global mind-set." In fact, the questionnaire formed part of a supplement to the London *Financial Times* called "Mastering Global Business" (February 27, 1998, part 5, p. 3).

In Rushdie's case, in fact, the subversion worked the other way. The British Conservative government sprang to Rushdie's defense and was more or less happy to support him against the hostility of the minority culture that his work really did attempt to subvert. Rushdie had forged for himself the cultural identity of the anti-racist spokesperson for Britain's ethnic minorities, promoting in his writing the liberal value of multicultural hybridization against an alternative that advocated a distinct culture with different cultural values: in other words, integration rather than separation. However, it was exactly these cultural values for which Rushdie was attacked by Muslims in Britain and elsewhere. With respect to any ethnic minority community, the issue remains: whose representations are represented and received, who authorizes them, and who controls them?

The gap between the representation and the represented does not only operate at the level of cultural values. The celebration of the "new ethnicities" also has participated in the tendency of identity politics in general to draw the political focus away from more mundane but material issues such as poverty, inequality, and disempowerment. Today in Britain the poor are the forgotten minority—the unglamorous other, deprived of their voice. Booker Prize winners notwithstanding, even fashionable ethnicity, wherever one goes in Britain today, still lives in the poorest part of town.

Notes

1. My thanks to Sadiq Ahmed for telling me this joke.

2. Cf. Laclau 1995, 105.

3. See Crenshaw 1996; see also Gaines 1996 and Williams 1991. My thanks to Emily Apter for our discussions about the differences between the United Kingdom and the United States in this regard.

4. A history rewritten in Gibson 1920; Nichols and Crogman 1925; Washington et al. 1900.

5. Tom Nairn, "Union Station," *Independent on Sunday*, September 30, 1998, p. 7 (emphasis in original).

Works Cited

Appiah, Kwame Anthony. 1992. *In My Father's House: Africa in the Philosophy of Culture.* London: Methuen.

Butler, Judith. 1990. *Gender Trouble: Feminism and the Subversion of Identity.* New York: Routledge.

Crenshaw, Kimberle, ed. 1996. *Critical Race Theory: The Key Writings That Formed the Movement*. New York: New Press.

Fanon, Frantz. 1986 [1952]. *Black Skin, White Masks*. Translated by Charles Lam Markmann. London: Pluto.

Gaines, Kevin K. 1996. *Uplifting the Race: Black Leadership, Politics, and Culture in the Twentieth Century*. Chapel Hill: University of North Carolina Press.

Gates, Henry Louis Jr., and Cornel West. 1997. *The Future of the Race*. New York: Vintage Books.

Gibson, John William. 1920. *Progress of a Race, or the Remarkable Advancement of the American Negro, from the Bondage of Slavery, Ignorance, and Poverty to the Freedom of Citizenship, Intelligence, Affluence, Honor, and Trust*. Revised and enlarged edition. Naperville, Ill.: J. L. Nichols and Company.

Gilroy, Paul. 1993. *The Black Atlantic: Modernity and Double Consciousness*. London: Verso.

Gobineau, Joseph Arthur comte de. 1853–1855. *Essai sur l'inégalité des races humaines*. 4 vols. Paris: Firmin Didot.

Hall, Stuart. 1987. "Minimal Selves." *Identity, The Real Me: Post-Modernism and the Question of Identity*. ICA Documents 6:44–46.

———. 1988. "New Ethnicities." *Black Film British Cinema*. ICA Documents 7: 27–31.

———. 1990. "Cultural Identity and Diaspora." Pp. 222–37 in *Identity: Community, Culture, Difference*, ed. Jonathan Rutherford. London: Lawrence and Wishart.

———. 1991a. "The Local and the Global: Globalization and Ethnicity." Pp. 19–39 in *Culture, Globalization, and the World-System*, ed. Anthony D. King. Bastingstoke, U.K.: Macmillan.

———. 1991b. "Old and New Identities, Old and New Ethnicities." Pp. 41–68 in *Culture, Globalization, and the World-System*, ed. Anthony D. King. Bastingstoke, U.K.: Macmillan.

Hebdige, Dick. 1979. *Subculture: The Meaning of Style*. London: Methuen.

Kellogg, Charles Flint. 1967. *NAACP: A History of the National Association for the Advancement of Colored People*. Vol. 1: 1909–1920. Baltimore: Johns Hopkins University Press.

King, Anthony D., ed. 1991. *Culture, Globalization, and the World-System*. Bastingstoke, U.K.: Macmillan.

Kureishi, Hanif. 1990. *The Buddha of Suburbia*. London: Faber and Faber.

Laclau, Ernesto. 1995. "Universalism, Particularism and the Question of Identity." Pp. 101–10 in *The Identity in Question*, ed. John Rajchman. New York: Routledge.

Mercer, Kobena. 1994. *Welcome to the Jungle: New Positions in Black Cultural Studies*. London: Routledge.

Nichols, J. L., and William H. Crogman. 1925. *The New Progress of a Race*. Washington, D.C.: A. Jenkins.

Rushdie, Salman. 1988. *The Satanic Verses*. London: Viking.

Selvon, Samuel. 1985 [1956]. *The Lonely Londoners*. Harlow, U.K.: Longman.

UNESCO. 1969 [1961]. *The Race Question in Modern Science: Race and Science*. New York: Columbia University Press.

Washington, Booker T., N. B. Wood, Fannie Barrier Williams et al. 1900. *A New Negro for a New Century*. Chicago: American Publishing House.

West, Cornel. 1993. *Race Matters*. Boston: Beacon.

Williams, Patricia A. 1991. *The Alchemy of Race and Rights: Diary of a Law Professor*. Cambridge: Harvard University Press.

CHAPTER EIGHT

REINCARNATING IMMIGRANT BIOGRAPHY

On Migration and Transmigration

AKHIL GUPTA

This chapter is inspired by a simple question: How does one write the life history of people who have experienced the dislocations of immigration from colonized or formerly colonized parts of the world to the metropolitan centers of the colonial world? How do transmigration and reincarnation, the eternal migration of a soul and its periodic reembodiment, trouble received (Western) canonical notions of autobiography, biography, life history, and the bourgeois novel? Exploring this question largely through the autobiography of one of the first prominent South Asian American writers, Dhan Gopal Mukerji, leads me to reflect on the specificities of immigrant experiences. Immigrant narratives depend on an implicit notion of the continuity of life that is itself brought into question by the rupture instantiated by immigration. I wonder, then, if through the category of transmigration, we may not be able to reimagine "immigrant biography." Is it possible to think of immigrant biography as not merely illuminating the lives of those who have been marginal to, or excluded from, conventional narratives of (national) history but as fundamentally challenging the narrative strategies by which the history of an individual life, and History as the biography of a nation, proceeds?

Reflecting on the temporality of displacement and the problem of representing immigrant experiences also raises questions of the analytical strategies by which efforts to go beyond dichotomies have proceeded. A new critical lexicon has enabled us to come to grips with the phenomenon of the global flows of people, capital, finance, ideas, images, technologies, and biota. Many phenomena, such as immigration, which had been put into a straitjacket by dualistic and nationalist conceptual frameworks divided, for example, into "sending" nations and "receiving" nations or motivated by "push" factors or "pull" factors, can now be reconsidered from perspectives that themselves historicize the nation-state, position immigration within a field of global capitalist relations, or interrogate the discrepant processes of globalization, in which the rapid rates of movement of finance contrast with the multiple controls put on the movement of people across national boundaries. If globalization is the name of an extremely uneven process, predicated, for example, on the highly unsymmetrical movement of people who have U.S. or European Community passports, versus those who have Indian or Sri Lankan passports, how is a theory of globalization to be formulated? By what concepts, metaphors, analogies, and habits of thinking is globalization itself to be grasped? What ideologies, histories, and intellectual traditions are privileged in the understanding and explanation of globalization? How are structural, systemic, cultural, and symbolic differences to be accounted for in the very terms in which globalization is described and understood? I address these questions by thinking about an alternative way by which to approach the life narratives of immigrants, one that fundamentally questions the ontological assumptions of the genre and the territorial assumptions of the category "immigrant."

When *Caste and Outcast* was published in 1923, Dhan Gopal Mukerji was thirty-three years old. The book, his first non-fictional work, was an instant hit, with five printings in the 1920s. It was published simultaneously in England, and French and Czech editions appeared in the next few years. Mukerji studied at Berkeley and Stanford and taught comparative literature briefly at Stanford. For the rest of his life, he was to become a member of the East Coast literary establishment, writing twenty-six books, mostly from 1922 until his death, by suicide, in 1936. Mukerji was a prominent defender of Indian nationalism in the United States, a close friend of Jawaharlal Nehru, and one of the preeminent translators and interpreters of Hindu philosophy and religious texts. Many of these ideas found their way into the dozen prize-winning books that he wrote for children, for which he is probably best remembered today.

Caste and Outcast opens by announcing the impossibility of its autobiographical project. How does one represent a Hindu's experience to a Western audience? Mukerji writes (1923, 3), "Though the early part of my life was much like that of other children of my caste, I find that in attempting to describe it to English readers, I am at once in a dilemma." The dilemma concerns the difficulty of constructing a narrative for readers who do not have the requisite background to understand "the real meaning" of even the simplest events. How is one to explain events from a radically different cultural and religious context to readers in the West? Mukerji (1923, 4) says: ". . . here is the dilemma to convey this in a manner consistent with the western idea of what a book ought to be. I fear it is impossible."[1] The narrative is doomed to digression and fragmentation, as events whose meaning might be obvious to any Brahmin boy have to be patiently explained to the uninitiated (Western) reader. The recuperation of the individual's life as a progressive project that is the hallmark of the genre of masculine autobiography is here frustrated by the difficulties of cultural translation (Smith and Watson 1992, xvii). This is only the first of many difficulties that Mukerji encounters as he bravely embarks on his "impossible" task.

Caste and Outcast is almost symmetrically divided: the first part describes Mukerji's life in India ("Caste"), and the second deals with his life in the United States ("Outcast"). The narrative closely follows the conventions of autobiography in being chronologically ordered, beginning with Mukerji's childhood.[2] We know that by the time *Caste and Outcast* was published, Mukerji had returned to India for a visit in 1921. However, the autobiography ends abruptly with Mukerji's student days at Berkeley, that is, sometime before 1914.

Apart from its chronological structure, Mukerji's autobiography shares little with the stereotypical U.S. immigrant narrative. His is not a tale of overcoming misfortune and enduring hardship to finally make it in this land of opportunity, nor is it an assimilationist narrative, in which the oppressive weight of tradition and the colorful customs of his past life are described in order to be cast off when he joins the American melting pot. He resists, too, the autobiographical imperative of Whiggishness, whereby his life story is one of personal growth and direction. He finds neither solace nor salvation in immigration, nothing that might enable him to find order or purpose in his life, but plenty of adventure and fresh experiences. He does not come to find wealth, political liberation, or personal freedom, and he does not find them. What we get instead is a curious, poignant tale of wanderlust, a story of a deep and an unfulfilled spiritual quest.[3]

Loss is intimated in the titles of the two halves of *Caste and Outcast*. The first part, "Caste," about his life in India, is saturated with the intimacy of community, family, and belonging. Unlike many other treatments of life in caste society, his is not a story of the unbearably oppressive weight of that institution. Of course, being a Brahmin placed him in a privileged position, but even privilege in a highly segmented society can take its psychic and emotional toll.

In contrast, the second part of his autobiography, "Outcast," about his life in the United States, is about being thrown out of community. "Outcast" carries with it the violence of expulsion, of being forsaken, rejected, ostracized; "outcaste," the term that is clearly being invoked by the pairing with "caste," is about removal from a caste community, something Mukerji hazarded in crossing the seven seas. But the title also is a reference to his life on the fringes of respectable society in the United States, among the anarchists, socialists, free thinkers, café intellectuals, farm workers, and hoboes of the San Francisco Bay Area.

Mukerji's description of his own journey in *Caste and Outcast*, then, cuts across the grain of the standard narrative authorized by the hegemonic ideology of immigration in the United States.[4] Instead of finding a new home in a new land, he concludes that America is "a continent fierce with homelessness" (1923, 301). He refuses the assimilationist credo by which he might have concluded that his new life was materially or spiritually more satisfying than the one he left behind, but he equally resists the nostalgic urge to describe his journey as primarily one of loss and longing. One particularly clear example of this is provided toward the end of the book (ibid., 298): "This was America neither worse nor better than India. All life was a wretched joke and every joke was a sordid travesty. I could bear it no longer." The epilogue sets out to compare India and the United States explicitly and offers this conclusion, which could scarcely have been comforting to nationalists in either country: "Both India and America are mad. India has been mad with peace and America is mad with restlessness. It is this madness that has drawn me to them both" (ibid., 303).

It would help to place Mukerji's journey in the larger history of South Asian migration to the United States. When Mukerji landed in San Francisco in 1910, he joined a very small number of men from the subcontinent (they were exclusively men), mostly from the north Indian state of Punjab. These men worked largely as agricultural laborers in the rich farmlands of California, and Mukerji spends a chapter in *Caste and Outcast* describing the time he spent as a farm worker with people from the subcontinent. But class, cultural capital, and language created a gulf between them too large for him to cross. He describes these South Asian laborers, from the perspective of one who is superior by virtue of cultural and educational capital, as people engrossed in the pursuit of material wealth with little regard for their spiritual condition. As it is this spiritual quest that he is obsessed with throughout the book, there is a certain flatness to his conclusions and observations about the United States. He finds a society preoccupied with the satisfaction of material needs, where even those thoughtful critics who are on the fringes of society are unconcerned with spiritual fulfillment.

From its first page, *Caste and Outcast* is shaped by the Orientalism of its implied (Western) reader. Nowhere is this more evident than in Mukerji's attempts to explain the "essential" difference in the Indian attitude toward death and the afterlife. The book is less a catalog of Mukerji's achievements and a description of the people he met on the road of life than the story of a quest told in a distinctively un-epic mold. It is therefore unlike an autobiography in the conventional sense: there is nothing heroic about its protagonist, no triumphant or teleological emplotment of his growth and accomplishments.

Mukerji constantly employs the Orientalist trope of "the East" to explain how the meaning of life itself differs in India. How does one explain the everydayness of reincarnation, transmigration, the eternity of souls, and the transitoriness of bodies to a Western audience? That is his challenge, and that is where Orientalist conceptions of a mystical East come in handy to legitimize the "exotic" ideas that he purveys in the book. Mukerji deftly conveys the centrality that these ideas have in the socialization of children and thus in his own childhood, which after all provides the context for his discourse. For example, speaking of the role that the infinite plays in the child's sense of self, he says, "In India all the prayers, such as, 'Lead me from the unreal to the real; from death into immortality' or 'It was never born; it shall never die,' guide the conscious mind to a sense of immortality. . . . This is what is called the education of the real self" (1923, 14). In the section of the book dealing with his life in India, this theme of transmigration and reembodiment is a constant presence. He writes about the time when his little sister died, at age twelve: "It was the plague, and at dawn the next day her soul set forth again on its eternal vagrancy" (ibid., 39). When he is preparing to be initiated into the profession of a Brahmin priest, his mother takes him for a holy dip in the Ganges. He expresses his unease at seeing the dead being cremated on the riverbank. His mother, whom he remembers fondly as an unlettered but a highly educated woman, replies, "But remember there is no death. . . . We throw off the body as man throws off worn-out garments for new ones. So does the soul rise out of the worn-out body." He asks her, "Why do you tell me this?" She replies, "How could I have given you life, if I could not explain death?" (ibid., 64). During his initiation, he is told, "Your parents are dead. Your relatives are dead. You are dead. Only one thing remains and that is your vagrancy for eternity" (ibid., 67). As a priest, he often is called upon to perform last rites. He recounts going around the funeral pyre seven times and reciting, "O you who are now homeless on earth, homeless on the waters, homeless in the deep, do not seek the vesture of flesh again, but go! . . . Take the path of silence where the sun wanders in quest of the ultimate truth" (ibid., 78).

To the extent that Mukerji is successful in portraying the pervasiveness of reincarnation and transmigration in the everyday lives of people in India and thus in his own life, he undermines the autobiographical project of his book. This is the place where the "impossibility" of his enterprise is most apparent, for if embodiment is indeed the temporary home of an eternally vagrant, living force, what reason could there possibly be to restrict the story of a life to an arbitrary period delimited by birth on one side and death on the other? Taking seriously Mukerji's claim of a culturally distinctive notion of the "real self," in which reincarnation and transmigration are seen as constitutive features of being, what do we make of the temporal horizons already inscribed into the practices of autobiography, biography, and life history? How can we even begin to grasp the nature of "lives" through narrative forms whose temporal structures incorporate certain strong ontological assumptions about "a life"?

Before I delve more deeply into this larger question, let me second Mukerji's observations and reiterate the continuing salience of reincarnation in contemporary India. My own interest in this topic arises from my interpellation in a reincarnation narrative told by a two-and-a-half-year-old girl in the village in North India where I was doing fieldwork. To many, if not most, people in South Asia, there is nothing extraordinary or fantastical about the phenomenon of reincarnation; it is a fact of life, no different from any other. When I heard people in rural India narrate their own or other people's life histories, they sometimes matter-of-factly included the story of their previous life: where they had lived, how they had died, and how, in this life, they located their families from their previous life.

It is my interest in the temporality of being that leads me to treat the otherwise dissimilar genres of autobiography, biography, and life history as one in this chapter, which I shall somewhat arbitrarily designate by the term *life narratives*. For all of their differences, their founding premise is that "a life," however it is narrated, is framed by the accident of birth and the finality of death. It is precisely this horizon of life that is brought into question by reincarnation. Consider for a moment the structure of a typical life narrative, beginning with birth. The timing, gender, and social class of a baby is always narrated as an accident, as something that is to be taken as a "given" in shaping the child's destiny. After that, the different stages of life, from infancy to childhood, adolescence, adulthood, and old age, follow in sequence. The narrative here is one of growing agency on the part of the developing person. In childhood, most things that happen are presumed to be external to the little person the child is, shaped by events and personalities who leave their impact on him or her but are not shaped significantly by the agency of the child; the growth of the child through successive stages until adulthood also is a narrative of greater agency, of a being who increasingly, if imperfectly, authors actions and events. This narrative of an authorizing presence is not infinite, however; it ends with the death of the author. In a biography, the death of the subject may already have occurred; in autobiography and life history, the death of the subject may not have literally come to pass but is prefigured in the structure of the narrative. Death itself may be represented as having a cause (disease, infirmity, "natural"), or it may be seen as accidental. Autobiographies and life histories are very often, although not always, written in the autumn of one's life and consist of a retrospective look at the accomplishments of one's lifetime. Birth and death, then, provide a specific structuration of "a life." Often, a great deal of the explanation of particular lives and personalities hinges on the periods closest to these extremes: by experiences of early childhood, on the one side (here I am thinking particularly of the psychoanalytic tradition), and the imminence or inevitability of death, on the other (here I am thinking particularly of existentialism).

At least since Margaret Mead's *Coming of Age in Samoa*, if not earlier, it has been a commonplace in anthropological explorations of other lives that there is nothing universal about the specific stages into which a life is divided in the West. Childhood seen as a stage of freedom and innocence, adolescence as a period marked by turbulence and an oscillation between juvenile and adult roles, adulthood marked by independence, professional achievement, and life in a nuclear family, and old age marked by physical infirmity and sometimes a childlike dependence on the care of others are culturally specific narratives of a life. Among anthropologists at least, there is such widespread agreement that there is nothing natural or universal about the division of life into these particular stages that it would not be worthwhile to belabor the point.

What I wish to emphasize here is that anthropologists' insights about the cultural distinctiveness of the stages of a life also can be extended to fundamentally rethink the cultural specificity of an idea of Being in which birth and death provide the horizons for life. Attempting to convey to his American audience the impact of ideas of reincarnation and transmigration on people's everyday lives, Mukerji says, "In India, we live with death on more intimate and friendly terms than in the West, and it makes less impression upon us" (1923, 40). It might be argued that the project of a life narrative in its various forms, autobiography, biography, and life history is an attempt to "extend" the life of the subject beyond the finality of death. Rememoration of "a life" through biography, in other words, is itself a culturally specific form of reincarnation.

The project of narrating a life, especially through the modes of biography and autobiography, is rendered unstable not merely because the boundaries of "a lifetime" and "the individual" have been brought into question. In contemplating immigrant life narratives, we have to think about the effect of boundaries of geographical and cultural contexts for concepts of the self as well. When Mukerji describes America as "a continent fierce with homelessness," he is not merely reflecting his own sense of displacement but suggesting the profound impact of immigration on notions of the self. The "home" has been a pervasive image in self-construction at least since the life narrative became an established genre in post–Renaissance Europe (Gusdorf 1980 [1956]). How does the notion of the interiority of the self relate to the idea of the body as home? What is the relationship of the origin of the concept of the bourgeois home as the private domain of the nuclear family and children's development of their sense of self? How exactly do we think of the rise of nationalism as an identity in connection to the conception of the nation as a "homeland"? Immigration often is about the loss of all of those homes: of land, family, community, and nation. If one's sense of self is closely tied to these constructions of home, then what does immigration do to notions of the self?

I ask these questions not because I can hope to answer them but because I wish to draw attention to one aspect of the life narrative that appears so natural as to be invisible. I am referring to the assumption that "a life" is constituted by the continuity of the subject. By this I mean simply the idea that the author of an autobiography, or the subject of a biography or life history, is assumed to be the same subject at different moments in time. The enterprise of the life narrative is built on the premise that subjects have continuous histories and biographies that can be narrated. Different experiences and ideas alter the subject whose life is being described, but the self who undergoes these changes is assumed to be continuous, if not coherent and unitary; otherwise, the entire project of narrating "a life" would be meaningless. How does this idea of the continuity of a life limit the ability to think of radical transformations of the self?

In his interviews with journalist Duccio Trombadori, Michel Foucault introduced the idea of "limit experiences," experiences that fundamentally transform the self, that constitute not a mutation of the subject but a rupture, a break so radical that it does not even allow us to speak of "the same" subject any longer. This poses a tremendous problem for life narratives: how does one describe the life of someone when it cannot be assumed either that it is the same "life" or that "the someone" whose life is being described is indeed the same "one"? Is it one of the legacies of historicism that we find it so difficult to even imagine the temporality of being outside of a metaphysics of continuity and succession?

Let us look at how Mukerji describes his immigration to the United States: "Finally I set forth again to meet this most tremendous change of all, having broken the ties of my country, my past and my caste" (1923, 162). This immigrant's experience is clearly one in which a sense of self is fundamentally shaken by his insertion into radically new relations with land, family, community, and nation. Immigrant biographies might thus enable us to begin the task of reevaluating the relevance of continuist narratives of self and to consider other possibilities for representing that experience. A writer who in the last decade has dealt with this question with great insight and sensitivity is Salman Rushdie. One of the central themes of that much-maligned novel *The*

Satanic Verses (1988) is precisely the immigration of black and brown people to the metropolitan centers of colonial rule. In this novel, particularly in its second half, Rushdie evocatively and imaginatively grapples with the difficulty of representing the discontinuities of the immigrant experience.

One of the central tropes in *The Satanic Verses* is reincarnation. The novel begins, in fact, with Gibreel Farishta falling from Air India Flight 420, flapping his arms wildly and singing a popular Hindi film song translated into English "in semi-conscious deference to the uprushing host-nation" (Rushdie 1988, 5). He and Saladin Chamcha, another actor, fall into the English Channel, "the appointed zone of their watery reincarnation." When he wakes up washed ashore on a beach, these are the first words he utters: "Born again, Spoono, you and me. Happy birthday, mister; happy birthday to you" (ibid., 10). In greeting Spoono with the words "happy birthday," Gibreel announces their rebirth.

Rushdie constructs his magically real world by deliberately confounding transmigration, the enchanted act of time travel, with immigration, the more mundane act of traversing space. Transmigration and migration: what do they have in common beyond their juxtaposition by a fanciful imagination? Rebirth bridges bodies across temporal distance; migration bridges spaces by the pathways traversed by a single body. To experience rebirth is to know that the past inhabits one's body as an immediate, tangible presence; to experience immigration or exile is to know the presence of another place in the here and now. If the body is defined not merely as a biological vessel but as a located entity whose identity derives from being situated in historical memory and constructed tradition, then both transmigration and exile can be seen as out-of-body experiences. Both are defined by displacement and detemporalization, by eviction from a located space, a physical home. Transmigration becomes the means by which the cultural landscape inhabited by the immigrant, the space carved by discourses of colonialism, race, and capitalism, can be described.

The experience of travel to colonial metropoles for immigrants from the Third World is defined by metamorphosis, transformation, and deterritorialization. These are the very processes that render a continuist narrative of the self problematical, and this is why the notion of transmigration seems so appealing as a "commonsensical" description of the dislocation experienced by many immigrants. Reincarnation serves as a better analytical framework to imagine immigrant life narratives than more conventional accounts of subjects traversing the geographical space of nations. It is my hypothesis that the more marginal a person is in global systems of power, the less likely are straightforward descriptions of immigration to adequately represent that experience. To write across that representational gap called immigration in a Third World subject's life is to risk erasing the difference between the journeys of people positioned in different geographical locales, on opposite sides of highly unequal and stratified systems of financial, social, and cultural capital.

Modernist notions of self, I have argued, are embedded in the multiple valences of "home," in what Liisa Malkki (1992) has called a "sedentarist metaphysics." Dominant narratives of immigration build on this sedentarist metaphysics, positing that migrants leave their old homes in order to build new ones in their new "homeland." In fact, renunciation of one's allegiance to an old "homeland" often is a necessary part of the legal requirements of citizenship in the new one; denunciation of one's affiliation with some other "homeland" may be an important part of the cultural or civic requirements of citizenship as well, but this model of immigration as a displacement of dwelling voluntarily undertaken by a subject in order to improve his or her life conditions rarely does justice to the experiences of immigrants. By uprooting the sedentarist assumptions of the dominant narrative of immigration, we can resituate it more fruitfully in terms of a notion of dwelling-in-travel (Clifford 1997).[5]

It is precisely this theme of dwelling-in-travel, of restlessness and vagrancy, that runs through *Caste and Outcast*. Mukerji's description of his life in India is replete with references to the vagrancy of the transmigrating soul and his own search for spiritual knowledge through pilgrimage. The peregrinations of the soul are mirrored in the wanderings of the seeker of knowledge of the soul, and Mukerji's idealistic description of Indian life consists largely of his journeys, the passage of various holy men that he comes to know; he even briefly mentions the pilgrimages undertaken by his parents. Wandering in search of spiritual enlightenment is portrayed as commonplace but not romanticized as yielding transcendental knowledge. He describes both of his parents as having left home to go on pilgrimages; his mother returned after three months, saying, "The Lord is within me, why should I go all over India to find Him?" In contrast, he reports that his father traveled for twenty years but never found the Lord (1923, 61).

A substantial portion of the book is taken up by Mukerji's description of his own experience of ascetic wandering after his initiation into the priesthood, which lasted two years, and in which he begged for food and slept wherever he could find shelter. He is captivated by the Himalayas, and after returning to his village and taking up the duties of a priest, he is filled with restlessness and dissatisfaction and thus takes up the trade of a shawl salesman to have an excuse to travel to the hills. He says of this decision, "I was free, thanks to the traditions of a race accustomed in child, in boy, in man, to the restlessness for God" (ibid., 126).[6] He describes his experiences in the hills thus:

> . . . at the end of the months of travel . . . I was still a wanderer, and no nearer the goal than when I had started. I had had some dim hope behind my youthful zest for adventure, that I might meet the supreme experience in the hills, and find, among the many hermits who flock to the Himalayas in search of God, a master greater than I had known before, who would tell me . . . the meaning of my life, and point out to me my way. But, alas, I did not find the mighty spirit wandering alone. (ibid., 136)

It is this same restlessness, the search for a higher purpose, that draws him to America; he is attracted to it precisely because it is a country "mad with restlessness" (ibid., 303).

Restlessness becomes the motif of the book, the only theme that links the two halves of the autobiography. Vagrancy and wandering define this journey; it is not a form of travel motivated by an immediacy of purpose but a pilgrimage with a transcendental and an ultimately elusive goal. The self here is defined not by the places where it comes to rest, neither its place of origin nor its place of settlement, but by the wanderings of a seeker searching for the mysteries of the vagrant soul. It is only fitting, then, that life itself be neither circumscribed by the boundaries of birth and death nor confined by the framework of nation-states. Writing the history of individual lives, then, also invites rethinking History as the biography of the nation.

NOTES

1. By "the western idea" of a book, Mukerji here is implicitly referring to a particular kind of book: an autobiography. Smith and Watson locate the difficulties elsewhere, arguing that the very process of writing autobiography transports the colonial subject into a situation where he or she might be obligated to "reproduce and re/present the colonizer's figure in negation" (1992, xix).

2. Caren Kaplan identifies other essential features of autobiography as including "the revelation of individuality, the chronological unfolding of a life, reflections and confessions, [and] the recovery and assertion of suppressed identity" (1992, 212).

3. I cannot explore in this chapter the possible connections between Mukerji's life narrative and other traditions of narrating stories about the self in India. Smith and Watson (1992, xviii) draw attention to the complicated connections between autobiography as a mode of writing and other genealogies of narrating the story of people's lives in different cultural traditions.

4. One need only contrast Dhan Gopal's autobiographical narrative with the more conventional account given by a more recent Indo-American author, Bharati Mukherjee.

5. Clifford (1997, 44) makes the point that, "Once traveling is foregrounded as a cultural practice, then dwelling, too, needs to be reconceived no longer simply the ground from which traveling departs and to which it returns."

6. Of course, Mukerji does not reflect here on the gendered nature of this freedom. Girls and women were not as free to travel because of the same "traditions."

WORKS CITED

Beverley, John. 1992. "The Margin at the Center: On testimonio (testimonial narrative)." Pp. 91–114 in De/Colonizing the Subject, ed. Sidonie Smith and Julia Watson. Minneapolis: University of Minnesota Press.

Clifford, James. 1997. Routes: Travel and Translation in the Late Twentieth Century. Cambridge: Harvard University Press.

Foucault, Michel. 1984 [1979]. "What Is an Author?" Pp. 101–20 in The Foucault Reader, ed. Paul Rabinow. New York: Pantheon.

Gugelberger, Georg M., ed. 1996. The Real Thing: Testimonial Discourse and Latin America. Durham: Duke University Press.

Gusdorf, Georges. 1980 [1956]. "Conditions and Limits of Autobiography." Pp. 28–48 in Autobiography: Essays Theoretical and Critical, ed. James Olney. Princeton: Princeton University Press.

Kaplan, Caren. 1992. "Resisting Autobiography: Out-Law Genres and Transnational Feminist Subjects." Pp. 208–16 in De/Colonizing the Subject, ed. Sidonie Smith and Julia Watson. Minneapolis: University of Minnesota Press.

Malkki, Liisa. 1992. "National Geographic: The Rooting of Peoples and the Territorialization of National Identity among Scholars and Refugees." Cultural Anthropology 7:1:24–44.

Mukerji, Dhan Gopal. 1923. *Caste and Outcast*. New York: E. P. Dutton.

Rushdie, Salman. 1988. *The Satanic Verses*. New York: Viking.

Smith, Sidonie, and Julia Watson, eds. 1992. *De/Colonizing the Subject: The Politics of Gender in Women's Autobiography*. Minneapolis: University of Minnesota Press.

Sommer, Doris. 1988. "'Not Just a Personal Story': Women's Testimonios and the Plural Self." Pp. 107–30 in *Life/Lines: Theorizing Women's Autobiography*, ed. Bella Brodzki and Celeste Schenck. Ithaca, N.Y.: Cornell University Press.

PART 3

TRANSLATING PLACES, TRANSLATING AMBIVALENCE

CHAPTER NINE

WARPED SPEECH

The Politics of Global Translation

EMILY APTER

The problem of translation and the global market fits into a larger project on literary *mondialisation*, or what might otherwise be termed, with reference to the *Dialectic of Enlightenment*'s famous fourth chapter, "Culture Industry, Enlightenment as Mass Deception: The Sequel." In applying the term *culture industry*, however, I want to shift the Horkheimer/Adorno emphasis on the supposedly corrosive influence of mass and popular culture to a more open-ended inquiry into the conditions of cultural globalization, specifically as they apply to the commodification of foreign authors within a niche market subsuming ethnics, immigrants, elite cosmopolitans, and the formerly colonized in a "multiculti" hodgepodge.

In taking up the globalization theme, I am keenly aware of the problematic way in which literary and cultural critics have appropriated the term from the economics of late capitalism. Though the economic analogy may be highly relevant to discussions of the corporatization of world culture—institutionally apparent in museum management, publishing, and long-distance learning enterprises—I would suggest that insufficient attention has been paid to the complicities between critical theories of postnationalism and corporate postnational practices, or even more pointedly, between a postnationalism seeking to question the preservation of national boundaries within disciplines and area studies, and a postnationalism presuming the subordination of nation-states to interstate global regulatory systems.

In addressing themes of global translatability and the internationalization of culture, I want to bear in mind Rick Livingston's caveat to the effect that "aesthetic products are anomalous commodities," their value poorly served by exclusive reliance on marketing models. Finally, I am concerned to avoid allowing the terms *translation* and *translingualism* to become pallid metaphors for any act of cultural negotiation. Rather, they should be invoked as a means of restoring the linguistic base to transnational aesthetics in the wake of reductive models of nation and identity.

Goethe was among the first to present translation as a threat to nationalist identifications when he associated the third and highest level of translation with an evacuation of the translator's nation of origin: "The goal of the translation," he wrote, "is to achieve perfect identity with the original, so that the one does not exist instead of the other but in the other's place. This kind met with the most resistance in the early stages," Goethe continues, "because the translator identifies so strongly with the original that he more or less gives up the uniqueness of his own nation" (1992, 61). In this scheme, as the target displaces the original nation it gives rise to a third typology: a language characterizable as "intranslation," which is worldly, cosmopolitan, and in some sense nationless. Goethe calls this urbane, denationalized prose a "third type of text for which the taste of the masses has to be developed" (ibid.).

My question at this juncture is whether, at the present time, this "third type of textuality" can be identified as, on the one hand, a userfriendly, non-nationally marked "translationese," or, on the other hand, as a form of literary transnationalism that defines itself through deviations from standard language (or what Gayatri Chakravorty Spivak (1992, 179) has called "fraying" or "rhetoricity").[1] Both, it would seem, respond in different ways to the condition that Arjun Appadurai diagnosed as *the end of the hegemony of territorial nationalism.* "No idiom," Appadurai writes, "has yet emerged to capture the collective interest of many groups in translocal solidarities, crossborder mobilization, and postnational identities. . . . The violence that surrounds identity politics around the world today reflects the anxieties attendant on the search for nonterritorial principles of solidarity" (1996, 58). Speaking of what he calls "trojan nationalisms," Appadurai evokes the "transnational, subnational, and, more generally, nonnational identities and aspirations ascribable to Haitians in Miami, Tamils in Sri Lanka, Moroccans in France, and Moluccans in Holland" (ibid.). These "carriers of new transnational and postnational loyalties," he implies, are up for grabs as cultural agents. They are not necessarily elites skilled at competing in the international culture industry but rather are less cultured ethnic, immigrant voices of a diaspora traversing national borders.

The point here is not to make categorical distinctions between high internationalism and "low" diasporism or between "bad" postnational globalization and "good" transnationalism. The point is, rather, to see how certain texts have mobilized translation in the service of language politics, thereby illustrating the extent to which transnationalism itself is a by-product of the migration of language communities that sponsor networks of cultural exchange, irrespective of national boundaries. In this vein, Edouard Glissant has recently explored translation as a kind of transnational racial claim. He assigns himself the task in *Faulkner, Mississippi* (1996) of "translating" the language of Faulkner's black characters into a Francophone, Afro-Caribbean context, thereby setting up a colloquy of the post-slavery Americas that ultimately bypasses metropolitan France. Eluding national affiliation in this way, Glissant brings the language of the bayou into alignment with archipelagian discourses.

Glissant's transnational Faulkner, it might be argued, thus sets affect free from the essentialist ties binding language to national voice. He denationalizes Faulkner as a quintessential Southern writer by re-regionalizing him in a different, comparative geopolitical frame. It is precisely this kind of movement on the map that I want to take up in more detail, focusing on several cases of regionally marked writers who have been successfully internationalized, despite their politically charged deviations from standard language.

How does a foreign, linguistically unconventional text go global? Irvine Welsh's 1993 best-selling novel, *Trainspotting*, made famous in the United States by the Danny Boyle film of the same title, exemplifies how language politics, no matter how iconoclastic, can be assimilated by the mainstream and made commercially lucrative through savvy merchandising and tie-ins. Welsh belongs to a group of contemporary writers, including Iain Banks, James Kelman, and Duncan McLean, who have created a fashion for Scottish "minor literature" by inventing an edgy, contemporary idiom orthographically transposed into what often seems to be another language, or at the very least a pseudo or an intralingual (English to English) translation. Taking over the folkloric tradition of regional accents in the British novel, amply used for local color in George Eliot's *Adam Bede* (1859) and culminating, perhaps, in Joyce's *Finnegan's Wake* (1969 [1939]), these "New Scotologists," as they have been dubbed, are classed among the white postcolonials of the British Isles.

David Lloyd (1987) has applied the term *minor literature* to writing by Britain's Irish cultural nationalists, borrowing the term somewhat problematically from Gilles Deleuze and Félix Guattari's book on Kafka. In a seminal chapter entitled "What Is Minor Literature?" Deleuze and Guattari analyzed Kafka's German as a pastiche of the "vehicular" tongue—meaning in this case the impoverished bureaucratese, the hollow state language imposed on Czechoslovakia by the Prussian state. According to their reading, Kafka subverted the vehicular by freighting it with unwelcome baggage, from Yiddish inflections to scraps of Czech vernacular. Now even if the newly edited and translated Malcolm Pasley/Mark Harman editions of Kafka reveal a very differently textured use of the German language from the one characterized by Deleuze and Guattari, their argument is still valid insofar as it is an attempt to rescue the immanent, "becoming-animal" Kafka from the postwar, "Darkness at Noon" grip of spiritual anti-Iron Curtain allegory.

Kafka's German may be compared to Irvine Welsh's minoritarian English in the way it allows the animality of language to shine through, whether it is in accent transliteration (the "goatiness" of the word "goat," the Scots pronunciation of "got") or in similes of embodied animation and ingestion (a smack-ingested phallus writhes like an ugly sea-snake; steak-mince and vomit stick in the craw; and the junkie beats his meat or vein, aiming for a hit). Language is the needle that pricks the reader into awareness of the deathliness of humanness, its proximity to meat or matter. Whether or not one interprets this raw immanence as part of a strategy to reveal hypocrisy festering within the humanist welfare state, what Welsh and the New Scotologists seem to have in common is the use of invective, honed to the bone of explosive regional utterance. Welsh's Scottish vernacular is not so much a transposition of accent and slang but a subcultural *Sprache* that has the effect of wounding Standard English with the slings and arrows of warped speech, at least for a Brit or an Anglophone reader outside of Scotland. At first glance, the obstacles to reading a page of *Trainspotting* create a shock to the system, since there is such a disjunction between eye and ear, such a preponderance of what Deleuze and Guattari call "tensors," or nodes of pain. The "incorrect use of prepositions; the abuse of the pronominal; the employment of malleable verbs; . . . the multiplication and succession of adverbs; the use of pain-filled connotations; the importance of accent as a tension internal to the word; and the distribution of consonants and vowels as part of an internal discordance" (1986, 23), these were the traits of the tensor, by which Deleuze and Guattari, following Wagenbach, distinguished Kafka's Prague German. Along these lines, Welsh's Edinburgh dialect can be seen as a tensored language deeply indebted to Joycean linguistic play. It was of course Joyce who most famously mined Irish brogue for its cache of puns and double entendres. *Finnegan's Wake*, in particular, fabricates a verbal fantastic out of vernacular expression, as in:

> His howd feeled heavy, his hoddit did shake. (There was a wall of course in erection) Dimb! He stottered from the latter. Damb! he was dud. Dumb! Mastabatoom, mastabadtomm, when a mon merries his lute is all long. For whole the world to see.
>
> Shize? I should shee! Macool, Macool, orra whyi deed ye diie? of a trying thirstay mournin? Sobs they sighdid at Fillagain's chrissormiss wake, all the hoolivans of the nation, prostrated in their consternation, and their duodisimally profusive plethora of ululation. (1969 [1939], 6)

In this scene of maudlin drunks fantasizing the erection of a corpse, Joyce encrypts the image of a randy, impotent, moribund Irish nation that anticipates Welsh's semi-ironic chapter title, "Scotland Takes Drugs in Psychic Defense." The word "duodisimally," with its spin on duodecimal (systems of accounts payable), the saddest twelve days of Christmas (duodecimal signifies twelfths), and stomach trouble (duodenum is the medical term for intestine), generates a psychic economy of dyspepsia and national melancholia. The play on "thirstay mournin," and on "Shize" and "shee," kneading together themes of inebriation and excretion, also underscores the image of a body politic overwhelmed by bodily functions, wallowing self-pityingly in its own shit. On this score, *Trainspotting*'s descriptions of "pungent showers" of "skittery shite, thin alcohol sick, and vile pish," of characters diving into toilets or complaining of flooded tampons, may be read as a 1990s' echo of Joycean billingsgate, though Welsh's language is less poetic and more faithful to everyday speech:

We're drinking on a balcony bar, and our attention is caught by a
squad of nutters entering the crowded pub below. They swagger in,
noisy and intimidating.

Ah hate cunts like that. Cunts like Begbie. Cunts that are
intae baseball-batting every fucker that's different; pakis, poofs, n
what huv ye. Fuckin failures in a country ay failures. It's nae good
blamin it oan the English fir colonising us. Ah don't hate the English. They're just wankers. We are colonised by wankers. We can't
even pick a decent, vibrant, healthy culture to be colonised by. No.
We're ruled by effete arseholes. What does that make us? The lowest of the fuckin low, the scum of the earth. The most wretched,
servile, miserable, pathetic trash that was ever shat intae creation.
Ah don't hate the English. They just git oan we the shite thuv goat.
Ah hate the Scots. (Welsh 1993, 94)

The trope of being "wanked by wankers" figures white colonization as a political state of abject servility: a psychic dependency, ultimately correlative with the narrator's dependency on heroin. The English are the Big Smack, assuming the guise of the bad mother, a.k.a.
Mother Superior, the street name for the local dealer, Johnny Swan.

Ah went tae take a shot. It took us ages to find a good vein. Ma boys
don't live as close tae the surface as maist people's. When it came, ah
savoured the hit. Ali was right. Take yir best orgasm, multiply the
feeling by twenty, and you're still fuckin miles off the pace. Ma dry,
cracking bones are soothed and liquefied by ma beautiful heroine's
tender caresses. The earth moved, and it's still moving. (ibid., 11)

The maternal leitmotif comes to the ear through the pronunciation of
"my" as "ma" and through reference to the "heroine's tender caresses":
an image of the social body seduced by a soporific matriarchal embrace.
Lulled by "the lady," depressed Scotland returns to a pre-Oedipal,
womblike state of libidinal depletion and ego loss. Internal colonization
is thus represented through a subcultural language of addiction and class
oppression. This amalgamation of prolespeak, drug argot, and pop-cul-
tural lingo also is used to draw attention to the neo-imperialism of
American global culture throughout Europe, as in a scene where Sick
Boy tries to humiliate two Asian tourists:

—Can I help you? Where are you headed? ah ask. *Good old-fash-
ioned Scoattish hoshpitality, aye, ye cannae beat it, shays the young
Sean Connery, the new Bond, cause girls, this is the new bondage* . . .

—We're looking for the Royal Mile, a posh, English-colonial voice answers back in ma face. What a fucking we pump-up-the-knickers n aw. *Simple Simon sais, put your hands on your feet . . .*

Of course, the Rent Boy is looking like a flaccid prick in a barrel-load of fannies. Sometimes ah really think the gadge still believes that an erection is for pishing over high walls. (ibid., 29, emphasis in original)

The "sh" sound signifies unhappy Scottishness. It may be read as a verbal tic of class resentment—smarmy, sarcastic and malevolent—erupting violently inside the words "hoshpitality" and "pish." The fear of impotence swirls through Sick Boy's speech; even the evocation of Scotland's only genuine action hero, James Bond, spirals self-defeatingly out of control in the form of a pun on girls in bondage. The schoolyard refrain, "Simple Simon says, put your hands on your feet," becomes the pathetic jingle of losers reduced to compensatory rape fantasy. Sick Boy's free-associating parapraxes articulate Scotland's servile relation to the United Kingdom and the United States, with James Bond (age) serving in the role of Scotland's prostitute-ambassador, the country's premier global export, alongside salmon and single malt.

If Welsh explores internal colonization as a kind of linguistic depressant, mired in the bog of poverty, class claustrophobia, addiction, and national self-hatred, his novel reaches a nonregional audience through its harrowing yet mesmerizing language of expletives and downbeat social realism. Salman Rushdie, Ken Saro-wiwa, and Raphaël Confiant have similarly experimented with postcolonial idioms doused with the spritz of social satire. In Rushdie's *The Satanic Verses* (1992 [1988]), Anglo-Indian prose rhythms collide with the alien vocabulary of American product lines, British brand names, global commodity fetishes, and Joycean neologisms in a self-parodic patois. Though his style has been accused of pandering to "coca-colonization," Rushdie has in turn repudiated his attackers as nation-based, anti-modern, spiritual recidivists. Their refusal to absorb idiolects of global popular culture, he asserts, renders them deaf to the Anglo-Indian renewal of literate English. This is the English clearly heard in this character sketch of Muhammad Sufyan:

prop. Shaandaar Café and landlord of the rooming-house above, mentor to the variegated, transient and particoloured inhabitants of both, seen-it-all type, least doctrinaire of hajis and most unashamed

of VCR addicts, ex-schoolteacher, self-taught in classical texts of
many cultures, dismissed from post in Dhaka owing to cultural differences with certain generals in the old days when Bangladesh was
merely an East Wing, and therefore, in his words, "not so much an
immig as an emig runt"—this last a good-natured allusion to his
lack of inches, for though he was a wide man, thick of arm and
waist, he stood no more than sixty-one inches off the ground. (1992
[1988], 243)

The Joycean play on "emig-runt" satirizes the runty status of the formerly colonized, even as it offers a condensed history of the inversion of
worlds experienced by Indian exiles.

The African and Afro-Caribbean writers Ken Saro-wiwa and
Raphaël Confiant have similarly employed postcolonial idioms that sur-
render the reader to a violent verbal world. Saro-wiwa's powerful novel
Sozaboy (1994 [1985]), subtitled *A Novel in Rotten English*, is akin to
Welsh's *Trainspotting* in its stretch from the local to the cosmopolitan
audience. Like Welsh, Saro-wiwa relies on a glossary at the back of the
book (where we learn, for example, that sozaboy = soldier and that
SMOG = "Save Me o God") to induct the reader into a postcolonial
order of language:

> Before, before, the grammar was not plenty and everybody was
> happy. But now grammar begin to plenty and people were not
> happy. As grammar plenty, na no trouble plenty. And as trouble
> plenty, na so plenty people were dying.
>   . . . The radio continue to blow big, big grammar, talking big
> talk. We continue to make big money, my master and myself.
>   . . . When I passed the elementary six exam, I wanted to go to
> secondary school but my mama told me that she cannot pay the
> fees. The thing pained me bad because I wanted to be big man like
> lawyer or doctor riding car and talking big big English. (1994
> [1985], 3, 11)

What is particularly striking here is the power ascribed to grammar; it
grows like speculator's money, out of itself, a plenty that begets plenty
but also "trouble." The "bigness" of grammar is proportionally related
to the size of political trouble.

In the short story "High Life," the predecessor text to *Sozaboy* in
which Saro-wiwa first used this brand of Nigerian ebonics, rotten English is used to flush out monolingualism as the linguistic superego whose
interpellative force "hails" the subject, bending him to ordinance. Much

like Welsh's *lumpen* orthographies, Saro-wiwa's intralingual idiolect exemplifies what Phil Lewis has called "abusive translation," referring to "the translatability that emerges in the movement of difference as a fundamental property of languages . . . a risk to be assumed: that of a strong, forceful translation that values experimentation, tampers with usage, seeks to match polyvalencies or plurivocities or expressive stress of the original by producing its own" (Lewis 1985, 41).

Narratively driven by a *Crying Game* conceit, whereby the narrator discovers that the prostitute he has taken home is a male transvestive, "High Life" introduces neologisms such as "prouding" and "shaming" to lend tropic force to states of affect.[2] While the short story deploys the theme of sex change to deflate the cult of hypermasculinity, *Sozaboy* ups the ante by internalizing sexual ambiguity within grammar itself:

> So that night, I was in the Upwine Bar. No plenty people at first. I order one bottle of palmy from the service. This service is young girl. Him bottom shake dey shake as she walk. Him breast na proper J.J.C, Johnny Just Come—dey stand like hill. As I look am, my man begin to stand small small. I beg am make 'e no disgrace me especially as I no wear pant that night. I begin to drink my palmy. The service sit near my table dey look me from the corner of him eye. Me I dey look am too with the corner of my eye. I want to see how him breast dey. As I dey look, the baby catch me.
> "What are you looking at?" is what she asked.
> "I am not looking at anything," was my answer.
> "But why are you looking at me with corner-corner eye?" she asked again.
> "Look you for corner-corner eye? Why I go look for corner-corner eye?" was my answer.
> "You dey look my breast, *yeye* man. Make you see am now."
> Before I could twinkle my eye, lo and behold she have moved her dress and I see her two breasts like calabash. God in Heaven. What kain thing be this? *Abi*, the girl no dey shame? (1994 [1985], 14)

Using a gender-inverted dative case—whereby possessive pronouns designating parts of the female body are masculinized—"him bottom shake," "the corner of him eye," Saro-wiwa depersonalizes the body, imaging it as a field of disparate, wildly associative, erogenous part-objects. A phrase such as "I dey look am too" or "my man begin to stand small" and acronyms such as J.J.C. ("Johnny-Just-Come") map a dispersed, bimorphic erotic animus that dissolves boundaries of subject

and object. A compilation he-woman, she-man emerges from the gen-
der-scrambled grammar, suggesting a phobic image of "queer Africa"
strategically deployed to flush out homophobia and political anxiety
around "Big-Manism" in Nigerian society.

In his prefatory note to *Sozaboy*, Saro-wiwa acknowledges the use
made of Nigerian Pidgin and conversational exchanges.[3] He quotes the
editor who anthologized "High Life" in a Penguin African Library edition of 1969 as saying "'the piece is not in true 'Pidgin' which would
have made it practically incomprehensible to the European reader. The
language is that of a barely educated primary school boy exulting in the
new words he is discovering and the new world he is beginning to
know.' Mr. Dathorne goes on to describe the style in the story as 'an
uninhibited gamble with language,' and 'an exercise in an odd style'"
(author's note). Though it is hard to ascertain here whether Saro-wiwa
is citing Mr. Dathorne's assessment of his prose approvingly or not, he
clearly endorses the classification of his style among "New Englishes"
that stridently and unapologetically lay claim to broken or "rotten"
Europhonic usage. Moreover, his assault on monolingual orthodoxy
might productively be placed in the broader context of his later career
as an environmental activist, especially if one reads his intralingual satire
of linguistic auto-colonization as prefigurative of his protest against
"indigenous colonialism" or "re-colonization," terms referring to the
complicity of the Nigerian military junta in the devastation of Ogoni-
land by the unobstructed mining practices of Shell Oil. As is well known,
Saro-wiwa paid dearly for his role as celebrity champion of the Ogoni
people's rights as a micro-minority. He was condemned to death and
executed by the Abacha regime in 1995.[4]

Sozaboy, one could argue, carries the seeds of the author's
untimely demise in its invention of a phantasmatic language whose par-
ticles carry the ghosts of the Biafran war, the stress marks and psychic
cavities of starvation, violence, humiliation, and colonial mimicry. The
phrase "Tan Papa dere" (translated as "stand properly there") is a
marker of the enduring elision between colonial paternalism and military psychology. The colonizer lives on, long after his official departure,
in such anachronisms. Or take the word "porson," the substitute for
person, in which the subject is effectively transliterated as a "poor-
son," that is, an average conscript forced into war by poverty and fear
of death, or as "poor sun," communicating the darkness of life at a
time of unmourned death, when bodies are replaced as soon as they fall
by the next round of human fodder. Even the book's structure partici-

pates in this ghostly chain of associations, its chapter divisions enu-
merated as "Lomber One," "Two," and so on. Though Lomber does
not exist as the pidgin equivalent of Number, it sounds like it might,
and this element of masquerade tricks the reader into projecting a
phantom country or land of ghosts, what Theresa Hak Cha calls a
"phantomnation." The homophony with the French "l'ombre" reinforces this line of interpretation by suggesting a textual haunting or
shadow book that makes its thematic apparition via the novel's representation of war. It falls once again to grammar to convey the disori-
enting prospect of war's physical theater: "Na just few of us remain. . . .
And we no know what is bomb or that aeroplane dey shit bomb wey
dey kill. And just that morning we see death. We all confuse. We no
know wetin to do" (Saro-wiwa 1994 [1985], 112). In the slippage
between no and knowing, between confusing and being confused,
between waiting and wetting, the psychosis of war takes shape. War is
personified in a figure of speech, a personage called "Manmuswak,"
whose name is a contraction of the phrase "a man must live or eat by
whatever means" (in a word, "shoot or be shot"). When the wounded
narrator regains consciousness in a hospital, his spirit is possessed by
this protean specter: "Manmuswak is here again. Oh, I cannot tell you
how my heart just cut when I see this Manmuswak in the hospital. He
is now nurse and chooking people with needle. What does all this
mean? Am I prisoner of war? What happened to me in that bush? And
why must I always see this Manmuswak man? (ibid., 118)

    As a kind of Nigerian Ebonics in which the spirit of a lost African
language gene runs amok in the syntactic corridors of Standard English,
Saro-wiwa's "rotten English" anticipates the heated controversies surrounding the Oakland School Board's 1995 resolution, which legally
designated Black English a separate language eligible for bilingual sub-
sidies. How far can a language diverge before it veers into another?
Before it warrants translation? These questions are of course equally
pertinent to creolized French, the object of many a High Surveillance
mission by the French Academy.

My concluding case will concentrate on thresholds of translatability in
a recent book by the "bad boy" of Martinican literature, Raphaël Confiant. Confiant's recent ten-franc novel, *La Savane des pétrifications*
[*The Petrified Savannah*] (1995), satirizes the plight of a local Caribbean
author, Hubert Badineau, who spends his time expostulating about the
multiple rejections of his manuscript by French publishing houses. At

one level Confiant casts a pitiless eye on the *arrivisme* of Caribbean intellectuals (perhaps including himself, since he himself switched from writing in Creole to French, presumably to gain wider recognition), while on another he sheds light on the neo-colonial politics of publishing, whereby "regional" authors, if they want to get anywhere, must necessarily route themselves through the metropole.

In *La Savane*, the language of the news media is inserted as a tertiary linguistic *couche* between Francophone in-jokes and exported Parisianisms. Creolisms are crossed with Anglo advertising jingles, producing ironic double entendres, as in "OMO-lave-plus-blanc," where the French laundry detergent OMO sounds out the gay-baiting pronunciation of "HOMO" in French, and where the whole phrase alludes to bleaching products targeted at non-whites. Allusions to infomercials, American politics, sitcoms, and products abound: an island "negro" is "vacciné-scolarisé" and "CD-Romisé"; a jumble of media brand names highlights the global relativism of a worldview filtered through CNN: "Bill Clinton, Mother Teresa, Whoopi Goldberg, Claudia Schiffer, Hussein of Jordan, Bernard Tapie, Mobutu Sésé Séko Wa Ndongo, and Madonna" (ibid., 83). Confiant also excels in macabre macaronics: rapes in Bosnia are euphemized through rhetorical preciosity, as "fornicatory dilations" (écartèlements fornicatoires). Tintin pokes his childlike head into a scene of atrocities: "I guarantee you, it will make a racket like the thunder of Brest over there" (ce fera un raffut du tonnerre de Brest là-bas, je t'assure) (ibid., 9). Turning the value system of the microcolony on its head, television provokes what the local sociologist diagnoses as an "ontological heart condition" (l'infarctus ontologique) (ibid., 37).

Auto-pastiche anchors the narrative's satire of the *créolité* language movement, a movement in which Confiant himself figured prominently as coauthor with Jean Bernabé and Patrick Chamoiseau of the flagship 1989 pamphlet *Eloge de la créolité* (*In Praise of Creoleness*). "Caught in its own trap between the teeth of belief and syntax," according to Derek Walcott, the manifesto is a schizoid text, written in French but extolling the virtues of Creole oral expression. In *La Savane*, an "éloge du fax" accompanies a withering portrait of a "hexagonal negrologue" specializing in *créolité*, Dr Jérôme Garnier de l'université de Triffoulis-les-Oies ("Rummaging geese" or "Head in the Sand"). We catch up with Garnier in the midst of a futile interrogation of a "native informant," who answers him contemptuously in language-lab English:

"Cher ami, pou . . . pourriez-vous me . . . me . . . con . . . confirmer que l'i . . . imaginaire créole ins . . . insuffle . . . ," répétait-il pour la vingtième fois.

"*What are you saying? You're nuts!*" répliquait le djobeur recyclé (grâce au laboratoire de langues de la chambre de commerce de la Martinique).

Accablé l'Hexagonal, qui avait bâti toute sa carrière universitaire sur l'étude de ce qu'il appelait, ses confrères et lui, la "littérature nègre" ou "négro-africaine" (comme s'il existait une "littérature blanco-européenne!," bande de rigolos, va!) et ne trouvait plus rien à pondre sur la négritude, fouinait depuis quelque temps dans les mangroves déroutants de la créolité. Quand les nègres se proclamaient nègres, écrivaient nègres, en un mot se réclamaient d'une écriture noire épidermiquement, noire stylistiquement, noire sémantiquement et tout le bazar, Garnier nageait dans le bonheur le plus parfait. Mais tout cessa d'aller pour le mieux dans le meilleur des mondes lorsqu'une bande d'hurluburlus à peine quadragénaires décréta qu'en plus d'être nègres, ils étaient blancs, amérindiens, hindous, chinois et levantins. Non mais? A-t-on idée d'inventer pareille idéologie macaronique, arlequinesque et patchworkienne?

["Dear friend . . . cc—could you . . . corr—corroborate that . . . th-the creole imaginary . . . re-resusci . . . ," he'd repeat for the twentieth time.

"What are you saying? You're nuts!" the retrained on-the-jobber replied in English (courtesy of Martinique's Chamber of Commerce language laboratories).

Crushed, the Hexagonal, who had constructed an entire university career around the study of what they (he and his colleagues) would call "Negro" or "Negro-African literature" (as if "White-European literature" existed, give me a break, band of jokers!), and who, having found nothing more on Negritude to ponder, had been rooting around for some time in the derailing mangrove swamps of creoleness. When the negroes proclaimed themselves negroes, wrote Negro, and, in a word, staked their claim on writing that was epidermically black, stylistically black, semantically black, and the whole bazaar, Garnier was awash in perfect bliss. But everything stopped being the best of all possible worlds when a band of hooligans, barely in their forties, announced that not only were they Negro, they were also white, Hindu, Chinese, and Levantine. You have to be kidding. Who could possibly come up with the idea of inventing an ideology as macaronic, carnivalesque, and patchworked as that?] (ibid., 41–42)

Foiling the white academic's obsession with the dermal blackness of
black language, Confiant vents his spleen against racial essentialism and
Europe's infatuation with stereotypes of the Other. To Garnier's consternation, blackness disintegrates into a dizzyingly variegated spectacle
of hybridity in this not quite "best of all possible worlds."

Confiant's *La Savane des pétrifications* is representative of a strategic translingualism revealing the collisions and collusions between postcolonial history and multicultural identity politics. Unlike linguistic anti-
imperialists such as Ngugi wa Thiong'o, who vowed (at least
provisionally) to give up writing in English in favor of his native Gikuyu,
Confiant places European and non-Western languages in abrasive contact, thereby cutting "target" and "source" along the bias to ensure their
mutual contamination. Africanizing metropolitan usage with the help of
ironic exoticisms, unpronounceable loan words, verbal calques, and
warped grammaticalities, Confiant both departs from and carries over
certain traditions initiated by the *négritude* poets of making the colonizer's language strange to itself. Though by now this "empire strikes
back" paradigm is no longer radical, it is perhaps still underestimated as
a tactic for resignifying Francophonia as a "glocal" phenomenon, no
longer pinned to the right side of the metropole-periphery model.

If I have concentrated here on writers hailing from geopolitical ter-
ritories in the process of surmounting legacies of colonial acculturation,
I will end on a futurological note, opening up for debate the problem of
what happens to ethnic and national literary voice in the global literary
market once that voice has become a regionally dislocated, overtrans-
lated caricature of cultural affect, shot at increasingly high speeds into
the post-national space of the Net.

Notes

1. Spivak writes: "The task of the translator is to facilitate love between
the original and its shadow, a love that permits fraying, holds the agency of the
translator and the demands of her imagined or actual audience at bay. The politics of the non-European woman's text too often suppresses this possibility
because the translator cannot engage with, or cares insufficiently for, the
rhetoricity of the original. . . . Without a sense of the rhetoricity of language, a
species of neo-colonialist construction of the non-western scene is afoot"
(1992, 178–79).

2. Saro-wiwa 1995, 73: "I undressed very quickly because I wanted to
make romantica with the woman. But all the time, she refused to pull her dress.

I thought she was *shaming* because of the light. So I quenched the electric. Then I went to the bed where she was sitting and removed her blouse. No breast. Ah-ah. What type of woman is this? Only artificial breast. Anyway that did not surprise me too much because I have heard that many women are using it. Then I began to remove the woman's loincloth. Although by this time I was feeling very hot inside and I was impatient, I took time to remove that loincloth. The next thing I found was that the woman was wearing short knicker. Ah-ah. What type of woman is this? is what I asked myself. Then I tried to remove the knicker. All this time, the woman said nothing at all. She was very very silent like church on Monday. Then the woman-man picked up all his-her things and gave me three sound slaps on the face and ran away."

3. A number of essays in Nnolim 1992 offer illuminating appraisals of Saro-wiwa's grammatical inventions. See, in particular, Augustine C. Okere, "Patterns of Linguistic Deviation in Saro-wiwa's *Sozaboy*," 9–15; Doris Akekue, "Mind-Style in *Sozaboy*: A Functional Approach," 16–29; and Asomwan S. Adagboyin, "The Language of Ken Saro-wiwa's *Sozaboy*," 30–38. See also Chantal Zabus' fascinating discussion of what she calls "pidgin in vitro," in Zabus 1991, 179.

4. For a trenchant account of Saro-wiwa's career and writings as a political activist, see Nixon 1996.

WORKS CITED

Appadurai, Arjun. 1996. "Off-White." *Architecture New York (ANY)* 16 (November): 58.

Confiant, Raphaël. 1995. *La Savane des pétrifications*. Turin: Editions Mille et une nuits.

Deleuze, Gilles, and Félix Guattari. 1986. *Kafka: Toward a Minor Literature.* Translated by Dana Polan. Minneapolis: University of Minnesota Press.

Eliot, George. 1859. *Adam Bede.* Edinburgh and London: William Blackwood and Sons.

Glissant, Edouard. 1996. *Faulkner, Mississippi.* Paris: Editions Stock.

Goethe, Johann Wolfgang von. 1992. "Übersetzung," in *Noten und Abhandlungen zum bessern Verständnis des westöstlichen Divans.* Translated by Sharon Sloan in *Theories of Translation: An Anthology of Essays from Dryden to Derrida.* Edited by Rainer Schulte and John Biguenet. Chicago: University of Chicago Press.

Joyce, James. 1969 [1939]. *Finnegan's Wake.* New York: Penguin Books.

Lewis, Phil. 1985. "The Measure of Translation Effects." Pp. 31–62 in *Difference in Translation*, ed. Joseph Graham. Ithaca, N.Y.: Cornell University Press.

Lloyd, David. 1987. *Nationalism and Minor Literature: James Clarence Mangan and the Emergence of Irish Cultural Nationalism*. Berkeley: University of California Press.

Nixon, Rob. 1996. "Pipe Dreams: Ken Saro-wiwa, Environmental Justice, and Micro-Minority Rights." *Black Renaissance/Renaissance Noire* 1:1 (fall): 39–55.

Nnolim, Charles, ed. 1992. *Critical Essays on Ken Saro-wiwa's Sozaboy: A Novel in Rotten English*. Port Harcourt, Nigeria: Saros International Publishers.

Rushdie, Salman. 1992 [1988]. *The Satanic Verses*. Dover: The Consortium.

Saro-wiwa, Ken. 1994 [1985]. *Sozaboy: A Novel in Rotten English*. Essex: Longman Group.

———. 1995. "High Life," in *A Forest of Flowers*. Essex: Longman Group.

Spivak, Gayatri Chakravorty. 1992. "The Politics of Translation." Pp. 177–200 in *Destabilizing Theory*, ed. Michèle Barrett and Anne Phillips. Cambridge, U.K.: Polity Press.

Welsh, Irvine. 1993. *Trainspotting*. New York: W.W. Norton and Company.

Zabus, Chantal. 1991. *The African Palimpsest: Indigenization of Language in the West African Europhone Novel*. Atlanta: Editions Rodopi.

CHAPTER TEN

NATIONAL IDENTITY AND IMMIGRATION

American Polity, Nativism, and the "Alien"

ALI BEHDAD

> Instead of noninterference and specialization, there must be
> *interference*, crossing of borders and obstacles, a determined
> attempt to generalize exactly at those points where general-
> izations seem impossible to make.
> —Edward Said in *The Anti-Aesthetic:*
> *Essays on Postmodern Culture*

In one of his campaign commercials during California's gubernatorial
race in 1994, Pete Wilson used footage of "illegal" border crossers at the
San Diego–Tijuana checkpoint. The advertisement opened with a black-
and-white video of a dozen presumably Mexican immigrants scurrying
across the border, dodging cars and running from the checkpoint, as the
voice-over announced, "They keep coming! Two million illegal immigrants in California. The federal government won't stop them at the border, yet requires *us* to pay billions to take care of *them*" (emphasis
added). Although the commercial sparked charges of immigrant bashing
by many Democrats and activists—who compared it to George Bush's

1988 presidential commercial that used murderer Willie Horton's story
to campaign against Michael Dukakis—Wilson's campaign continued to
run the commercial for about two weeks, claiming it was "a real commercial about real issues."[1] Ironically, less than a decade earlier, Wilson
had successfully lobbied as a pro-immigration leader. He supported the
continuation of farm labor from Mexico as a way to appease Western
growers, who were concerned that the employer sanctions imposed by
the Immigration Reform and Control Act of 1986 would raise labor
costs and damage their earnings. In his 1994 campaign, however, Wilson claimed to be a crusader against illegal immigration, fighting against
foreigners stealing Californians' jobs, services, and tax dollars.

Wilson's commercial is a striking example of how the current anti-
immigrant frenzy in the United States, as a response to the fear of an
alien invasion, is articulated through the binary logic of us and them.
Despite the Wilson campaign's claim that the pronoun "they" is a reference to "illegal immigrants," the phrase "they keep coming" is broad
enough to be a reference to immigrants in general. As Darry Sragow,
campaign director for Democrat John Garamendi, correctly pointed out,
"The word *they* is obviously a veiled reference to a specific group of
people who tend to be perceived as having certain attributes in common.
One of those attributes, of course, is that if they are illegal, they don't
belong in this country. But in the perception of most voters, these people also are not white and don't speak English as a first language" ("Wilson Ad Sparks Charges of Immigrant-Bashing," *Los Angeles Times*,
May 14, 1994). In spite of America's foundational myth that it is an
immigrant nation, the country's latest nativist spasm reveals a *differential* mode of national identification. By "differential" I mean a binary
form of cultural and political classification in which national identity is
articulated through and depends on an alien other who, by threatening
to invade, helps define the citizen as a white, English-speaking person
who, as the commercial went on to point out, "work[s] hard, pay[s]
taxes, and obey[s] the laws."

To be sure, the sentiment that this commercial expressed so bluntly
is not merely that of an opportunist politician exploiting cultural anxiety about immigration to get reelected, as most immigrant rights
activists claimed. It also is that of a broader nativist population, ranging
from second- and third-generation immigrants and members of labor
unions to older citizens and people who classify themselves politically as
"moderate" to "conservative." Cautious as one should be of the empirical knowledge produced by polls and surveys, they are still useful in

illustrating the national anti-immigrant consensus today. According to most surveys—from the Gallup Poll to the American Institute of Public Opinion, Associated Press-NBC, the *New York Times*, and Roper and Harris Surveys—an overwhelming percentage of Americans, close to 80 percent, wish to limit legal immigration and stop "illegal" immigration to the United States.[2] More ironically, if not disturbingly, a 1992 nation-wide survey showed that 75 percent of Mexican Americans believed that too many immigrants were arriving.[3] Why such a broad-based, anti-immigrant consensus? How can a "nation of many nations," to use Walt Whitman's description of America (1959, 36), deny so adamantly the fact of its immigrant formation?

Many sociologists and most immigrant rights advocates view the current anti-immigrant frenzy as rising from the country's economic condition. Echoing the economism of the restrictionists, they argue that the present hostility toward "aliens" is an ephemeral and a cyclical reaction to the nation's swelled unemployment and economic slump. These observers cite the juxtaposition of periods of receptivity with periods of exclusion—for example, the "open door" era of 1776–1881 before the era of regulation of 1882–1924 or the post–World War II admission of political refugees before the 1954 "Operation Wetback" that sanctioned the mass deportation of Mexican farm workers—to demonstrate the schizophrenic pattern of welcoming immigrants when they are needed and turning against them when times are hard. The conventional liberal wisdom about the public reaction to immigration is: "When things are going well and there's a shortage of labor, people either look the other way or are actively supportive of bringing cheaper labor into the United States. But when jobs are tight, and the cost of supporting people goes up, then we suddenly redo the calculus."[4]

Empirically convincing though such an economic view of anti-immigration consensus may be, it fails to address immigration as both a necessary mechanism of social control in the formation of the state apparatus and an essential cultural component of national identification. What the view of cyclical anti-immigration misses is that immigration as a practice and discourse of exclusion has *always* been a part of American polity (though it may occasionally be exacerbated by a poor economy). Contrary to Wilson's claim to have spearheaded the new agenda of immigration control, the practice and discourse of excluding aliens are hardly new. Even during the so-called era of the open door, anti-immigrant sentiment ran high against newcomers: against Germans for their "clannishness," against Jews for their "parvenu spirit" or radicalism, against the

Irish for their "low and squalid" way of life, against Italians and Poles for their Catholicism, and against the Chinese for their "criminality" and inability to assimilate.⁵ The discourse and practice of exclusion, as I will discuss briefly, also is nascent in the writings of the "founding fathers," whose fear of seditious foreigners led at least some of them to pass the early Alien Act of 1798, which invested the president with the power to exclude undesirable aliens and delineated the requirements for U.S. citizenship. These requirements, in spite of their apparent leniency, embody the regulatory exercise of state power and are symptomatic of the nation's anti-immigrant sentiment.

To acknowledge the prevalence of anti-immigrant consensus since the beginning of American national consciousness, however, is not to suggest an unchanging attitude toward immigration throughout U.S. history. Indeed, as some scholars of immigration have recently pointed out, crucial shifts, such as the Chinese Exclusion Act of 1882, the Immigration Act of 1917, or the McCarran-Walter Act of 1952, have transformed the ways in which the United States as a nation-state has treated its immigrants, gradually moving from a more lenient and receptive tendency to a more restrictive and regulatory one.⁶ These critical moments constitute ruptures in the nation's discourse and practice of immigration, and as such they demystify linear histories of immigrant America. Neither successive nor continuous, the nation's response to its immigrant formation and its immigrants has always entailed a complex and often contradictory transformation of relations. I will return to these shifts in policy and public perception later, but for the moment I wish to make a broader, more theoretical point about the ways in which immigration has functioned throughout American history as a nodal point for the exercise of state power and as a differential mode of national identification. My contention here is that the United States, as a modern nation-state, has always relied upon the phenomenon of immigration to construe and delineate its national, geographical, and political boundaries. The old cliché about America being a nation of immigrants and the myth of America as a "promised land" obscure the history of immigration in the United States as a disciplinary and differential relation between the nation-state and its "alien" subjects. In what follows, I hope to demonstrate that immigration in America offers a cultural discourse through which the nation imagines itself and a field of sociopolitical practices whereby the state exercises its disciplinary power. Located at the interstices of national consciousness and state apparatus, immigration makes the ambivalent concept of the "nation-state" imaginable in America:

while the figure of the "alien" provides the differential signifier through which the nation defines itself as an autonomous community, the juridical and administrative regulations of immigration construe the collective sovereignty of the modern state. The circulation of social and political energy between these polar forces of identification and regulation allows for an ambivalent form of national consciousness that bridges the split between the nation and the state with its so-called cyclical history of tolerance and exclusion. I use the word "ambivalent" as opposed to "contradictory" to suggest a form of opposition that is not unified or about returning to an undifferentiated state. Whereas contradiction implies an imaginary unity and the idea that opposite forms of consciousness arise out of each other to form a more inclusive totality, the notion of ambivalence suggests an irreconcilable debate between competing notions of identity. To unpack the ambivalent structure of American nationalism, it is necessary to consider both the social history of "nativism" and the legal history of immigration law in the United States.

In the seventh of his papers entitled, "Examination of Jefferson's Message to Congress of December 7th, 1801," Alexander Hamilton, a West Indian by birth, wrote:

> The message of the President contains the following sentiments: "A denial of citizenship under a residence of fourteen years, is a denial to a great proportion of those who ask it, and controls a policy pursued from their first settlement, by many of these States, and *still believed of consequence to their prosperity. And shall we refuse to the unhappy fugitives from distress, that hospitality which the savages of the wilderness extended to our fathers arriving in this land?* Shall oppressed humanity find no asylum on this globe? Might not the general character and capabilities of a citizen, be safely communicated to *every one* manifesting a bona-fide purpose of embarking his life and fortune permanently with us?"
>
> . . . The pathetic and plaintive exclamations by which the sentiment is enforced might be liable to much criticism, if we are to consider it in any other light than as a flourish of rhetoric. It might be asked in return, Does the right to *asylum or hospitality* carry with it the right to *suffrage and sovereignty*? And what, indeed, was the courteous reception which was given to our forefathers by the savages of the wilderness? When did these humane and philanthropic savages exercise the policy of incorporating strangers among themselves on their first arrival in this country? When did they admit them into their huts, to make part of their families? And

when did they distinguish them by making them their sachems? Our histories and traditions have been more than apocryphal, if any thing like this kind and gentle treatment was really lavished by the much-belied savages upon our thankless forefathers. But the remark obtrudes itself. Had it all been true, prudence requires us to trace the history further and ask what has become of the nations of savages who exercised this policy, and who now occupies the territory which they then inhabited? Perhaps a lesson is here taught which ought not to be despised. (quoted in Grant and Davidson 1928, 45–57)

I have quoted Hamilton at length because his text offers a prototypic example of the country's ambivalence toward immigrants: on the one hand is Jefferson's powerful myth of America as an asylum for immigrant masses who come here in search of liberty, freedom, and opportunity; on the other hand is Hamilton's equally potent fear of foreigners corrupting and invading the polity. The "Grecian horse," as Hamilton called new immigrants, would destroy the polity through their "insidious intrigues and pestilent influence," to quote another founding father.[7] Contradictory though they may seem, these founding myths share a common repressive mechanism. What is repressed in both Jefferson's and Hamilton's references to the founding of the nation is the genocide of Native Americans by the English forefathers of these founders. While Jefferson consigns to oblivion the brutality of English forefathers toward the country's indigenous people (to posit the myth of America as an asylum, hospitable to "the unhappy fugitives from distress"), Hamilton celebrates the forefathers' colonialist usurpation of the land from Native Americans—a celebration forgetful of the immigrant status of pilgrims, which enables him to advocate an anti-immigrant position to maintain the nation's homogeneity and coherence. This repression allows the benevolent president to rationalize as hospitality the colonial interest of early settlers in immigrants to claim land and expand capital, while helping the reactionary politician make a case for his anti-immigrant stance. "Forgetting," as Ernest Renan remarked, "is a crucial factor in the creation of a nation," and "unity is always effected by means of brutality," which often is repressed in the official national history (1990, 11). The repressed history of colonial America is a crucial component of American nationalism, in keeping with Renan's notion of nation building as an act of forgetting: the nation disremembers its violent beginning to fashion itself and define a homogeneous community. Repressed in both narratives is that uprooting communities—in one case, the Native Americans' and in another, the European immigrants'—is the precondition for the formation of national consciousness. Uprooted from their national communities, "pilgrims" brutally displaced Native Americans in order to build a nation and create a sense of nationalism that would unite diverse and disparate communities. In the nation's historical memory, or its foundational myth, Europeans' experiences of exile and violence in establishing their polity are always disremembered. In short, exile and displacement are not the opposite of nationalism but the necessary requisite to imagining a national community in America.

More crucial in the context of my argument in this chapter, however, is how the debate between Hamilton and Jefferson exposes the ambivalent formation of nationalist sentiment in the United States. Students of American history often have argued that American polity legitimizes ambiguity and "embraces contradictory values" (Lipset and Raab 1970, 20). The notion of ambivalence that I am positing here, however, is neither about ambiguity nor contradiction but instead implies a productive difference between competing notions of national identity. Jefferson's and Hamilton's different views of immigration are not contradictory; rather, they both work out of a desire to imagine a national identity and a nation-state through an act of forgetting. The difference that they express is symptomatic of an ambivalent form of national consciousness at once insecure and confident, vigilant and inattentive toward the fact of its immigrant formation. Hamilton's and Jefferson's remarks are founding examples of the competing discourses of nationalism in the United States—that is, the country as a refuge for displaced masses versus the nation as a homogeneously Anglo-Saxon and Protestant community—and constitute an ambivalent nationalism that simultaneously acknowledges the nation's immigrant formation and ethnic heterogeneity and disavows them. The incommensurable difference between America as an immigrant heaven and a "pure" nation is a function of what these opposing myths repress, a repression that demands their repetition as new historical and social crises appear. To unpack the ideological functions of this "neurotic" compulsion to repeat, a discussion of the two poles of American nationalism is in order.

On the one hand, as Hans Kohn remarked, "The character of the United States as a land with open gateways, a nation of many nations, became as important for American nationalism as its identification with the idea of individual liberty and its federal character" (1957, 135). Jefferson's and George Washington's notion of America as an asylum for the oppressed and needy of the globe has been consistently interpreted as one of the nation's most important founding myths, and as such has been repeated throughout the country's political and social history.[8] Beginning with J. Hector St. John de Crèvecoeur's glorification of America as an "every person's country" in 1782,[9] through the celebration of the country as a heterogeneous community in the poetry of Ralph Waldo Emerson, Emma Lazarus, and Walt Whitman in the nineteenth century, to the more recent claims of twentieth-century scholars such as Louis Adamic, Milton Gordon, Oscar Handlin,[10] and Hans Kohn, every generation has repeated and thus perpetuated the founding myth. Even Ronald Reagan, whose administration helped the passage of the Immigration Reform and Control Act of 1986, polemically asked in his nomination speech in 1980, "Can we doubt that only a Divine Providence placed this land, this island of freedom here as a refuge for all those people in the world who yearn to breathe freely, Jews and Christians enduring persecution behind the Iron Curtain, the boat people of Southeast Asia, of Cuba and Haiti, victims of drought and famine in Africa."[11] There is no doubt that at least until the late nineteenth century, the United States was mostly hospitable toward newcomers and maintained an open-door immigration policy. But like every national myth, the discourse of asylum is forgetful of the historical context of its formation. What the myth of the nation as a refuge for the oppressed of all nations represses is that until very recently, "it was applied only to whites from Europe," and that "it was driven primarily by capital seeking labor in pursuit of wealth and by the desire to clear Indians from their own lands" (Fuchs 1992, 40). Latent in Jefferson's benevolence toward immigrants is a colonialist will to appropriate the land and a capitalist desire for expansion. Indeed, it is worth noting that the debate among the founding fathers about immigration did not revolve around the issue of human rights (or the "needy") but focused instead on the advantages and disadvantages of immigration as a solution to the new nation's need for labor. For instance, did the advantages of naturalizing immigrant mechanics, professionals, and farmers outweigh the disadvantages of their cultural and political differences?

Not only does the myth of America as an asylum disremember the ideological underpinnings and the political context of America's production, it also represses the fact of nativism in defining the nation. I will return to the history of nativism below, but for the moment I will only note that even Jefferson, who carried the banner of pro-immigration, spoke disparagingly about the immigrant "mobs of great cities" in the East and against "German settlements" in the Midwest for preserving "their own languages, habits, and principles of government."[12] The notion of cultural and political assimilation always underlies the myth of the immigrant-loving nation, as newcomers are expected to lose their old national "skins" in order to become Americans. As John Quincy Adams bluntly put it, "They [immigrants to America] come to a life of independence, but to a life of labor—and, if they cannot accommodate themselves to the character, moral, political, and physical, of this country with all its compensating balances of good and evil, the Atlantic is always open to them to return to the land of her nativity and their fathers. . . . They must cast off the European skin, never to resume it" (cited in Gordon 1964, 268). Repressed in the myth of asylum is the notion of ethnic diversity and difference. As Lawrence Fuchs observes, "It was not until well into the twentieth century that 'melting pot' implied ethnic diversity" (1992, 40). To be accepted as an immigrant, the newcomer had to forsake his or her ethnicity and relinquish her or his political and religious differences.

What the exclusion of diversity and difference suggests is that nativism is not contradictory to the nation's myth of asylum but a repressed component of its formation. As histories of American nativism have demonstrated, the nation's benign image of itself as a haven for the "oppressed and persecuted of all Nations and Religions," to quote Washington, has always coexisted with intolerance and racism toward new immigrants. In his compelling social history of American nativism, *Strangers in the Land: Patterns of American Nativism 1860–1925* (1955), John Higham locates three main currents in America's anti-foreign consensus: anti-Catholicism, as the product of the Reformation; anti-radicalism, as the fearful effect of the French Revolution; and racial nationalism, as the ideology of Anglo-Saxon racial superiority. The early English colonizers' heritage of anti-Catholicism, nourished by their struggle against the two hostile Catholic empires of France and Spain, contributed greatly to emerging national consciousness in America. Mostly latent until the arrival of large numbers of Catholic immigrants in the 1850s, anti-Catholicism constitutes, according to Higham, the oldest and most powerful anti-foreign tradition in America, a tradition that transforms the patriotic tinge of the Protestant revolt into a new form of nativist nationalism in the New World. An equally important European event, the French Revolution, worked to produce a second nativist tradition in the late eighteenth century: anti-radicalism. In this tradition, claims about European "disloyalty" and a penchant for revolution helped produce a national form of identification that viewed opposition to the status quo as profoundly "un-American." And, finally, the essentialist claims about the racial superiority of the Anglo-Saxon race offered a third current to define American nationality. While the first two currents used differential frames to identify the nation—America as anti-Catholic and anti-radical—the latter theme in the history of American nativism introduced a mimetic form of national identification: the appeal to one's racial origin in imagining a nation. Benjamin Franklin, to cite an example, asked, "Why increase the sons of Africa by planting them in America, where we have so fair an opportunity, by excluding all blacks and tawnies, of increasing the lovely white and red?" (Grant and Davidson 1928, 26–27). Informed later by the racial nationalism of such intellectuals as Sharon Turner (1907), Horace Bushnell (1915), and Frederick Saunders (1855), this current of nativism claimed the Anglo-Saxon "race" as the source of America's greatness and demanded protection against the mixed tide of immigration.

Schematic though Higham's narrative may be, it offers a useful historical view into the ideological underpinnings of America's nationalist consciousness and its differential effects on the anti-immigrant penchant. The nativist traditions that his narrative posits contravene the cyclical hypothesis by demonstrating the prevalence of anti-foreign sentiment since the beginning of national formation. The periodic reappearances of these currents, cyclical though they may appear, do not constitute a linear nationalism but rather a complex process of identification in which every upthrust of nativist tendency makes a distinct mark on how America imagines itself. The movement, in other words, is never static or cyclical but maintains a dynamic function through which the nation constantly reimagines itself and by which social and political crises are contained.

Higham's narrative offers a persuasive thesis about the interdependence of American nationalism and the rise of nativism, defined broadly here as an "intense opposition to an internal minority on the ground of its foreign (i.e., 'un-American') connection" (1955, 4). But the ambivalent movement of national consciousness that I am suggesting is a corrective to the causal relationship between nativism and American nationalism that Higham constructs. It is not that American nationalism emerged as an effect of nativism, or even that nationalism causes nativism. Rather, nationalism has always embodied a nativist or an anti-foreign component to manufacture an imagined sense of community (i.e., the nation). Nativism does not constitute a contradiction to the national myth of asylum; rather, it is the culmination of what the latter conveniently represses, namely, the nation's self-interested benevolence toward immigrants. Nativism is the limit of nationalism as an exclusionary mode of identification.[13] The three currents of nativism that Higham outlines point to a differential and exclusionary mode of national identification in which the figure of the foreigner is invested with values contradictory to the American polity.

"American nationality," Arthur Mann (1979, 47) remarks, "is purely ideological."[14] By this, he means that the founding of the nation-state in the late eighteenth century was not based on traditional prerequisites for nationhood, such as territorial integrity, a long and legendary history, the sharing of an ancient folklore, or any racial and religious commonality. Instead, citizenship based on such politically contingent keywords as democracy, liberty, and freedom became the foundation of national identification. Although, as Benedict Anderson suggests in passing, we ought to be wary of the idea of nationalism as an ideology, Mann's definition of American nationalism offers a valuable insight into the differential role of the immigrant in the articulation of national consciousness in the United States (1983, 15). What anti-Catholicism, anti-radicalism, and Anglo-Saxon racial superiority have in common is their reliance on an ideological notion of national consciousness defined through the identification of immigrants with political dissidence.

Reflected in the short-lived Alien and Sedition Acts of 1798, imposed by the Federalist administration of John Adams, the association of foreigners with violent opposition to the status quo has been a fundamental component of American nationalism. To possess "the genuine character of true Americans," as John Adams claimed, was to "have no attachments or exclusive friendship for any foreign nation" (Grant and Davidson 1928, 6). To be an immigrant by definition implied a certain attachment to one's native country, an attachment consequently marked as "un-American." The figure of the foreigner as a menacing source of sedition, discontent, insurrection, and resistance, articulated repetitively, therefore manufactures a consenting, though imagined, sense of national community. This figure, however, does not remain the same, for historical epochs rotate representations of the seditious foreigner. The late-eighteenth-century fear of foreign radicals was reproduced over and over: in the mid-nineteenth century's anti-foreign parties' claims about "disloyal" Irish and Germans, in the 1880s' labor movements' demands for "the exclusion of the restless revolutionary horde of foreigners,"[15] in the Big Red Scare of 1919–1920, in 1950s' McCarthyism, and in our current association of Middle Eastern immigrants with terrorism and fanaticism. My aim in enumerating these cases of anti-alien sentiment is not to undermine their rather different and complex histories but to point out their productivity in propagating a sign of difference through which the nation imagines itself as an autonomous unit.

What we encounter in every anti-immigrant claim is the assertion that a fundamental difference exists between a patriotically imagined community and a disrupting alien other. The Know-Nothings' Manifesto, to cite an example, uses the "language of Washington" to claim that "the maintenance of the Union of these United States" is "the primary object of patriotic desire" and declares its members' total "obedience to the Constitution" before it advocates laws regulating immigration (*Platform* [1855]). What caused the Know-Nothings to act against Catholics was not their religion, for the American Party advocated the protection of religious opinion and worship, but Catholics' affiliation with an autocratic, hierarchical, and centralized institution that was viewed as anathema to American democracy and individual rights. Catholics were thus viewed as a subversive community whose support of "popish despotism" made them both unassimilable into the national community and antithetical to Republican ideas of freedom and liberty. The Know-Nothings' anti-Catholicism was, in other words, a form of anti-radicalism. What we encounter in the American Party's manifesto is an exclusive form of nationalism that is articulated through the differential role of immigrants as unassimilatable and dissident. Nativists, in other words, identify themselves as "true" Americans by distinguishing themselves from immigrants who represent "un-American" values and ideas.

The Know-Nothings may have disappeared from the political scene by 1856, but their anti-immigrant agenda was perpetuated. Later in the century, for example, fears of immigrant radicalism became a powerful force in forming national identity as labor discontent swept the nation. When the Haymarket Square violence erupted in Chicago during the "eight-hour" strikes of May 1886, for which Chicago authorities sentenced to death six immigrants and a native American, the figure of the immigrant proved useful again in preserving nationalist fervor. The big daily newspapers editorialized about the "danger that threatens the destruction of our national edifice by the erosion of its moral foundations," claiming that the "invasion of venomous reptiles [i.e., immigrants]" endangered "our National existence" as well as "our National and Social institutions."[16] Similar anti-immigrant sentiment was expressed after the bombing of the home of Mitchell Palmer, the new attorney general, in 1919, leading to a series of raids by the newly created General

Intelligence Division in the Department of Justice to gather information about foreign radicals. The *New York Times'* editorials claimed that "the sentimental notion of America as the asylum of the oppressed has disappeared in the alarmed instinct of self-preservation," and that "no economic or financial consideration has any standing in comparison with the imperative patriotic need of guarding against enemies of order and the emissaries of destruction" (June 19, 1919, quoted in Simon 1985, 197). Like earlier nativist claims, these editorials point to the productivity of anti-alien claims in perpetuating patriotic sentiments and nationalist fervor. The figure of the immigrant is the sign of all that stands in opposition to being American and to the notion of the American polity.

Immigrants play a productive role in the formation of nationalist fervor not only as political dissidents but also as contaminators. In the mid-nineteenth century, for example, the nativist groups and an overwhelming percentage of the general public opposed the arrival of Germans, Eastern Europeans, and other immigrants on the grounds that the newcomers were poor, mentally and physically ill, or criminal. Immigrants, according to these restrictionists, were a source of contamination that threatened the well-being of the nation. The Massachusetts Sanitary Commission, to cite a sample, warned the nation against the danger of an open-door immigration policy:

> The stream of emigration has continued to increase, and seems to gain a new accession of strength in every passing year. . . . Each [mercenary ship-owner and manager of a pauper-house] smiles at the open-handed but lax system of generosity which governs us. . . . And yet a greater calamity attends this monstrous evil [of the open-door policy of immigration]. . . . Our own native inhabitants, who mingle with these recipients of their bounty, often become themselves contaminated with diseases, and sicken and die; and the physical and moral power of the living is depreciated, and the healthy, social and moral character we once enjoyed is liable to be forever lost. Pauperism, crime, disease, and death stare us in the face. ("Report of a General Plan for Promotion of Health, April 25, 1850," in Abbott 1926, 596–600)

As in the anti-immigrant discourse of the late twentieth century, immigrants are inextricably linked here with the nation's serious and costly social ills. But beyond the simple scapegoating of newcomers, the commissioner's remarks posit a fundamental binary relation between the national self and the alien other through which a defensive and an exclusionary form of nationalism is advocated. What concerns this public official is the way in which new immigrants contaminate the national community, not only physically and mentally but also socially and morally. The difference between the healthy and prosperous citizen and the diseased and poor immigrant is transformed by the end of the passage into an ethical distinction between a national self conforming to established norms of right conduct and a threatening alien violating the nation's ethical principles.

More significantly, however, the cases of anti-immigrant sentiment that I have cited above bring into focus a repetitive process of disavowal that produces what is referred to as "our National existence," as well as the discriminatory regulation and control of immigrants by the state. Along with the nationalistic sentiment during these and subsequent periods came demands by a broad range of organizations—from the Order of Railway Conductors to such patriotic societies as the Grand Army of the Republic and the Patriotic Order of Sons of America—for legislation to completely suspend immigration to the United States. The fear of anti-radicalism and the anxiety over the contaminating immigrant are always followed by demands for regulation and control of national borders. Two more recent editorials about immigration elucidate the consequential relation between the dichotomous perception of American cultural identity and demands for exclusionary immigration laws:

> We must choose how many people to admit, and which ones. That can be done only if we can control the borders. Otherwise, a population troubled by hard times will slam the Golden Door. ("Immigration and Purity," *New York Times*, December 16, 1982)

> The bombing of the World Trade Center in New York should cause Americans to realize that terrorism is one of the prices paid for lax immigration control and inadequate border security. ("Open Borders and Weak Laws Invite Terrorists," *Border Watch*, April 1993)

The binary relation between us and them, implicit in these commentaries, is construed often in terms of a national crisis. The immigrant other threatens the very foundation of the American polity, creating a state of national emergency that can only be overcome with more rigid regulation and control of the border. The fear of the radical or the contaminating other is thus productive in manufacturing a national consensus against immigration. The redundancy of claims about the menace of immigrants demands a conception of the U.S. history of immigration in keeping with Walter Benjamin's insight that "the 'state of emergency' in which we live is not the exception but the rule" (1969, 257). The so-called crisis of immigration is neither a historical exception, as Governor Wilson claims, nor a series of cyclical eruptions of a unique disorder, as some social scientists have argued. Rather, the state of siege is the rule in the narrative of nationalism: it is what legitimates national authority and state power. The repetitive scapegoating of immigrants in the United States, though perpetuated in each instance by different historical conditions, underscores the productivity of crisis in imagining a nation-state. The perpetual crisis of immigration reinscribes a notion of difference on the national community and its others, a difference that must be constantly maintained to propagate a space of contestation where concepts of nationality as citizenship and state as sovereignty can be rearticulated and reaffirmed. The crisis of immigration, in other words, awakens the community to self-consciousness as a nation while legitimating the state apparatus to guard its sovereignty.

The crisis of immigration and its binary logic do not imply a uniform response to the issue of immigration, nor do they suggest a monolithic notion of nation-state. On the contrary, nationalist sentiment and the state's regulation of immigration in the United States have always been articulated ambivalently. As Elizabeth Hull remarks, "From Colonial times, [Americans'] idealism [e.g., America as an asylum or sanctuary for masses of immigrants] has coexisted with intolerant and even xenophobic attitudes that have also represented a resilient strain in the American psyche" (1985, 9). Many historical examples attest to the nation's ambivalence about its immigrants: during the 1830s and 1840s, when the country was benevolently accepting Irish immigrants fleeing the potato famine and German refugees escaping economic depression, it also encouraged a powerful anti-Catholic movement (reflected in the "No-Popery" agitation and in the rise of the American Party and later the American Protective Association, which championed a notion of national homogeneity). Similarly, in the late nineteenth century, when a broad range of labor and patriotic organizations in Northeastern cities were demanding the exclusion of immigrants from the industrial workforce, and West Coast nationalist zealots were lynching, boycotting, and expelling the Chinese, Americans also, as Higham demonstrates, embraced a "cosmopolitan interpretation of their national mission," defined as a humanitarian assimilation of the wretched of the earth who had endangered their lives in their long journeys to become free subjects in the New World (1955, 22).

The humanitarian acceptance of immigrants, however, does not constitute an oppositional moment in the formation of American national consciousness, for it too carries the binary logic of us and them in a symbolically violent discourse that reproduces the stereotype of the immigrant as the "wretched refuse" in need of help from benevolent Americans.[17] In this narrative, the stereotype of the immigrant is not so much of a menace as of a poor and miserable figure in need of assistance by the imaginary America. Stereotype, as Homi Bhabha has demonstrated in another context (1986), is an "ambivalent mode of knowledge," one that ensures its repetition across historical periods and masks its excess through a strategy of individuation. The discourse of immigration is fraught with contradictory stereotypes. On the one hand, the immigrant is weak and wretched, on the other hand, powerful and dangerous; on the one hand, an opportunist who steals our jobs, on the other hand, a lazy parasite who abuses our social welfare funds. As examples of cultural fetishism, these stereotypes point to the ambivalence of the nation toward its immigrants, an ambivalence marked by both knowledge and disavowal, control and defense, exclusion and amnesty, and acceptance and rejection. What we encounter in the national discourse about immigration is a mode of discriminatory power that embodies a repertoire of conflicted and split positions. It is a discourse that depends on a system of multiple beliefs to constantly produce a state of emergency in which the nation rearticulates itself as an imagined, democratic community, a community that is always differentially identified against the threatening aliens. The shifting and ambivalent images of the immigrant are a sign of the productivity of the discourse of immigration: the images are what give the discourse its authority, ensure its hegemony through a claim to democracy, and perpetuate its repetition by the split reaction they engender in national consciousness.

Were it not for the state's parallel ambivalence about the issue of immigration, my remarks about the split identity formation of American nationalism might have appeared as a theorization of just a confused public's contradictory reactions toward new immigrants. But legal histories of immigration confirm the centrality of ambivalence to the imagining of the nation-state in the United States. American immigration law and policy, as both Hull (1985) and Edwin Harwood (1986) have suggested, have demonstrated a great deal of uncertainty about the country's mission: "Should the United States be a refuge for the 'tired and the poor,' or an outpost, properly off-limits to the 'wretched refuse' of the world?" (Hull 1985, 9) Again, there are many examples to cite here. The early Alien and Sedition Act of 1798, imposed by Adams, which authorized the president to deport any immigrant considered dangerous to the state's security, was abandoned two years later when Jefferson and his Democratic Republican supporters took control of the White House and Congress. The 1921 National Origins Act and the Johnson–Reed Second National Origins Act of 1924, while attempting to restrict the number of "undesirable" immigrants and restore an "optimal" ethnic configuration by imposing a strict quota system, established no quota for Mexican and Latin American immigrants, an exception that facilitated the migratory movement of a large body of farm workers. The Immigration and Nationality Act of 1965 eliminated the race and ethnic biases of previous acts but also created a new system of visa allocation that reduced the number of immigrants from Mexico, colonies, and dependencies. And, finally, the 1986 Immigration Reform and Control Act attempted to control the flow of undocumented immigrants by expanding border enforcement efforts and sanctions against employers who hired "illegal aliens," while at the same time offering an extensive amnesty and legalization program for undocumented immigrants. Listing the state's ambivalent responses to immigration together is not meant to hide their important differences. Rather, my aim is to emphasize how parallel the state's ambivalence about controlling immigration is to the public's split reaction toward immigrants. The parallel attests to the *circulatory* relationship between the state's apparatus of social regulation and the nation's mode of identification. The regulation of the immigration crisis by the state, I suggest, is at once a response to the nation's concern about the intruding other and productive of a differential mode of identification through reaffirming the claim to sovereignty. The relation between the nation and the state, as Etienne Balibar has demonstrated (1990), has been conventionally viewed in terms of "reflecting": it is either the state that creates the nation in response to political and economic constraints, or the nation that constitutes the state "as a way of fulfilling the needs of its collective consciousness, or of pursuing its material interests" (ibid., 332). Critical of these myths of origin, I posit the circular relation between the state and the nation around the issue of immigration in consonance with Balibar's insight that "a state always is implied in the historic framework of a national formation" (ibid., 331). I take this remark to define a notion of nation-state that neither reduces their relation to causality nor is forgetful of their autonomy. The formations of state and nation are mutually implicated in each other, and yet they are conceptually and socially distinct.

The history of immigration law in the United States offers a compelling context in which to consider how the nation, as an imagined community, and the state, as an ideological and a repressive apparatus, inform each other. While the imagined community of the nation has led the state to legislate a juridical and an administrative structure for regulating immigration, the state's regulations have perpetuated a disciplinary context for the nation's sense of collective sovereignty and a differential mode of national identity. The state's regulation of immigration has always relied on the nation's consensus. By this I mean not only that immigration control has a popular base, but that the state's regulation of immigration entails a consensual perception of immigration as a crisis by the national community. The state solicits the nation's consent in regulating immigration while contributing, as I discuss below, to the popular perception of immigration as a national problem. The ambivalent regulation of immigration in the United States calls into question both the instrumentalist and structuralist models of the state: the state is neither the "instrument in the hands of the ruling class for enforcing and guaranteeing the stability of the class structure" (Sweezy 1942, 243), nor can its function be reduced to simply reproducing the capitalist system's social structure.[18] The history of U.S. immigration law and the state's regulatory apparatuses, such as the INS and Border Control, suggests a notion of state that is at once autonomous, acting occasionally against the interests of the ruling class, and productive in mediating and managing the nation's social crises to enable a sense of national culture.[19]

As the colonialist myth of the frontier disappeared in the late nineteenth century and the general public became less hospitable toward new immigrants for bringing down wages by increasing the supply of labor and requiring extra social welfare expenditures, the state, specifically the federal government, was forced to move toward a more regulatory and restrictive immigration policy. Until 1882, authority over immigration was exercised by individual state governments and local officials, allowing each state to legislate and exercise jurisdiction over immigrants according to its labor needs. During the so-called Open Door Era (1776–1881), states with large ports of entry, such as New York, Maryland, Massachusetts, and Pennsylvania, were given the authority to individually legislate laws concerning the inspection, integration, recruiting, and welfare of their immigrants. But with the passing of the Immigration Act of August 3, 1882, the federal government established the administrative, bureaucratic, and regulatory machinery to control immigration. This act levied a head tax of fifty cents on each immigrant to cover the cost of immigration welfare, blocked the entry of certain undesirable aliens and, more important, made the Treasury Department responsible for enforcing immigration laws. Supported by the Supreme Court's ruling in the 1875 case of *Henderson v. Mayor of New York*, which declared unconstitutional individual states' laws regulating immigration, the 1882 Act practically transferred the authority and practice of immigration from states to the federal government, marking thus a crucial stage in the development of immigration as an important site for the state's regulatory practices in the United States. The state simultaneously took charge of immigration by providing individual states with funds to cover immigrant welfare while building the administrative machinery to regulate and control immigration. A few years later, with the Immigration Act of 1891, Congress created the Office of Immigration, the predecessor to today's INS, to oversee the regulation of immigration. This new state apparatus was a disciplinary institution from its very genesis, monitoring the flow of new arrivals, supervising the individual states' regulation of contract labor laws, and deporting excludable aliens. The investing of the Office of Immigration with the authority to supervise and control aliens and Congress' active role in legislating new immigration laws shifted the practice of immigration regulation from a regional and particular issue to a national and general problem. As the federal government's role in regulating immigration increased, immigration was generalized as a national problem to be regulated and controlled by state apparatuses.

The year 1882 is a crucial date in the history of U.S. immigration policy, not only because it inaugurated the state's active role as the primary agent of immigration control but also because Congress yielded to the Western states' demand to exclude orientals. It passed the Chinese Exclusion Act, which prohibited the entry of Chinese workers and barred all foreign-born Chinese from acquiring citizenship. Although an act in 1870 had extended the privilege of citizenship to "aliens of African nativity and persons of African descent," now Congress used the Naturalization Act of 1790, which limited citizenship to "free white persons," as its legal base for excluding Chinese. This and the Immigration Act of 1882 were the beginning of the era of regulation in the history of immigrant America, an era characterized by a more interventionary role for the federal government in legislating and exercising jurisdiction over immigration. These acts signal at once the emergence of the state as the agent of regulation and the beginning of a new notion of citizenship defined hereafter in terms of racial identity. Congress not only built the state apparatus for a regulatory practice of immigration but, as the legislative component of the state, it also enabled the articulation of citizenship in racial terms by identifying an "unassimilable" race and banning it from entry and citizenship. The Chinese Exclusion Act ended the idea of citizenship as a status that could be gained through the immigrant's own acts of immigration and naturalization, transforming it instead into a privileged rank reserved for certain ethnicities whose racial and cultural identities made them assimilable in the polity.

To be sure, the issue of race has always been an important keyword in defining national identity and culture in the United States, for as historians of American nativism have demonstrated, a notion of Anglo-Saxon racial superiority informed much of the nation's discourse of immigration since the late eighteenth century. But the shifts that I have been discussing here point to a new mode of racial identity in defining the national self as *citizen*. It was not that race did not matter before 1882, given that citizenship was until the late nineteenth century limited to free white people, but the new laws of that year were crucial in making race a key site for the state's exercise of disciplinary power, thus enabling an exclusionary form of nationalism, as the "native" was interpolated as citizen by the state. Historians of American nativism consider the rise and fall of the Ku Klux Klan in the 1920s as traditional nativism's last stance, pointing to the decline of anti-alien sentiment after the Great Depression.[20] Considering the Johnson Act of 1924 as the temporal marker of this change, Walter Benn Michaels (1997) has argued further that since the mid-1920s, a cultural notion of national identity (defined in terms of family and racial inheritance) has displaced the ideological notion of American identity in which belonging is defined as a status that could be achieved through one's own actions, such as immigration and naturalization. The Johnson National Quota Act of 1924, he argues cogently, recast the very notion of American citizenship, "changing it from a status that could be achieved through one's own actions (immigrating, becoming 'civilized,' getting 'naturalized') to a status that could better be understood as inherited" (ibid., 32). My argument about the interpolation of natives as citizens by the state is in accordance with Michaels' insight about the racialization of citizenship, but I view it as a complex process that began fifty years earlier with the Chinese Exclusion Act and with the shift in the state's role as the arbitrator of immigration issues. As the state consolidated its authority over immigration in the 1920s with the passing of National Quota Acts, it became invested with the power to mediate new notions of national identity and culture through its racialization of the immigrant and by defining citizenship in terms of racial inheritance—notions that, as I will discuss below, are articulated ambivalently. In other words, the seeming disappearance of nativism in the post–depression era is a consequence of the emergence of the state as a key player in the debate over national identity and culture. In the so-called era of regulation (1882–1924), notions of national identity and culture became interlocked in and were mediated by the state and its legislation and exercise of regulatory immigration laws.

The notions of race and culture as key words in defining citizenship are, however, ambivalently articulated in the state's regulation of immigration. The Immigration Act of 1917 and the National Quota Acts of 1921 and 1924, which finally consolidated the federal government's power over immigration, provide examples of the state's split reaction to immigration control. Based on the findings of the Dillingham Commission of 1910, and in response to the intense pressure from citizens and labor organizations on the West Coast, the first act made a literacy test a requirement and excluded laborers from the "Asiatic Barred Zone," while the other two acts provided a quota system that limited the annual number of immigrants from each admissible nationality to 3 percent of the foreign-born of that nationality, based on the census of 1910, privileging Western European immigrants over Eastern European and Asian newcomers. These new immigration laws signal the consolidation of the state as the principal "guardian" of national culture, investing it with the power to regulate the country's racial configuration, as the individual states were robbed of autonomy in managing their immigration predicaments. These acts also marked the state establishing a policy of restriction based on a hierarchical order of eligibility that favored those immigrants thought to be more assimilable because of their racial and cultural background.

Like the Chinese Exclusion Act, these restrictive and exclusionary policies, as responses to the importuning of such civil organizations as the American Federation of Labor (AFL) and other national societies as well as demands by racial nativists of the West Coast and the South to restrict the flow of new immigrants, underscore the consensual character of the state's regulatory practices. The state, in other words, did not necessarily act in the interests of capitalists and employers whose need for a cheap supply of labor made them supportive of lax immigration laws. Instead, it yielded to a broader public demand for federal regulation of immigration, a drive that symbolically began in California and other Western states, where the myth of the frontier ended with the immigration of unskilled and low-wage laborers from China. Caught between the demands of organized labor to curtail the flow of immigration and the needs of employers and capitalists to gain a cheap source of labor, the state proved to be more ambivalent, however. A series of statutes was included in these acts that exempted Mexicans from both the literacy test and quota system. Responding mostly to pressure from Southwestern agricultural growers, the state acknowledged their demands, legislating a law at once restrictive and accommodating. The ambivalent immigration laws of 1917–1924 at once quelled the general public's desire for regulation and catered to the capitalists' need for cheap labor. The state simultaneously acted independently of the ruling class while intervening politically to maintain the stability of the capitalist social structure.

The state's ambivalent legislation and regulatory practices of immigration have continued ever since. We encounter, for example, a similar split reaction to the nation's immigration dilemma by the state with the passing of the Immigration Reform and Control Act of 1986 (IRCA). In response to widespread public pressure to curtail the flow of illegal immigration across the U.S.–Mexico border, the new act included an employer sanctions measure that for the first time made the hiring of undocumented workers illegal and punishable. And yet, as Kitty Calavita aptly observes, "concerned not to 'harass' employers, Congress crafted employer sanctions that were largely symbolic" (1992, 8). Not only did the law include provisions such as Special Agricultural Worker and Replenishment Agricultural Worker, which made it possible for growers to employ temporary Mexican workers, it also included an "affirmative defense" clause that "protects employers from prosecution as long as they request documentation from workers, regardless of the validity of the documents presented" (ibid., 169). Like the immigration acts of 1917–1924, the IRCA simultaneously responded to the general public's demand to restrict the flow of illegal immigration across the southern border, acting as such against the interests of agricultural and service employers, while paying attention to the latter's lobbying for sanctions not so onerous as to disrupt their business. Again, the state did not serve solely the interests of the ruling class, nor did it assume an imposing role in relation to the general public. Rather, its regulatory and exclusionary practices were produced consentingly in response to contradictory demands made by the national community and the capitalist class.

More significantly, the state's juridical and administrative rationality played a crucial role in the cultural and ideological fields that constituted the nation's consensus and its reaction toward immigrants. "Every social formation," Louis Althusser has demonstrated, "must reproduce the conditions of its production at the same time as it produces, and in order to be able to produce" (1971, 128). The state is no exception to this rule: its regulatory apparatus is productive of the consensus it elicits from civil society at the same time it produces such apparatuses of regulation as the police, the prisons, the INS, and the Border Patrol. The state's manufacturing of social consensus is achieved not only through the exercising of hegemony over such ideological apparatuses as the schools, political parties, legal system, and so on but also by perpetuating a popular and violent form of vigilantism through the uses of patriotic rhetoric and nationalist discourse. As a result, the state's legislation and regulation of immigration in the United States have often perpetuated, instead of soothed, the general public's patriotic fervor and exclusionary attitudes. There are many examples to cite here. For instance, the passing of the Chinese Exclusion Act of 1882, rather than diminishing the public's anxiety about the "yellow peril," was followed by a series of violent riots against "orientals" on the West Coast. Demonstrations against the Chinese occurred throughout Arizona, California, Oregon, Washington, and Wyoming. In the fall of 1885, for example, twenty-eight Chinese were murdered and hundreds were wounded and driven away from their homes in a single evening in Rock Springs, Wyoming, while in Washington, a Tacoma mob burned down the community's Chinatown and drove out its residents.[21] Similarly, the Espionage and Sedition Acts of 1918, instead of lulling postwar vigilantism, intensified it. Tolerated by the government, secret voluntary organizations, such as the American Protective League, took the law into their own hands to police the public: carrying out investigations of "disloyal" behavior and utterances, locating draft evaders, spotting violators of food and gasoline regulations, and even checking up on people who did not buy Liberty bonds.[22] And finally, the 1986 Immigration Control and Reform Act, instead of appeasing the public about the nation's immigration crisis, helped the emergence of a broad range of regulatory practices by watchful citizens who have voluntarily produced and participated in such organizations as the Federation for American Immigration

Reform (FAIR), the American Immigration Control Foundation (AICF), and the Center for Immigration Studies, trying to create a "Nation of Americans." Not only have these voluntary organizations been instrumental in perpetuating the current anti-immigrant frenzy, through such projects as "Light the Border," they have also "commissioned academic studies on the economic impact of immigration and financed opinion polls that reflect a growing public resentment of illegal immigration."[23] In addition, these organizations regularly lobby Congress to pass stricter immigration laws and file amicus briefs in suits that deal with undocumented immigration. The success of these organizations points to the dynamic function of the state as an ideological apparatus that can produce and perpetuate the consensus it elicits from its citizens by interpolating them as patriotic subjects. Anti-immigration is a form of defensive patriotism today, for opposition to immigration is always articulated in terms of a defense against the eroding of "American" values and the disintegration of national unity.

Moreover, as I have demonstrated elsewhere (Behdad 1998), the micro-practices of immigration and border control play a crucial role in generating and perpetuating a culture of surveillance marked by a sense of permanent and constant visibility.[24] The Border Patrol may not be successful in keeping all of the "undesirables" out, but it has been instrumental in establishing a pattern of social control and a generalized mode of surveillance at least in the border region, if not throughout the country. The rise in the active public support of immigration enforcement in the form of protests (such as the project "Light the Border") as well as tips on undocumented workers sent to the INS by ordinary citizens demonstrate the powerful effects of the state's disciplinary practices in transforming the average citizen into a patriotic vigilante.

Elaborating on the immigration deal forged between the Clinton administration and Congress in the spring of 1996, Rahm Emanuel, White House immigration advisor, remarked, "We're a nation of immigrants and a nation of laws, and this agreement respects both those ideas."[25] Emanuel's comment is remarkable, not only for acutely capturing the split nature of the recent bill but also for offering a symptomatic expression of the nation's ambivalent discourse about immigration: on the one hand, the pole of national identification: "We're a nation of immigrants"; on the other hand, the state's exercise of disciplinary power: "We're a nation of laws." By law, Emanuel seems to be referring at least partially to the propositions in the bill: doubling the Border Patrol, installing fences and barriers along the U.S.–Mexico border, streamlining the deportation process, creating pilot projects to verify the immigration status of job applicants, and imposing tougher penalties on smugglers of immigrants. What the state legislates as immigration law, at least according to the bill's propositions, is nothing less than an extension of its disciplinary exercise of power: the surveillance of its immigrants, the policing and controlling of its borders, and the toughening of its exclusionary and regulatory practices.

And yet, the acknowledgment that we are a nation of immigrants, while repeating the general cliché about America's national identity, points to a veiled recognition of the state's inability to control the flow of immigrants, a recognition that is disavowed in the regulatory propositions that the state legislates: "They keep coming, and we have to keep regulating them." The cliché of America's immigrant identity is predicated as much on the nation's salutary mode of self-identification as on the country's anxiety about its immigrants. The nation's mode of identification is thus ambivalent: on the one hand, we are a nation of immigrants; on the other hand, we identify ourselves against our immigrants as we try to control them. It is on the site of such an ambivalence that the state's strategies of discipline, normalization, and regulation are produced in collaborative ways with the political and economic exigencies of the nation. The ambivalent discourse of immigration is, in sum, productive of the polity that we call nation-state.

NOTES

An earlier version of this chapter was published in *Diaspora: A Journal of Transnational Studies* 6:2 (fall 1997): 155–78.

1. For a brief report of the controversy, see "Wilson Ad Sparks Charges of Immigrant-Bashing," *Los Angeles Times*, May 14, 1994.

2. See Cornelius 1982.

3. See "Tensions on Hereford Drive," *Los Angeles Times*, March 4, 1996.

4. The quotation is by Bruce Cain, a political scientist and the associate director of the Institute of Governmental Studies at the University of California, Berkeley, but the idea it expresses is a common argument made by many economists, sociologists, political scientists, and immigrant rights activists: "Hospitality Turns into Hostility," *Los Angeles Times*, November 14, 1993. See, for example, Cornelius and Bustamante 1989.

5. See Gordon 1964 and Higham 1955.

6. See, for example, Hull 1985.

7. Hamilton's reference appears in his article "Pacificus," published in the *Gazette of the United States*, July 17, 1793; the second reference is from John Adams' letter of January 22, 1795, to Jefferson (Grand and Davidson 1928, 41, 13, respectively).

8. I am referring here to Washington's description of America as "an asylum . . . to the oppressed and needy of the Earth," quoted in Rischin 1966, 44.

9. *Letters from an American Farmer*, extract reprinted in Abbott 1926, 16. As will become evident in my discussion of the country's nativism, the historical accuracy of Crèvecoeur's alluring portrait of America as a hospitable and kind nation to immigrants is questionable, but the letters were nonetheless so popular that several editions and numerous reviews appeared within only a few years.

10. See, for example, Adamic 1938; Gordon 1961; Handlin 1959.

11. *Congressional Quarterly* 1980, p. 2066; quoted in Fuchs 1992, 40.

12. The first reference appears in his "Notes on Virginia" and the second in a letter of September 12, 1817, to George Flower (Grant and Davidson 1928, 62, 70).

13. In this sense, the kind of claim that I make about U.S. nationalism can be broadened to include other forms of national identification elsewhere, but for the sake of specificity, my discussion focuses on American nationalism.

14. This point also has been made by Richard Hofstadter (1965) and Hans Kohn (1957).

15. Peter Dinwiddie Wigginton, *America for Americans: Declaration of Principles of the American Party*. Fresno: Daily Evening Expositor Steam Print, 1886: 1–2. Quoted in Higham 1955, 56.

16. These statements are drawn from *Public Opinion* I (1886), III (1887), and V (1888), quoted in Higham 1955, 54–55.

17. A good example of this type of humanitarianism is Emma Lazarus' poem to boost the fund-raising campaign for the Statue of Liberty:

> Give me your tired, your poor,
> Your Huddled masses yearning to breathe free,
> The Wretched refuse of your teeming shore,
> Send these, the homeless, tempest-tost to me,
> I lift my lamp beside the golden door!
> (Lazarus 1889: I, 202–03)

18. As an example of the structuralist approach, see Mandel 1978.

19. For a discussion of the state's autonomy, see Skocpol 1979.

20. See, for example, Bennett 1988, 199–237.

21. For an early account of the Chinese Exclusion Act and the violence against "orientals," see McKenzie 1928.

22. See Higham 1955, 211–12.

23. *Los Angeles Times*, November 24, 1993.

24. My claim has been corroborated by Timothy Dunn's findings about the changes in U.S. immigration policy since the late 1970s. See Dunn 1996.

25. Quoted in the *Los Angeles Times*, September 29, 1996.

WORKS CITED

Abbott, Edith, ed. 1926. *Historical Aspects of the Immigration Problem: Selected Documents*. Chicago: University of Chicago Press.

Adamic, Louis. 1938. *My America, 1928–1938*. New York: Harper.

Althusser, Louis. 1971. "Ideology and Ideological State Apparatuses (Notes Towards an Investigation)." Pp. 121–73 in *Lenin and Philosophy and Other Essays*, trans. Ben Brewster. New York: Monthly Review Press.

Balibar, Etienne. 1990. "The Nation Form." *Review* 13:3 (summer): 329–61.

Behdad, Ali. 1998. "INS and Outs: Producing Delinquency at the Border." *Aztlan: A Journal of Chicano Studies* 23:1 (spring): 103–13.

Benjamin, Walter. 1969. *Illuminations*. Translated by Harry Zohn. New York: Schocken Books.

Bennett, David H. 1988. *The Party of Fear: From Nativist Movements to the New Right in American History*. Chapel Hill: University of North Carolina Press.

Bhabha, Homi K. 1986. "The Other Question: Difference, Discrimination, and the Discourse of Colonialism." Pp. 148–72 in *Literature, Politics, and Theory*, ed. Francis Barker et al. London: Methuen.

Bushnell, Horace. 1915. "The True Wealth or Weal of Nations." Pp. 3–15 in *Representative Phi Beta Kappa Orations*, ed. Clark Northrup et al. Boston: D.C. Heath and Company.

Calarita, Kitty. 1992. *Inside the State: The Bracero Program, Immigration, and the I.N.S.* New York: Routledge.

Cornelius, Wayne A. 1982. "America in the Era of Limits: Nativist Reactions to the 'New' Immigration." *Working Paper in U.S.–Mexico Studies* 3. San Diego: University of California Press.

Cornelius, Wayne A., and Jorge A. Bustamante, eds. 1989. *Mexican Migration to the United States: Origins, Consequences, and Policy Options*. La Jolla, Calif.: Center for U.S.–Mexican Studies, University of California, San Diego.

Dunn, Timothy. 1996. *Militarization of the U.S.–Mexico Border 1978–1992*. Austin: CMAS Books.

Fuchs, Lawrence H. 1992. "Thinking about Immigration and Ethnicity in the United States." Pp. 39–65 in *Immigrants in Two Democracies: French and American Experience*, ed. Donald L. Horowitz and Gérard Noiriel. New York: New York University Press.

Gordon, Milton. 1961. "Assimilation in America: Theory and Reality." *Daedalus* 90:2 (spring): 263–85.

———. 1964. *Assimilation in American Life: The Role of Race, Religion, and National Origin*. New York: Oxford University Press.

Grant, Madison, and Charles Stewart Davidson, eds. 1928. *The Founders of the Republic on Immigration, Naturalization, and Aliens*. New York: Charles Scribner's Sons.

Handlin, Oscar. 1959. *Boston's Immigrants*. Cambridge: Harvard University Press.

Harwood, Edwin. 1986. *In Liberty's Shadow: Illegal Aliens and Immigration Law Enforcement*. Stanford, Calif.: Hoover Institution Press.

Higham, John. 1955. *Strangers in the Land: Patterns of American Nativism, 1860–1925*. New Brunswick, N.J.: Rutgers University Press.

Hofstadter, Richard. 1965. *The Paranoid Style in American Politics*. New York: Alfred Knopf.

Hull, Elizabeth. 1985. *Without Justice for All: The Constitutional Rights of Aliens*. Westport, Conn.: Greenwood Press.

Kohn, Hans. 1957. *American Nationalism: An Interpretive Essay*. New York: Macmillan.

Lazarus, Emma. 1889. *The Poems of Emma Lazarus*. Boston and New York: Houghton, Mifflin and Company.

Lipset, Seymour Martin, and Earl Raab. 1970. *The Politics of Unreason: Right-Wing Extremism in America 1790–1970*. New York: Harper & Row.

Mandel, Ernest. 1978. *Late Capitalism*. London: Verso.

Mann, Arthur. 1979. *The One and the Many: Reflections of the American Identity*. Chicago: University of Chicago Press.

———. 1983. *Imagined Communities: Reflections on the Origin and the Spread of Nationalism*. London: Verso.

McKenzie, R. D. 1928. *Oriental Exclusion: The Effect of American Immigration Law, Regulations, and Judicial Decisions upon the Chinese and Japanese on the American West Coast*. Chicago: University of Chicago Press.

Michaels, Walter Benn. 1997. *Our America: Nativism, Modernism, and Pluralism*. Durham: Duke University Press.

Platform of Principles of the American Party in Connecticut, adopted June 28th, 1855. [1855] N.p.

Renan, Ernest. 1990. "What Is a Nation?" Pp. 8–22 in *Nation and Narration*, ed. Homi K. Bhabha. New York: Routledge.

Rischin, Moses. 1966. *Immigration and the American Tradition*. Indianapolis: Bobbs-Merrill.

Said, Edward. 1983. "Opponents, Audiences, Constituencies." Pp. 135–59 in *The Anti-Aesthetic: Essays on Postmodern Culture*, ed. Hal Foster. Port Townsend, Wash.: Bay Press.

Saunders, Frederick. 1855. *A Voice to America: or, The Model Republic, Its Glory or Its Fall*. New York: E. Walker.

Skocpol, Theda. 1979. *States and Social Revolution*. Cambridge: Cambridge University Press.

Simon, Rita J. 1985. *Public Opinion and the Immigrant: Print Media Coverage, 1880–1980*. Lexington, Mass.: Lexington Books.

Sweezy, Paul. 1942. *The Theory of Capitalist Development*. New York: Monthly Review Press.

Turner, Sharon. 1907. *History of the Anglo-Saxons*. London: Longman, Hurst, Rees, and Orme.

Whitman, Walt. 1959. "Song of Myself," in *Complete Poetry and Selected Prose*. Boston: Houghton Mifflin.

CHAPTER ELEVEN

RICHARD WRIGHT AS A
SPECULAR BORDER INTELLECTUAL

The Politics of Identification in Black Power

ABDUL JANMOHAMED

The following analysis of Richard Wright's *Black Power* (1995 [1954]), the journal of his visit to Ghana, and in particular Wright's presentation of himself as an intellectual on a mission to establish solidarity with Kwame Nkrumah and the Ghanaian anti-colonial struggle is in some ways an extension of the notion of the "specular border intellectual" that I articulated in an article on Edward Said (JanMohamed 1992). In that article on Said, which argues that his entire oeuvre is centered around a tension produced by his location between cultures—a tension that manifests itself as the complex equilibrium of his intellectual stance, between "worldliness-without-world," on the one hand and "homeless-ness-as-home," on the other hand—I argued that to the extent that all groups define their identities through some form of binary opposition to other groups, the very process of *suturing* the (relative) "homogeneity" that is crucial to the definition of that group's "identity" (as well as to its attempt to suppress differences within the group that is to be homogenized) also simultaneously constitutes the process of rupturing various subjects on its borders: the border subject becomes the site on and

through which a group defines its identity. That is, the body and consciousness of the subject caught between two groups are cleaved by
those groups, and hence the ruptured body of that subject becomes the
text on which the structure of the identity of the groups is written in
inverted form—the *in*-formation of a group's identity is inscribed on the
body/consciousness of the border subject via his or her *inclusion-as-an-
excluded-being*. The relation between the "individual" and the "group,"
or between individual and collective subjectivity, as Mikkel Borch-
Jacobsen points out in his critique of the Freudian subject, is mutually
constitutive: "The group is thus at the origin (without origin) of the individual. Neither simply undivided nor simply divided, neither One nor
Other (the One in differ*a*nce from the Other, to borrow from Derrida),
the ego is then inaugurated as (the) group" (1988, 192). If the group
"inaugurates" the individual by fundamentally inhabiting his or her origin and constitution, then the group cleaves the border intellectual at its
margins, producing what Du Bois called the "double consciousness" of
black Americans. Thus the border intellectual willing to read his or her
own body or consciousness, his or her in- and out-formation, has ready
access to the structures and values of the groups in question as well as
to alternate possibilities of individual and collective subject formation.

A writer such as Wright then is a border intellectual, in that he is
caught between two groups, that is, between the racialized construction
of white and black groups, with neither of which he could fully identify
or disidentify: he felt simultaneously included and excluded by both
groups. Rather than passively suffering his fate, Wright ended up dedi-
cating his life to an investigation of the border space between the two,
and in so doing he in effect became an archaeologist of the site of his
own formation, devoting most of his fiction to deconstructing the formation of the black (male) subject on the racial border and hence re-
forming his own subjectivity-as-a-writer around his project of archaeo-
logical excavation. In other words, Wright's identity as a *constituting*
subject comes to be formed around his commitment to deconstructing
the black male subject (the "Black Boy" of his autobiography) as a *constituted* pseudo-subject. In short, Wright's fiction constitutes a systematic specular reading of the political economy of his own identificatory
investments as these are involved in the formation of racialized identities. His journalistic writing, however, takes the opposite tack: instead of
deconstructing the formation of the individual subject, it is deeply motivated and structured by a desire to find or define a viable, coherent community to which the individual can belong in some "organic" and

"unambiguous" fashion. Although the utopian desire to find a viable community remains constant in these texts, the possibility of finding and defining such a community becomes increasingly tenuous, hence supplying the pathos that characterizes Wright's journalistic writing. One of the most fascinating versions of this quest, *Black Power* is particularly poignant: at the invitation of Kwame Nkrumah, the leader of the Convention People's Party at the time and later the prime minister of independent Ghana, Wright visits the British colony in order to witness the process through which the colony would gain "independence" from British control. At the time, of course, the prospect of "independence" aroused powerful utopian visions among many intellectuals from the colonies and elsewhere.

Black Power, however, has received relatively little scrutiny. Paul Gilroy's chapter on Wright in *The Black Atlantic* (1993, chapter 5) constitutes one of the most fruitful, substantive, and theoretically provocative examinations of *Black Power*. Gilroy is fundamentally correct, it seems to me, in his claim that Wright's "travel books," as he calls them, "offer much more than a series of failed attempts to make the condition of chronic rootlessness habitable." Wright's journalistic writing, he feels, can be viewed as an "extended exercise in intercultural hermeneutics which has important effects on Wright's theories about 'race,' modernity, identity, and their interrelation" (ibid., 150). In addition to his comments on Wright's revision of the Du Boisian notion of "double consciousness," on Wright's "anti-essentialist" preoccupation with "race," and so forth, Gilroy claims that, "Wright's life bears witness to the value of critical perceptions that could only have been gained through the restlessness, even homelessness, that he sometimes manages to make into an analytic opportunity" (ibid.). While this seems entirely true to me, I would put a very different emphasis on the function of homelessness in Wright's work: I would argue that homelessness almost always subtends Wright's fiction and journalism—from his first published short story, "Big Boy Leaves Home" (1936) to Fishbelly's exile in his last published novel, *The Long Dream* (1958). Wright's own life also is characterized by a series of flights from potential "homes." The homelessness that characterizes the man and his entire literary production is central to my attempt to define him as a border intellectual, as an intellectual who is always capable of turning his own border condition into an analytic opportunity.

While I am not concerned with Wright's engagement with modernity, I feel that Gilroy's characterization of *Black Power* is apposite: "The ambiguities that stem from Wright's uncomfortable position—

inside but not organically of the West—become unbearable in *Black Power* . . . and other works where he spelled out his understanding of the relationship between precapitalistic, traditional societies and the dynamic, imperial structures of technological and philosophical modernity" (1993, 151). I am concerned more with the "unbearableness" of the ambiguity in Wright's book about the dawn of "independence" in Africa and the putative end of British colonial domination. An index of the painful nature of the ambiguities can be found in Gilroy's reluctance to examine or define them more fully. While insisting that Wright's journalistic writings have been unjustly neglected by all of his critics, Gilroy himself devotes only a small portion of his chapter on Wright to these texts, preferring to concentrate instead on the richer vein of Wright's fiction. Also symptomatic of this refusal is Gilroy's hesitation in articulating one side of the homelessness that produces the excruciating ambiguity in *Black Power*. While it is perfectly true that Wright is "inside but not organically of the West," as Gilroy argues, it also is the case that Wright is inside but not organically of the West African societies and cultures of which he is a guest, and that he has enormous difficulty in identifying and sympathizing with his host country.

As Wright negotiates his "subject position" between Euro-America and Africa, as he negotiates his location in this "intercultural border space" between two sets of "racial," cultural, and political differences, he relies as much as possible on his consistent view that "race" is a social construct. And this view involves the corollary that, as Gilroy puts it, "the groups that we know as races are associated with the repression of differences within those races. Literary and other cultural forms thus provide him [Wright] with [a] chance to comprehend that a race may differ from itself. Notions of typicality and racial representativeness in aesthetic and political judgement are rejected because they arrest the play of differences" (1993, 153). Now it seems to me that neither Wright nor any other human being is capable of living for long in a Hereclitian stream of the infinite play of differences. The practical (or rather the political) business of living necessarily requires one to arrest or punctuate that infinite play of differences. To put it another way, the infinite play of *identificatory exchanges*—that is, Wright's ambivalent identification with Euro-America as well as with the African desire for "independence"—that traverse *Black Power* is arrested by that extra-linguistic punctuation mark that we call "identity." Wright does arrest the play of differences by making judgments—aesthetic, moral, political, and so on—that are not explicit or formal but implicit, and they manifest themselves in his repeated failure to sympathize adequately with so many of the Africans he meets. It is this failure of sympathy, which I shall examine below, that I think most readers find puzzling, painful, and, all too often, unbearable. Of course, the failure or success of the attempt to sympathize is profoundly linked to the politics of identification: as Mikkel Borch-Jacobsen points out in his critique of Freud, one does not identify because of sympathy; rather, one sympathizes because of identification (1988, 189). As Gilroy insists so correctly, Wright's identification with and sympathy for his African hosts are profoundly ambivalent and ambiguous. As much as Wright tries to avoid foreclosing judgments, he cannot avoid the process of significant and substantive identifications (and disidentifications) regarding both the West and the West African cultures. However, what is most valuable about *Black Power* is that he foregrounds, sometimes consciously and sometimes unconsciously, the politics of identification as such, and it is to that politics that I want to turn now. If the ambiguity of Wright's identifications and disidentifications is unbearable, I feel that it should *bear scrutiny precisely because it is unbearable.* And I feel that this form of scrutiny—a clear, unsentimental, *hard* examination of that which is unbearable—is one that Wright would very much appreciate, as I hope will become clear later.

In examining the politics of Wright's ambivalent identifications, I will be utilizing the Freudian distinction between primary and secondary identification, which Lacan has rearticulated as the difference between "imaginary" and "symbolic" identification, and which Jacques Alain Miller has further glossed as the difference between "constituted" and "constitutive" identification.[1] It may be useful to gloss briefly the particular ways in which I will be employing these distinctions. An elaboration of the fundamental constitution of the subject in the "Mirror Stage," imaginary identification structures the ego by identification with something/someone outside and opposed to the subject. Such identification thus structures the subject as a rival against itself, producing an identificatory relation that is full of aggressivity and alienation. Slavoj Zizek's formulation of imaginary identification is apposite: "Imaginary identification is identification with the image in which we appear likeable to ourselves, with the image of 'what we would like to be.'" In contrast, in symbolic identification, we identify "with the very place *from where* we are being observed, *from where* we look at ourselves so that we appear to ourselves likeable, worthy of love" (1989, 105). It is a process in which we identify with the position of agency through which we are observed and judged and through which we observe and judge ourselves; it is a process in which we identify with the *structure* of the process that identifies us; in Freudian terms it is identification with the superego, and in Lacanian terms with the (negating) Law of the Father. Using this theoretical framework, I will employ the term *identity* to designate the point at which the identificatory process is frozen, either in an "imaginary identity" or a "symbolic identity." In the latter case, "identity" can be thought of as being analogous to the "point de capiton," a "punctuation mark" that retroactively makes clear the syntax of intersubjective investment or cathexes and that consequently gives meaning to the process through which identifications are negotiated. If we keep the distinctions between imaginary and symbolic identifications in mind, then the unbearable ambiguities of Wright identificatory politics become relatively clear and, hopefully, more bearable. I will thus argue that Wright's attempt to identify with his African hosts fails terribly on the imaginary register and yet succeeds on the symbolic register. However, since the bulk of *Black Power* is articulated on the imaginary register and strenuously attempts to cement an imaginary identification between the author and his hosts, the impression of failure easily overwhelms the success of symbolic identification.

The problem in Wright's attempt at imaginary identification with his prospective African hosts manifests itself at the very inception of the suggestion of his possible trip to Ghana. Even before he has agreed to undertake the trip to Ghana, his mind rapidly rehearses the fundamental options—from the most "positive" to the most "negative"—within the realm of imaginary identification available to him. He is broached by Dorothy Padmore, at the end of a Sunday lunch in Paris, with the suggestion that he might visit Ghana at a point when the Ghanaian struggle for independence is reaching its climax, and she assures him that a personal invitation from Kwame Nkrumah could be procured for him. After he gets over the initial shock produced by this idea (he gaped at the suggestion, he tells us), Wright finds himself profoundly distracted by the implications of such a trip. As Dorothy and Ellen, Wright's wife, continue to persuade him to go, his "mind and feelings," he tells us, "were racing along another and hidden track." That hidden track, Wright makes it quite clear, is the specter of an essentialist racial identification with Africans: "*Africa!* Being of African descent, would I be able to feel and know something about Africa on the basis of a common 'racial' heritage? Africa was a vast continent full of 'my people.' . . . *But, am I an African?*" (Wright 1995 [1954], 4, emphasis in original). However, Wright quickly dismisses this possibility of a profound essential-ist/imaginary identification, of a resemblance based on "racial" and therefore genetic kinship. This possibility is quickly displaced by what Wright calls "my habitual kind of thinking," in which "racial identity" is "conditioned by the reaction of human beings to a concrete social environment" (ibid., 6). However, what is most fascinating about Wright's thinking, or rather his "feelings," is that these two moments of contemplation about the processes that define and produce "racial iden-tity" are dramatically cleaved by what for Wright is a profound source of disidentification with Africans, namely, the specter of slavery. As he thinks about the historical disjunction between Africans and African Americans produced by slavery, he throws some of the blame on the Africans (and some on Europeans as their "trading" partners): "Had some of my ancestors sold their relatives to white men? What would my feelings be when I looked into the black face of an African, feeling that maybe his great-great-great-grandfather had sold my great-great-great-grandfather into slavery?" (ibid., 4).

It must be emphasized that Wright is not concerned here with "mere" theoretical possibilities; this particular disidentification carries a deep and complex negative investment for Wright, which can be mea-sured in the first place by the fact that the particular form in which Wright raises the issue of slavery marks at least a double and possibly a triple disidentification. The first of these is the initial historical disjunc-tion, the one supposedly perpetrated by the African ancestor who denies kinship and resemblance/identification through the act of selling his rel-ative. The second disjunction exists potentially in the future, in the moment when Wright will face the descendant of the "relative" who sold his ancestors into slavery. And finally, the third moment exists in the present, in Wright's act, deliberate and conscious or otherwise, of resurrecting the ghost of that initial disjunction/disidentification pre-cisely at the moment when Dorothy Padmore is implying the possibility of a rapprochement, of a rearticulation of a kinship/identification between Africans and African Americans. The depth of this negative cathexis also is underscored by the correlation between Wright's deci-sion to (partly) blame his African ancestors for the pain and suffering produced by slavery and his similar decision, evident in his autobiogra-phy as well as in his fiction, to blame his black American ancestors for the pain and suffering that he endured at the hands of Jim Crow society. In other words, this negative cathexis of Africans can be seen as an extension of Wright's view that his parents were not only responsible for their failure to prevent Jim Crow racism's attempt to stunt his subjective formation—Jim Crow society's attempt to confine his formation to that of a "Black Boy" (the title of the first volume of Wright's autobiography)—but indeed that they were *responsible for collaborating* with Jim Crow racist restrictions.[2] The depth of this cathexis also surfaces in *Black Power* in shockingly explicit terms: "The fortuity of birth," Wright tells us, "had cast me in the 'racial' role of being of African descent, and that fact now resounded in my mind with associations of *hatred, violence, and death*" (1995 [1954], 5, emphasis added). Thus the aggressivity and alienation that characterize imaginary identification surface quickly and explicitly in *Black Power*. However, hatred, violence, and the threat of death are not factors that Wright arbitrarily injects into his imaginary identification with Africans. I cannot demonstrate it in detail here, but I would contend that violence and the threat of death/lynching were the central mechanisms of Jim Crow racist subjection, mechanisms the effects of which are deeply internalized in the process of racialized subjectification and which provide the twin engines of Wright's archaeology of the racialized (male) subject.

So strong is Wright's preoccupation with slavery and his feeling of being betrayed by his African ancestors that it dramatically marks his arrival and departure from Ghana, thus furnishing a strong narrative bracket or closure for his entire experience of Ghana. The experience contained within and by the brackets consists almost entirely of the painful and almost unbearable articulation of his highly ambivalent imaginary identification with the Africans—that is, an identification that is sympathetic at the conscious level but hostile at the subconscious/unconscious level. It is thus an identification that operates through a process of classic disavowal. This narrative organization, which brackets and firmly contains the imaginary identification, is deliberately structured, consciously or otherwise, since the expression of symbolic identification is contained on either side of the brackets, that is, in the prologue, articulating Wright's state of mind (supposedly) prior to his departure for Ghana, and in what functions as the epilogue, the open letter he addresses to Nkrumah as he leaves the shores of Ghana.

The bracket at the beginning of Wright's travelogue is in fact an explosive manifestation of his anxiety about how he would handle an encounter with a descendant of the Africans who had betrayed Wright's ancestors. Thus his anxiety turns out, as happens so often in Wright's work, to have been prophetic; as a self-fulfilling prophecy, Wright's anxiety becomes an index of a compulsive preoccupation with ancestral responsibility. The particular target that Wright chooses for his wrath toward the ancestors also reveals the (unconsciously) deliberate nature of the anxiety that surrounds his imaginary aggression toward and alienation from the Africans. Upon first setting foot in Ghana, Wright is greeted by a wealthy personal friend of Nkrumah, whose task it is to put Wright on a bus to the interior. But the second person Wright meets, a lowly store clerk who, in a gesture of friendly hospitality, insists on establishing ties of kinship with Wright, quickly becomes the target of disidentification that Wright has been nursing. The clerk easily identifies Wright as an American and then asks if Wright knows where in Africa his ancestors came from. Wright demurs that he has no answer, thereby provoking the clerk's credulity: "Didn't your mother or grandmother ever tell you what part of Africa you came from, sar?" the clerk persists, and again: "Haven't you tried to find out where in Africa you came from, sar?" To which Wright finally responds: "'Well,' I said softly, 'you know, you fellows who sold us and the white men who bought us didn't keep records'" (ibid., 39–40). The encounter quickly fades into silence, embarrassment, and avoidance. Thus immediately upon arriving, Wright establishes the tense and contradictory structure of imaginary identification: articulation of resemblance, on the one hand (upon disembarking from the boat, Wright is elated to see that the policemen, firemen, engineers, and so on are all black, and that whites are in the minority), and aggressive articulation of alienation, on the other hand.

The bracket that closes the travelogue returns more ritualistically and deliberately to the scene of disidentification between "Africans" and those about to be shipped off to eventually become, after enduring slavery and Jim Crow society, "African Americans."[3] The last chapter of *Black Power* is neatly divided into two: the second half, consisting of the open letter addressed to Nkrumah, is full of counsel about how to deal with British colonialism and how best to manage the coming independence of Ghana. The first half, however, contains Wright's description of three infamous castles—Christianborg, Cape Coast, and Elmina—which were the final staging posts on the African side of the slave trade and from which slaves were sent across the Atlantic. At each site Wright imaginatively rehearses scenes of identification and disidentification. First he asks the guides detailed questions about where the slaves were kept prior to transportation, where they stood, who was observing them, how they were treated and transported to the Americas, and so forth; Wright is so insistent on identifying with the slaves that he tells us with relish: "I was told that the same iron bolts which secured the doors to keep the slaves imprisoned were the ones that my fingers now touched" (ibid., 382). Wright also tries to imagine how the chiefs who sold their subjects into slavery would have observed the transportation from their hidden vantage points, how the slaves might have felt as they were being led out to the waiting ships, and so on. In these instances Wright is clearly trying to get as close to the experience of the slaves as he can, thus identifying with those of his ancestors who were shipped out as slaves. Then in a disidentificatory gesture he imagines those of his ancestors who were responsible for selling the slave to the colonial powers: "I tried to picture in my mind a chief, decked out in cowrie shells, leopard skin, golden bracelets, leading a string of black prisoners of war to the castle to be sold. . . . My mind refused to function" (ibid., 383). On his final visit to Elmina castle, Wright reverses, with profound irony, his castigation of the chiefs who had betrayed the slaves. He now imagines the fate of an African chief who had resisted the colonial onslaught: "King Premphe I was kept in a large bare room in one of the towers [of the castle] by the British. I stood gazing into that room and wondered what could have passed through his mind. . . . *How he must have prayed to his ancestors for help!*" (ibid., 385, emphasis added).

After working his way through this series of imaginary identifications, Wright brings the first half of the chapter to a close with the most moving gesture of disavowal that simultaneously links and distinguishes imaginary identification from symbolic identification. Wright tells us that the contemporary Ghanaians around Elmina castle believe that a golden treasure lay hidden somewhere in the castle, and then he continues:

> If there is any treasure hidden in these walls, I'm sure that it has a sheen that outshines gold—a tiny, pear-shaped tear that formed on the cheek of some black woman torn away from her children, a tear that gleams here still, caught in the feeble rays of the dungeon's light—a shy tear that vanishes at the sound of approaching footsteps, but reappears when all is quiet, hanging there on that black cheek, unredeemed, unappeased—a tear that was hastily brushed off when her arm was grabbed and she was led toward those narrow, dank steps that guided her to the tunnel that directed her feet to the waiting ship that would bear her across the heaving, mist-shrouded Atlantic. (ibid., 385)

This is how the section on slavery ends, and Wright immediately follows it up with his open letter to Nkrumah:

Dear Kwame Nkrumah:
My journey's done. My labors in your vineyard are over. The ship that bears me from Africa's receding shores holds a *heart* that fights against those *soft, sentimental feelings* for the suffering of our people. The kind of *thinking* that must be done cannot be done by men whose hearts are swamped with emotion. (ibid., 385, emphasis added)

These two passages, or really one continuous passage with a strong caesura, contain a disavowal that perfectly marks the structure of imaginary identification. As the silent, suffering mother, who is the figure of all human suffering in Wright's work,[4] sails off into slavery, so Wright sails with her, thus establishing a profound identification and sympathy between the two. As he writes the letter from his departing ship, he writes it as a "slave" addressing a modern African chief (Nkrumah) who will presumably be different from those chiefs who sold their subjects into slavery. On the other hand, Wright firmly rejects the emotions that he has just evoked with his finely crafted, lyric description of the maternal figure being torn out of all the social relations—being severed from ancestors as well as descendants—that have been a part of her "identity" until that moment. For Wright, these "soft, sentimental" *emotions* must be firmly separated from the "kind of *thinking* that needs to be done." Thus the identification just established has to be negated, or to use the more appropriate Hegelian term, it has to be sublated: imaginary identification has to be sublated so that it can become symbolic identification. Wright makes this turn in the next paragraph:

While roaming at random through the compounds, market places, villages, and cities of your [Nkrumah's] country, I felt an odd kind of *at-homeness, a solidarity* that stemmed not from ties of blood or race, or from my being of African descent, but from the quality of deep hope and suffering embedded in the lives of your people, from the *hard facts* of oppression that cut across time, space, culture. I must confess that I, an American Negro, was filled with consternation at what Europe had done to this Africa. (ibid., 385, emphasis added)

The identification—the feeling of "at-homeness" and "solidarity"—is now to be based neither on race, ancestry, nor even emotional sympathy, if by sympathy one means, as Wright tends to imply, something "soft" and "sentimental," bordering on pity and pathos. Identification is now to be grounded on a rational ("the kind of *thinking* that has to be done") appreciation and articulation of "*hard* facts." Through the alchemy of sublation, specific and contingent experiences (i.e., soft and sentimental emotions) have to be dialectically transformed into a more universal and rational understanding of oppression in general—into the "hard facts" that "cut across time, space, and culture." An adequate appreciation of how this transformation constitutes "symbolic identification" depends on one's understanding of the function of "hardness" as a multivalent trope in Wright's work generally, as well as in *Black Power*. However, before proceeding to that trope, I would like to elaborate on several specific instances of imaginary identification in *Black Power* that also will be useful in elucidating the trope of hardness.

Generally, the travelogue between the opening and closing brackets is a long and frustrating series of attempts by Wright to understand and sympathize with his hosts, yet the vast majority of these attempts, which fail quite miserably, fall into one of two categories. The first one is characterized by Wright's lack of diplomacy. Anxious to rapidly understand this alien culture in clear, rational terms, Wright repeatedly attempts to interrogate his hosts with bluntly analytic questions that tend to offend them and lead to their withdrawal from him. Because his hosts cannot analyze their own cultural practices in terms that are adequately rational and mechanistic to satisfy Wright's surgical demands, he feels that they are uncooperative and secretive, that they see him as an outsider and an intruder. Thus under the umbrella of Wright's official sympathy with Ghanaians, which brings him to Ghana in the first place and fuels his urgent inquiries, the relations between the guest and hosts are marked by mutual distrust and hostility. The other category of incidents is in effect the obverse of the first: Wright's experience of "organic" communities is so inadequate that he fails to understand imaginatively the operations of Ghanaian society. This is most evident, and painfully so, given Wright's political interest, in Wright's repeated attempt to understand the political movement organized by Nkrumah and the Convention People's Party (CPP) in terms of Wright's own experience with the American Communist Party. However, the rather mechanistic and hyperconscious organizational principles and practices of the party, which provided Wright with his most "communal" experience, do not furnish him with a model that can adequately explain the complex mixture of indigenous religions, traditional tribal allegiances, modern political practices, and so on that combine to form the operative structures of the CPP. So in spite of Wright's genuine political sympathies, he fails to understand much about Ghanaian anti-colonial struggles. His inability to step outside of his own assumptions and values makes him feel even more alienated from his hosts. It is the pervasiveness of these types of failures that creates the impression of unbearable ambiguity in *Black Power*.

In the midst of this general tension produced by the "contradictions" of imaginary identification are two specific incidents, both of which ultimately involve Wright's bodily discomfort, and clarify the profound alienation underlying the superficial identification. The latter is unable to overcome the multitude of cultural differences between various African cultural practices and Wright's own Western formation—albeit a formation strongly contained by racism. While he had clearly prepared himself for his trip by voluminously reading sociopolitical and historical literature about colonialism and Ghana, he seems to have been totally unprepared to comprehend West African cultural practices. Thus his sense of alienation, of "homelessness," in a context in which he had somehow expected to feel at home, and his own astonishment at this sense of homelessness are drastic. As he says, "faced with the absolute otherness and inaccessibility of this new world, I was prey to a vague sense of mild panic, an oppressive burden of alertness which I could not shake off" (ibid., 44). Those readers familiar with Wright's first major novel, *Native Son*, will recognize that the "vague sense of panic" and the "oppressive burden of alertness" are the same emotions Bigger Thomas experiences when he first approaches the otherness and inaccessibility of white American society.

One particular aspect of this otherness tends to bother Wright more than the rest: the ubiquitous presence of half-naked African women. While Wright tells us and himself that this nakedness is perfectly "natural," his discomfort is strong enough to make him wish that this alienating experience could be a fantasy that could disappear in the blink of an eye. "As the bus rolled swiftly forward," he tells us, "I waited irrationally for these fantastic scenes to fade: I had the foolish feeling that I had but to turn my head and I'd see the ordered, clothed streets of Paris" (ibid., 42). The ordered, clothed streets of Paris function here as the opposite of the "chaotic, naked (and streetless) countryside" of Ghana. Wright feels as homeless in Ghana as he did in the United States; ironically, Paris, that heaven of exiles, is about as close as he can get to a sense of "home."

The other, deeper, and more troubling instance of disidentification quintessentially illustrates Wright's habit of mind: a tendency to turn any event into a specular occasion for self-analysis. This habit is paradigmatic of Wright's function as a "homeless" border intellectual, but it may well be paradigmatic for other border intellectuals as well. The event in question concerns Wright's reaction to what he perceives as the similarities between African and African-American dancing. Wright is totally confounded by the continuity of these practices across the ocean. So powerful are the emotions aroused by this hint of a continuing "identity" that Wright totally forgets his context—that he is riding in a car with Nkrumah, and that they are on their way to an important political rally. Later that day, he tries to explain his feelings:

> The bafflement evoked in me by this new reality did not spring from any desire to disclaim kinship with Africa, or from any shame of being of African descent. My problem was how to account for this "survival" of Africa in America when I stoutly denied the mystic influence of "race," when I was as certain as I was of *being alive* that it was only, by and large, in the concrete social frame of reference in which men lived that one could account for men being what they were. I sighed: this was truly a big problem. (ibid., 73–74, emphasis added)

Here the emotions are being rationalized as a theoretical problem of defining cultural continuity if one subscribes to the notion of "race" as a social construct and not as a "natural," essential structure. This is clearly a way of containing the "big problem" of identification. What is curious, however, is that Wright utilizes his "being alive" as an anchor for certainty, thus in a sense unconsciously grounding the problem of kinship in his own bodily vitality. Yet if we return to the immediate and spontaneous specular meditation that is provoked in Wright by the dancing, we can see that in effect he "solves" the problem by denying his own bodily vitality, because he cannot deny the evidence of cultural identity. This denial of the body is fascinating enough to warrant a lengthy citation:

> How much am I a part of this? How much was I a part of it when I saw it in America? Why could I not feel this? Why that peculiar, awkward restraint when *I* tried to dance or sing? The answer to this did not come until I penetrated deep into the African jungle. . . . On we rode. The crowd surged, danced, sang, and shouted, but I was thinking of my mother, of my father, of my brother . . . I was frankly stunned at what I saw; there was no rejection or condemnation; there was no joy or sorrow; I was stupefied. Was it possible that I was looking at myself laughing, dancing, singing, gliding with my hips to express my joy? . . . Had I denied all this in me? If so, then why was

it that when I tried to sing, as a child, I'd not been able to? Why had
my hands and feet, all my life, failed to keep time? It was useless to
say that I'd inhibited myself, for my inability to do these simple
things predated any desire, conscious or unconscious, on my part. I
had wanted to, because it had always been a part of my environment, *but I had never been able to*! (ibid., 63, emphasis in original)

What is most fascinating about this complex and convoluted negotiation of resemblance is that faced with a cultural similarity/identity
that he could no longer deny, Wright turns to the supposed inertia of his
own body in order to use it, in the guise of an interrogation, as both an
alibi and a symptom, as a cause and effect of his denial of cultural kinship: in effect, he avoids identification by denying kinship indirectly via
the denial of his own body. What is ultimately telling about this proce-
dure is that it forces Wright indirectly to affirm "racial identity" as an
essentialist concept in the very process of trying to deny it as such. That
is, Wright firmly forecloses the possibility that his inability to dance may
have been a product of "inhibition," of awkwardness, nervous tension,
or bodily inertia, which may all be produced by "social construction."
He similarly also denies the possibility that the "survival" of African
dancing in America may be a product of social, cultural continuity
rather than "racial" continuity. By denying these possibilities and by
insisting so fervently that his bodily inertia predates any (social) construction of desire (which is a logical impossibility), Wright in effect
"elevates" the inertia onto a "natural," ontological register, that is, onto
the same register on which "racial identity" as an essentialist concept is
articulated. Thus the convoluted logic of Wright's imaginary identification with his African hosts forces him to simultaneously affirm and deny
essentialist "racial identity." It is this "contradiction" that fuels the
excruciating nature of Wright's ambiguous feelings.

Yet Wright's systematic and tactically crucial privileging of his (ontological) inability to dance in a sensuous manner should alert us to its
overdetermined nature, for the inability connotes a kind of bodily rigidity,
a "hardness." Wright's privileging and raising of hardness to the ontological plane return us to what I had earlier defined as the site of Wright's symbolic identification. An examination of the hardness trope, which is central
to Wright's process of symbolic identification, reveals that it is not simply
the (universal) "facts" of oppression that are "hard," but that the very
means through which these "facts" have been produced are themselves
"hard," as are most of the effective means of resisting the oppression.

The prologue, to some extent, and the epilogue in particular—that is, those sections of *Black Power* that fall outside of the trope of slavery that brackets the bulk of the text—are devoted to the articulation of hardness and symbolic identification. In the preface, Wright clearly identifies the genealogy of hardness, that is, the type of hardness that not only precedes but also, through a process of racial and colonial exclusion, produces the hardness he valorizes as a means of resistance. "The Western world," he tells us in the preface, "does not even yet know *how hard and inhuman* its face looks to those who live outside of its confines" (ibid., xxxvii, emphasis added). In the letter to Nkrumah, he admits that if the West had treated Africans differently, then "the question of 'hardness' would not have presented itself to me" (ibid., 386).

In the face of this hard oppression, Wright proposes a solution that is in some ways an "imitation" or a reflection. Of course, he does not advocate an imitative reproduction of the "oppression" but rather of the quality of "hardness." He is advocating a quasi-Newtonian moral imperative as a form of resistance: every hardness must be met with equal and opposite hardness. Thus his letter to Nkrumah continues to warn the latter of the problems facing him and advises him how to overcome them:

> African culture has not developed the personalities of the people to a degree that their egos *are stout, hard, sharply defined*; there is too much cloudiness in the African's mentality, a kind of sodden vagueness that makes for lack of confidence, an absence of focus that renders that mentality incapable of grasping the workaday world. And until confidence is established at the center of African personality, until there is an inner reorganization of that personality, there can be no question of marching from the tribal order to the twentieth century. . . . At the moment, this subjective task [of hardening the African personality] is far more important than economics! (ibid., 385–86, emphasis added).

The antidote to the "sodden vagueness" is the development of hardness: against the background of colonial oppression, says Wright, "one refrain echoes again and again in my mind: *You must be hard*! While in Africa one question kept hammering at me: Do the Africans possess the necessary hardness for the task ahead?" (ibid., 386, emphasis added). Hardness is necessary for resistance to colonial dominance: ". . . if the choice is between traditional Western domination and hardness, take the path of hardness!" However, unlike the hardness that is "externally" imposed by the processes of enslavement and colonization, this hardness must be self-imposed: "Africa needs this hardness, *but only from Africans*" (ibid., 392, emphasis added). Wright himself would be willing to accept such discipline: "Be merciful by being stern! If I lived under your regime, I'd ask for this hardness, this coldness" (ibid., 388). Along with subsidiary formulations such as the "need to militarize African life," the trope of hardness becomes a mantra that repeatedly punctuates the letter to Nkrumah, and like a typical mantra, it can seem quite vague after a while.

The genealogy of this trope in Wright's entire work can rescue it from its relatively vague deployment in *Black Power*. I cannot recapitulate that entire genealogy here, but perhaps a few glimpses will suffice to clarify how the trope forms the core of symbolic identification for Wright. The development of a hard subjectivity, which becomes one of the central ingredients of Wright's strategy of resisting the processes of racist subjection, first manifests itself in one of Wright's early short stories, "Long Black Song" (1940 [1936]). Here the hardness of the Jim Crow racist society is resisted by the inculcation of its mirror image, a hardness that permits the protagonist, a prosperous black farmer, to choose heroic and honorific (and somewhat romantic) death rather than succumb to the dictates of that society, dictates that would require him to become a virtual slave once again. Silas, the protagonist, vows that he will be as "hard" as the whites who have come to lynch him for beating a white salesman who had seduced/raped his wife. Barricading himself in his house, he shoots as many of them as he can before they set fire to his house, and he burns to death without uttering a sound. While this mode of resistance is somewhat romantic in this story, Wright later modifies the function of (the fear of) death in the process of resistance. It also is at this point that Wright begins to genderize this trope: hardness is masculinized in association with Silas, while its opposite, "softness," is associated with his wife, whose preoccupation with and investment in the mundane pleasures of life come to signify unconscious collaboration with the racist society, denial of the severity of racism, and escapism through material consumption in general.

This stylized, genderized dichotomy resurfaces in *Native Son* in Bigger's callousness and his and Wright's tendency to conflate what we might call "political hardness" (as it manifests itself in the letter to Nkrumah) with sexual/phallic hardness. This conflation then goes a long way toward explaining (though not justifying or excusing) the misogynistic tendency that permeates Wright's fiction. This "stylization" also manifests itself in

Black Power, precisely at the point where Wright wants to make the transition from "soft" and "sentimental" emotions elicited by the plight of the slave mother—emotions that Wright has deliberately evoked in order to then negate them in contrast—to the "hard thinking" and "hard subjectivity" that he advocates as a political solution. In Wright's autobiography, the trope is articulated via the figure of Wright himself, who has won a certain kind of freedom because of his hardness, in contrast to his father, who has remained a "Black Boy" and whose personality is described in terms remarkably similar to those that Wright employs to describe the "African personality" in *Black Power*.

By the time Wright deploys this trope in *Black Power*, its role in the process of symbolic identification becomes fairly clear. "Imitation" of Euro-American hardness permits a mimetic identification not with the content of that culture but with its structure, in particular, with the means it deploys to enhance its power. This kind of identification differs from the imaginary type, because by facilitating an identification with the *position* from which we are observed (and observe ourselves) as being worthy of love, symbolic identification makes it possible for us to (re) appropriate the agency that otherwise controls our destinies. In short, symbolic identification permits an identification with the Law and, via the subsequent access to the process of (political) signification, the capacity to occupy an active place in an intersubjective symbolic/political network. According to Zizek's (1989) reading of Lacan, the transition from imaginary to symbolic identification is marked by a moment of "*le point de capiton*," that is, a "quilting" point that, like a punctuation mark, retroactively fixes the meaning of a given signifying chain.

Thus if we treat the trope of hardness not as an empty mantra but as a metalinguistic punctuation or "identity" mark that, by punctuating the processes of identification, retroactively grants meaning to the syntax of identification, then we might be in a better position to understand its function in the process of resistance as well as in the production of Wright as a specular border intellectual. In the first place, it is clearly evident that the valorization of hardness, as a mimetic process, is profoundly specular. Wright uses his oppressors as mirrors in order to better chart and evaluate his own resistance to them. It also is specular in another, more crucial sense. As a process of symbolic identification, it privileges the imitation not of content, values, and so on but of structures and processes that can be used to quite different ends than those for which the oppressors use their "hardness." It enables, in short, a significant process of deterritorialization. For Wright, the most important form of deterritorialization centers on development of a "hard subjectivity," as he so clearly insists in *Black Power*. The advice he proffers to Nkrumah has been worked through by Wright in terms of his own subjectivity.

Wright tells us in *Black Boy* (1945, 215, emphasis added) that he "could not make subservience [to racist demands] an *automatic* part of my behavior. I had to feel and think out each tiny item of racial experience in the light of the race problem, *and to each item I brought the whole of my life*." Now in order for subservience to be *automatic* it cannot be conscious; it has to become a part of one's unconscious behavior pattern, and precisely at the point where one's behavior is unconsciously controlled by a prevailing form of subjection, one has succumbed to that prevailing cultural hegemony. Wright's personal imperative is diametrically opposed to the demands of racist subjection: he wants to *understand* each racial incident that he experiences in light of the entire social, political, and ideological system of racism and slavery, and to each incident he devotes his entire life and *consciousness*. Wright thus constantly "reflects (on)" the processes of subjugation and then deterritorializes these processes. So where racist society demands an imitation of the model of "a black boy" at an unconscious, noncritical level, that is, where it demands imaginary identification, Wright's specular project requires an analytic rearticulation of those mimetic demands at a conscious, critical level: it thus transforms the demand for imaginary identification into an imperative for symbolic identification. And the success of his specular deterritorialization depends on a hard, cold, and unsentimental analysis of his own formation—it depends, for instance, on an analysis of the role his fear of death plays in the process of his own collaboration in his subjection and subjectification. The trope of hardness thus not only defines the entire political field in which Wright operates but also defines the core of his subjectivity. The trope demands a certain hardness; it produces a certain stiffness; it robs him of sensuality; it prevents him from dancing; and it forces him to construct fictional characters, such as Bigger Thomas, who misrecognize their hardness as an essential feature of their "identities." Hardness, in short, is a punctuation mark that retroactively defines Wright's entire literary project as well as his subjectivity: Wright is a specular border intellectual whose subjectivity and body coagulate around hard reflection and hard identification. The hardness that Wright offers to Nkrumah as a gesture of solidarity in effect constitutes a reading of his own body and subjectivity as a specular border intellectual. It constitutes a gesture of profoundly specular/symbolic identification.

NOTES

This chapter was previously published in Korean in *An-kwa-Bak: Yongmi-munhak-yonku* ([In]Outside: English Studies in Korea) 8 (April 2000): 270–96.

1. For Miller's distinction, see Zizek 1989, 105.

2. See JanMohamed 1987.

3. These ritualistic scenes are quite drawn out and elaborately patterned; I can only touch upon some highlights here.

4. See JanMohamed 1987 for an elaboration of maternal suffering as the paradigmatic form of suffering in Wright's autobiography.

WORKS CITED

Borch-Jacobsen, Mikkel. 1988. *The Freudian Subject*. Stanford: Stanford University Press.

Gilroy, Paul. 1993. *The Black Atlantic: Modernity and Double Consciousness*. Cambridge: Harvard University Press.

JanMohamed, Abdul. 1987. "Negating the Negation As a Form of Affirmation in Minority Discourse: The Construction of Richard Wright As Subject." *Cultural Critique* 7 (fall): 245–66. Reprinted in *Richard Wright: A Collection of Critical Essays*. Edited by Arnold Rampersad. Englewood Cliffs, N.J.: Prentice Hall, 1995.

———. 1992. "Worldliness-without-World, Homelessness-As-Home: Toward a Definition of the Specular Border Intellectual." Pp. 96–120 in *Edward Said: A Critical Reader*, ed. Michael Sprinker. Oxford: Basil Blackwell.

Wright, Richard. 1940 [1936]. "Long Black Song." Pp. 103–28 in *Uncle Tom's Children*. New York: Harper & Row.

———. 1945. *Black Boy: A Record of Childhood and Youth*. New York: Harper & Row.

———. 1995 [1954]. *Black Power: A Record of Reactions in a Land of Pathos*. New York: Harper and Brothers.

Zizek, Slavoj. 1989. *The Sublime Object of Ideology*. London: Verso.

CHAPTER TWELVE

BEYOND DICHOTOMIES

Translation/Transculturation and the Colonial Difference

WALTER D. MIGNOLO AND FREYA SCHIWY

INTRODUCTION

Perhaps the most common and widely discussed problem of dichotomies
in Western thought[1] is the pervasive logic that underlies them. Although
dichotomies could be identified in communities and societies either
before or next to the macro-narrative of Western civilization, our concern
here is with the reshaping of the hierarchical and contradictory
dichotomies imposed through the expansion of Western civilization.[2]
Dichotomies, in the modern/colonial world (i.e., since 1500, with the
emergence of the Atlantic commercial circuit), have been organized (and
are still being reproduced) as colonial differences. Our thesis is that
"translation" could allow us to think about possible futures, beyond
dichotomies, in which the "lower end" of the colonial difference would
no longer be the place of shame and ignorance but of epistemic potential.

It is our assumption that translation is more than a syntactic and
semantic transaction between two languages. It also involves historical
and geopolitical configurations: historical, because a given language has
not only a grammatical logic but also a historical memory engrained in

it, and thus forms the subjectivity of its speakers. For that reason, translation in the domain of language is at the same time a phenomenon of transculturation. Furthermore, transculturation goes beyond language and involves people and objects at levels beyond language proper, as we will see in more detail below. "Transculturation" was introduced by the Cuban anthropologist Fernando Ortiz so it could carry the weight of his nationalistic program. We are aware of that and have no intention of promoting Ortiz's national ideals. While Ortiz used transculturation in the contradictory scenario of nation building in Latin America, where national homogeneity implied biological and cultural *mestizaje*, our own use of transculturation is centrifugal rather than centripetal. We suggest that transculturation is a necessary concept to think all kinds of social and political relations of forces in a transnational world. Transculturation is a necessary concept to remove translation from its linguistic conception. This idea is closely tied to the alphabetic conception of language engrained in modernity and crossing the entire idea of Western civilization, from the Greek invention of the alphabet to the current assumption linking the alphabet to democracy (Havelock 1982; Hill Boone and Mignolo 1994).

Our argument presupposes the historical structure of the modern/colonial world and the complicity between translation/transculturation and the making of the colonial difference, which in turn goes hand in hand with the construction of a hierarchical gender binary. It further assumes that in this structure, the colonial difference is the logic of colonial dichotomies. Finally, we argue for a change of directionality in the work of translation and transculturation that could help in thinking and moving beyond dichotomies, politically and ethically.

TERRITORIAL THINKING AND TRANSLATION/TRANSCULTURATION IN THE MODERN/COLONIAL WORLD SYSTEM

It is fair to say that critical reflections on translation in the last fifty years have been done in the realms of linguistics, literature, the philosophy of language, and anthropology. Linguistic, literary, and philosophical reflections on translation presuppose the macro-narrative of Western civilization from the Greek invention of the alphabet to modern/colonial and European languages.[3] The second, anthropology, presupposes cross-cultural understanding brought about by coloniality and modernity.[4] That is, the expansion of the Western world in the name of modernity justifies coloniality. Although anthropology is a nineteenth-century invention, missionaries and men of letters faced the same kind of problem in the sixteenth century and set the stage for what later on would be codified by anthropology as an emerging social science.

Between the ninth and twelfth centuries, the intense traffic of ideas and linguistic interaction between Arabic, Greek, and Latin implied a constant work of translation and transculturation. However, the underlying structure of power was not the same as the one that would operate after 1500, with the emergence of the modern/colonial world. Since 1500, translation contributed to the construction of hierarchical dichotomies imposing certain rules and directionalities of transculturation. Translation contributed to building the colonial difference between Western European languages (languages of science and knowledge and the locus of enunciation) and the rest of the languages on the planet (languages of culture and religion and the locus of the enunciated). Translation was indeed unbalanced. Conversion to Christianity in the sixteenth century offered the general frame for the construction of dichotomies and for establishing the directionality of translation and transculturation. During the Renaissance, this translation in the context of conversion intersected with debates over the body that were establishing the idea of fixed, dichotomous, and unchangeable gender identities, no longer subject to the medieval conceptions that explained gender as a result of body heat, capable of sudden change.[5] These medical debates were linked to the issue of colonialism, as the New World continued for some time to function as a space where undecided gender identities could continue in their ambiguity. The life of Catalina de Erauso may be a case in point; the anxiety about Amazons may be another (Mott 1992; Montrose 1991). At the time of conquest land was conceptualized as feminine, a territory to be penetrated and governed by masculine rule. The inhabitants were children or Amazons, both extremes of the imagery of women, either as helpless and in need of male guidance, or as a threat in her assumption of masculinity, a threat that needed to be contained and submitted. By the end of the Renaissance, these ambiguities were translated and fixed into the dichotomous designs that differentiated men and women, self and other. In the nineteenth century, Eurocentric definitions of colonial relations again employ a gendered imagery to construct progress, development, science (knowledge), and Europe (or in Latin America, the European-oriented city) itself as masculine. The rural space of barbarity, populated frequently by Amerindian peoples, was landscaped as the city's/Europe's binary other, identified as static and again fitted with female-identified characteristics. Until recently, the rural/urban divide that allocates knowledge within an urban and a public geographic sphere continued to firmly associate the private and rural with femininity (Massey 1994).

This logic that conceives of differences in terms of hierarchical dichotomies continues to operate today, although the visible scenario has changed. Feminist criticism is debating the status of gender difference in the face of hegemonic beliefs about the existence of two biological sexes. At the same time, although neoliberalism is of course not Christianity, its logic is similar, as "conversion" remains a hidden principle while the strategies have changed. Today it is issued as a total conversion to global market relations and consumerism that politically wants to leave no space for alternative designs.

Translation from Greek to Latin or from French to Spanish is one thing; translation from Aymara to Spanish is something different (Harrison 1989). From Hindi to English, it is still another thing. There is, of course, more translation from English to Hindi than vice versa. However, the question is not just translating from one language to another in some indeterminate history of humankind; translation is enacted within particular structures of power. The main thrust of this chapter is to reflect critically (some will say "theorize") on translation, transculturation, and the coloniality of power in which colonial difference is embedded. We locate the coloniality of power and the colonial difference in what Immanuel Wallerstein (Quijano and Wallerstein 1992) has called "the modern world-system" and, following the contributions of Latin American theorists such as Anibal Quijano (1998), what we will call the "modern/colonial world system." Translation was indeed the place where the coloniality of power articulated the colonial difference in the modern/colonial world. Franciscans and Dominicans in Mesoamerica in the first half of the sixteenth century and Jesuits in China toward the end of the sixteenth century planted, so to speak, the banner of the modern/colonial world imaginary in terms of translating knowledge and establishing the principles of epistemic colonial power. This translation machine entailed an enormous effort to write grammars of non-European languages, to adapt them to the Latin grammar, or to translate the concepts and ideas of other cosmologies to the Christian one that emerged in the New World (Mignolo 1995, chapter 1). Here the question was not simply the incommensurability of different worldviews but of different worldviews tied up by the coloniality of power in the making of the colonial difference. By "coloniality of power," we simply refer to the kind of power exercised in the classification of people and cultures and in the historical and colonial dichotomies implied in such classifications. Translation and interpretation designated one particular epistemic/theological perspective as "correct," conceiving as deviant and insufficient other forms of knowledge, whether Confucianism or Buddhism in China (Jones 1999; Hart 1999) or unnamed forms of knowledge among the Aztecs and the Incas (Mignolo 1995, chapters 2 and 3). With this move, the subjects of other knowledges were denied the masculinity that now reasserted itself as a prerequisite for participation in the process of translation and knowledge production. Knowledge other than the kind articulated in the religious orders and in European universities was erased by the translation machine at the inception of the modern/colonial world system. Jean Franco (1990) has shown how women needed to translate their knowledges into the acceptable framework of the Church in colonial Mexico,[6] a project not open to indigenous women. At the same time, Christian missionaries initiated a massive project of writing grammars and vocabularies of Amerindian languages. The approximately fifty years (1528–1578) that Franciscan Bernardino de Sahagun devoted to translating Nahuatl into Latin and Spanish, along with the time many religious orders devoted to translating Spanish and Latin into Nahuatl for the purpose of conversion, constitute the most dramatic and exemplary case of translation for assimilation. It is the most dramatic and exemplary because it became a model that was later reconverted and adapted by subsequent religious orders in the colonization of Africa and Asia since the nineteenth century. We locate translation and transculturation within the overall frame of the colonial difference in the modern/colonial world system, as a process grounded in an ethno-racial, gendered, and epistemological foundation.

BORDER THINKING AND THE ZAPATISTAS' TRANSLATION/TRANSCULTURATION MODEL

If the missionaries set a model of translation in the sixteenth century, the Zapatistas drastically changed this model at the end of the twentieth century and contributed to a new theory of translation/transculturation. The missionaries' project consisted of translating Amerindian languages and masculine voices into Spanish with the purpose of assimilation (of both men and women) and of translating Spanish into Nahuatl with the purpose of conversion. Missionaries' translations were always performed from the hegemonic perspective of local Christian histories projecting and enacting global designs (e.g., to Christianize the world). The Zapatistas' theory of translation and the project attached to it underline, on the contrary, that the missionaries' translation constructed the colonial difference at the same time they intended to erase it by assimilation (i.e., conversion). The Zapatistas instead brought the colonial difference as well as the issue of gender to the foreground as a place of epistemic and political intervention (Mignolo 1997). The dictum "Because we are all equal we have the right to be different" is the most concise and clear formula of the colonial difference as a place of translation/transculturation from a perspective of subalternity. The Zapatistas' enactment and theory of translation (as Subcomandante Marcos explained and as we will develop below) was performed from the subaltern perspective of local Marxist and Amerindian histories resisting and transforming global designs. The Zapatistas' performance and theory of translation is not just from one language to another, but it is indeed a complex and double movement. First, there is the double translation/transculturation of Marxist into Amerindian cosmology, and vice versa. Second, this double translation is not isolated but emerges in response and accommodation to the hegemonic discourse of the State which, in 1994, was identified as neoliberalism. We explore this schema and explain our perspective on translation/transculturation and the colonial difference by "listening" to Mayor Ana María's opening address to the Intercontinental Encounter in the Lacandon Forest in August 1996.

> For power, the one that today is globally dressed with the name of neoliberalism, we neither counted nor produced. Did not buy or sell. We were an idle number in the accounts of Big Capital. Here in the highlands of the Mexican Southeast, our dead ones are alive. Our dead who live in the mountains know many things. Their death talked to us and we listened. The mountain talked to us, the mace-hualo, we the common and ordinary people, we the simple people as we are called by the powerful. We were born war [sic] with the white year, and we began to trace the path that took us to the heart of yours, the same that today took you to our heart. That's who we are. The EZLN. The voice which arms itself so that it can make itself heard. The face which hides itself so it can be shown. The name that keeps quiet in order to be named. The red star which calls to humanity and the world, so that they will listen, so that they will see, so that they will nominate. The tomorrow that is harvested in

the yesterday. Behind our black face. Behind our armed voice. Behind our unspeakable name. Behind the we that you see. Behind us we are [at] you [*Detras de nosotros estamos ustedes*]. (Mayor Ana María 1996)

The last sentence, "Detras de nosotros estamos ustedes," is a case in point. First, we have the word order in Spanish between "we" and "you." "Detras de ustedes estamos nosotros" could have been translated as "We are behind you." Second, we have the agrammatical use of "estamos" (are) instead of "somos" (are), which dislocates the possibility of a simple transference that could be rendered as "we are you." Instead, the "estamos" creates a fracture in Spanish that has to be rendered by the "nonsense" (in Spanish and English!) "we are at you." The important point here is not whether Ana María should gloss and explain (to those who do not speak Tojolabal) what she "means" (in Spanish or English), but that the fracture in the sentence is produced by the presence and intervention of the "other" grammar, the grammar of Amerindian languages. Two interrelated elements deserve attention: one is the grammar and the other is the cosmology out of which grammar exists or which grammar mirrors. In this fracture produced by translation, as here from Tojolabal to Spanish to English, the cosmologies of grammar highlight the dimensions of colonial difference, which include those of ethnicity/race and gender.

Carlos Lenkersdorf (1996) describes Tojolabal as an intersubjective language, and by that he means that it is a language which, unlike Spanish or English, does not have direct or indirect objects. In a language such as Spanish, the grammar places a certain portion of the world, including persons, outside of the speaker's realm of interactions. Amerindian languages, such as Tojolabal, are based in a cosmology in which persons, living systems, and nature are not objects but subjects. This interaction between grammar and cosmology, which informs a given worldview, has been noted in other Amerindian cosmologies. As long as we keep grammar, cosmology, and language interrelated, translation/transculturation cannot be mastered and controlled by one type of correlation between language, worldviews, knowledge, and wisdom. Vine Deloria Jr. has devoted many essays to redrawing the map of translation/transculturation since the sixteenth century, which has been dominated by a hegemonic view of Spanish and English cosmology, language, and epistemology. Deloria also is speaking from his own Native American experience and not only as a scholar or outside intellectual observer. Deloria is closer to Mayor Ana María in this respect; closer,

also, to Lenkersdorf and Subcomandante Marcos as intellectuals educated in Western institutions. "Relatedness" is the word used by Deloria to describe Native Americans' experience of the world, instead of
"isolation," which is the word used to describe Spanish or English patterns of experience.[7] It should be remembered, for the clarity of the argument, that the colonial difference articulates the external borders of the
modern/colonial world system, not its internal-imperial conflicts.

Dichotomies have been articulated differently in each new phase of
modernity/coloniality (including the kind of global coloniality we are
living in today). The logic, however, remains constant. An argument
similar to the one we are making with reference to the New World and
China in the sixteenth century could be made with reference to the
Islamic world. If we think in terms of the modern/colonial world system
and consider the fact that, since the sixteenth century, God and later
Reason (but without eliminating Christianity) became the anchor of the
overarching imaginary of the modern/colonial world and the West, then
the question of translation/transculturation is no longer that of dualism.
We are no longer facing the question of "the West and the rest," but "the
rest in the West." This is the reinscription of the colonial difference from
the perspective of subalternity that the Zapatistas have been teaching us
and that impinges on the ways in which translation/transculturation can
be theorized and enacted in the future.

Western Christian rationality, an imaginary that also is identified
as "Occidentalism" (Deloria 1998 [1978]), confronts "multiple others"
that have been elaborating alternative engagements with Reason, both
on its interior and its exterior borders. The rethinking of gender
dichotomies, for instance, challenges binaries on the inside by proposing
that gender is a socially assigned category and ultimately a performance
of identity (Butler 1990). Postcolonial feminist critics such as Chandra
Talpade Mohanty (1988) or bell hooks challenge the category "women"
across the external borders of the modern/colonial world system by
pointing to the different positions that this system has assigned to
women because of their ethnicity or geopolitical location, both in economic as well as in epistemological terms. The thesis of incommensurable cosmologies begins to be rethought in terms of an intervention in
the colonial difference from a subaltern perspective rather than as equal
and incommensurable cosmologies. The concurrency of these critiques
provides the link that creates the basis for their impact; dichotomies are
dissolved because these multiple others challenge the center and critically engage with each other on its interior and exterior borders.

Cosmologies, Cultural Practices,
and Translation/Transculturation

Mayor Ana María's discourse and Lenkersdorf's observation on the
Tojolabal language unlock a history of repressive translation since the
sixteenth century. We provide another example, this time from Aymara;
we apologize for jumping from Tojolabal in southern Mexico to
Aymara in Bolivia, but we do not have substantial archives in these
matters as we do for the vehicular or main colonial languages of the
modern world system. The Aymara word *Pachakuti* caused missionaries and anthropologists in the twentieth century a lot of headaches. The
problem was to find the right translation and interpretation for
Pachakuti: what kind of "god," after all, was he? Ethnographic information was very complex, and the full understanding of Pachakuti was
very elusive. Recently, however, a different understanding about
Pachakuti began to be provided by French, British, and Bolivian
anthropologists Thérèse Bouysse-Cassagne, Denise Arnold, Tristan
Platt, Olivia Harris, and Veronica Cereceda (Bouysse-Cassagne et al.
1987; Arnold, Jiménez, and Dios Yapita 1992).

A simple but accurate description of Pacha is to say that it con-
denses Western notions of space and time. Kuti, on the other hand,
means a shift of opposites when contrary terms are irreducible to one
another. Contrary terms are compacted in another term, Tinku, which
means the encounter of contrary terms. If, then, Kuti is the shifting of
contrary terms, Pachakuti is turn, revolt, a violent turnaround of events.
Thus it was natural to refer to the situation created by the arrival of the
Spaniards as Pachakuti. So after all, there was not a "god" named
Pachakuti, but an interlocking of words and meaning to describe intersubjective relations. Languaging[8] for the Aymara speakers was slightly
different than for a Spanish speaker: the Aymara speaker was not naming but establishing relations with the world, and the world was not
divided between human beings, objects, and gods (as objects) but rather
conceived as a network of living interactions, including those with
nature, gods, and—to the occidental eye—seemingly lifeless objects.[9]
Perhaps we can understand Mayor Ana María in this sense when she
states that "our dead ones are alive. Our dead who lie in the mountains
know many things. Their death talked to us and we listened. The mountain talked to us." Perhaps this also refers to the way that space is a
visual archive of knowledge that contains memory, that is time (Rappaport 1998, 161–73; Salomon and Urioste 1991).

As with Pachakuti, which conflates space and time, the discourse of Zapatismo and Ana María trans-lates (tras-ladar) the past into the present. The Amerindian memories of the past are transformed by the perspective of today. They conflate, in a specific manner, the past into the necessities of the present. At the same time, the translating subject, Ana María, also trans-lates the Amerindians into the present of global time. She claims coevalness, as has Rigoberta Menchú, with the West. As such, she unravels metaphorical attachments between nature, femininity, stasis, and indigenous peoples.[10] Amerindians are not primitives located on a temporal axis of development and occupying a moment of pre-modernity. Amerindians and Amerindian memories are present, but there is no primeval authenticity. They are present in and through the colonial difference as the place where transculturation and the coloniality of power are constantly at work. Ana María wears a *pasamontañas* (the black ski mask of the EZLN [Ejército Zapatista de Liberación Nacional]). This transculturation takes place on Amerindian terms; there is no integration to the nation on national terms. There is a particular kind of translation/transculturation going on here, in which a dense history of oppression and subalternization of language and knowledge is being unlocked.

There is a fundamental difference between what goes on in the case of the Zapatistas and recent academic approaches to translation, even when they are grounded in postcolonial principles.[11] The difference is that the geopolitical directionality of translation and the relations between language, knowledge, and power are not questioned. While the Zapatistas' political visions stem from the translation of Western thought into Maya cosmo-vision and Maya cosmo-vision into Western thought confronted with the hegemony of the state, postcolonial approaches to translation (Niranjana 1992, Liu 1999) seem to be out to prove something else, that is, an original way of thinking that is multiple and legitimized in its existence by the European master's deconstructions. This need for legitimization, however, limits the postcolonial critique: the logic of dichotomies is reinstated in the act of criticizing their content.

The Zapatistas' theoretical revolution in the domain of translation/transculturation offers an attractive way to think beyond the dichotomies constructed in and by the imaginary of the modern/colonial world. We pause, this time, on a statement signed by the Comité Clandestino Revolucionario Indígena-Comandancia General (CCRI-CG) of the EZLN.

When the EZLN was only a shadow creeping between the fog
and darkness of the mountain, when the words justice, freedom,
and democracy were just words; merely a dream that the elders
of our communities, the real custodians of the words of our
ancestors, had given us right at the moment when day gives way
to night, when hate and death were beginning to grow in our
hearts, when there was only despair. When the times turned back
over their own selves, with no exit the authentic men talked, the
faceless, the ones who walk the night, those who are mountains,
so they said: It is the reason and will of good men and women to
search and to find the best way to govern and self-govern, what
is good for most is good for all. But not to silence the voices of
the few, rather for them to remain in their place, hoping that
mind and heart will come together in the will of the most and the
inspiration of the few, thus the nations composed of real men and
women grown inward and grown big, so that there could be no
exterior force capable of breaking them, or of deviating their
steps toward different roads. In this way our strength was born
in the mountain, where the ruler obeys, when she or he is authentic, and the one who obeys commands with the common heart, of
the genuine men and women. Another word came from far away
for this government to be named, and this word, called "democracy," this road of us who moved forward before words were able
to walk. (EZLN 1994, 175–76)

"Democracy" (the word also could have been "socialism") has a
double edge: the word is being universally used, but its meaning is no
longer universal. "Diversality," a term introduced by Francophone intellectuals, seems to grasp the kind of multiple renegotiations implied by
the paragraph just quoted.[12] The concept for the EZLN's particular base
democracy existed in Tojolabal before encountering the Spanish term; as
the Zapatistas said, "another word came from far away for this government." It is now translated, made to coincide with a Tojolabal understanding. The translation of democracy into Tojolabal will be "to rule
obeying at the same time," which does not put a premium on the "people" but on the relations between them, the changing roles, and the mov-
able field of forces.[13] The appropriation of democracy, from a subaltern
perspective, to mean "ruling at the same time as obeying," is at the same
time appropriating the vehicular and dominant language, in this case,
Spanish. There is a particular form of translation at stake here, which
we would like to call "transculturation" (and not just "cultural translation") as the politics of border thinking.

The appropriation of "democracy" into the Amerindian languages/cosmologies is rendered in Spanish. It is a process of double translation, a historical condition of subaltern languages for political intervention. Let us explain. In the sixteenth century, as we said, the missionaries translated both Amerindian languages into Spanish and Spanish into Amerindian languages. Amerindians initially assisted in these projects, but translations were controlled and manipulated and in the hands of the dominant group. They did not transform the imperial design but were absorbed into its logic. Syncretic practices may indeed indicate a long-standing strategy of translation/transculturation that has worked in the opposite direction of imperial translations. A tradition of syncretic practices may therefore be the foundation that allows the Tojolabales to perceive the Marxist/Leninist guerillas as a revolutionary potential adequate to their (the Tojobalales') needs. In the case of the Zapatistas, however, the subaltern group manipulates translation, but now in multiple directions. What is at stake, then, are different ways of translating in several directions. First, translation occurs between the four Amerindian languages of the Zapatista movement. Second, and most importantly, translation from Amerindian languages to Spanish is no longer simply a translation of Amerindian language into Spanish concepts and systems of understanding. Rather, an Amerindian understanding is rendered in Spanish syntax, becoming transformed in the process and not entirely losing its difference from Western understanding. In the other direction, from the Spanish/Western language to Amerindian languages, Spanish/Western thinking is transformed, its words inserted and interpreted on the grounds of Amerindian cosmologies.

Subcomandante Marcos (Marcos et al. 1997) has talked about these various levels of translation. For Marcos, translation is not just interlanguage but intercosmologies. He uses the term "translator" ("traductor") to refer to the "indigenist element" that made communication between the Marxist–Leninist guerilla forces and the indigenous communities in the Chiapan highlands possible. Crucial to this translation was the transportation of concepts, thoughts, and ultimately revolutionary needs and goals from one cultural context to another. This transport did not go primarily in the direction it has traditionally taken when revolutionary actors equipped with Western knowledge have confronted "the masses." Marcos explains that the Marxist–Leninist revolutionary organization encountered a reality that could not be explained by Western concepts. The organization therefore realized that it needed to "listen." According to Marcos, the EZLN thus transformed itself from a revolutionary vanguard into an army of the indigenous communities.

The translation of Marxism into Amerindian cosmology and Amerindian into Marxist cosmology is what, according to Subcomandante Marcos, made Zapatism possible:

> We [the urban intellectuals, as Marcos defines himself and his group] believed in all the possible formulas and commonplaces that is it possible to imagine. But, after the EZLN gets in contact and interaction with the indigenous communities and becomes part of the indigenous resistance, it gets contaminated and subordinated to the indigenous communities. Indigenous communities appropriate the EZLN, they place it under their control. We surmise that what allowed EZLN to survive was to accept that defeat. The [a new] EZLN was born from the very moment that it realized that there is a new reality for which it has no answer and to which it subordinates itself to be able to survive. (Marcos et al. 1997, 149)

Marcos calls the moment when these two cultures come together a "choque," a clash, but rather than a moment in time, this clash produces a space of contact and conflict where translation takes place. The EZLN notices that it needs to learn rather than teach. A space opens up where knowledge flows from the Mayan indigenous communities into the thinking of Marxist–Leninist revolutionaries. The pressure for this flow is created because the Amerindian components become a majority in the political organization. Marcos calls this process "translation." It is facilitated and encouraged by translators, principally Old Man Antonio and the leaders of the communities.

Marcos's encounter with Old Man Antonio (*El viejo Antonio*) goes back to 1984. Old Man Antonio is the first translator, or at least the one who makes Marcos aware of the need for translation. Now from the perspective of urban intellectuals, the process of translation turns into a process of re-education. "And that is where Old Man Antonio and the leaders of the communities and the indigenous guerrilleros became the teachers of this military-political organization [the EZLN]" (Marcos et al. 1997, 148):

> We went through a process of re-education, of re-modeling. It was like they unarmed us. As if they had dismantled all the tools we had—Marxism, Leninism, socialism, urban culture, poetry, literature—everything that was a part of ourselves, and also that we did not know we had. They dismantled us and put us together again, but in a different configuration. And that was for us [urban intellectuals] the only way to survive. (ibid., 151)

Marcos asserts that this process of translation also "indianized" the urban part of the EZLN. Again, the existence of subjects connected to Amerindian knowledge and traditions who were simultaneously taking part in the occidental urban culture of the cities is crucial. This is, in other words, how "the indianization of the EZLN tactically displaced itself ["se traslado," which means transplaced and translated itself], contaminated the urban part, and indianized it as well" (ibid., 150). Old Man Antonio emerged on the Zapatistas' horizon in the first Amerindian town that the EZLN encountered, in 1985. What he did was explain to the urban intellectuals "who we were and what we sh[ould] be doing" (ibid., 154). It was Old Man Antonio "who gave us the indigenous elements that you find in Zapatistas' languages when we address ourselves to the Mexican or the world audience" (ibid., 155).

But Marcos himself also is a translator. More than that, since the moment of encounter with Old Man Antonio, he has transformed himself into something else. Precisely as Rafael Guillén begins to be erased, Marcos transforms himself into what the Amerindians want him to be: a paradigmatic case, indeed, of translation/transculturation transacting the colonial difference and the coloniality of power from a subaltern perspective. Marcos became a transculturated/translated new persona who did not have much to do with the person behind him. He converted himself into someone used by the Amerindians. Marcos, as translator, is the window through which to look inside and to look outside (ibid.). "What happened," explains Marcos, "is that the glass of that window is dirty, and people began to see themselves in it, and it is at that moment that Marcos becomes a symbol, that persona that is being constructed since 1994" (ibid.). However, the temptation of underlining Marcos's *vita* instead of what the transformation of Rafael Guillén into Marcos means in political terms may take us away from the major point of the argument:[14] that is, that translation and transculturation (not just "cultural transformation") lead to a theoretical revolution, in political as well as ethical terms.

If the window of translation/transculturation is dusty, as Marcos emphasized (1997, 155), it also reflects what is left of Rafael Guillén, and perhaps as well a struggle over whose Amerindian perspective engages in the translating process among the men and women actively figuring in the EZLN. With the protagonist Old Man Antonio, Marcos establishes a masculine genealogy in which Old Man Antonio is the primeval translator now transformed into the voice of Marcos, who prolongs the process, publishing the EZLN perspective for the national and international audience. So this process of translating and alerting to the colonial difference blurs the voices of the women *guerilleras*, such as Major Ana María, themselves engaging in a process of double translation not through Marcos but next to him.

Nevertheless, the failure to understand the scope of such transculturation/translation in redrawing the colonial difference and revealing the coloniality of power ends up in lamentable misunderstandings and in the reading of Marcos' and the Zapatistas' theoretical revolution in terms of the old models of the "self" and individual-family.

An "indigenous" uprising with a new language was and is a social movement yet difficult to process within either the neoliberal frame of mind of the Mexican government or that of intellectuals (such as, early on, Octavio Paz) but also from orthodox Marxist, leftist, and even feminist positions.[15] It is an epistemological revolution that has an impact on how to talk about and think translation/transculturation. Zapatism, indeed, began to be defined by the indigenous intellectuals with previous political experience, such as Tacho, David, Zevedeo, and Maribel. They are, according to Marcos, the true creators of Zapatism and the leading theorists for new conceptions and enactments of translation/transculturation: "The true creators of Zapatism are the translators, translators such as Mayor Mario, Mayor Moises, Mayor Ana María, all of those who also had to be translated from dialects [Marcos is referring here to indigenous languages], such as Tacho, David, Zevedeo. They are indeed the Zapatistas' theoreticians, they built, they are building a new way for looking at the world" (1997, 338–39).

Translation/Transculturation from the Borders

There are, therefore, a series of issues that the Zapatistas' theoretical revolution helps us in framing and arguing. First, the links between language and nation and between language and writing can no longer be sustained. Second, the way language and location are tied to epistemology and the link between real and metaphorical gender and knowledge are coming unglued. Third, the potential for intercultural communication in border spaces, which requires reflection not least of all on academic practice, is opening.

The Zapatistas call for redefining the concepts of translation and transculturation. Both terms have a close link to imperial and national beliefs and assumptions, as we outlined at the beginning of this chapter.

Translation, in terms of translating texts and literatures, was redefined in the modern world (from the Renaissance) under the presupposition of the unity and distinctiveness of certain languages held together by their grammar. In the modern world, grammatical treatises based on alphabetic literacy and the expansion of Western Christianity (generally referred to as "Western expansion"), which are translated into the unity and distinctiveness of certain (other) languages, proliferate. As self-contained entities, they are placed in dichotomous relations that are not equal or even complementary to each other but defined hierarchically by the geopolitical location of the language as nation. Talal Asad has insisted on keeping in mind the inequality of languages when it comes to cultural translation in the production of anthropological knowledge. The Zapatistas opened up new possibilities: those of speaking and writing Amerindian languages through Spanish or using and appropriating Spanish as the official language of the nation. Such possibilities also have important consequences for indigenous movements in Latin America, from Bolivia and Ecuador to Guatemala and Mexico, as well as for international and interlingual relations in the production of knowledge and its political consequences. Amerindian debates within the nation-state, but also across the Latin American continent, take place in Spanish, while English, as in the case of the Zapatistas, allows indigenous peoples to communicate at a global level.

For three centuries, from 1500 to 1800, Amerindians—in the best of all possible worlds—were targeted to be converted to Christianity and to learn Spanish. Translation was part of a project of transculturation, and transculturation was understood and described as "conversion." Today we would say "assimilation." During the process of nation building after 1800, Amerindians were marginalized as the targets of bilingual education from the perspective of Spanish. That is, Amerindians had to learn Spanish, but the Creole elite in power did not have to learn Amerindian languages. If not known, this fact will surprise no one. What is more interesting is that now some Amerindians, such as Cojti Cuxil in Guatemala, are no longer interested in learning Spanish, but English. The Creole elite in power, intellectuals, and journalists of nationalist persuasion could consider this inappropriate. However, from Cojti's perspective, Spanish was the language that oppressed Amerindians; English could be the language that liberates them from Spanish and its ties with the nation-state.[16] "Transculturation" is here best described as a social conflict between languages and cosmologies in hegemonic and subaltern positions, respectively.

There is, therefore, another dimension to the inequality of languages, not only between English and Swahili or Aymara, as Talal Asad implies, or between Tojolabal and Spanish, but the inequality of imperial languages—in this case, Spanish, vis-à-vis English. Roughly, Spanish is, among the imperial languages of the modern world (Spanish, Portuguese, French, English, and German), a subaltern language. This is part of a complex spectrum of the inequality of languages in the modern world system because, again roughly speaking, there is, on the one hand, the hierarchy among imperial languages of the modern world system and, on the other hand, the hierarchy of languages at its borders. Arabic, for instance, is not the same as Aymara or Nahuatl, although both of them are outside of the system, so to speak. The result is that translation from English or French into Arabic is very common, although not into Aymara. For the same reason that links language to knowledge, Arabic translations into English or French are less common than in the opposite direction. The same happens with Spanish or Portuguese. Translations from German, French, and English into Spanish abound. There are not many translations in the opposite direction, we are sure. What gets translated is literature, but literature, we know, falls within the intellectual distribution of labor within the system: Third World or Third World-like countries produce culture, not knowledge.[17] If this frame is kept in mind, then Talal Asad's final recommendation makes sense:

> I have proposed that the anthropological enterprise of critical translation may be vitiated by the fact that there are asymmetrical tendencies and pressures in the languages of dominated and dominant societies. And I have suggested that anthropologists need to explore these processes in order to determine how far they go in defining the possibilities and the limits of effective translation. (1986, 164)

This conclusion and recommendation are made with a particular scenario in mind: the anthropologist from the United States going around the world and coming back to translate such knowledge for the academic community. As we have shown, language translation concerns the hierarchies of power between nations and, above all, it is shaped by the coloniality of power and the colonial difference, from early colonial states to modern nation-states. We can revamp the notion of "internal colonialism" here to understand how the coloniality of power and the colonial difference works in the nation-building process. Modern nation-states reproduced, within the territorial frontiers, the structure of power put into place by the colonial model. That is why the coloniality of power is not a question only related to colonial "periods," here and there, but to the modern/colonial world system, from its inception to its current form of global and transnational coloniality.

Hegemonic languages were not only tied to the empire and to the nation but were also the expression and means of transportation for knowledge. The epistemological dimensions opened by the Zapatistas cannot be divorced from the geopolitics of knowledge and the colonial difference: the new scenario for translation/transculturation. It is within the Cold War "area studies" framework that such observations make sense. The question for us is, what about anthropologists in Bolivia or Argentina, working and living in the Andes? Is this situation similar to those that became the paradigmatic examples of area studies: Third World culture translated into First World anthropology? Do they experience the ideological underpinnings of area studies for anthropological knowledge in the same way?[18] This apparent detour into anthropology and area studies takes us back to the question of translation/transculturation and nation building after decolonization, or the moment in which the coloniality of power is inscribed into nation building and the colonial difference reproduced as internal colonialism.

Briefly stated, the concept of transculturation, introduced in 1940 by Cuban anthropologist Fernando Ortiz, was intended mainly to correct the one-direction process of translation and acculturation in British anthropology, in this case, as articulated by Bronislaw Malinowski (Asad 1986). "Transculturation" indirectly underlined (even if for Ortiz it was a tool to think nation building in a society where homogeneity had to account for *mestizaje*) that cultural transformations go not only from East to West but also from West to East or North to South and South to North. The fact remains that transculturation was, for Ortiz, a process perceived from a postcolonial society. This was more difficult to see for Malinowski, a Pole educated in England, who only saw acculturation (Coronil 1995). When Ortiz talks about transculturation in terms of human communities, he is thinking in terms of cultural diversity—so to speak—in Cuba. But when Ortiz talks about transculturation of commodities, of the social life of things, he goes beyond the nation. He is thinking here in terms of what later on will be conceptualized as the modern world system but which, from Ortiz's perspective, could be relabeled the modern/colonial world system (Mignolo 2000). Ortiz said all of this in Spanish, a good reason to remain untranslated in the field of knowledge, and a significant case study for understanding translation and epistemology across imperial languages and across imperial and national conflicts. Cuba, remember, emerged as a nation after the imperial war between the United States and Spain. From the end of the eighteenth century on, knowledge production has been translated from English to Spanish, which remained a language for the consumption of knowledge in hegemonic imperial languages rather than for knowledge production sustainable transnationally, across the internal and external borders of the modern/colonial world system.

But let us return to Ortiz's worldly concept of transculturation. Tobacco reached the Christian world along with the revolutions of the Renaissance and the Reformation, when the Middle Ages were crumbling and the modern epoch, with its rationalism, was beginning. One might say that reason, starved and benumbed by theology, to revive and free itself, needed the help of some harmless stimulant that should not intoxicate it with enthusiasm and then stupefy it with illusions and bestiality, as happens with the old alcoholic drinks that lead to drunkenness. For this, to help sick reason, tobacco came from the Americas, and with it came chocolate. From Abyssinia and Arabia, at about the same time, came coffee. And tea made its appearance from the Far East. Nicotine, theobromine, caffeine, and theine—these four alkaloids were put at the service of humanity to make reason more alert (Ortiz 1995 [1940], 206–07).

Following Ortiz, transculturation is at work in the social life of things, and it works in both directions. It trans-lates objects that transform modes of being and thinking, which at the same time transform the "original" uses and life of the object, like the transculturation of African drums when they got to Cuba, which Ortiz wrote about later in life. Now in neither case was Ortiz translating languages from distant cultures; rather, he was thinking transculturation as a world process that made Cuba what it was, as a nation, in the first half of the twentieth century. In this sense, he was thinking in terms of the larger picture of the modern world system: in the sixteenth century, a new commercial circuit was created that linked Cuba, the Mediterranean, and the Atlantic. This commercial circuit created the conditions for the slave trade from Africa and provided—among other things—the foundation for Cuba's demographic profile.

Ortiz was writing from a position of suspension between two contradictory frames of reference. The demand of scientific anthropology was centered on objectivity, rationality, and masculinity—prerequisites that were opposed to the feminine-identified space and genre of Ortiz's writing. If Latin America, as the designated object of study, intervenes to be heard, "translating" itself onto itself to produce anthropological knowledge, it poses the non-subject as subject. Ortiz advocates rationality and objectivity, free of interests and emotions such as "enthusiasm," but he writes the *Counterpoint* from the perspective of culture and literature, the feminine-identified genre, to launch a contribution to knowledge that entails a different take by a new subject of knowledge. To gain admittance, however, he would have to successfully question the location of knowledge production and the claim to a universal scientific objectivity. This is not possible for Ortiz, nor is there a global context that would support such a translation. In this sense, he is still not at the point where a mutual cross-fertilization with Afro-Cuban intellectuals will be possible and bring the results we find in the Zapatistas.

TRANSLATION FROM THE BORDERS, TRANSCULTURATION ON THE BORDERS

How does the change of direction in translation/transculturation from a Zapatista perspective become possible? What makes the Zapatista discourse forceful in the "war of interpretation"? We argue that the global situation at the end of the twentieth century witnessed a certain preparation of the terrain significantly different from the conditions of possibility in the sixteenth century, and even from those at the time of Ortiz's reflections on transculturation. The Zapatistas allow for a conceptualization of indigenous knowledge as sustainable knowledge, intersecting the knowing power of colonial languages and epistemology. That intersection is already a translation/transculturation inscribed in the heart of the colonial difference, revealing the coloniality of power. The sixteenth century provided a model for the subalternization of knowledge based on establishing hierarchical dichotomies, then reconverted after the eighteenth century and inscribed upon the nation-state ideology. At the end of the twentieth century, we witnessed a desubalternization or, if you wish, a decolonization of knowledge that placed translation/transculturation in a different epistemological level and structure of power. That some translations/transculturations are no longer reproducing the coloniality of power and colonial difference is perhaps not entirely new. The Zapatistas, however, are acting from the colonial difference itself, which explains one of their famous dictums: "Because we are all equal, we have the right to be different," as we have already mentioned but find useful to repeat here. As we have seen, at the immediate and local level, the translation of Amerindian knowledge becomes a matter of urgency, both in terms of physical survival and the survival of revolutionary potential. In this process, it transforms at least some of the blind spots in Marxist–Leninist revolutionary ideals and brings to light their limitations. Border thinking emerges here not as a representation of anything or as a happy hybrid surrounded by repressive purity but as a place of epistemic and political confrontation with the neoliberal thinking of the state. At the same time, border thinking undoes the dichotomies that sustained the modern/colonial world system and its hegemonic epistemology. It is precisely here that the Zapatistas' theoretical revolution is located: where the colonial difference emerges as the locus for the epistemic potential of border thinking, and where translation/transculturation has to be remapped.

Our notion of border thinking is here related to Gloria Anzaldúa's exploration of consciousness and borderlands. In the chapter "La conciencia de la mestiza," Anzaldúa (1987) wrote:

> In a constant state of mental nepantlism, an Aztec word meaning torn between ways, la mestiza is a product of the transfer of the cultural and spiritual values of one group to another. Being tricultural, monolingual, bilingual or multilingual, speaking a patois, and in a state of perpetual transition, the mestiza faces the dilemma of the mixed breed: which collectivity does the daughter of a dark-skinned mother listen to? (ibid., 25)

In this paragraph Anzaldúa addresses several crucial problems. She proposes to think identity as a cultural product. Her references to bodily experience rooted in biological features ("the mixed breed," "the daughter of a dark-skinned mother") do not imply that Anzaldúa is assuming biological determinism; rather, she is allowing for its cultural effects. She insists that the transformation from racism as a religious difference in the sixteenth century to racism as a biological difference in the nineteenth century was based on the physical differences among people around the planet, and that they continue to affect the way people are perceived, categorized, and treated. Identity, for Anzaldúa, is at once a state as well as a movement. It is a state of being in a border-space, a place where different cultural values intersect. But it also is a movement between cultural places, "a state of perpetual transition," where differing values achieve hegemony. Identity thus becomes a shifting, a movement between the meanings attached to biological characteristics, between the cultural values prescribed by differing groups and between the contradictions inherent in these values and created precisely by their intersection. "Nepantlism" is neither a harmonious synthesis nor a happy hybridity. It means being "torn between ways," and it implies the colonial difference. Border thinking as a new perspective to think translation/transculturation is precisely this double consciousness from a subaltern perspective in confrontation with hegemony.

Most importantly, Anzaldúa asserts that the self also makes choices about how and what to accept of these values that tear between ways. The choice arises from an act of listening, but it is not only listening; it is a need for translation, both in a direct and in a metaphorical sense, that opens options. Anzaldúa emphasizes that it is not sufficient to engage in a counterculture, since "reaction is limited by, and dependent on, what it is reacting against" (78). In a border-space (or borderland) of multiple intersections (Chicano, working class, academic, female, lesbian, etc.), the counterreaction in itself leaves things unresolved; there is no one place in which to be against all of these different cultural values. Anzaldúa herself asserts that a crucial component must be "tolerance for ambiguity," a third element that is "greater than the sum of its severed parts"; this is what she terms "mestiza consciousness." Mapping out the way to this new consciousness, Anzaldúa frames a progression: examining the cultural traditions available to her, "bote lo que no vale" (throw out what is not useful) but "aguarda el juicio, hondo y enraizado, de la gente antigua" (guard the profound and rooted judgment of the ancient people). In English, Anzaldúa concludes with the need to "reinterpret" history, using new symbols that become available by making herself "vulnerable to foreign ways of seeing and thinking." Here is the act of translation in a metaphorical sense. It is never literal—elements get lost on the way—but most importantly it is allowing the foreign way to make itself visible in the known. It is a call to traditions and other ways of knowing in order to inscribe them in the present and thus to transform them and the dominant and hegemonic epistemic space.

In *Borderlands/La Frontera* (1987), Anzaldúa begins this task by retelling, "translating" Chicano history (itself a product of the civil rights movement and the forging of a communal identity among the heterogeneity of Mexican Americans) by letting it become infused with feminist perspectives. She translates pre-Colombian history, against the dominant Mexican nation-making version that became famous through Octavio Paz's *Labyrinth of Solitude*, by inserting both Chicano and, again, feminist perspectives. She does not discard any of the "identifications" that are only partially available to her but uses them with and against each other to construct a concept of identity that seeks to go beyond biological fixation, constructivist disembodiment, and harmonious homogeneity. It is a space for ambiguity in constant transition that "translates" (in order to make sense in a new value system) that cultural baggage that seeks to define and fix her. Translation is thus tied intimately to the opening up and listening of the translator. It is not the attempt to "translate to Anglos, Mexicans and Latinos, apology blurting out of our mouths at every step," but an offering of a different reading to those willing to translate for themselves. Feminist rewriting is crucial to this translation, but its knowledge is not rooted in Western discourse alone. Similarly, Ana María and Comandante Ramona are reworking Maya "identity" by translating "feminism": a translation going from Mexico (itself already a reworking, a constant negotiation of "white" feminism) to Amerindian languages and back into Spanish, where the CCRI-CG becomes "feminist" both in person and in discourse.[19]

Thinking translation/transculturation from the perspective of the Zapatistas makes clear that the war of interpretation being waged at the national level in Mexico can no longer be contained by the boundaries of a nation-state. If the government and its media seek to codify the indigenous people as primitive or infantile, they base themselves on a traditional/colonial translation that, moreover, anachronistically reiterates masculinity as a requirement for citizenship: an obvious Enlightenment framing that gathers children, women, the insane, and (Europe's) racial Others into the group lacking this masculinity. But the Zapatista discourse reverberates with developments at a supranational level that cannot be isolated from thinking in Mexico itself.

Border-spaces bring new perspectives beyond a binary thinking that has been saturated with gender attributes. Feminist discourses themselves have gained purchase in the production of knowledge, making it harder to exclude Amerindian discourse on the basis of an equation of geographical stasis (femininity) with rural and indigenous populations.

If Guatemalan Rigoberta Menchú was awarded the Nobel Prize in 1992, Amerindian thinking has been valorized at least to a certain degree, since we shall be reading more than a "peace" manifesto. If testimonio as a narrative genre (as a means of transporting/translating subaltern voices) emancipates itself from ethnography and becomes a challenge to the disciplines of literature and history, it may still be allocated within the poetic realm. But on its borders, it is now breaking open the

dichotomies of fiction and science, of Self and Other, toward a continuity of knowledge and memory, opening up not only the directionalities
of translation but also writing as its genre. Marcos emphasizes that the
first communities that the guerilla entered into contact with (in the second half of the 1980s) were "the most isolated" (1997, 151). With this
he implies that traditional knowledge was well preserved. However, the
Lacandon forest constitutes a place of migration, deeply heterogeneous
(Solano and Franco 1996). It may well be understood as a "borderlands" (Anzaldúa 1987) that precisely enables the processes of translation and the elaboration of a new transculturated cosmo-vision. This
contradiction points to a tension that Marcos is still partially caught in.
The terrain on which indigenous voices are heard/understood is still
informed by a need for authenticity on the part of the West, a need that
indigenous peoples cater to while simultaneously undoing it.

As we elaborated on earlier, the Zapatistas are speaking from a
feminine-identified space, but they are making contributions to public
discourse, both in the language of violence (a-rational) and in the language of poetics (literary), as well as in terms of political resolutions (a
public language). They are translating/transculturating Western languages into Amerindian knowledge and enunciating it back in Spanish
(and English and German translations) at a global audience. They are
profoundly undoing the binaries at the base of their subalternity, creating border-spaces for translation/transculturation from the epistemic
potential of the colonial difference. They are at the other end of the spectrum, so to speak, from early missionaries in the New World and in
China. There is a proliferation of the border-spaces to which we have
referred, which has been contributing to a further undoing of the binaries underlying the anchoring of translation in area studies.

The significance of this view on translation/transculturation lies in
the following: if Western concepts are transformed and integrated into
Amerindian cosmologies, it becomes possible to be both Amerindian
and always already a protagonist of history (such as Rigoberta
Menchú), but also Amerindian and revolutionary, local and regional,
ultimately Amerindian and powerful, thus breaking a powerful semantic attachment between power and masculinity, itself created and maintained within the colonial difference and the coloniality of power.

The colonial difference in the modern/colonial world is the location of cosmologies in conflict articulated by the coloniality of power.
Thus the concept of translation/transculturation that we are developing
here is related to borders established by the colonial difference. Our con-

ceptualization runs contrary to the concept of translation/transcultura-tion generally known and defined in the territorial internal domain of empires (translations, say, between English and Spanish), as well as to the one direction/translation on the external borders of the modern/colonial world system where the colonial difference operates (translations, say, between English and Hindi, English and Arabic, and English and Chinese, or, if you prefer, between Spanish and Aymara or Nahuatl). The coloniality of power structures the colonial difference in the external borders. Imperial conflicts within modernity structure the internal borders of the modern world system. Translation/transcultura-tion in one or another terrain is indeed, to use a common expression, a different ball game.

We now can emphasize that the translators emerge out of border-spaces where contact has already been taking place without subsuming the actors to the tale of integration (translation/transculturation as acculturation), whether this contact be the quincentennial relations between Spaniards, Mexican Creoles, and mestizos in the modern world order or the more recent national conflict between Mexico and the United States, formalized in 1848 by the Guadelupe–Hidalgo treaty and the drastic relocations of the national frontiers. In both cases, the Zap-atistas and the emergence of a Chicano/a consciousness, we face the emergence of a border-space that rearticulates the colonial difference from a subaltern position and makes the new kind of translation/tran-sculturation possible. It creates experiences that open up new ways of thinking, not as inescapably or necessarily so but as possibilities (Moya 1997). The discourses emerging from the Lacandon reverberate with the voices/challenges issued from other borderlands that together constitute the broader ground for the epistemological impact of translation/tran-sculturation on Zapatista terms.

TRANSLATION/TRANSCULTURATION
AND DISCIPLINARY KNOWLEDGE

The anthropological work that consists of "studying" Aymara or Quechua communities, that is, translation from Aymara and Quechua into Spanish, is already an interesting case because the three languages are alive and well as languages of the nation, although only Spanish is recognized as the offi-cial language of the nation-state. But not only that—the emergence of an Amerindian intellectual community in academia complicates issues further.

It is here that—at least as a projection toward the future—the Zapatistas' theoretical revolution begins to make sense, since it becomes a model both for academic-institutional work and for theoretical production. It is not only a communication between peasants and scientists but the communication between different versions of intellectual knowledge, translating and transculturating each other.[20] The "disadvantage" of epistemic subaltern languages—languages that are not "sustainable" from the perspective of the production of knowledge—began to offer an epistemological potential unfamiliar and strange to the epistemic/hegemonic languages, and that, precisely, is one of the aspects that we tried to underline in the Zapatistas' theoretical revolution that is related to translation and transculturation (not to cultural translation), which we have explored in this chapter. In all of these cases, including the emergence of Amerindian intellectuals (of which the Workshop for Oral History in Bolivia has been a very important institutional site), translation and transculturation as epistemic and political practice are moving beyond area studies and beyond the modern/imperial versions of translation/transculturation. There is a geohistorical sequence that shall be displaced, and that is the following:

1. translation of Amerindian languages into Spanish in building "Occidentalism";

2. the translation of Arabic, Hindi, or Chinese into English and French—the second phase of the modern world system, building "Orientalism"; and,

3. area studies and the rise of the social sciences and the reconversion of anthropology, in which discipline "became" a crucial issue and which reelaborated epistemic sites in the polar distinction of subject and object of knowledge.

There is still another aspect of translation, transculturation, subaltern languages, and knowledge that we would like to consider in the colonial horizon of modernity, or the colonial horizon of the modern world system. The question here is no longer between Aymara and Spanish or Aymara and English—that is, the anthropologist translating an Amerindian to a colonial language—but the translation between two colonial languages. In this particular case, the issue is further complicated by the transformation of civil society, as well as the configuration of the scholarly community: Spanish, like English an imperial language of the modern world system, is a minority language in the United States.

Therefore, the area studies anthropologist and Andean specialist has a specific issue to resolve with Spanish and the "Hispanic" component in the United States and within the U.S. academic community. On the other hand, if the anthropologist studying the Andes deals with Aymara or Quechua, the question is again Spanish, which gets between the language and culture "studied" (Aymara or Quechua), and the language and culture from which the former is "studied" (English and the U.S. anthropologist). Writing in Spanish for the Andean-speaking community (which includes Aymara and Quechua speakers) is an ethical responsibility and a political imperative—if, of course, the anthropologist is not only interested in appropriating knowledge and information from the culture that is the object of his or her study. Thus Spanish, in this case, is part of the object of study but also part of the language of scholarship. Translation can no longer be understood as a simple question of moving from object language A to subject language B, with all of the implications of the inequality of languages. Rather, translation becomes a trans-languaging, a way of speaking, talking, and thinking in between languages, as the Zapatistas have taught us. This "trans-languaging" is a form of border thinking, opening up new epistemic avenues beyond the complicity between national languages and cultures of scholarship established in the modern/colonial world system and in which the "modern" concept of translation was articulated (Mignolo 2000, chapter 6).

BEYOND DICHOTOMIES: THE FUTURE TERRAIN OF TRANSLATION/TRANSCULTURATION

If we think this configuration from the perspective of emerging Amerindian intellectuals and social movements, the epistemic relations between languages and disciplines as conceived and enacted in anthropology since its inception, we realize that it is undergoing a drastic transformation. Anthropology emerged as a discipline at the moment in which translation was tied to the idea of the unity of language, nation, and literature, on the one hand, and the unity of language, culture, and race, on the other hand. Anthropology, as the discipline in charge of negotiating the external borders of the modern/colonial world system, was at the same time in charge of translating subaltern languages/knowledges to a hegemonic epistemic language/knowledge and of finding the space of transculturation for the anthropologist. This was needed in order to understand the "native culture." The colonial difference was certainly recognized but not enacted. Early Occidentalism and later Orientalism, the visible landscapes of the colonial difference, were remapped in the domain of "culture" rather than "civilization." The reverse process was blocked: there was no expectation that the "native" would become transculturated into the culture of the anthropologist. After all, anthropologists were scientists, not missionaries! Now once the anthropologist is no longer such but also an activist, like Marcos, and Amerindian languages and knowledges are no longer conceived as an object of study but as a space of negotiation and interaction, the situation changes. Translation and transculturation become the space of/for alliances on the borders and from the borders confronted by the territorial epistemology underlying the discourses of the state. Amerindians are placing claims on the nation-state by mobilizing solidarity not only within but also beyond the nation's borders. In this sense, they are bypassing the state at the same time they are affirming the continuous relevance of the state for their struggle. Here there is no longer Marxism against Liberalism as a totality but Amerindian totality in alliance with Marxism, enacted in a border-space, a space in which the gendered imaginary of the colonial difference is negotiated as well. If the difference between Occidental and Other has been conceptualized according to a gender dichotomy (masculine vs. non-masculine), this dichotomy is breaking open as masculinity as a requirement for citizenship, or revolutionary struggle is unhinged. Indeed, gender as the fundamental dichotomy that structures Occidental thought is revealing itself as a construction and an enactment whose properties have been discursively assigned in the process of forming the modern/colonial world system.

Something similar is happening to the ties between language and nation and between language and memory. Language is no longer equivalent to nation as multiple languages and knowledges transculturate, or break open the dichotomy of nation and Other. On the other hand, although language is linked to memory and may shape understanding, this link is not ontologically so. As the appropriation of Spanish by Tojolabal shows us, language in translation also can become the means of transportation for other knowledges and memories. The same may be said for English: English language does not necessarily go with English memory. This presupposition, based on national ideology, is no longer sustainable in a transnational world. Rosario Ferre, writing in English and in Puerto Rico (*The House on the Lagoon*, 1995), filling and transforming English with Spanish memories, is a case in point. So are the claims to indigenous identity by people who no longer speak indigenous languages, such as many of the Paez (Nasa) in Colombia. If English is the hegemonic language in a transnational world, it shall also be the transnational language in which positions of subalternity can be rearticulated. Simultaneously, however, Spanish continues as well, on a regional level, as the means of transnational communication, and indigenous languages are being recuperated through the bilingual educational efforts of indigenous social movements. If networking, information systems, and technoglobalism are shaping the world today, they also are being appropriated by those who work toward social transformation from the perspective of the colonial difference,[21] relocating neoliberal global coloniality from the perspective of subalternity, which is not to say that Ferre is offering the "right answer," but rather that she is contributing to the asking of new questions offering a critique of the national language assumptions upon which modern approaches to translation have been operating.

The theories of translation/transculturation that we foresee are coming from a critical reflection on the colonial difference and seeking to overcome the national-language ideological framework in which translation was conceived, practiced, and theorized in the modern/colonial world. Modern concepts and theories of translation assumed the unity and purity of language and linked it to national culture and national literature, ranking languages through space and subjectivity to arbitrary and sometimes changing associations with binary-gendered imageries. This was one possible scenario. The other was the anthropological translation of non-Western languages and cultures to the main languages of scholarship that were, at the same time, hegemonic imperial and national languages. The future of theories and practices of translation, we surmise, will come from the perspective of coloniality and the colonial difference.

The position we have developed from the theoretical foundations offered by Gloria Anzaldúa's *Borderlands/La Frontera* and by the Zapatistas' conceptualization and enactment of translation/transculturation links translation/transculturation to border thinking from a subaltern perspective. We surmise that this direction will keep gaining ground in the future, as intellectual production is recognized beyond the academe and theories are where you can find them. The possibility of going beyond dichotomies presupposes an-other logic, not only a reconfiguration of the content.

NOTES

1. By Western thought, we mean the geohistorical macro-narrative from Ancient Greece to the current North Atlantic.

2. One could say, for instance, that the logic of Andean thought (e.g., Aymara and Quechua) was dichotomous. However, their logic made them complementary rather than contradictory hierarchical units. See, for example, Estermann 1998. Our argument here will focus on how binary thinking is being shaped in the spaces where different traditions of knowledge and thinking intersect. In this sense, the dissolution of binary thinking may affect Amerindian conceptions as well.

3. Robinson 1997 is a recent attempt at reworking this tradition that remains nevertheless within its geopolitical limits. He offers a critical engagement with the latest thinking about translation from postcolonial and feminist perspectives. However, Robinson does not think beyond translation processes pertaining to the written field proper, where the translator also is a publisher. Since his horizon remains within the internal borders of the modern world, translation, for him, remains mainly a business within colonial languages. In the end, translation here remains uncoupled from knowledge and the coloniality of power.

4. In a brief 1998 working paper, Alexandrov, for example, conceives of translation as part of a global communicative network that ties different parts of human culture together. He therefore opens up translation to a global perspective, including nonimperial languages. Nevertheless, he fixes a binary distinction between the Western self and the self in non-Western cultures as he reiterates Eurocentric notions of progress and civilization. According to Alexandrov, only Western conceptions of the self are able to conceive of change as they embody progress. The hybridization of non-Western cultures—that is, what we here refer to as the space of translation/transculturation and the rearticulation of colonial difference—is, for Alexandrov, an adaptation to the forces of Western cultural models. Alternatives will disappear since they are static, according to his reading of cultural psychology.

5. See Huarte de San Juan 1977 [1594]; Vallbona 1992; Mott 1992; Montrose 1991. The medical tradition conceived of basically four different genders, depending on the degree of body heat and amount of bodily fluid. Sudden changes in body heat were understood to produce hermaphrodites by causing the vagina to reverse to the outside.

6. See Harding 1990. For accounts from a North American perspective on how modern science has operated with a similar masculine bias, see Keller and Longino 1996.

7. Deloria's formulation, as the one offered by Lenkersdorf, may sound like a reinscription of Western dualism or the reproduction of the "incommen-

surability" in translating worlds or cosmologies, as Roger Hart (1999) correctly criticizes in J. Gernet's "incommensurablity" thesis on the confrontation of two cosmologies (assuming, of course, that Taoism, Buddhism, and Confucianism are part of the same cosmology or episteme). Our point of engagement, in any case, is not with the incommensurability between cosmologies but with the negotiation across the colonial difference (Hart 1999).

8. See Mignolo 2000 for a detailed account of the term *languaging*.

9. See Estermann 1998 for a similar account of Quechua thinking.

10. See Massey 1994 for the production of gendered spaces; see Schiwy 2000 for the link between gendered spaces, temporalities, and indigenous peoples.

11. See again Robinson 1997; Alexandrov 1998. See also von Flotow 1997 for a feminist critique of translation. See Niranjana 1992 and Liu 1999 for a postcolonial approach to translation. Liu situates the problem of translation in the context of coloniality. She combines linguistics (Saussure) and semiotic theory (Baudrillard) with Marxist notions of exchange value to signal broader contexts of power difference that inform the relations between China and the West. She argues that a theory of translation needs to take colonial contexts into consideration in terms of circumstantial meetings of languages and peoples based on interactive and conflictual processes rather than fixed identities. The centrality of the concept of exchange value in Liu's argument allows her to emphasize and include in the volume contexts of translation, not only as an exchange of verbal and symbolic concepts but also of material objects—"tokens," as she calls them. The terms seem useful in order to think translation/transculturation as a situated practice that includes various forms of engagement. Other than our explorations of Zapatismo in Mexico, however, Liu (as do most of the articles in her volume) capitalizes on the violence accompanying colonization and colonial relations as well as the cooperation of colonial intellectuals in translating from English to Chinese, as has been the focus of much postcolonial work in the past decades.

12. The term has been offered by Edouard Glissant. For a discussion of its context and significance, see Mignolo 2000, chapter 5.

13. The ideas about base democracy issued from the perspective of the Zapatistas could possibly be brought into communication with attempts to elaborate base democracy in other geopolitical locations and from other memories, as in the case of the Green Party in Germany. It would indeed be interesting to see how issues of populism and popular ethics that are not always desirable (such as the call for the death penalty in Germany) are resolved by the Zapatistas.

14. Such as the misguided biography written by two journalists, one from Spain and the other from France (La Grange and Rico 1998). Mexican sociologist Pablo González Casanova has pointed out the same blindness among the

European left by commenting on the Italian former director of *Il Manifesto*, Rosana Rossanda. Rossanda described Marcos as Leninist and Castrist, adding that Latin American revolutionaries are "Leninist" by definition, almost as a biological or psychological destiny (González Casanova 1998, 33). The colonial difference cuts across and reveals the silence occupied by universal theories, (neo) liberal or (neo) Marxist. Obviously, these theories were aware of the colonial difference, although not recognizing that the colonial difference is an epistemic location, not only a space for expansion of capital and of the proletarian revolution guided from the space occupied by modernity and modern epistemology. Translation and transculturation were caught in the same limitations.

15. See Rojas 1994–1995; Rovira 1997.

16. Cojti expressed this position during his talk at a conference on the relocation of languages, Duke University, spring 1997.

17. Marcos' writings exploit precisely this tension as he disguises a political discourse as magical realism. Nevertheless, his writing consistently escapes this frame: fictional writing mixes with Amerindian knowledge and political declarations that are backed by a mortal war between indigenous peoples, landowners, and the Mexican army in Chiapas.

18. There has already been an interesting discussion in *Current Anthropology* 35:1 (1994) of these issues, provoked by Starn 1994 (comments by Olivia Harris, David Nugent, Stephen Nugent, Benjamin S. Orlove, S. P. Reyna, and Gavin Smith, pp. 27–33; reply by Starn, pp. 33–35). We cannot summarize this discussion here, but we will take it as a reference point to draw on our own knowledge and experiences regarding the issue.

19. Zapatismo offers a new perspective on what may be called feminism. See Rovira 1997.

20. See Hess 1997 for recent approaches in developmentalism that attempt to acknowledge the existence of indigenous knowledge but nevertheless restrict importance at the local level.

21. The use of the Internet by the Zapatistas is of course a case in point, as is the use of video and television by indigenous peoples from Australia to Latin America (Ginsburg 1994; Schiwy 2000).

WORKS CITED

Alexandrov, Vladimir A. 1998. "Lotman's 'Semiosphere' and Varieties of the Self." Working Papers and Pre-Publications, Centro Internazionale di Semiotica e di Linguistica. Serie C 270. Urbino: Università di Urbino.

Anzaldúa, Gloria. 1987. *Borderlands/La Frontera*. San Francisco: Aunt Lute.

Arnold, Denise, D. Jiménez, and Juan de Dios Yapita. 1992. *Hacia un orden andino de las cosas*. La Paz: Hisbol.

Asad, Talal. 1986. "The Concept of Cultural Translation in British Social Anthropology." Pp. 141–64 in *Writing Culture: The Poetics and Politics of Ethnography*, ed. James Clifford and George E. Marcus. Berkeley: University of California Press.

Bouysse-Cassagne, Thérèse, Olivia Harris, Tristan Platt, and Veronica Cereceda, eds. 1987. *Tres reflexiones sobre el pensiamento andino*. La Paz: Hisbol.

Butler, Judith. 1990. *Gender Trouble: Feminism and the Subversion of Identity*. New York: Routledge.

Cheyfitz, Eric. 1991. *The Poetics of Imperialism: Translation and Colonialism from* The Tempest *to* Tarzan. Oxford: Oxford University Press.

Coronil, Fernando. 1995. Introduction to Ortiz, Fernando. 1995 [1940]. *Cuban Counterpoint: Tobacco and Sugar*. Translated by Harriet de Onís. Durham: Duke University Press. ix–lxi.

Deloria, Vine Jr. 1998 [1978]. "Civilization and Isolation." Pp. 135–44 in *For This Land: Writings on Religion in America*, ed. James Treat. New York: Routledge.

EZLN (Ejército Zapatista de Liberación Nacional). 1994. *Documentos y Comunicados*. Vol. 1. Mexico: Grijalbo.

———. 1995. *Documentos y Comunicados*. Vol. 2. Mexico: Grijalbo.

Estermann, Josef. 1998. *La pilosofia andina*. Quito: Abya-Yala.

Ferre, Rosario. 1995. *The House on the Lagoon*. New York: Farrar, Strauss, and Giroux.

Franco, Jean. 1990. *Plotting Women: Gender and Representation in Mexico*. New York: Columbia University Press.

Garg, Pulin K., and Indira J. Parikh. 1995. *Crossroads of Culture: A Study in the Culture of Transience*. New Delhi: Sage Publishing.

Ginsburg, Faye. 1994. "Embedded Aesthetics: Creating a Discursive Space for Indigenous Media." *Cultural Anthropology* 9:3:365–82.

González Casanova, Pablo. 1998. "La Democracia de Todos." Pp. 23–33 in *Democracia sin exclusiones ni excluidos*, ed. Emir Sader. Caracas: Nueva Sociedad.

Harding, Sandra. 1990. "Feminism, Science, and the Anti-Enlightenment Critiques." Pp. 83–106 in *Feminism/Postmodernism*, ed. Linda Nicholson. New York: Routledge.

Harrison, Regina. 1989. *Signs, Songs, and Memory in the Andes: Translating Quechua Language and Culture*. Austin: University of Texas Press.

Hart, Roger. 1999. "Translating the Untranslatable: From Copula to Incommensurable Worlds." Pp. 45–73 in *Tokens of Exchange*, ed. Lydia H. Liu. Durham: Duke University Press.

Havelock, Erick. 1982. *The Literate Revolution in Greece and Its Cultural Consequences*. Princeton: Princeton University Press.

Hess, Carmen. 1997. *Hungry for Hope: On the Cultural and Communicative Dimensions of Development in Highland Ecuador*. London: Intermediate Technology Publications.

Hill Boone, Elizabeth, and Walter D. Mignolo, eds. 1994. *Writing without Word: Alternative Literacies in Mesoamérica and the Andes*. Durham: Duke University Press.

Huarte de San Juan, Juan. 1977 [1594]. *Examen de ingenios para las ciencias. Donde se muestra la diferencia de habilidades que hay en los hombres y el genero de letras que a cada uno responde en particular*. Madrid: Nacional.

Jones, Andrew F. 1999. "The Gramophone in China." Pp. 214–36 in *Tokens of Exchange*, ed. Lydia H. Liu. Durham: Duke University Press.

Keller, Evelyn Fox, and Helen E. Longino. 1996. *Feminism and Science*. Oxford: Oxford University Press.

La Grange, Bertrand de, and Maite Rico. 1998. *Subcomandante Marcos: La genial impostura*. Madrid: El País/Aguilar.

Lenkersdorf, Carlos. 1996. *Los Hombres Verdaderos: Voces y testimonios tojolabales*. Mexico: Siglo XXI.

Liu, Lydia H., ed. 1999. *Tokens of Exchange: The Problem of Translation in Global Circulations*. Durham: Duke University Press.

Marcos, Subcomandante et al. 1997. *El sueño Zapatista. Entrevistas con el subcomandante Marcos, el mayor Moisés y el comandante Tacho*. Edited by Yvon Le Bot and Maurice Najman. Mexico City: Plaza y Janés.

Massey, Doreen. 1994. *Space, Place, and Gender*. Minneapolis: University of Minnesota Press.

Mayor Ana María. 1996. "Discurso Inaugural de la Mayor Ana María en el Primer Encuentro Intercontinental por la Humanidad y contra el Neoliberalismo." *Chiapas* 3:101–05.

Mignolo, Walter D. 1995. *The Darker Side of the Renaissance: Literacy, Territoriality, and Colonization*. Ann Arbor: University of Michigan Press.

———. 1997. "The Zapatistas' Theoretical Revolution: Its Epistemic, Ethic, and Political Consequences." Keynote address at the conference *Comparative Colonialisms: Pre-Industrial Colonial Intersections in Global Perspective*. Binghamton University: Center for Medieval and Renaissance Studies.

———. 2000. *Local Histories/Global Designs: Coloniality, Subaltern Knowledges, and Border Thinking.* Princeton: Princeton University Press.

Mohanty, Chandra Talpade. 1988. "Under Western Eyes: Feminist Scholarship and Colonial Discourse." *Feminist Review* 30:65–78.

Montrose, Louis. 1991. "The Work of Gender in the Discourse of Discovery." *Representations* 33:1–42.

Mott, Luiz. 1992. "As Amazones: um mito e algumas hipotesis." Pp. 33–57 in *America em tempo de conquista*, ed. Rainaldo V. Vainfar. Rio de Janeiro: Jorge Azhar.

Moya, Paula. 1997. "Postmodernism, 'Realism,' and the Politics of Identity: Cherrie Moraga and Chicana Feminism." Pp. 125–50 in *Feminist Genealogies, Colonial Legacies, Democratic Futures*, ed. Chandra Talpade Mohanty and M. Jacqui Alexander. Bloomington: Indiana University Press.

Niranjana, Tejaswini. 1992. *Siting Translation: History, Post-Structuralism, and the Colonial Context.* Berkeley: University of California Press.

Ortiz, Fernando. 1995 [1940]. *Cuban Counterpoint: Tobacco and Sugar.* Translated by Harriet de Onís. Durham: Duke University Press.

Quijano, Anibal. 1998. "The Colonial Nature of Power and Latin America's Cultural Experience." In *Sociology in Latin America*, ed. Roberto Briceño-León and Heinz R. Sonntag. Montreal: Service de l'information et des relations publiques de l'UQAM.

Quijano, Anibal, and Immanuel Wallerstein. 1992. "Americanity As a Concept, or the Americas in the Modern World-System." *International Social Science Journal* 44:4 (November): 549–58.

Rappaport, Joanne. 1998. *The Politics of Memory: Native Historical Interpretation in the Colombian Andes.* Durham: Duke University Press.

Rengifo Vásquez, Grimaldo. 1998. "Education in the Modern West and in Andean Culture." Pp. 172–92 in *The Spirit of Regeneration: Andean Culture Confronting Western Notions of Development*, ed. Frédérique Apffel-Martin, with PRATEC (Proyecto Campesino de Tecnologías Campesinas). London: Zed Books.

Robinson, Douglas. 1997. *What Is Translation?* Ohio: Kent State University Press.

Rojas, Rosa, ed. 1994–1995. *Chiapas, y las mujeres qué?* 2 vols. Mexico City: Ediciones la correa feminista.

Rovira, Guiomar. 1997. *Mujeres de maíz.* Mexico City: Ediciones Era.

Salomon, Frank, and George L. Urioste, trans. 1991. *The Huarochirí Manuscript: A Testament of Ancient and Colonial Andean Religion.* Austin: University of Texas Press.

Schiwy, Freya. 2000. "Camerografos indigenas, ecoturistas y la naturaleza. El papel del género sexual en las geopolíticas del conocimiento." Pp. 263–83 in *La reestructuración de las ciencas sociales en América Latina*, ed. Santiago Castro-Gomez. Bogota: Centro Editorial Javeriano.

Solano, Xochitl Leyva, and Gabriel Ascencio Franco. 1996. *Lacandonia al Filo del Agua*. Mexico City: Centro de Investigaciones y Estudios Superiores en Antropologia Social.

Starn, Orin. 1994. "Rethinking the Politics of Anthropology: The Case of the Andes." *Current Anthropology* 35:1:13–38.

Vallbona, Rima de, ed. 1992. *Vida I sucesos de la monja alferez. Autobiografia atribuida a Doña Catalina de Erauso*. Tempe: Arizona State University Center for Latin American Studies.

von Flotow, Luise. 1997. *Translation and Gender: Translating in the "Era of Feminism."* Manchester, England, and Ottawa: St. Jerome and University of Ottawa Press.

CONCLUSION

THE UNFORESEEABLE
DIVERSITY OF THE WORLD

EDOUARD GLISSANT
(translated by Haun Saussy)

When we look around us—at the world realized in its totality, only now so stunningly given to our awareness—we see and feel its extraordinary diversity, which changes and inspires us.

If we say that we write, henceforth, in the presence of all the world's languages, all of them, leaving none out of consideration (one of the most unusual motifs of our imaginative world), if we rediscover the fact that we can change through exchange with others, without losing ourselves or our true nature, then we are able to glimpse what I would like to call worldness, which is our common condition today.

To *glimpse* that condition, because this earthly totality that has now come to pass suffers from a radical absence, the absence of our consent. Even while we of the human community experience this condition, we remain viscerally attached to the origins of the histories of our particular communities, our cultures, peoples, or nations. And surely we are right to maintain these attachments, since no one lives suspended in the air, and since we must give a voice to our own place. But I also must put this place of mine in relation to all the places of the world.

Worldness is exactly what we all have in common today: the dimension I find myself inhabiting and the relation we may well lose ourselves in.

The wretched other side of worldness is what is called globalization or the global market: reduction to the bare basics, the rush to the bottom, standardization, the imposition of multinational corporations with their ethos of bestial (or all too human) profit, circles whose circumference is everywhere and whose center is nowhere.

What I would like to tell you is that we cannot really see, understand, or contest the ravages of this globalization in us and around us unless we activate the leaven of our worldness.

Whether we get there through the intimate, inward, introverted route, or whether we throw ourselves in gales and breakers across the landscapes of the world, whether we ceaselessly repeat our single theme or venture into another's, whether we plot our stories or investigate chaos in all of its grandeur, the fact is that we meet ourselves in this fermentation.

The lesson is that a plural, multiplying, fragmented identity is no longer given or thought as a lack of identity but rather as a huge opening and new opportunity of breaking open closed gates.

What we would call a healthy Excess is just this: an astonishing expansion of personal or collective identity throughout the field of the world's unforeseeable variations.

Moreover, we can no longer lay claim to any sort of model in the collective estimation of measure and excess. What I find right and measured is excessive for another, and vice versa. For us, for example, the gradual unfolding of a Nô play takes a great effort to follow, and I know few people unfamiliar with Africa or the Caribbean who could endure a whole night of piercing and ceaseless drumming.

What I am calling the measure of time is no different. We tumble down the rapids of time, we sink into gulfs of memory, we crawl forth in the pale light of our theories, which are none other than the twitching of our juxtaposed sensibilities. For all of these reasons, the world totality never presents itself to us in a total or totalitarian fashion. I leap over the boulders in my time, while others float placidly down their time as down a river; I force my memory to retain and reorganize what has long since broken up into a collection of absences, while others are barely able to live with the burden of a too-heavy, too-vividly-present memory; I build up stone by stone my wavering, ambivalent, or fragile vision of this worldness, that is, I act as the theoretician or anthropologist of myself, while others fashion and try to manage the world system. But we are all bound to this unbounded excess, wherein we remain and where we go.

How can anyone deny that this is common to all of us: atavistic cultures that once generated a myth of the world's creation, a Genesis buried in the mists of time, and composite cultures that emerged from the movement of history and therefore find themselves naturally inclined to sharing, to exchange, to change?

Among the myths that have plotted the path toward historical awareness, we must distinguish between founding myths and another class of myths that elucidate, that offer underground explanations, that create contacts (and perhaps also endless self-reflection) among the various elements of a given culture's social structure.

The sole purpose of founding myths is to consecrate the presence of a community on a territory, by establishing this presence, this present, in a legitimate line of descent from a Genesis or an act of world creation. Consciously or not, the founding myth gives confidence in the seamless continuity of this inheritance and thereupon authorizes the community it addresses to consider its territory as being absolutely its own. As an extension of the principle of legitimacy, it may be that, in passing from myth to historical consciousness, the community decides that it is its given right to extend the limits of its territory. That was one of the founding principles of colonial expansion; colonialism thus appeared to be strongly tied to the idea of universality, that is, to the idea of the general legitimation of an absolute that had its first beginnings in a chosen particular. You can now see why it is important that the founding myth should be based on a Genesis, should demand two motors (inheritance and legitimacy, which guarantee the force of legitimation), and why it should suppose a single end, the universal legitimation of presence. Is this not the model of the working of what people call history with a big H, whatever may be the nature of the philosophy that underwrites it?

History with a big H is really the daughter of the Founding Myth and on the path that leads to history myth will be accompanied, then hidden, and finally replaced by myths that are elucidating, explicative, or self-referring, or by those stories and tales that look forward to the history of the future; finally, it will be accompanied by stories, poems, and reflective texts that will proclaim, sing, or silently meditate on History.

Wherever founding myths appear, in what I am calling atavistic cultures, the notion of identity grows up around the axis of filiation and legitimacy, which gives no room to the Other as a participant.

One may go on to suppose that though this process orality will come to be thought of ontologically, so that it naturally comes to its conclusion in that realization of the absolute that will be performed by writing and scripture.

What will historical conscience then be if not the generalized sentiment of a mission to be performed, a family tree to maintain, a legitimacy to be kept pure, a territory to expand?

In those societies where no founding myth functions, unless it is a borrowed one, and by these I mean composite societies brought together by creolization—here the notion of identity will be built up on the basis of Relation, where the Other is understood and implicitly included.

Such cultures begin directly with storytelling, and storytelling is, paradoxically, full of detours. What storytelling causes to make a detour is the tendency to link oneself to a Genesis, the inflexibility of pedigree, the long shadow of basic legitimacies. And when the orality of storytelling develops into the fixedness of writing, as it has done in the Caribbean and in Latin America, it clings to this star-patterned detour that takes writing off into a different direction and shapes narrative into a different configuration from which ontological absolutes are absent.

What will historical consciousness be, then, if not the chaotic pulsing toward these meetings of all histories, none of which can claim (due to the inherent qualities of chaos) to have an absolute legitimacy?

We must reconcile the writing of myth and the writing of storytelling, the memory of Genesis and the foreknowledge of relationship, and that is no easy task. But what other task can compete with this in beauty?

I call creolization the meeting, interference, shock, harmonies, and disharmonies between the cultures of the world, in the realized totality of the earth world.

Creolization has the following characteristics: the lightning speed of interaction among its elements; the "awareness of awareness" thus provoked in us; the reevaluation of the various elements brought into contact (for creolization has no presupposed scale of values); and unforeseeable results. Creolization is not a simple crossbreeding that would produce easily anticipated syntheses.

There are many examples of creolization. I point out that they take shape and develop better in archipelagos than on continents.

My proposition is that today the whole world is becoming an archipelago and becoming creolized.

In atavistic societies, where creolization happened so long ago the memory of it is replaced by myths, the community arms itself with a set of stories confirming the legitimacy of their relation to the land they occupy. In composite cultures, creolization is happening before our eyes.

These cultures do not lead to a creation of the world; they do not have such a foundation myth. They begin in what I call a digenesis.

But it is noticeable that composite cultures tend to become atavistic, that is, they aspire to the permanence and the long historical past that every culture seems to need before it can have the energy and boldness to express itself. National liberation struggles, which demand an ardent certainty about who and what one is, encourage this process.

Inversely, atavistic cultures tend to become creole, that is, they tend to question (or dramatically defend) their legitimacy. A generalized creolization pushes them to do this.

This leads to two concepts of identity that I have tried to present through the images of the solitary root and of the rhizome (after Deleuze and Guattari).

European and Occidental cultures have spread through the world a sublime and fatal conception of identity as a sole and an exclusive root. That single root plants itself in a soil that thus becomes territory.

A notion of identity as a rhizome that goes to meet other roots is today alive in all composite cultures. In this way, what was territory becomes earth once again.

As long as the earth totality had not been realized, as long as there were still countries to be discovered, this impulse to expand one's territory seemed to be an ontological necessity for the peoples and cultures that thought it their job to discover and rule the word. And they did.

Today, in the physically realized world whole, where creolization has replaced the impulse to expand terrain and the legitimization of conquest, the poetics of relationship allows us to grasp the difference between an earth (the unavoidable place of every being) and a territory (the traditional and now infertile revendication of Being).

When I say that our world is creolizing, that the cultures of present-day humanity are reacting on one another, with this startling power of instantaneous things, with the total awareness that we have of it all, I also and incessantly mean to say that this creolization, forming novel connections, will bear unforeseeable results. Creolization is not a synthesis. Segalen long ago warned us away from "boring syntheses." Creolization is not the simple mechanics of a crude mixture of distinct things, but it goes much farther—what it creates is new, unheard-of, and unexpected.

This is what is difficult for us to imagine and accept, for we sense there a mutation out of control. We leave behind the formerly fertile certainties of Being and enter into the variability of what is. The permanence of being, now so mortal, yields to the movement and change of what is. Essence fades away in the process. But can one endure a perpetual becoming? Do we not need the reassurance of anchoring our identity in a territory, a law, a founding myth? That question bears on literature and poetry—it is the question of measure and excess.

The question becomes even more involved if one reflects on the concrete state of the world, where genocides and oppressions continue, where cultures are threatened, negated, or ravaged in their very identity. How can one suggest that an oppressed community throw itself into a perpetual becoming, an infinite process of change? How would one inspire a homeless black American who inhabits a fortress of cardboard on the frozen pavements of New York to stand up for creolization? His only recourse must be to plant himself more deeply in the particular form of identity that has determined his oppressed condition. It may be the cruelest effect of the hell he is forced to live in that he is cut off from affirming his share in the world totality and its movement.

Just as there were those who benefited from the privileges of the philosophy of Being or the privileges of writing (the transcribed word of a god and the mark of his law), just as some have benefited from technology, which is perhaps the inscription of writing in the materiality of the things of this world, so too might there be beneficiaries of creolization, certain cultures that might be better placed to enjoy its most extreme possibilities? Let us beware of underrating the peoples of the world.

Let me repeat (for repetition is one modern form of knowledge), creolization is neither a mechanism nor a system. It conceives and receives those who still need an anchor in their present time and place; it even conceives those who keep themselves tightly closed up, every Switzerland that stands aloof from the noise of the world, but creolization opens for everyone the unfenced archipelago of the world totality. I see a sign of this in the fact that certain oppressed communities, such as the Amerindians of Chiapas in Mexico or the Gypsies of the former Yugoslavia, are motivated to fight this oppression in the name of an openness, a relation, an intertwining that would be more just and balanced.

The question of Being is no longer asked in the profitable solitude to which the thought of the Universal has shrunk. The Universal has toppled into, and is now jostled by, Diversity.

This means that the question of Being no longer automatically supposes its own legitimacy, being disoriented by the onslaughts of its concurrent diversities.

In other words, it is no longer the old universal Law that makes the rule but rather the piling up of Relations. This should be clear enough from the play of current international politics where law, once again, must be gradually and with difficulty defined and then upheld by the pressure of monolithically organized armed forces, lined up against subversive forces that are slowly worn away.

The constitution of these new Laws, or Law, is the very sign of the obsolescence of the old universal Law, which never needed to justify its nearly ontological extension. The new Law is purely institutional, armed, which means that it no longer uses cunning, no longer hides, and hardly sublimates at all. In any case, the question of Being has been evacuated from it.

It dawns on us, through the drama of multiple hegemonies, that the generalizing and *a priori* Universal has broken down, and that What Is bursts forth to the great surprise of the embattled permanence of Being.

A trace presupposes and bears not the thought of Being but the meandering of what is. Today the avenue of history is barricaded with obscure turnings, apparent new beginnings wherein the peoples and communities that gave birth to the idea of History can churn their uncertainties.

They have confronted not merely the Other, the different, but what is harder still, the turbulence of empty space. The white spaces on the maps are now covered over with darkness. That has broken permanently the absolute of history, which was primarily a project and projection anyway. Since then, history comes apart in its very concept, while it continues repeating its various "returns"—the return of identity politics, the nation, fundamental belief—the more obsolete, the more narrowly sectarian.

In contrast to this retreat to old paths, the trace is the trembling shoot of what is always new. What the trace gives a glimpse of is not virgin land, a virgin forest, as the discoverers wildly fantasized it. To tell the truth, the trace does not go to complete totality; it allows the conception of what cannot be said. Permanent novelty is not the last thing to be discovered before the totality can be made whole; it is what needs to be made yet more fragile in order truly to scatter totality, or more accurately, to accomplish it at last.

We find that the place where we live and from which we speak can no longer be extracted from this mass of energy, which is completely in motion for us, in the world totality. The "exclusive section" that might be our place would leave us unable to express its exclusivity if we turned it into exclusion. Then we would be able to conceive of a totality that would approximate totalitarianism. No. We establish relation.

And not through an abstraction or idealization of everything, as if we had discovered in our own place the reflection of a universal and profitable benefactor. We have sworn that off as well. The ambition of extracting a universal from a particular no longer moves us. The very matter of all of those places and the minute or infinite detail and the inspiring combination of all their particularities ought to be set down. To write is to awaken the savor of the world.

The idea of the world is not enough. A literature about the idea of the world may be clever, ingenious, may seem to have "seen" the whole (this is, for example, what in English is known as world literature), but it will ramble on in our places and never amount to more than ingenious destructuration and pale recomposition. The idea of the world ought to be founded on the imagination of the world, intertwined poetics that would allow me to guess how my place connects to other places, adventures outside without moving, and carries me with it in its immobile movement.

Fragments of poetry are manifest, left behind people who came to sing their languages, perhaps before they disappeared from the rough treatment of the international sabirs. For all of these languages of orality—disregarded and imprisoned—the adventure is only beginning. There are traps to avoid—fixation, transcription—but also the inscription of these languages into a social formation that may tend (or be forced to tend) toward the use of a major communicative language. The world's diversity needs the world's languages.

The regained glory of oral literatures has not come to replace written records but to change their order. Writing amounts to opening oneself up to the world without dispersing or diluting oneself, and as well to harness the powers of orality that are so good for expressing the diversity of all things—repetition, restatements, circular speech, spiral-formed cries, voices that break.

What is a novel? What is a poem? We no longer think of the story as the natural form of writing. History as told and learned was not so long ago the twin of history used to make a dominant history. The latter was the guarantee of the former, for the Occidental peoples, and the former was the legitimate brilliance of the latter. Something remains of this solidarity in the vogue for popular fiction in Europe and in the United States. Other scores tempt us. The explosion of the world totality and the eruption of audio-visual techniques have opened the field to an infinite variety of possible genres that we cannot even imagine. In the meantime, the poetics of the world combine genres and reinvent them.

What might writing mean today? It is not just writing histories to amuse or move people; it may be, above all, a matter of looking for the frail but trustworthy link between the wild diversity of the world and the balance and knowledge we desire to have. Every day the world knocks us off balance, and we must try to find our place here. The artist and writer help us in this. Their work bears the marks of this vocation.

First of all, they should be sensitive to the totality of the world and to everything we owe to modernity: the knowledge of other civilizations that enriches our own; the techniques of orality that are making their way into writing; the knowledge of foreign languages, which bends and changes our ways of using our native language. Herein is an enormous magma of possibilities for the artist and writer, making it hard to follow a path and to maintain a career.

This diversity of the world causes the writer to gradually give up the old division of literature into genres, which formerly resulted in the unfolding of so many masterpieces. Readers, too, enjoy these mixed genres—novels that are historical essays, biographies that are exact and scrupulous but that resemble novels, monographs in natural science or astrophysics or marine biology that can be read as poems or meditations or adventure stories. For the time being, the poetics that have come forth delight in combining genres, which is one way to reinvent them.

In truth, we write in a wild and hurried way, as befits the pace of this world and the rapidity of technical progress, in the flux of which we are plunged. It may be that the writer is like an exploiter of the Internet and its waves of information. But we write in a placid, quiet way too, as when the writer, without ever ceasing to be a part of the world's movement, tries to become solitary, for instance, like a reader isolated in his house. In this case, the writer brings all of the patience he can to his work, because he sees in front of him the book he will finish, and he cannot imagine that humanity will not need it some day.

About the Contributors

Emily Apter is Chair of the Department of Comparative Literature and Professor of French and Francophone Studies at the University of California at Los Angeles. Her publications include *Continental Drift: From National Characters to Virtual Subjects* (1999) and *Fetishism As Cultural Discourse* (co-edited with William Pietz, 1993). A book entitled *The Translation Zone: Language Wars and Literary Politics*, is in progress, as is a volume, *Decadence and Modernity Around 1900*. Apter also is the editor of a book series, *Translation/Transnation*, and she serves on the editorial boards of *PMLA, Comparative Literature, October, Signs,* and *Emergences*.

Ali Behdad is an associate professor of English and comparative literature at the University of California at Los Angeles. He published *Belated Travelers: Orientalism in the Age of Colonial Dissolution* in 1994, and his *The Forgetful Nation: Reflections on Immigration and Cultural Identity in the United States* is forthcoming. He has published many articles and essays and edited the special issue of *L'Esprit Créateur*, entitled *Orientalism beyond "Orientalism"* (1994).

Arif Dirlik is Knight Professor of Social Science and Professor of History and Anthropology at the University of Oregon. His recent publications include *Postmodernity's Histories* (2000), *The Postcolonial Aura: Third World Criticism in the Age of Global Capitalism* (1997), and *After the Revolution: Waking to Global Capitalism* (1994). He is also the editor of *Postmodernism and China* (2000, with Zhang Xudong), *History after the Three Worlds* (2000, with Vinay Bahl and Peter Gran), and *Places and Politics in an Age of Globalization* (2001, with Roxann Prazniak).

Emmanuel Chukwudi Eze is a visiting professor in the Department of Philosophy, Mount Holyoke College. He previously taught at the University of Nigeria, Nsukka, and at Bucknell University. He is the author of *Achieving Our Humanity: The Idea of the Postracial Future* (2001), and he has edited *African Philosophy: An Anthology* (1998), *Postcolonial African Philosophy: A Critical Reader* (1997), and *Race and the Enlightenment* (1997). Eze is the editor of the journal *Philosophia Africana* and an elected member of the American Philosophical Association's Committee on Blacks in Philosophy (1997–2001).

Edouard Glissant is currently a distinguished professor at the City University of New York Graduate Center and vice president of the Writers' International Parliament. His influential teaching centers around the questions of creolization and *métissage*, Caribbean identity, cultures in contact, local cultures, and globalization. He has received numerous prestigious literary prizes and honorary doctorates. His recent publications include the novel *Sartorius* (1999); the essays *Faulkner, Mississippi* (1996) and *Traité du Tout-Monde* (1997); *Poèmes complets* (1994); and the play *Le Monde incréé* (2000).

Akhil Gupta is an associate professor of anthropology at Stanford University. He is the author of *Postcolonial Developments: Agriculture in the Making of Modern India* (1998) and the editor (with James Ferguson) of *Culture, Power, Place: Explorations in Critical Anthropology* (1998) and *Anthropological Locations: Boundaries and Grounds of a Field Science* (1997). An edited book (with Gordon Chang and Purnima Mankekar), *Caste and Outcast*, has just been published (2002). Gupta was a fellow at the National Humanities Center in 2000–2001 and also has received the Fulbright–Hays Faculty Research Abroad Grant, a fellowship from the Woodrow Wilson Center, and an Agrarian Studies Fellowship at Yale University. He has served as an associate editor of the journal *American Ethnologist.*

Abdul JanMohamed is a professor of English at the University of California, Berkeley. His publications include *Manichean Aesthetics: The Politics of Literature in Colonial Africa* (1983) and *The Nature and Context of Minority Discourse* (ed., with David Lloyd, 1990). He is currently working on a book on Richard Wright that focuses on his investigation of the different forms of resistance that are called forth by Jim Crow society's use of death, the fundamental mode of coercion.

Eileen Julien is Professor of French and Comparative Literature and Executive Director of the David C. Driskell Center for the Study of the

African Diaspora at the University of Maryland. Her teaching and research focus on the literatures of Africa, France, and the Americas in their relationships to one another. Among her publications are *African Novels and the Question of Orality* (1992), a special issue of the *Yearbook of Comparative and General Literature* on African literatures (1995), and a recent co-edition, *Atlantic Cross-Currents/Transatlantiques* (2001). She is currently completing a study, *Modernity and Multiple Imaginaries in Literature and the Arts*. In 1993–95, she was founding director of the West African Research Center, Dakar, Senegal.

Walter D. Mignolo is William H. Wannamaker Professor and Director of the Center for Global Studies and the Humanities at Duke University. His recent publications include *The Darker Side of the Renaissance: Literacy, Territoriality, and Colonization* (1995), *Local Histories/Global Designs* (2000), introduction to and compilation of *Capitalismo y geopolitica del conocimiento: La Filosofia de la liberacion en el debate intelectual contemporaneo* (2001), and introduction and afterword to the English translation of Jose de Acosta's *Natural and Moral History of the Indies* (2001).

Elisabeth Mudimbe-Boyi teaches French and Francophone literatures in the departments of French/Italian and Comparative Literatures at Stanford University. Her publications include *L'Oeuvre romanesque de Jacques-Stephen Alexis: une écriture poétique, un engagement politique* (1992), a special issue of the journals *L'Esprit Créateur* and *Callaloo,* as well as numerous articles in Francophone literature from Africa and the Caribbean.

Mary Louise Pratt is a professor in the Department of Spanish and Portuguese and in the Department of Comparative Literature at Stanford University. Her publications include *Imperial Eyes: Travel Writing and Transculturation* (1992), *Women, Culture, and Politics in Latin America* (1990), and the monograph *Amor Brujo: The Image and Culture of Love in the Andes* (1989).

Haun Saussy is an associate professor in the Department of Asian Languages and in the Department of Comparative Literature at Stanford University. In 1996 he was awarded the René Wellek Prize of the American Comparative Literature Association for *The Problem of a Chinese Aesthetic* (1993). His other publications include *Women Poets of Tradi-*

tional China (with Kang-i Sun Chang, 1999), *Great Walls of Discourse and Other Adventures in Cultural China* (2001), *An Anthology of Chinese Women Poets from Ancient Times to 1911* (ed., with Kang-i Sun Chang, 1997), and *The Cult of the Hand* (1987).

Mineke Schipper is a professor of literary theory and comparative literature at Leiden University, where she also is chair of intercultural literary studies. She has published two novels: *Conrads rivier* (1994) and *De zieleneters* (The Soul Eaters, 1998). Her academic publications include *Imagining Insiders: Africa and the Question of Belonging* (1999), *Source of All Evil: African Proverbs and Sayings on Women* (1991), and *Beyond the Boundaries: African Literature and Literary Theory* (1990). She recently edited *Poetics of African Art*, a special issue on the connections between African verbal and visual arts of the journal *Research in African Literatures* (2000).

Freya Schiwy holds a master of arts degree from Goethe University (Frankfurt), and she is currently a doctoral candidate in the Department of Romance Studies at Duke University. She is finishing her dissertation, "(Re)Framing Knowledge: Indigenous Video, Gendered Imaginaries, and Colonial Legacies." Her recent publications include "Intelectuales subalternos? Notas sobre las dificultades de pensar un dialogo intercultural" (2002), and an introduction to *Knowledge and the Known: Andean Perspectives on Capitalism and Epistemology* (2002).

Michel-Rolph Trouillot is a professor of anthropology at the University of Chicago. He has taught at Duke University and Johns Hopkins University. His books include *Ti dife boule sou Istoua Ayiti*, a history of the Saint-Domingue/Haiti slave revolution in Haitian Creole (1977), *Haiti, State against Nation: The Origins and Legacy of Duvalierism* (1990), and *Silencing the Past: Power and the Production of History* (1995). His latest publications deal with the anthropology of the state and the ongoing wave of historical apologies.

Robert J. C. Young is a professor of English and critical theory at Oxford University and a fellow at Wadham College, Oxford. He is the author of *White Mythologies: Writing History and the West* (1990), *Colonial Desire: Hybridity in Culture, Theory, and Race* (1995), *Torn Halves: Political Conflict in Literary and Cultural Theory* (1996), and *Postcolonialism: An Historical Introduction* (2001). Young also is general editor of *Interventions: The International Journal of Postcolonial Studies*.

INDEX

Absolutism, 25
Achebe, Chinua, 140
Action: communicative, 49–62; rational orientations of, 53, 55
Adamic, Louis, 207–208
Adams, John, 209, 211, 217
Adebayo, Diran, 162
Adorno, Theodor, 54, 64n9, 185
Aesthetics: anthropophagic, 40; athnographic, 41; frontier, 41; nonurban, 40
Africa: as ahistorical, 53; anti-colonial struggle in, 231; attempts to identify with, 236; colonialism and, 49, 50, 56; common denominators in, 131; competing versions of, 55; conceptualization of nature in, 58; cultural practices in, 242; disidentification with, 237; fictioning of, xviii, 129; gender issues in, 139, 140, 141; Habermas on, 51–62; as "haunting," 130; here/there, 131; hyphenated identities and, xx; independence in, 234, 236; inferior forms of reason in, 56; inside-but-not-of, 234; lack of sympathy for, 235; lack of uniformity in, 134; as Limit, 54; limited access to, 131; masculinity of, 136, 137, 138; as monolithic construction, 131; as more civil place, 137; mythologizing of, 53, 54, 58, 129, 130; as "negative" principle,

63n3; as Other, 54, 56; perceptions of, 135; postcolonial literature in, xix; prerational states in, 56; "presentist" conception of, 53; racial identification with, 236; realistic vision of, xvii; reality of, 131; relations to Europe, 51–54, 55, 56; romanticization of, xviii; as symbol, 131; "traditional," 65n16; understanding Europe and, 49–62; worldview of, xvi
African Americans: fictioning of Africa by, 129–146; gender identity and, 134; identity, 159; impediments to understanding Africa for, 131; limits of symbolism of, 132; oppression and, 131
African literature, 192–195
Afrocentrism, 16
Ahmad, Aijaz, xiv, 17
Alien and Sedition Act (1798), 204, 211, 217
Alienation: articulation of, 239
Althusser, Louis, 223
Amado, Jorge, 41
Ana María, Mayor, 256, 257, 259, 265
Anderson, Benedict, 211
Andrade, Mario de, 40
Andrade, Oswald de, 40
Androcentrism, 28
Angell, Norman, 5, 6
Angelou, Maya, 132–146